C000135350

IN QUEST FOR GOD AND FREEDOM

To my father Eduard Zelkin, my mother Elena Shatrovataya and my husband Magomed Galaev

ANNA ZELKINA

In Quest for God and Freedom

The Sufi Response to the Russian
Advance in the North Caucasus

HURST & COMPANY, LONDON

Published in the United Kingdom by
C. Hurst & Co. (Publishers) Ltd.
38 King Street, London WC2E 8JZ
© Anna Zelkina, 2000
All rights reserved
Printed in Malaysia
ISBN 1-85065-384-4

ACKNOWLEDGEMENTS

As a famous Russian military leader once put it, 'Each victory has many fathers, but only one person bears the responsibility for a failure.' While I assume all responsibility for the way the present book is written, it would have not been the same without the help and advice of many friends and colleagues, to whom I would like to express my deepest gratitude.

I am extremely grateful to my supervisor, Dr Derek Hopwood, for his guidance, patience and encouragement. Throughout the years of my research not only has he given me invaluable academic advice, but I was always able to rely on his support and professional opinion when I needed them most.

I am also greatly indebted to Prof. Albert Hourani, whose death in the second year of my research was a tragic loss both in personal and academic terms. I believe myself to be extremely fortunate to have enjoyed knowing and working with him. His gentle remarks and thoughtful questions have continued to illuminate me – as well as his numerous other pupils – long after his passing.

The writing of my D.Phil., which laid the foundation for this book, was the culmination of a long process of learning, begun in 1983 at the Oriental Faculty of St Petersburg University. I would like to take this chance to express my warmest gratitude to many wonderful teachers who opened up to me the rich world of Middle Eastern history and Muslim culture.

I was extremely fortunate to have been able to continue my studies at Oxford University. There I came to know many scholars who generously shared with me their professional knowledge, and extended personal friendship.

I am extremely grateful to Dr H. Shuckman, my college adviser, and his wife. Rarely does one come across such great warmth and wisdom as I have found in Dr Shuckman. His house has always been open to me and I often turned to him for support and advice. I also warmly thank Dr C. Andreev for her constant help and friendship.

I am very grateful to Dr Marie Bennigsen-Broxup, who gave me access to her personal archives and the library of the Central Asian and Caucasian Centre, of which she is the director.

I would like to thank the Soros Foundation for granting me a scholarship which brought me to Oxford as a visiting scholar. I am grateful to the Anne Arbib Trust, AJA and BFUW Trust for providing me with grants. In the second year of my research I was granted a full scholarship by an organisation which has wished to remain anonymous; I am most grateful to its members for their generosity. Special thanks are also due to Mr and Mrs Karten and their private foundation for their financial support and kind friendship.

My life would have not been the same without the many friends I have made in this country. My warmest gratitude goes to Mrs E. Jewell, Mr and Mrs Nettler, Prof. and Mrs Murphey, Prof. and Mrs Hewitt, as well as my other friends who shared many happy and difficult days with me and my husband. It would be impossible to mention every name, but I would like especially to thank Mrs and Dr Eshraikh and Dr Irina Anita for their constant friendship and support.

Above all, my gratitude goes to the members of my family, to whom I owe everything. My parents and my husband have not only given me all their love and support but were also a constant source of help, encouragement and advice. Seldom does one come across such love, support and devotion as I have enjoyed from my family. I have no doubt that without them not only my life but also my research would not have been the same. It is to them that I dedicate this book as a sign of my great love and appreciation.

School of Oriental and African Studies,   A. Z.
London
November 1999

CONTENTS

MAPS

ILLUSTRATIONS

between pages 8 and 9

Aerial view of Daghestan

Ghaybakh deserted village, Chechnya

between pages 156 and 157

Martyrs' cemetery in Gimrah, Daghestan

Mausoleum of the first imam, Ghazi Muhammad, Gimrah

The site of Ghazi Muhammad's death, Gimrah

The tombstone of Ghazi Muhammad

Imam Shamil in Russian captivity   *facing page* 234

GLOSSARY

abrek. An outlaw. Traditionally a person who has to leave his commune for the fear of blood-revenge. In Russian usage it became equivalent to bandit or robber.

'adat. Customary law.

'alim (pl. *'ulama*). A Muslim scholar.

amanat. A hostage handed over for a certain period of time as security for an agreement.

amir al-mu'minin. Commander of the Faithful: the title of Muslim rulers which implied full sovereignty.

aul. Mountain village in the North Caucasus.

baraka. Blessing, benediction, spiritual protection.

batin. Inward dimension, hidden knowledge.

bayt al-Mal. Treasury.

bek, bey. A man of noble origin, dignitary.

bid'a. Harmful innovation that corrupts the true nature of Islam.

burka. A sheep-skin cloak.

Daghestan. 'Mountain country'. From *Dagh* – mountain.

Dar al-Islam. The domain of Islam where warfare is not permitted as opposed to *Dar al-Harb*, the domain of non-Muslims, where warfare is legitimate.

dhikr. Lit. remembrance, recollection. In Sufism, a ritual which involves the repetition of certain phrases either aloud or in the mind accompanied by particular breathing and physical movements. The ritual aims at gaining the presence of God throughout one's being.

dibir. Muslim religious functionary. Identical to *Mullah* (Ar.).

Divan-Khaneh (otherwise known as *Majlis al-Shura*). The official supreme legislative and judicial power established by Shamil in his imamate.

ekzekutsiya (ekzekutsii). A from of punishment which implied quartering of soldiers in the houses of offenders at the owner's expense.

fiqh. A branch of traditional Muslim scholarship on jurisprudence.

ghazavat. Lit. conquest. In the Caucasus a holy war for the sake of Islam, identical to *jihad*.

gyaur. An infidel.

hajj. Pilgrimage to the holy cities of Islam: Mecca and Medina.

hajji. A title of one who has performed the *hajj*.

haqq or *al-haqq*. Lit. truth, essence. In Sufi tradition God, the Ultimate Reality.

haqiqa. Used as opposed or complementary to the *shari'a*, i.e. the inward dimension of the Divine Reality.

hijra. Prophet Muhammad's emigration from Mecca to Medina in 622 AD. The beginning of the Muslim era.

ijaza. Licence granted by a sheikh to his *khalifa* to spread the *tariqa* and initiate his own *murids*.

ijma'. A consensus of Muslim experts in legal matters.

ilm (pl. *'ulum*). Muslim knowledge.

imam. Lit. leader in prayer. In the North Caucasus, a political and religious leader, head of state.

imamate. Theocratic state in the North Caucasus governed by the *shari'a* and headed by the imam.

jama'at. A rural commune in Daghestan, made up of one or more adjacent villages. It usually formed an economic and political unit with the borders defined by natural boundaries (river, canyon, slope, hollow, etc.).

janka. Son of a khan born by a common woman.

kanly. Blood feud, or parties involved in blood feud.

khalifa. Deputy, caliph. In Sufi terminology, a deputy of a Sufi sheikh in a specific area with or without the full authority to initiate *murids* into the *tariqa*.

khalwa. Seclusion. In Sufi terminology, the retirement of a Sufi sheikh for prayer and reflection. In some Naqshbandi branches, the practice that accompanied initiation into the order.

khanaqa or *tekke*. A Sufi lodge.

kharaj. Land tax in Islamic law.

khawaja. Master of knowledge. A title mostly used in Central Asia, where it became synonymous with sheikh. It was also sometimes applied to men of noble origin.

khums. One fifth of booty, which, according to the *shari'a*, belongs to the ruler.

kibin. Bride money in Daghestan. Identical to *Maghar* (Ar.).

Kurban-Bayram. Muslim Festival of Immolation, blood sacrifice. Identical to *'Id al-Adha* (Ar.).

ma'azun. Before the creation of the imamate, a public crier. In Shamil's imamate the deputy of a *naib*.

Madhhab. One of the four legal schools in Islamic jurisprudence.

madrasa. Muslim educational institution, school.

Mahdi. Lit. 'rightly-guided'. In Islamic tradition the *Mahdi* will appear at the end of the world to fill the world with justice. Similar to the Messiah in Jewish and Christian traditions.

mahkama. A *shari'a* court.

maktaba. A primary religious school. library, bookstore.

maqam (-*at*). A lasting stage in a mystical spiritual journey which man reaches through persistent and lengthy exercise (unlike *hal* – a state, which descends upon man's heart from God at God's choice).

Mawlid. Celebration of the Prophet's or a saint's birthday, usually accompanied by prayer and chanting of hymns in honour of the celebrated person.

Mehq-Qel. Lit. Council of the land. The council of elders where all Vaynakh *tuqums* were represented. It was held occasionally to discuss matters which involved all Vaynakh *tuqums*.

mirnyi. Peaceful, subdued.

mudir. The highest military-administrative rank in Shamil's imamate. Head of a province consisting of several *vilayats*.

muhajir (-un). Those companions of the Prophet Muhammad who emigrated with him from Mecca to Medina. In the North Caucasus, those who emigrated from the pacified areas under Russian control to the imam-held territories.

muhtasib. Lit. auditor, inspector. In Shamil's imamate, a member of the imam's secret police.

mufti. Official expounder of Islamic law. In the Russian Empire, the head of a Muslim Directorate.

mujaddid. Renovator of Muslim faith sent by God at the end of each Muslim era.

mullah. Religious functionary.

munafiq. Hypocrite.

muraqaba. Awareness, surveillance or contemplation of God. A certain degree attained on a Sufi path which is generally regarded as that proceeding the degree of *mushahada*.

murid. Lit. aspirant. Adept of a Sufi brotherhood. In the Caucasus also a warrior in *ghazavat*.

muridizm. In Russian historiography, the equivalent of the Sufi movement in the North Caucasus.

murshid. A Sufi spiritual guide. In the North Caucasus the ultimate head of the Naqshbandi order.

murtaziq(-a). Lit. hired, kept. In the North Caucasus, the cavalrymen in the personal service of the imam or his deputies, who formed the regular army units in Shamil's imamate.

mushahada, shuhud. Witnessing of God. A special mystical type of knowledge, gnosis, which can only be acquired through spiritual practice and exercise.

naib. Lit. deputy. In the North Caucasus, a governor of a province, military political official in Shamil's imamate.

Naibstvo. Russian name for a province in Shamil's imamate.

nisba. Lit. lineage. Initiatory affiliation with a particular Sufi tradition.

nizam. Lit. order. In the North Caucasus, a system of laws and regulations introduced by Shamil in addition to the *shari'a*.

nuker. A member of the Daghestani hereditary rulers' and local dignitaries' private army.

papakha. Astrakhan hat.

pristav. Bailiff, police officer.

pristavstvo. A system of local administration introduced by the Russian government.

qadi. A *shari'a* judge. In Daghestan before the imams, the term *qadi* referred both to Muslim judges and, in some areas, to the head of a *jama'at* (e.g. the *qadi* of Akusha, the *qadi* of Tabarsaran).

qadiyat. A political entity ruled by a hereditary dynasty of *qadis* (e.g. the *qadiyat* of Tabarsaran).

rabita. Lit. link, connection. In Sufi terminology, a spiritual communication between a disciple and his guide which results in the absorption of a *murid* into his sheikh.

ruhaniyya. In Sufi terminology the spirituality or spiritual being of a living or a deceased sheikh, which can enter into spiritual contact with a living man.

sadaqa. Almsgiving, charity.

salik. Lit. pilgrim on a Sufi path. A Sufi adept.

sayyid. A real or fictitious descendant of the Prophet Muhammad.

shahada. Profession of faith, which implies reciting the declaration that there is no deity but God and Muhammad is His Prophet.

shaman. A pagan priest, magician, witchdoctor.

shamkhal. The ruler of Targhu, one of the main Daghestani principalities. Sometimes also referred to as the *wali* of Daghestan.

shari'a. Islamic law.

Sheikh al-Islam. The Chief *mufti* of Istanbul and the Ottoman Empire.

shura al-'ulama. A gathering of religious and secular authorities, which was held at times of the election of the imams and for the discussion of the most important matters in the imamate.

silsila. Chain of transmission of a particular Sufi tradition. A lineage of spiritual descent.

stanitsa. A Cossack settlement.

suhba. Lit. company with somebody. In Sufism the traditional way of transmitting Sufi knowledge through personal association of a *murid* with his sheikh.

sufi. A Muslim mystic.

sufism or *tasawwuf.* Islamic mysticism.

sunna. Lit. Custom. Normative example of the Prophet Muhammad. One of the main sources of Muslim law.

sura. Chapter of the Qur'an.

tafsir. Commentary on the Qur'an.

tariqa. Mystical path pursued by Sufis in the search of God. A Sufi order.

tariqa murid. In the Caucasus, a term describing a Sufi adept proper as opposed to a *naib* or imam's *murid* – i.e. one who pursues service to God not through spiritual purification but participation in the *ghazavat*.

teip. A tribe among the Vaynakh (Chechens and Ingush).

tekke. A Sufi order.

toqum. A tribe among the Lezgs in southern Daghestan. Not to be confused with the Vaynakh *tuqum*.

tuqum. A rural commune formed of one or several villages among the Vaynakh (Chechens and Ingush).

turkhq. A public crier in the Vaynakh communes, similar to *ma'azun* in Daghestan. At the time of Beybulat and Tashou Hajji, an elected official in a *tuqum*. In the Qadiri order, a head of the local Sufi network in a village or village quarter.

Uezd. Province in the Russian administrative system.

umma. World Muslim community. A nation of Islam.

umykanie. Elopement.

utsmiy. A title of Tabarsaran rulers.

Utsmiyat. A political entity ruled by a hereditary dynasty of *utsmiy* (e.g. the Utsmiyat of Tabarsaran).

uwaysi. A mystic who has attained illumination through the spiritual being of a living or deceased sheikh.

uzden'. A free man of common origin.

Vilayat (from Ar. *Wilaya*). A province in Shamil's state.

vol'ny. Lit. free. In Russian sources applied to the unsubdued communes of the North Caucasus.

Wali. Ruler, governor. In the North Caucasus this title was applied only to the *shamkhal* of Targhu.

waqf. Religious endowment.

wujud. Existence of finding the existence of God.

Yurt. A low-land village in the Caucasus.

zakat. Alms tax in Islamic law.

NOTE ON TRANSLITERATION AND USAGE OF NAMES

This book is written on the basis of sources in two foreign languages – Russian and Arabic. It is also concerned with an area known for its linguistic complexity and a period when Arabic was the dominant written language. Thus local names and geographic terms are given in transliteration from their Arabic forms. Those names and geographical terms which were originally introduced in Russian – 'Chechens', 'Ingush' etc. – are transliterated from Russian. A few which are commonly known in the West are rendered as in English, e.g. 'Ossets', 'Circassians'. Personal names of Russian officials and authors of foreign origin (Polish, German, French etc.) are transliterated from their Russian forms.

References to the Bibliography are given in transliteration from the language in which they were written. Names of Russian archives are also given in Russian transliteration.

The transliteration of Russian words is based on the standard system as used by the *Slavonic and East European Review*. The transliteration of Arabic words is based on the standard system as used in *IJMES*.

The bibliography is presented in *American Anthropologist* style. Works with no known author are listed in the bibliography by their date of publication.

MAPS

The Caucasus range.

Source: M. Bennigsen-Broxup (ed.), *The North Caucasus Barrier*, London: Hurst, 1992

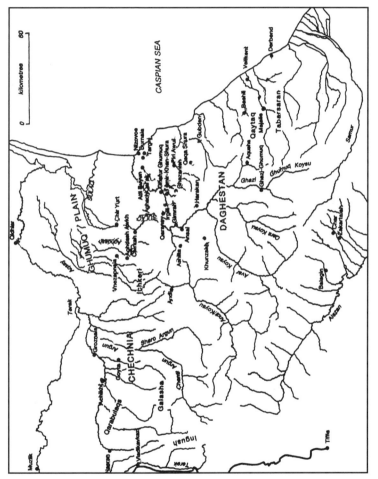

Chechnya and Daghestan.

The source of this and the two following maps is Moshe Gammer, *Muslim Resistance to the Tsar*, London: Frank Cass, 1994.

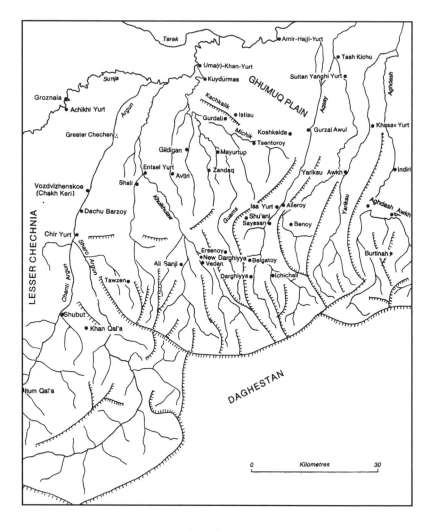

Chechnya

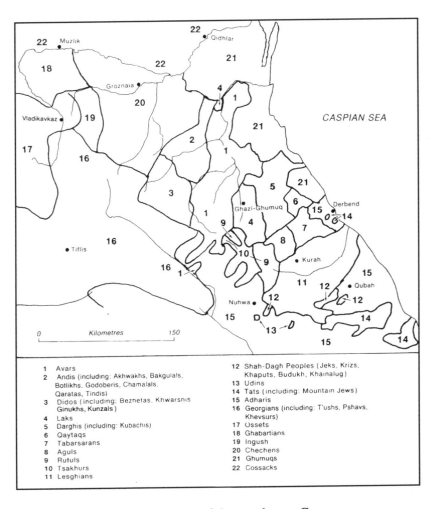

1   Avars
2   Andis (including: Akhwakhs, Bakgulals,
    Botlikhs, Godoberis, Chamalals,
    Qaratas, Tindis)
3   Didos (including: Beznetas, Khwarsnis
    Ginukhs, Kunzals)
4   Laks
5   Darghis (including: Kubachis)
6   Qaytaqs
7   Tabarsarans
8   Aguls
9   Rutuls
10 Tsakhurs
11 Lesghians

12 Shah-Dagh Peoples (Jeks, Krizs,
    Khaputs, Budukh, Khainalug)
13 Udins
14 Tats (including: Mountain Jews)
15 Adharis
16 Georgians (including: T'ushs, Pshavs,
    Khevsurs)
17 Ossets
18 Ghabartians
19 Ingush
20 Chechens
21 Ghumuqs
22 Cossacks

Ethno-linguistic map of the north-east Caucasus.

xxiii

INTRODUCTION

The present book treats the relationship between the realm of ideas and the realm of matter – specifically the way in which a religion can reshape a society in its cultural values, social organisation and legal culture. Without entering into a theoretical debate on the matter, I have adopted a 'historical' and, to a certain extent, 'theological' approach to the subject. This is a case-study of the impact of a Muslim mystical order (the Naqshbandi Sufi *tariqa*) upon the social, religious and political life of the peoples of the North Caucasus, the Chechens and Daghestanis, in the first half of the nineteenth century.

The transformation of North Caucasian society is studied here on the basis of the analysis of the social structure, legal system and religious and political history of nineteenth-century Chechnya and Daghestan alongside the doctrine and practices of the Naqshbandi order – the main driving force behind this transformation. Each of these elements constitutes a major theme in its own right. The North Caucasus as a relatively small region within the Russian empire has not been of research interest to scholars of Islam; similarly, as a non-Russian, Muslim area of the Russian empire, it has been overlooked by historians of imperial and Soviet Russia. Only recently – due to intense media attention towards Chechnya driven mainly by the devastations of two Russo-Chechen wars – did the name of this small republic become familiar to the Western public. Yet, the complaint expressed almost half-a-century ago by a scholar of the North Caucasus that 'though the Caucasus lies so near to Europe that some geographers are inclined to consider it as belonging to that continent...it remains the least known of lands in the world. The Caucasus is indeed so near, yet so far away', is still relevant.[1]

Only one aspect of the history of the nineteenth-century North Caucasus attracted Western scholars, namely the Russo-Caucasian war (1825-59/61). One can single out two comprehensive works on the subject – Baddeley from the early twentieth century[2] and a recent publication by Gammer[3] (a classic as soon as it appeared). However, while these works recognise the significance of a Sufi element in organising and leading the North Caucasian resistance, they concentrate mainly on the military aspect of resistance. In contrast, the present book focuses on the religious and social dimensions of the Naqshbandi movement.

Research which was carried out by Russian and Soviet scholars was

---

[1] Luzbetack, 1951, p. 2.

[2] Baddeley, 1908.

[3] Gammer, 1994.

subject to strong ideological pressure.[4] The official line that dominated Russian and later Soviet historiography had to conform to the thesis that various North Caucasian peoples had voluntarily joined Russia in the early eighteenth century, thus portraying the resistance movement as a revolt of 'bandits' and 'fanatics'. Moreover, almost all Russian and Soviet scholars treated the Naqshbandiyya as an isolated 'sectarian' movement unique to the North Caucasus and denied any all-Muslim dimension to it, to the extent that the terms 'Sufi' and 'Naqshbandi' were replaced by a misleading term '*Myuridism*' (after *murid*, a Sufi adept: from Arabic – 'a seeker' [of the Divine truth]).

Unwilling to admit the destabilising effect of the Russian expansion in the area as one of the main factors that led to the longevity and ferocity of the North Caucasian resistance, the pre-Revolutionary Russian historians resorted to the concept of an inherent Muslim fanaticism and inclination towards banditry (lawlessness), which were allegedly reinforced by the intrigues and conspiracies of the foreign powers, mainly Ottoman Turkey and Persia (with some assistance and inspiration from the Western imperial rivals of Russia, namely Britain and France).[5]

Soviet historians, after a brief flirtation with the idea of national liberation movements in the atmosphere of total disengagement from the Russian colonial past immediately after the Bolshevik revolution,[6] revived in the mid-1930s the pre-Revolutionary view of the North Caucasian resistance movement. In the resolution of the State Commission on Historical Issues (*Gosudarstvennaya Komissiya po Voprosam Istorii*) adopted in August 1937, the tsarist conquest of the North Caucasus was described as 'a lesser evil' for it had saved the North Caucasian peoples from annexation by other imperialist countries and brought them into direct contact with the 'progressive' Russian proletariat, thus allowing them to benefit from the later Bolshevik revolution. The return to the pre-Revolutionary line was completed in the early 1950s when Islamic fundamentalism and foreign conspiracy again became the official interpretation. This is best illustrated by the book published by the People's Commissariat for Internal Affairs (NKVD), *Shamil – Stavlennik Sultanskoy Turtsii i Britanskikh Kolonizatorov* (Shamil the Stooge of Ottoman Turkey and the British Colonialists).[7]

The discussion about the 'progressive-regressive' character of the Caucasian resistance movement was resumed three years after Stalin's

---

[4] For a detailed description of the historiography of the question see M. Broxup, 1886, pp 5-17.

[5] With some degree of variations this thesis can be found in all pre-Revolutionary Russian works of such authors as Potto, Dubrovin and Volkonskiy – to name but the most famous.

[6] The best example of such an approach can be found in Pokrovskiy, 1923.

[7] Tsagareshvili (ed.), 1953.

death in 1956, when, following the opening of a debate in the Soviet press,[8] a number of conferences and sessions took place both in Moscow and in the North Caucasus that revealed the tension between Russian and North Caucasian historians. As a result of a two-year discussion Soviet historians reached a compromise according to which the 'social motives of the movement as directed against the local landlords and Russian colonisers' were to be separated from its 'ideological religious cover'.[9] Thus, while the resistance movement was accepted as '*narodnoe i progressivnoe*' (popular and progressive), the religious ideology under which it was fought was labelled as '*antinarodnoe i reaktsionnoe*' (anti-popular and reactionary).[10]

This two-dimensional approach has never been resolved and, even after the liberalisation started by Gorbachev, Soviet (and now post-Soviet) historians have continued to dismiss the universal Islamic nature of the Naqshbandi movement in the North Caucasus and treat it exclusively in the context of the anti-colonial political struggle.[11]

In one respect of one must agree with the Russian/Soviet scholars: that the North Caucasus is unique in its ethnic, social and geographical nature, which when combined with the dramatic changes brought about by the Russian expansion in the area, arguably contributed to the astonishing rise of the Naqshbandi brotherhood to such a prominent position.

One can argue that the very setting of the North Caucasus, its nature and landscape, accounted for a great deal of the region's political and social complexity. Writing about the political geography of the nineteenth-century North Caucasus is challenging in itself. The area does not lend itself easily to an orderly description, for it had never existed as a united political entity with clearly defined borders. The geographical and political content of the terms Daghestan and Chechnya themselves tended to vary significantly from one author to another.[12]

Projecting the present-day borders into the reality of the nineteenth century is not helpful either, for these have experienced a series of changes and revisions due to the volatile history of the region under tsarist and Soviet rule. Although the present-day borders of Daghestan correspond by and large to those defined by the Russian authorities in

8 Pikman, 1956; Daniyalov, 1950.

9 Smirnov, 1963, p. 28.

10 *Ibid.*, p. 30.

11 This attitude was particularly evident at an International Symposium in the memory of Ghazi Muhammad, the first imam of the North Caucasus, held in Mahachqala, October 1993.

12 See for example *Obozrenie Rossiyskikh Vladeniy za Kavkazom v Etnograficheskom, Statisticheskom i Finansovom Otnosheniyakh* (Hereafter *Obozrenie...*) 1836 p. 187; Bronevskiy, 1823, pp. 58-9, 293-4, Zubov, 1835, p. 221.

1860 shortly after the conquest and have remained largely unchanged,[13] those of Chechnya have seen many dramatic changes and revisions, especially during the period under consideration; the conquest of Chechnya was accompanied by the colonisation of the newly conquered areas by Cossack settlers that changed the geographical definition of the term Chechnya. Following the Russian conquest, Chechnya – unlike Daghestan – was not treated as a single province of the Russian empire but, rather, as several districts within the Terek province.

Nevertheless, many historians and ethnographers continued to treat all the territory inhabited by the Chechen and Ingush tribes as a single cultural, if not political entity, a treatment I find totally justified. Therefore, I apply the term Chechnya to all the lands occupied by the Chechen and the Ingush tribes prior to and at the time of the Russian conquest, whereas Daghestan is the area within the borders defined by the Russian administration in 1860.

Defining the social and political composition of the nineteenth-century North Caucasus has been a research topic in its own right. Aside from work on family and family law[14] and anthropological research limited to the north-western, mainly Circassian lands, which borrowed heavily from Soviet scholarship,[15] this subject has received very little scholarly attention in the West.

Although there was a great deal of material published on the subject by Russian and Soviet scholars, it was largely produced under strong political and ideological pressure. The Russian scholars working on the subject were mostly concerned with practical needs, namely providing the Government with information on the social structure to enable the Russian authorities to work out an appropriate system of administration in the area. This often resulted in their treating local elders and hereditary rulers in terms similar to Russian landowners and gentry and the rest of the mountain peoples as Russian serf peasantry. At the same time, driven by the need to justify the appropriation of land into the Russian treasury, Russian scholars denied the existence of any forms of private property in certain Daghestan and Chechen areas.[16]

During the Soviet period, there were constant attempts to make the mountain societies fit into 'classical' Marxist formation theory. Depending on the ideological requirements of the moment, Soviet historians and ethnographers argued that the North Caucasian peoples were at different stages of their development[17] which corresponded to either

---

[13] Khashaev, 1961, p. 6.

[14] Luzbetack, 1951.

[15] Lemercier-Quelquejay, 1992.

[16] See *TsGVIA*, fond 718, opis' 2, delo 758, list 7, 8; fond 80, opis' 2, delo 4, list 133.

[17] For the overview of the controversy see Khashaev, 1961, pp. 126-34.

primitive,[18] feudal[19] or even capitalist formations.

Despite these drawbacks, Russian and Soviet historians provided extensive material by recording, translating and publishing local codes of '*adat*, which are the most valuable source material for research on the subject of the social and judicial structures in the North-eastern Caucasus. However, in treating the subject, one inevitably encounters the problem of the lack of uniformity in terms of reference. To avoid confusion caused by the artificially constructed theories of class-struggle and class-differentiation in nineteenth-century North Caucasian society, I have introduced, or rather adopted, the terms as used by the North Caucasian people themselves and explained them in my own words. I have also provided their standard Russian definition in the footnotes.

The legal structures in the nineteenth-century North-eastern Caucasus defy categorisation in the same way as the society itself. For the purpose of my research, I have grouped them into two broader categories on the basis of the extent to which Islam had defined the legislation of a particular group of people.

Writing on the history of the Islamisation of the North Caucasus has been a challenging task. The fundamental problem that faces a researcher is the lack of local written sources, the only exception being in southern Daghestan, particularly Derbend.[20] This lack of local written sources is only partly compensated by foreign travellers' accounts and epigraphic and archaeological evidence. Unfortunately, most of the travellers failed to penetrate the high mountains of Daghestan and Chechnya, so their accounts are confined largely to coastal Daghestan. The archaeological data on Daghestan were processed and published, but in Chechnya due to the political sensitivity surrounding the whole issue of Chechen history, both distant and recent, conducting fieldwork and collecting evidence were technically impossible.[21] Hence, it is not surprising that the history of Islamisation among the Chechen and Ingush people remained under-researched not only in Western, but also in Soviet historiography. I have tried to utilise all available material, both written and oral although I recognise its limitations.

The events and processes described in the book took place against the background of the Russian expansion into the area. Moreover, one can argue, that had it not been for the external threat of a European Christian power, the Naqshbandi message would not have had as profound and far-reaching effects as it did. Therefore, although a detailed description of the Russian military campaigns in the North Caucasus is outside

---

18 Bushuev, 1956, p. 74; Tsagareshvili, 1953, p. iii.

19 Yushkov, 1939, pp. 66-70; Khashaev, 1961, p. 127.

20 Lavrov, 1966; *idem*, 1968; Shikhsaidov, 1984.

21 Particularly after the deportation, the Soviet authorities put a prohibition on any archaeological or ethnographic work in the Chechen mountains.

the scope of my thesis, I give a brief outline of the main stages of the Russian expansion into the area. Similarly, I describe the military campaigns of the North Caucasian religious leaders only in as much as I see it as necessary for the adequate understanding of the rationale of their religious and political activities.[22]

The first North Caucasian leader who combined religious preaching with anti-Russian military struggle was Sheikh or Imam Mansour. The fact that his Naqshbandi credentials are less then certain and that he did not leave any coherent Naqshbandi, or other Sufi, framework do not lessen his achievements. Furthermore, his activities highlight the importance of the Naqshbandi framework to the similar efforts of the later Naqshbandi imams, while his failures can in part be explained by the fact that he had no such infrastructure on which to rely.

Researching the movement led by Sheikh Mansour is a most challenging task. Parallels can easily be drawn between his and other reformist movements elsewhere in the Muslim world. Yet, this apparent resemblance requires particular care to avoid making broad generalisations and unfounded assumptions. The difficulty of carrying out adequate research is aggravated by the nature of the sources and published material available. Although the Russian archives contain a fair amount of the eighteenth-century material directly related to Sheikh Mansour and his teaching, they are far from exhaustive or even reliable.

From the very beginning the Russians saw Sheikh Mansour as 'nothing more than an impostor and an Ottoman stooge'.[23] This attitude heavily influenced all their accounts, where his role of independent religious leader was belittled or rejected altogether.

Even Sheikh Mansour's own testimony of his life and preaching given during his interrogation by the *Taynaya Komissiya* (Secret Committee) after he was captured in 1791, can hardly be seen as a fully reliable source, due to the circumstances in which it was made. To refute the Russian accusations, Mansour played down his role as a religious and military leader and denied any political aspirations.[24]

The Ottomans (who present an alternative source) also met the news of the appearance of the 'new prophet' with hostile suspicion and after an investigation dismissed him as 'a false prophet and a liar'[25] with 'nothing extraordinary or supernatural about him'.[26]

More reliable are the Russian and Ottoman accounts of the military campaigns undertaken by Sheikh Mansour and his supporters both in

---

[22] For a wider military political context of the movement see Gammer, 1994, which is an exellent source of reference on the subject.

[23] Report of Prince Potemkin in *TsGADA*, razdel. XXIII, chast' 10, list 161.

[24] *TsGADA*, razdel VII, delo 2777, list 1-22.

[25] Bennigsen, 1964, p. 183.

[26] *Ibid.*, p 182.

the eastern and western Caucasus. They are, however, beyond the scope of the present book. Despite their deficiencies and limitations, the Russian archives provided valuable source material for the life and religious activities of Sheikh Mansour, which I cross-referenced with the data from the Ottoman archives processed and published by A. Bennigsen,[27] the only Western scholar to carry out research on Sheikh Mansour.

The dispute over the origins of 'Caucasian *myuridism*' has preoccupied generations of Russian and Soviet scholars, who usually depicted it as a heresy and deviation from the Sufi tradition. Yet far from being a heresy or a unique, home-grown phenomenon as was hitherto claimed by Russian and Soviet scholars, it was a mainstream Naqshbandi outlet in the region. Well within the Sufi tradition, the North Caucasian Naqshbandis preserved a strong spiritual and institutional link with their predecessors.

The chapters on the history and practices of the Naqshbandi doctrine are written on the basis of both the Western works on Sufism in general and the Naqshbandi brotherhood in particular, as well as the published writings of the Naqshbandi sheikhs in the Arabic language. Although some of the published sources in Arabic that I have used have been available for scholarly examination before, they escaped the attention of almost all Russian and Soviet scholars, for the sole reason that they denied this phenomenon a wider Islamic dimension. I have for the first time fully translated the writings of Jamal al-Din al-Ghazi Ghumuqi and that of Iliyas al-Tsudaqari, Abd al-Rahman al-Thughuri (al-Sugratli)[28] which I cross-referenced with those written by Naqshbandi sheikhs elsewhere in the Muslim world.[29]

Although from the very beginning the new movement became embroiled in the complex political situation in the North Caucasus, with the political Naqshbandiyya remaining at the forefront of the events, it was the spiritual–mystical dimension of the brotherhood that provided and maintained the momentum for the far-reaching religious and social reforms in the area.

From the first decade of its existence in the North Caucasus, the dissemination of Naqshbandi ideas occurred on two distinct levels – the 'spiritual' and the 'political'. This split between the two was overcome only in the persons of the North Caucasian Naqshbandi imams, who combined the powers of military-political leaders with those of the supreme religious authority in the area. Apart from its political sig-

---

27 *Ibid.*, pp. 159-204.

28 Due to limited space in the present work I have used only the core chapters of the above mentioned treatises. It is my hope that before too long I will be able to publish a work on the spiritual history of the Naqshbandi order in the North Caucasus with the English translation and commentary of these manuscripts.

29 Al-Khani, 1308; Sahib, 1334; Thughuri, 1907; al-Tsudaqari, 1904.

nificance, the assertion of the new style of leadership by the Naqshbandi sheikhs was equally, if not more important, in its social effects. It came into conflict with the traditional institutions of power and challenged the legitimacy of the tribal and communal rulers.

The transformation of the nature and sources of power in the North Caucasian tribal societies was a gradual process. The first to appreciate the Naqshbandi appeal as a far stronger source of legitimacy than adherence to tribal values and principles was Beybulat Taymi, the leader of the Great Chechnya Revolt of 1825-7. Being a traditional tribal warlord, Beybulat could not realise the Naqshbandi potential to the full. His movement is a clear illustration of the controversial and painful process of gradual transformation in the nature of power and in social organisation in the North Caucasus.

This evolution finally permitted the Naqshbandi sheikhs to assume military-political and religious authority, and on the basis of the Sufi structure the first North Caucasian state emerged. This transformation of a religious structure in the form of a Sufi brotherhood into a political movement and state structure was not unique to the North Caucasus. At the time of the growing confrontation with hostile European powers and internal political crisis, the Sufi orders provided a ready-made platform for the first stage of the modern Islamic reformation, known as 'Neo-Sufism'. It was not until later that the Islamic reformers came to deny the legacy of Sufism and accuse Sufis of heresy and corrupting the 'true spirit of Islam'. In the early nineteenth century, the Sufi orders were crucial in providing both the structure and the ideology for anti-colonial resistance. Nowhere was that role more apparent than in state-less environments similar to the North Caucasus. The Sanusiya in the Sahara desert, the Qadiriyya in Algeria and the Naqshbandiyya in Kurdistan are the closest examples of similar phenomena.

For a long time it was the political activities of these orders and the anti-Western resistance they inspired that attracted scholarly attention, and only recently did works on their religious and intellectual basis begin to appear.[30] It is my hope that the present book makes a contribution to both the study of the intellectual history of Sufi Islam and that of the North Caucasus.

---

[30] Such as the work by Knut S. Vikør (1995) on the Sanusi order and M. Chodkevicz's work on the Spiritual Writings of 'Abd al-Qader (English translation, 1995).

Aerial view of Daghestan.

Ghaybakh deserted village, Chechnya.

Part I. PEOPLE AND LAND

1

GENERAL DESCRIPTION OF THE NORTH CAUCASUS

The Caucasus is situated at the crossroads between Asia and Europe. It is approximately 1,000km. across from the Taman Peninsula in the Black Sea in the north-west to the Apsheron Peninsula in the Caspian Sea in the south-east. The main chain of the Caucasian Mountains divides the area into two: Transcaucasia (consisting of Georgia, Armenia and Azerbaijan) to the south, and the North Caucasus which is populated by numerous ethnic and linguistic groups and presently divided into numerous administrative units within the Russian Federation.

Geographical description of the North Caucasus[1]

The present work deals primarily with the North-eastern Caucasus which, in the early nineteenth century, was inhabited by the Vaynakh (Chechen and Ingush) and Daghestani peoples. The whole area may be regarded as a triangle bounded by the Caspian Sea to the east, the main Caucasian mountain range to the south and south-west, the rivers Kura, Sunja and Terek to the north and north-west. In geographical terms, the area can be divided into high mountains, lower mountains, foothills and lowlands.[2]

The high mountains of the Vaynakh lands, formed by the first ridge of the main Caucasus range, are called *bash-lam* ('melting mountains' in Chechen), for their peaks are snow-covered all year. In the foothills the snow melts by the end of May giving way to Alpine meadows. Except for the Terek and Sunja ranges, which are completely bare, most of the mountainous area of Chechnya is forested.

[1] On the Geography of the North Caucasus see Bronevskiy, 1823, part I; Berzhe (Berge), 1859, pp. 8-64; Gul, 1959; Khashaev, 1958; Khashaev, 1961, pp. 6-12; Gvozdevskiy, 1958; Litvinov, 1884, pp. 149-64, 304-20, 328-46; Maksimov, 1893, pp. 7-18; Berg, 1950; Maslov, Gozulov and Ryazantsev, 1957; Nadezhdin, 1895; *Obozrenie...* part IV; Olshevskiy, 1850; Terterov, 1959, Tikhonov, 1958; Zubov, 1834-5; Gammer, 1994, pp. 11-17.

[2] The geographical classification is derived from Khashaev, 1961, pp. 6-12. The distinction between the high and low mountains is drawn to differentiate between the distinct types of societies inhabiting them.

9

The high Andi range separates the Vaynakh lands from Mountain or Inner Daghestan, which is completely surrounded by ranges 2,000-3,000m. high, cut through by numerous mountain rivers. 'This one lofty massif intersected by deep gorges, Inner Daghestan, is a country so gloomy, severe and infertile as no other.'[3] Most of the outward facing slopes of its ranges are rocky and bare. Only the inward looking slopes in the north and east, especially in Qaytaq and Tabarsaran, are covered with forests, although nowhere in Daghestan are the forests as extensive and dense as in Chechnya.

To the west, Inner Daghestan gradually rises to 3,500-4,000m. with the mountain summits always covered with snow feeding numerous mountain rivers.[4] To the east the mountain ranges of Inner Daghestan gradually descend to the semi-arid Qumyq plain in the north and the Caspian Sea in the south. There the Caspian lowland runs as a long strip fro 500km. along the Caspian coast from the mouth of the river Sulak in the north to the mouth of the Samur in the south, and range from 20 to 200km. wide. From the western to the southern border runs a 250km.-long curved range of foothills rising to 500-600m. high, which in the vicinity of Derbend and Targhu (present-day Mahachqala) runs parallel to the cost of the Caspian sea. Further from the sea the ranges rise to 1,000-1,200m.

The Caspian lowland is separated from Inner Daghestan by the Andi, Salataw and Qara-Syrt ranges, with the only passage between the two running along the confluence of the Avar and Andi Koysu, where the river Sulak forms a narrow canyon.

Ethnic and linguistic composition[5]

Perhaps nowhere in the world can one find such ethnic and linguistic diversity as in the North Caucasus.[6] It became standard practice to classify the North Caucasian peoples according to language or dialect, and on this basis the inhabitants of the North Caucasus have been divided into two main categories – 'aboriginals' (those speaking various Ibero-Caucasian languages)[7] and later foreign migrants.[8]

---

[3] *Obzor Dagestanskoy Oblasti za 1911 God*, 1912, p. 2 (hereafter *Obzor...*).

[4] Khashaev, 1961, pp. 6-9.

[5] Geiger, 1959; archival material published in Khashaev and Kosven, 1958; Komarov, 1873; Khashaev, 1961, pp. 12-23; Kosven, 1955; Luzbetac, 1951, Narody Dagestana, 1955.

[6] On theories which try to a account for such diversity see Adighe, 1957; Klimov, 1965; Khashaev, 1961, pp. 20-2; Luzbetac, 1951; Lavrov, 1951; Bokarev, 1961, Uslar, 1888.

[7] Otherwise known as the Japhetic, the Ibero-Caucasian linguistic group falls into three separate branches: the southern, spoken by the Kartveli Georgians, Mingrelians, Svans and Laz; the north-western, spoken by the Abkhaz, Circassians and the Kabard; and the north-eastern, spoken by the Chechen, Ingush, and the 'aboriginal' Daghestani peoples.

[8] These include peoples speaking Turkish, Persian and Semitic languages as well as

In ethnic terms, the population of the Vaynakh lands (Chechnya and Ingushetiya) is homogeneous and comprised of Vaynakh tribes[9] speaking several dialects of a common Nakh language which belongs to the north-eastern branch of the Ibero-Caucasian group of languages.[10] The terms 'Chechen' and 'Ingush' were defined by the Russians in the late seventeenth century. They derive from the names of the two large villages where the Russians first encountered them – Chechen-*aul* and Angusht (Ingush in the Russian version). Following the conquest of the North Caucasus the Russian authorities, divided the Vaynakh on the basis of dialect into two different peoples – the Chechen and Ingush.[11] In the context of the eighteenth and nineteenth centuries these definitions do not reflect a social reality, for at that time the Vaynakh had not yet developed a strong sense of common identity, but rather described themselves in terms of their clan affiliation. Moreover, the Russian classification introduced a certain confusion with some tribes referred to as both Chechen and Ingush,[12] while others formed yet another separate group – the Qarabulaq (or Orstkhoy).

Unlike Chechnya, which was named after its inhabitants, Daghestan was given a geographic name which can be translated as 'the mountain country'.[13] It held the lion's share of the North Caucasus' ethnic and linguistic diversity with more than thirty ethno-linguistic groups inhabiting the area, some being confined to the population of a single village.[14]

The largest ethnic group in Daghestan were the Avars, who initially formed two separate groups on the basis of the two dialects spoken. The Ma'arulal group in the north spoke the Khunzakh (Khunz) dialect,[15] while the Bagulal group in the south spoke the Antsaqul dialect.[16] The Avars occupied the central part of Daghestan bordered by Chir-Yurt village in the north and Zakartalah (Zakataly in Russian) in the south.

---

later Slav settlers.

9 Some of the Vaynakh tribes were formed by ethnically different outsiders who with the passage of time assimilated into Vaynakh society and adopted the Nakh language as their own. The Tarkoy (Targhoy) tribe, for example, most likely originated from Targhu in Daghestan, and the Batsay tribe – from Tsov-Tushetia in present-day Georgia. See Avtorkhanov, 1831, no. 4, p. 26.

10 Uslar, 1888, p. 33.

11 *Ibid.*

12 Thus, for example the Akki tribe was referred to as Ingush by Genko, 1930, and as Chechen by Arskhanov, 1959.

13 'Dagh' in Turkish means 'mountain'.

14 Khashaev, 1961, pp. 17-20; Goroda i Okruga Dagestanskoy oblasti. Statisticheskie dannye o naselenii Zakavakzskogo kraya izvlechennye iz poimennykh spiskov, 1886, part IV (hereafter, Goroda i okruga...).

15 Named after the political centre of the northern Avars, the Khunzakh-*aul.*

16 Named after the political centre of the southern Avars, Antsaqul.

Their territory ran as a long strip from north to south through the whole of Inner Daghestan dividing it into two parts.

The area to the north-west of the Avars along the northern reaches of the Andi Koysu was inhabited by people ethnically close to the Avars but speaking a distinct Andi dialect, which gave the name to these people (who called themselves Qwannowr or Qwannal).

The area to the south of Andi and west of the Avars along the south bank of the Upper Andi Koysu river was inhabited by a small ethnic group known as the Didoy (who called themselves Tsezibi or Tsezi).

To the east of the Avars lay the valley of the Koysu river inhabited by the Laks, a coherent ethnic group who spoke a distinct dialect of the Dargho-Lak group.

The area east of the valley of the Koysu river was inhabited by the second most numerous people after the Avars, the Darghins. Up to the twelfth century the people of Dargho (Dargintsy in Russian) lived on the Caspian plain, but were later forced out by the Qumyq into the mountains. In the eighteenth century they came to occupy middle Daghestan in the mountain plains at a medium altitude, bounded by the River Gerga to the north, the Ulu Koysu to the south, the valley of Koysu to the west and the Qumyq plain in the east.

Alongside the people of Dargho in the mountains of the southern part of the Ulu Koysu valley lived another ethnic group closely related to the people of Dargho but speaking a distinct dialect – the people of Qaytaq.

Southern Daghestan was inhabited by several ethnic groups speaking the Samur group of the north-eastern branch of the Ibero-Caucasian languages. The Lezgs occupied the whole of the south-eastern part of Daghestan in the basin of Guilgeri-Chay, the middle and lower reaches of the Samur and Shakhnabad rivers; the Aghuls inhabited the Samur basin to the west of its confluence with the Qara Samur and the southern slopes of the Caucasian mountains in the area of Ilisu (Elisu in Russian); the Rutulal people lived near the confluence of the rivers Samur and Qara Samur; and the people of Tabarsaran inhabited the Upper Rubas-Chay and Upper Chirah-Chay.[17]

While the inaccessible mountains helped to preserve the ancient type of Caucasian aboriginals almost in their pure form (with some insig-

---

[17] Several theories have ventured to provide an explanation of such linguistic and ethnic variety. One suggested that it was the geographical isolation that led the parent Caucasian language to develop into smaller branches and dialects. Berzhe, 1858; Komarov, 1873; Kovalevskiy, 1890, vol. 2; Bokarev, 1961; Klimov, 1965. This theory, however, does not explain why the inhabitants of two neighbouring villages on the plain, only 2-3km. away from each other, speak different dialects or even languages. More plausible seems the theory according to which '...these numerous languages were not the creation of specific Caucasian conditions...but rather the result of a gradual process of the expansion of the ancient peoples of the south into the Caucasian mountains.' Marr, 1916, no. 5, pp. 1379-1408.

nificant admixture of foreign ethnic elements), the lowlands of eastern Daghestan, more open to foreign migrants, witnessed the creation of new nations. When coastal Daghestan was overrun by the Turkic speaking tribes,[18] the Qumyq[19] and Noghay[20] ethnic groups were formed; these came to occupy a considerable part of the northern and eastern plain of Daghestan between the mountains and the coastal area.

In the south the émigrés from Shirwan and Kubah (in northern Azerbaijan) formed a considerable Azeri (south-western or Oghuz Turks) community in Derbend.

The Tats (Persian-speaking Jews) and Persian émigrés who throughout history came to settle in the North Caucasus lived in ethnically defined communities, mainly in Derbend and in the *aul* of Miskinjy (Miskindzhi) in the country of Dargho.

Following the Arab conquests in the late seventh and, particularly the first half of the eighth century a number of Arab fortresses were built around Derbend such as Kamah, al-Muhammadiyya and Dar-Waq.[21] These were populated by Arab warriors, builders, merchants and craftsmen,[22] alongside the small number of later immigrants from Syria, Baghdad and, particularly, Yemen, most of whom were Muslim scholars and missionaries; they preserved their language and tribal association up to the eighteenth century.[23]

---

[18] This process falls into several periods. The first penetration of the Turkic elements came from the north in the second century AD. The second and more significant inflow dates back to the tenth-eleventh centuries AD. See Fedorov and Fedorov, 1978; Shiksaidov, 1984, pp. 400-3.

[19] The Qumyq people were formed in the twelfth century in the process of the assimilation of the Qypchaq Turks with the local Ibero-Caucasian people of the northern Steppes of Daghestan.

[20] The Noghay people were formed at the time of the disintegration of the Golden Hord. According to the two dialects spoken, the Noghay tribes were divided into the Noghay proper and the Qara Noghay.

[21] See Yaqubi, 1927, vol. III, IV; Genko, 1941, pp. 81-111.

[22] Al-Qadari, 1903, p. 25. For more on the Arabs in Daghestan see Shiksaidov, 1984, pp. 397-400; Shikhsaidov, 1969, p. 93; Genko, 1941, pp. 97-9.

[23] Bakikhanov, 1926; Genko, 1941, pp. 85-93; Gerber, 1958, pp. 307-8; Zeydlits, 1894, pp. 51-2.

2

THE SOCIAL STRUCTURE[1] AND POLITICAL MAKE-UP[2] OF THE NORTH CAUCASUS

The ethno-linguistic diversity of the North Caucasus was matched by the political structure of the area, which prior to the Russian conquest in the nineteenth century, had never been united under the rule of one people or one dynasty. In contrast to this remarkable ethnic and political diversity, the social and economic structures of the various North Caucasian peoples had many common features.

The social structure of North Caucasian society was based on the clan (or tribal) system. At the lowest level was the extended family – *dözal* or *tsa'* in Vaynakh,[3] *ahyu* or *kuflet* in Tabarsaran etc. – which included up to thirty people (the head of the family, his wife, families of their grown-up male children and grandchildren).[4] All members of an extended family shared common property and joint responsibilities. The head of the family regulated all economic activities, distributed jobs, gave his authorisation for marriage or divorce and was responsible for the well-being and good behaviour of the whole family. He petitioned for his family, mediated in disputes and represented it at trials.[5]

After the death of the head of the family the succession did not necessarily pass to the eldest son, but to the most capable and respected.[6] In some Daghestani societies the widow of the head of the family was

[1] This description of the social structure of the North-eastern Caucasian peoples is derived from the following sources: Akhriev, 1871; Aliev, 1970; Alimova, 1992; Avtorkhanov, 1931; Berzhe, 1858; Berzhe, 1859, Berzhe, 1859(a); Berzhe, 1876; Golovinskiy, 1878; Ippolitov, 1868; Ivanenkov, 1910; Khashaev, 1956; Khashaev, 1957; Khashaev, 1961; Kosven, 1963; Kovalevskiy, 1890, vol. 1, 2; Laudaev, 1872; Magomedov, 1957; Marr, 1920; Martirosyan, 1940; Medzhidov, 1992; Petrushevskiy, 1934; Pozhidaev, 1926; Volkova, 1989; Yakovlev, 1928; Yashinkov, 1958.

[2] In addition to the above sources, on political formations see Mekhtulinskie Khany, 1862; Shamkhaly Tarkovskie, 1869; A.K. 1869; Butkov, 1958; Kotsebu, 1958; Scherbachev, 1958.

[3] On the social structure among the Vaynakh see Mamakaev, 1973; Kovalevskiy, 1890, vol. 2.

[4] Kosven, 1963; Kovalevskiy, 1888.

[5] Dalgat, 1929, pp. 308-9.

[6] *Ibid.*, p. 308.

allowed to take his place if the members of a family so agreed.[7] This was never the case in Vaynakh families, where authority was strictly confined to the male members.[8]

The family dwellings of the mountain Vaynakh were centered around a common traditional tower (*ghal*),[9] while on the plain and in Daghestan the members of a large extended family lived in one house divided into a number of isolated rooms with separate entries, each facing a common courtyard. By the end of the eighteenth century some large families came to live in separate houses in one neighbourhood, which allowed its members greater autonomy, but did not free them from subordination to the head of the family, whose authority still applied to all members of the extended family.

Several extended families closely related to each other formed a clan – *gar* or *neq'i* among the Vaynakh, *sihil, qa'am, jins* in southern Daghestan etc. Their blood kinship was based on an actual common ancestor, whom they all knew and could name. Several *gars* formed a tribe – *teip* among the Vaynakh, *haldan* or *hamadan* among the Rutul, Ahtin and Tsakhur; *tabun* among the Qumyq, *uhtsi* or *urtshi* in Kubachi, *toqum* among the Lezg, *dzhegala kante* in Akusha, *evled, jins, qoum, utzi-urmi* in Qaytaq.[10] Members of a tribe claimed blood relationship and traced a common ancestry, but unlike that in a clan, this could have been actual or putative. The number of clans united in a tribe differed from one area to another – in Tabarsaran a *toqum* could consist of two to six *sihl's* (clans); in Qara Qaytaq – five; in the Upper Qaytaq – nine; in Kubachi – seven etc.[11]

The formation of tribes and clans was a continuous process, and tribal and clan identity were capable of transformation. When leaving their *teip* and resettling in new territory, clans could preserve their tribal name and blood association (as was the case with the Chechen Akki-Aukh tribe) or lose the sense of common identity (as happened in the case of Benoy, Tsentaroy and some other Chechen *teips* which came out of the Nohchimahkoy tribe and eventually lost any affiliation with it). The North Caucasian tribes were named after a real or putative ancestor, or could bear the name of the most famous man in a tribe or the toponym of its origin.[12]

The Vaynakh as well as most of the Daghestanis (apart from the Noghay nomads) were sedentary agricultural and pastoral peoples, who

---

7 See Alimova, 1992, pp. 130, 131-3.

8 Dalgat, 1929, p. 310.

9 On the Vaynakh dwellings and villages see 'Chechensky Aul', 1862; Grabovskiy, 1870; Kobychev, 1982.

10 See Documents in Khashaev 1965.

11 Kovalevskiy, 1890, vol. 1-2; Khashaev, 1965.

12 Kovalevskiy, 1890, vol. 2, p. 249; Dalgat, 1929, p. 308; Khashaev, 1965, p. 5.

lived in villages (*aul* – mountain village; *yurt* – lowland village). Several villages formed a rural commune[13] – *jama'at* in Daghestan; *tuqum* – among the Vaynakh. In the mountains communal borders were defined by the natural boundaries (river, canyon, slope, hollow etc.), while on the lowland *tuqums* and *jama'ats* comprised several adjacent villages.

Originally, the most widespread type of settlement in the North Caucasus comprised one tribe. Later settlements included several tribes, through the merging of a number of tribal settlements, the migration of new tribes from areas affected by war or devastation, or the branching out of a large tribe into several smaller independent ones.[14] Thus, the rural commune in the late eighteenth-early nineteenth centuries became a socio-political and territorial entity, united by common economic and defence aims, rather than a purely tribal one.

In all Vaynakh *tuqums* and most of the high-mountain Daghestani *jama'ats*, the tribe continued to be a main source of identification and to act as the subject of economic and legal relationships within the commune, which hence can be described as the tribal association. The villages were divided into quarters along tribal lines; members of one tribe jointly owned arable land and acted as a single body in all inter-tribal dealings. Members of one tribe shared common responsibility for and enjoyed the protection of their tribe, which ensured strict adherence to all regulations imposed by the clan and tribal authorities. These rules can be summarised as the following moral code: first, an obligation of each member of a tribe to follow principles laid down by the tribe; second, a right to an equal share in the communal land-holding; third declaration by the whole tribe of blood revenge on another clan for the killing or public humiliation of one of its members; fourth, rendering assistance to a family in need; fifth, unconditional implementation of the tribal regulations of the social and moral code; and finally, uncon-ditional adherence to the decisions made by the tribe's elders.[15]

Conversely, in many Daghestani *jama'ats* tribal identity was eroded, and the extended family emerged as the principle economic and legal nucleus. The tribal principle of settlement within a village was abandoned, so that the arable land belonged to the extended or even individual families rather than tribes, and each family represented itself in legal matters without the mediation or patronage of their tribe.[16]

Among the Vaynakh, the *tuqum* was the ultimate political entity. At the end of the eighteenth century there were 130 *teips* which the Russians referred to as Chechen. Two-thirds of these formed nine *tuqums* – Akkiy, Melkhiy, Nohchimahkoy, Terloy, Chantiy, Cheberloy, Sharoy and

---

[13] In Russian terminology, *sel'skaya obshchina*.

[14] Alimova, 1992, pp. 83-6.

[15] This short summary is based on Mamakaev, 1973, pp. 28-41.

[16] Khashaev, 1965, pp. 6-9.

Shoatoy, while the Ortskhoy (or Qarabulaq) occupied a midway position between the Chechen and Ingush and was assigned to both or regarded as a separate group altogether. The remaining one third of the Chechen *teips* each formed their own *tuqum* (Zurzuqoy, Maistoy, Peshkhoy, Sadoy etc.).[17] *Teips* referred to as Ingush made up five more *tuqums*, the most numerous of which was Ghalghay.[18]

In Daghestan the main political entity was an association of several *jama'ats* which formed a military alliance – *bo* among the Avars,[19] *mahall* (magal in Russian sources) in southern Daghestan. Russian scholars defined this as '*vol'noe obshchestvo*' (free association). The *jama'at* associations were formed on the basis of territory and united neighbouring *jama'ats* that were often inhabited by people belonging to different ethno-linguistic groups. The *jama'ats* within such an association while acting in unison *vis-à-vis* other associations and outside parties, continued to exist as separate economic and administrative entities which maintained autonomy in running their own affairs.[20] In the late eighteenth century there were about sixty *jama'at* associations whose composition was subject to constant change.[21]

At times of serious external threat the *jama'at* associations formed loose confederations (in the Russian definition '*soyuz volnykh obshchestv*' – the union of the free associations). Only two of the latter – Akusha and Dargho Confederations – became permanent.[22]

System of rule and administration

Being the principle economic and administrative entity, the rural commune was the focus of legal and administrative powers, with ultimate authority vested in the elected council of elders. The council of elders was composed of the representatives of each clan and tribe living in the commune. They were elected on the basis of *duces exvirtute summit*, with the main criteria being courage, military competence, energy and a deep knowledge of the local codes of '*adat*.

Decisions on the most important issues concerning all members of the commune were based on the general consent expressed at the people's assembly at which all adult males had the right of free voice and vote.

[17] Mamakaev, 1973, pp. 18-24.

[18] On tribes and communes among the Vaynakh see Avtorkhanov, 1931; Berzhe, 1859; Kusheva, 'Chechnya i Ingushetiya v XVI-XVII vekakh (manuscript, hereafter' Chechnya i Ingushetiya..); Laudaev, 1872; Mamakaev, 1936; Mamakaev, 1973.

[19] The local names of these associations, e.g. *bo* literally means 'army' which indicates the military basis of the original alliances.

[20] For a description of these unions see Kovalevskiy, 1890, vol. 2, pp. 153-63.

[21] Khashaev, 1965, p. 4.

[22] Some scholars compared the *jama'at* association with a republic and confederation with the federal republic. See Komarov, 1873, vol. 8, p. 6.

In some communes one vote against the decision was enough in principle to revoke it altogether, although in practice to put oneself against the whole commune was dangerous and could result in expulsion.[23] Thus, to advocate a different point of view, one had to solicit some support from at least several other members of the commune.

In the Vaynakh *tuqums*, the council of elders had no elected or hereditary heads and possessed only legislative power. In most Daghestani *jama'ats* the council of elders had a head of the council elected by its members from 'the wisest of the elders' (in Qaytaq) or simply 'the wisest of men' (in Tabarsaran), and approved at the people's gathering. The main criteria at these elections were the candidate's qualities as a military leader and his knowledge of the *'adat*, which was essential since he enjoyed the ultimate administrative and judicial authority within the *jama'at*.

In the *jama'at* association supreme power rested with either the head of the council of elders of the most powerful *jama'at* or the one elected at the joint gathering of the *jama'ats*' council of elders. Such a head of the *jama'at* association had the authority to declare war or conclude peace on behalf of the whole association, assemble a people's army and lead it in battle. He also exercised the supreme legal authority within the association. In the confederation of *jama'at* associations, this power rested upon the head of the Confederation (e.g. the Qadi of Akusha).

In the Vaynakh lands matters which involved all Vaynakh *tuqums* were dealt with by the *Mehq-Qel* (lit. 'the council of the land') – the council of elders where all Vaynakh *tuqums* were represented.

In some Daghestani *jama'at* associations the office of the head of the association gradually became vested within one particular clan or family (e.g. in the Rutul, Tsakhur and Kurah *jama'ats*) or evolved into a hereditary position. In the latter case the *jama'at* associations turned into more centralised political formations, which in Russian terminology were defined as *vladenie* (lit. holding).[24] In nineteenth-century Daghestan there were fifteen such holdings, the most powerful of which were the Avar khanate, with its centre in Khunzakh;[25] the khanate of Ghazi-Ghumuq, which united some of the Lak, Lezg, Avar and, at times, Dargho *jama'ats*;[26] the *qadiyat* and *maysumiyat* of Tabarsaran (with two distinct dynasties in the north

---

[23] As registered in 'The 'Adat of Rustem Khan' – the Avar ruler of the eighteenth century. For the Russian translation see Khashaev, 1965.

[24] Khashaev, 1965, introduction, p. 4.

[25] In the nineteenth century the Avar khanate comprised the territory bordering on the khanate of Mehtuli in the east, Ghazi-Ghumuq in the south-east, Jaro Belokany *jama'at* in the south-west and the Koysubu Avar *jama'at* in the north. See Khashaev, 1958, p. 146; *Materialy po Istorii Chechni i Dagestana*, 1940, pp. 185-6.

[26] Khashaev, 1961, p. 186.

and south);[27] the *utsmiyat* of Qaytaq with the centre in Majalis which consisted of the *jama'ats* of Qara Qaytaq, Qaytaq, Ghamri-Dargho, Terkeme and Kaba-Dargho;[28] *shamkhalat* of Targhu in the northern Daghestan which united ·some of the Qumyq, Avar and Lak peoples, the sultanate of Ilisu in the southern Daghestan, etc.[29]

No hereditary dynasties were formed among the Vaynakh. Only for a short period of time, in the second half of the sixteenth century, did some of the Chechen tribes of the eastern lowland areas fall under the political domination of their powerful Qumyq neighbours and had to pay tribute to the *shamkhal* of Targhu and Ghazi-Ghumuq,[30] while the Kabardian (Ghabarta) knights imposed tribute on the Ingush tribes of the western lowlands.[31] The period of both the Qumyq and Kabardian domination was short-lived and their protectorate was denounced already in the late sixteenth-early seventeenth centuries.[32]

In Daghestan, the way in which ruling dynasties came into being varied from one *jama'at* to another. Most commonly the elected office gradually became fixed within one clan and subsequently one family.[33] Alternatively, members of the established ruling families were initiated as mediators into some *jama'ats*, which in turn accepted their authority.[34]

---

[27] On Tabarsaran see Alimova, 1992; Khashaev, 1961.

[28] In the early nineteenth century the *utsmiyat* of Qaytaq comprised the territory from the Caspian sea in the west up to the Qaytaq mountains in the east and was divided into two distinct areas – the lowland Qaytaq and the Upper Qaytaq, with the first populated almost exclusively by the Qumyq and the latter by the people of Dargho. Khashaev, 1961, p. 172.

[29] Khashaev, 1961; Kozubinskiy in Khashaev (ed.) 1958; Shamkhaly Tarkovskie, 1868.

[30] Butkov 1850, p. 134; Maksimov, 1893, p. 25; Laudaev, 1872, pp. 2-5; Kusheva, 'Chechnya i Ingushetiya...', p. 35.

[31] Kusheva, 'Chechnya i Ingushetiya...', pp. 33-4.

[32] Maksimov, 1893, pp. 26-7.

[33] The *utsmiy* of Qaytaq had originally been elected at the people's gathering. Gradually the choice of the *utsmiy* became restricted to the members of one clan and then became hereditary. However, in tribute to the old tradition, a new *utsmiy* was to be confirmed at the assembly of the people when the most respected elder put a small hat (similar to the Jewish cap) on the head of a new *utsmiy*. After the confirmation ceremony the new *utsmiy* distributed presents – money, cattle and sheep – among the elders and most respected families and arranged a party for the whole *jama'at*.
The hereditary titles of *maysum* in southern Tabarsaran and *qadi* in northern Tabarsaran were also reconfirmed at people's gatherings. The ritual was similar to that in Qaytaq, the only difference being that instead of a cap the most respected elder 'crowned' a new ruler with his *papakha* (Astrakhan hat). For a discription of the ritual see Alimova, 1992, p. 25.

[34] In the fifteenth century the people of Aymaq invited a member of the family of the Ghazi-Ghumuq Khans, Mehti as a mediator and a judge. Thus, emerged a new *jama'at* association known as the khanate of Mehtuli, which existed until its dissolution by the Russian administration – in 1860. Mekhtulinskie khany, 1869, pp. 56-9.

Some *jama'ats* were subjugated by force.[35]

The hereditary rulers were the supreme judicial and administrative authorities in their land. They regulated inter-*jama'at* relations, introduced taxes and fines, made peace, declared war and assumed supreme military authority during wartime.[36]

Central rulers often appointed governors – *naibs* or *beks* – to *jama'ats* under their authority, and in turn they formed the local gentry. In their administrative role the *bek* replaced the elected head of the *jama'ats* council of elders. In most *jama'ats* and *jama'at* associations the power of a central ruler over the *beks* was far from being authoritarian; the former's position was that 'of the eldest in the clan and a mediator, rather than sovereign'.[37]

Beks and central rulers largely depended upon the military class of *nukers*, with the *bash-nuker* ('chief *nuker*') in command. Chosen from the people loyal to a *bek* or central ruler, they played the role of domestic police force in peacetime and formed the nucleus of the army in war.

The power of local rulers was far from absolute. *Jama'ats* which had submitted to the central power of a hereditary ruler still preserved a considerable degree of their traditional self-rule. Moreover, some confederations elected mediators to deal with the disputes between the *jama'at* and central ruler. In Tabarsaran, for example, all *jama'ats* within the *maysumiyat* elected three supreme judges (*ahi-kevk*) who mediated in disputes between *jama'ats* within the *maysumiyat*, as well as those between *jama'ats* and the *maysum*. The decision of the *ahi-kevks* was final and indisputable.[38]

The equilibrium between the power of a hereditary ruler and that of the *jama'ats* within the association was easily upset which led to long-lasting power struggles between them. To overcome the resistance of the *jama'ats*, who tried to preserve their independence and extend their authority over them, the hereditary rulers often appealed to foreign powers.[39] In return the *jama'ats* constantly strove to dismiss the power of the central ruler and as soon as they gained strength and sensed the ruler's weakness denounced his authority.

---

[35] The Sultanate of Ilisu was created on the basis of Alazan valley *jama'ats* conquered by the people of Tsakhur. Yashinkov, 1958, pp. 304-5.

[36] *TsGA Dagestana*, fond 150, opis' 1, fond 150, delo 1, list 15.

[37] Shikhsaidov, 1969, p. 151.

[38] Alimova, 1992, pp. 181-4.

[39] The Sultans of Ilisu were able to gain the upper hand in their struggle for hereditary power only after they appealed for support to the Persian rulers. Later they concluded agreements with both the Persians and Ottomans, depending on who was more influential at a particular time, and finally signed an agreement with the Russians, who gained the upper hand in the struggle for power in the region. The same kind of power game was played by almost all other local rulers. See Chapters 8-10 on Russian Colonisation.

3

THE ECONOMIC STRUCTURE OF NORTH CAUCASIAN SOCIETY[1]

All the territory belonging to a particular *jama'at* or *tuqum* was traditionally divided among arable land and a small area of common pasture in the immediate proximity of the village, hayfields on the lower slopes and alpine pastures in the high mountains.

With slight modifications from one rural commune to another, land ownership took two main forms: private and communal. Arable fields were owned by the extended family, while pasture land constituted the joint and undivided property of the whole commune.

Even private ownership of arable land was not unconditional but was regulated by strict rules which guaranteed the right to acquire a neighbour's allotment. In the rare case of neighbours not being interested in the acquisition of land on offer, it was permissable to sell it to another clan – even one living in a different village – but never outside the *tuqum* or *jama'at*.[2] Moreover, individuals and even whole clans or tribes who had been expelled from the commune or simply left it were deprived of all rights to the land which had formerly belonged to them.[3] These rules prevented land from passing into the hands of a member of another confederation, for both the individual tribe and the tribal union strictly guarded the integrity of their land.

Economic activities in the commune were regulated by common rules. In Daghestan private arable land after the harvest was used as winter pasturage by the whole confederation; for this transition to be effective, special dates were observed for the beginning of sowing ('opening of the field') and the end of harvesting ('closing of the field'). No one was allowed to start sowing or harvesting in his own land before the public announcement of the requisite date for 'opening' or 'closing'.[4]

---

[1] Aglarov, 1988; Gavrilov, 1868; Grabovskiy, 1870; Kantariya, 1986; Magomedov, 1957; Maksimov, 1893; Malyavkin, 1893.

[2] In the Dargho *jama'ats*, a member who sold his land to an outsider had to pay one bull every day this land was owned by this outsider. The same law applied if the land was given as a dowry. See Aglarov, 1988, p. 83.

[3] Kovalevskiy 1890, vol. 2, pp. 142-5.

[4] See Aglarov, 1988, pp. 58-9; also on the *'adat* laws see Kovalevskiy, 1890, vol. 2, p. 135.

This practice did not apply to *tuqums* in the Vaynakh lands, since unlike in Daghestan, arable land was never used as pasture.[5] This does not imply that the regulations governing the use of land were any less restrictive. Originally, those who had developed and cultivated virgin land (which involved an enormous effort in clearing the land of trees and stones, fertilising and in some areas the construction of terraced fields) held personal and hereditary rights to it. By the eighteenth century this practice had been abandoned due to the shortage of arable land, and no one had the right to cultivate any piece of land without the permission of the *tuqum*'s or *jama'at's* authorities.[6]

In some communes, arable land which had been vacated by migrating clans/tribes or confiscated from serious offenders against the tribal code of conduct became part of communal property.[7] Allotments from this newly appropriated land were usually distributed among the most needy members of the commune (widows, orphans etc.) or rented out, but never sold. Only full members of the *tuqum* or *jama'at* had the right to rent such land, unlike outsiders temporarily employed as shepherds or blacksmiths or those staying as guests or taking refuge.

Hayfields were also the property of the whole *tuqum* or *jama'at*. Allotments were distributed annually by the council of elders among all members of the commune who had satisfied all the tributes and regulations of their clan, tribe and commune. Alternatively, allotments in the hayfields were distributed among tribes of the union, and then either further apportioned to the members of the tribe by the tribal authorities or used communally.

The most important communal property comprised the summer and winter pastures. The mountain pastures were used by all members of the commune, while those close to the village only by the inhabitants of that village. The pastures were strictly guarded with special fines levied for any damage. If cattle or sheep from another commune were found in one's pasture lands, the whole of that commune was held responsible.[8]

Daghestani *jama'ats* which formed *jama'at* associations shared political and military aims, but always preserved their territorial and economic integrity and independence. Thus, all laws concerning *jama'at* and outsiders applied to the other *jama'at* members within the association.[9]

---

[5] On the agricultural techniques of the Vaynakh see Kantariya, 1986, pp. 41-70.

[6] See Kovalevskiy, 1890, vol. 2, p. 62.

[7] Priority over such lands belonged to the clan of a previous owner, but in case his clan was for some reason not interested or had migrated to another area, this land became communal property.

[8] Aglarov, 1888, p. 64.

[9] See documents in the *TsGA Dagestan*, fond 150, opis' 1, delo 1, list 7; fond 2, delo 139a, list 9.

Some communes owned mountains with summer pastures and hayfields jointly and regulated their use at general meetings. Those who did not have their own summer or winter pastures rented them from others, exchanged winter for summer pastures,[10] or rented them in exchange for services. Thus, weak *jama'ats* rented part of their communal lands to a stronger one in exchang for its help and protection. Concluded orally, such agreements often led to confusion which could result in bitter land disputes between the *jama'ats* involved.

The use of distant pastures frequently resulted in the establishing of new, temporary or permanent settlements. These often attained the status of an independent *tuqum* or *jama'at*, which inevitably led to a conflict with the original rural commune over property rights and regulations. The shortage of land combined with the rigid regulation of land use and ownership which could not accommodate the constant evolution of North Caucasian society produced bitter and long-lasting conflicts between numerous tribal unions.[11]

Water, forests and other natural resources were also 'owned' and distributed by the *jama'ats*. Thus, water belonged to the commune which used it, rather than to that which controlled the territory of its source.

Land donated as *waqf* property (either arable or hayfields) constituted yet another distinct category of communal property. In high-mountain Daghestani *jama'ats* and virtually all Chechen *tuqums*, the arable land which was referred to as *waqf* property was rented out or even sold to the members of a commune. Those who bought *waqf* land became automatically responsible for all the duties which were associated with the *waqf* property. They could sell, rent or give this land in a dowry, but any new owner had to pay a land tax to the mosque, usually equivalent to half the harvest.[12]

In the Vaynakh and mountain Daghestani societies there was no class of landlords, and the only form of unconditional private ownership was of livestock, which hence became the main gauge of the wealth of a particular household. The working animals used in life were kept in byres or on the common close to the village the rest (mainly sheep) were sent out to the high mountain summer pastures and brought down only at the onset of winter.

Private land ownership developed only in the Daghestani *jama'ats* governed by hereditary rulers. Apart from the khans, *sultans* and others, the class of Daghestani landlords included their appointed governors – *beks*. Originally the *beks* received land from the central ruler as payment

---

[10] Kuynuk-Rubas, Ersi-Rubas, Chuvk-Rubas etc. exchanged pastures; Akki rented summer pastures from Qaytaq. See Alimova, 1992, pp. 48-56.

[11] For examples, see Aglarov, 1988, pp. 80-1.

[12] According to the documents the Kwankhi quarter mosque in the Chokh village, received revenues from forty ploughed fields. Aglarov, 1988, p. 80.

for their service. With the passage of time the land gradually became their unconditional hereditary property.[13] In southern and central Daghestan the class of landlords also included the *janka-beks* (children born of a *bek* and a common woman) who occupied a mid-way position between *beks* and *uzdens* (free men of common origin).[14]

Private land generally consisted of winter and/or summer pastures and, much more rarely included arable land due to the strict *jama'at* regulations. The landowners generally rented their land to the *jama'ats*. This repeatedly led to clashes between them, which at times ended in the *jama'ats* confiscating a khan's or *bek*'s lands. On the other hand, central rulers and their governors constantly sought the means to extend their domain into the territory of the weaker *jama'ats* and if possible to appropriate their land.

An overview of the geographical and ethno-linguistic composition of the North Caucasus reveals a great degree of diversity. That this did not create isolated communities among the peoples of the region was due to the fact that most of the people could speak at least two or three languages. A certain pattern was established according to which people inhabiting the territory higher into the mountains knew the language of their neighbours living in an area below, while Azeri Turkish was the *lingua franca* of the eastern Caucasus, or at least Daghestan. Furthermore, among the educated *'ulama* (again mainly in Daghestan) Arabic played its usual role as the language of education, scholarship and correspondence.

The topography of the North Caucasus, inaccessible mountains, deep forests and rocky slopes, combined with a lack of roads would seem to imply difficulties (if not impossibility) in communication between various tribal units. In practice, numerous mountain paths (which to the Europeans would have seemed impassable) and well trained horses provided the local peoples with all the means they needed to travel freely throughout the area. This remarkable ease of communication between various confederations, was noted by a Russian traveller who observed that people and news travelled throughout the North Caucasus much quicker than in the vast Russian steppes.

One must see the local ways of communication, have a close look into all natural boundaries laid down by the nature to separate people – and yet people communicate with each other much more easily, than for example people living on our [Russian] plain or steppe villages...the information travels as quickly as if the country were criss-crossed by telegraph wires.[15]

---

[13] Similar to the Turkish beys.

[14] See documents in *TsGA Dagestana*, fond 150, opis' 1, delo 1, list 2, 3, 4(ob).

[15] Voronov, 1868, pp. 19-20.

Social structures in common to North Caucasian society produced some sense of shared identity. This, however, was felt almost exclusively in the context of confrontation with the outside world. Once the North Caucasians were left to their own devices, the tribal structure of their society resurfaced, dividing them into numerous groups, each holding to its own self-seeking economic and political interests.

The existence of ruling dynasties in some parts of Daghestan instigated power struggles between them and the elected tribal authorities. In the course of these power struggles new alliances were made and broken which added to the generally complex nature of relationships between various *tuqums, jama'ats, jama'at* associations, etc.

The shortage of arable land and pastures stirred up antagonism between rural communes and led to constant clashes between them. With no centralised authority to mediate and with each tribe, rural commune (Daghestani *jama'at* and Chechen *tuqum*) and union of rural communes (*bo, mahall*) trying to secure its interests by all means available, a peaceful solution was difficult if almost impossible to reach.

Once conflict arose, it was difficult to end on account of the principle of collective responsibility whereby the entire tribe or commune was held responsible for the misdeeds of a single member, which left little room for compromise and retreat. In the Vaynakh lands, the situation was further aggravated by the lack of permanent judges and executive authorities. When a ruling was given, it was left to the tribe and clan to ensure that the decision was complied with. In case such a decision contradicted the interests of a certain clan or tribe, there were no judicial or law-enforcing bodies to impose it.

This led to the emergence of the deeply-rooted enmity and centuries-long confrontation between the various North Caucasian tribes and political formations.

Part II. ISLAM AND MUSLIM INSTITUTIONS IN THE NORTH CAUCASUS

4

ISLAM IN DAGHESTAN

The history of Islamisation [1]

The Islamisation of the North Caucasus was a complex and long-lasting process. The diffusion of Islam in Daghestan alone took almost 1,000 years and by the early nineteenth century revealed diverse patterns in various *jama'ats*.

The first stage of Islamisation ran parallel with the Arab conquests. In 733 AD, Umayyad Caliph Hisham's (r. 724-743 AD) brother, Abu Maslama, conquered Derbend and established it as a stronghold of the Arab-Muslim caliphate in the Caucasus.[2] By the time of Hisham's rule the religious policy of the caliphate had become one encouraging the conversion of all the peoples in the conquered areas and their acceptance as being of equal status to the Arabs.[3] Thus, the domain of Islam in Daghestan largely coincided with the area under Arab political influence.

Various Daghestani *jama'ats* and even some Chechen *tuqums* traced the time of their Islamisation to the conquest of Abu Maslama,[4] whom they often confused with Abu Muslim of Khorasan.[5] The ruling dynasties

---

[1] The history of the Islamisation of Daghestan is based on the following sources: Al-Qarakhi, 1929; Bakikhanov, 1926; *Derbend-nameh*, 1898; Lavrov, 1966; Lavrov, 1968; Minorskiy, 1953; Shikhsaidov, 1957; Shikhsaidov, 1958; Shikhsaidov, 1969; Shikhsaidov, 1974; Shikhsaidov, 1979; Shikhsaidov, 1984; Yaqubi, 1927.

[2] Shikhsaidov, 1969, pp. 5-11.

[3] Lapidus, 1991, pp. 63-4.

[4] See Shikhsaidov, 1957, pp. 67-8; Khanykof, 1847, p. 118.

[5] Abu Muslim of Khorasan was a popular leader of the uprising in 749 AD which resulted in the fall of the Ummayad dynasty and the ascendance of the Abbasids. Later Abu Muslim became a symbol of religious and social opposition often seen as a precursor of the messiah.

of the *shamkhals* in Ghazi-Ghumuq,[6] *utsmiys* of Qaytaq,[7] and *maysums* of Tabarsaran[8] all claimed to be the descendants of the Arab governors of noble origin.[9] It is probably best to regard such claims as legendary for the title of *shamkhal* was first mentioned in the thirteenth century[10] and that of *utsmiy* only in the sixteenth,[11] while the Islamisation of the Avar and other peoples inhabiting Inner Daghestan, let alone the Vaynakh tribes, did not even start until several centuries after the Arab conquests.

The Arab expansion in the area was confined to south-eastern Daghestan, including Derbend, Tabarsaran, Qaytaq and lowland Kura, which had previously been under Persian political and cultural domination. The more remote areas of Akusha, Khunzakh, Ghumuq and Ashty remained largely beyond the Arab-Muslim reach. The effect of the military campaigns into Inner Daghestan of Abu Maslama and his successors (at the time of Caliph Marwan ibn Muhammad (r. 744-50 AD) proved to be superficial and short-lived, and in the late eighth century the Khazars and Daghestanis jointly expelled the Arabs from all the areas above Derbend, Derbend itself falling for a short time under Khazar rule in 799 AD.[12]

Under the Abbasid caliphate, the grip of the central rulers on the Caucasian frontier gradually weakened. The Hashimid dynasty established itself in Derbend as *de facto* independent rulers only nominally accountable to the Shirwan-shahs.[13]

The first major stage in the Islamisation of Daghestan was completed in the tenth century. By that time Derbend had become a predominantly Muslim city and a stronghold of Islam in the area; the Lezgs and the people of Tabarsaran were Islamised more superficially; the rest of

---

[6] The legend claims that Abu Maslama appointed a nobleman from Syria (Sham in Arabic) as his regent, which gave the name to the ruler's title. Thus, later the Lak rulers claimed to be descendants of the Syrian Arabs, and derived the title of *shamkhal* from the name of the country their 'ancestors' had allegedly come from. *Debend-nameh,* 1898, pp. 174-5; Shamkhaly Tarkovskie, 1868, p. 56.

[7] A similar story explains the title of *maysum* of the Qaytaq rulers, which they derived from the Arabic '*ism, ismi* (honourable, noble), and claimed that the founder of the *utsmiy* dynasty was a noble Arab appointed by Abu Maslama as a regent. Shikhsaidov, 1969, pp. 19-22.

[8] In this case the local tradition ascribed it to the Arab root *asam* – 'pure'.

[9] The Avars also claim Arab descent for their rulers and pride themselves in allegedly being Islamised second, after the Laks, and directly at the hands of Abu Maslama. This claim is disputed by the people of Dargho who maintain that the *aul* Qurush in their lands was founded by a Qureishi Arab in the time of Abu Maslama. Al-Qarakhi, 1929, pp. 22-4; Bakikhanov, 1926, p. 44; *Derbend-nameh,* 1898, pp. 78-80.

[10] Shikhsaidov, 1984, p. 388.

[11] This title was granted to the rulers of Qaytaq by the Timurid sultan, Ahmad Khan (d.1578/88 AD) who had protectorate over Qaytaq.

[12] Shikhsaidov, 1969, pp. 29-35.

[13] Shikhsaidov, 1957, p. 72.

Daghestan remained pagan with influence from Christianity in the northern mountain areas, Judaism in the Khazar lands and Zoroastrianism
in Zerihgeran (Kubachi).

The second period of the Islamisation of the North Caucasus started
in the tenth century and was associated with Muslim missionaries and
merchant travellers who carried Islam to areas which had never been
under Arab rule. Situated on the crossroads of trade routes from China
and Central Asia to Byzantium (the famous Silk route) and from Asia
and the Middle East to eastern Europe (the fur trade route),[14] coastal
Daghestan became heavily involved in international trade, and Derbend
assumed great importance as a trade centre and port. The increasing
contacts with Muslim traders strengthened Islam in coastal Daghestan
and furthered the Islamisation of inner Daghestani *jama'ats*, with the
Muslims of Derbend now becoming increasingly involved in dispatching
missions into the mountain areas and winning for their city the title of
Bab al-Jihad (Gateway of Jihad).[15]

In the tenth-eleventh centuries it was the Turks who took over the
mission of propagating Islam in Daghestan. In the words of Bartold
'the victory of the Turkish element was accompanied by the victory
of Islam and Muslim culture'.[16] The rise to power of a Turkic Saljuq
dynasty (1038-1194 AD) encouraged further Islamisation, for 'after gaining strong positions in Persia, the Saljuqs became powerful and turned
their attention to Shirwan and Daghestan. During their rule many *jama'ats*
of high- and lower-mountain Daghestan became Muslim.'[17] It is most
likely that the spread of the Shafi'i *madhhab* throughout the eastern
and central Caucasus was due to Saljuq influence.

The Mongol conquests (particularly in eastern and southern Daghestan
which led to the incorporation of those areas into the Golden Horde
empire) hampered the process of Islamisation. However, after Khan
Berke converted to Islam (1257-66 AD), the Mongol Khans themselves
encouraged Islamisation in their domains. With the victory in 1385 of
the famous Khan Timur (Tamerlane) over Tohtamysh, his pagan governor
and rival in the North Caucasus, the Islamisation of the area became
inevitable.[18]

To become firmly established Islam had to compete in Daghestan

[14] Belyayeva and Leskov, 1990; Shikhsaidov, 1958, p. 129. For a description of the
Daghestani harbour see Istarkhi, as translated in Minorskiy, 1953, pp. 127-8.

[15] Shikhsaidov, 1958, pp. 133-4.

[16] Bartold, 1928, p. 19.

[17] Bakikhanov, 1926, p.54.

[18] In 1836 Timur undertook a number of military campaigns into the mountain Daghestan
(Salataw, Qaytaq, etc.). Like most of his campaigns, apart from the military aims, these
pursued the Islamisation of the newly conquered areas. For more information, see Tizen-
gauzen, 1941, vol. I, pp. 74-5, 116.

not only with pagan beliefs[19] but also with Zoroastrianism, Judaism (in eastern Daghestan) and, especially, Christianity which had for centuries dominated the religious life of the area.[20]

The ousting of Christianity and other religions by Islam was a gradual and lengthy process which is reflected in epigraphic inscriptions and local oral tradition. For instance, thirteenth-century Muslim tombstone engravings from southern and central Daghestan contain Christian names.[21]

Ample evidence portraying the clash between Christianity and Islam is to be found in mythology, which preserved the stories of struggle between the white (Muslim) and the black (Christian) angels, and maintained two pantheons of jinns: the good (Muslim) and the evil (Christian) ones fighting each other over people's souls.[22]

The expansion of Islam in the North Caucasus continued throughout the fourteenth and fifteenth centuries. By the late fourteenth century Zerihgeran, in which all three monotheistic religions and Zoroastrianism had been widely practised, became a predominantly Muslim city, and ever since, became known as Kubachi (Turkish for the original Persian name, meaning 'chain-mail armour makers').[23]

In Qaytaq the struggle between Christianity and Islam lasted till the end of the fifteenth century when Islam finally became the dominant religion.[24] The Islamisation of the Avar, who from the sixth century AD were under particularly strong Christian influence, started in the twelfth century, but became more profound only after Timur's reign (1370-1405 AD).

The fifteenth century was a turning point in the process of Islamisation of the North Caucasus. From this time onwards it was carried out mostly by local agents. Among the latter, the Laks became the most ardent proselytisers of Islam through their active participation in Timur's military campaigns. This was recognised in their newly acquired name:

[19] On pre-Islamic beliefs, in addition to the sources already mentioned, see Bulatova, 1988; Khalilov, 1988; Gadzhieva, 1985; Khanykoff, 1847.

[20] In the early centuries (six-ninth) the spread of Christianity was associated with Byzantium, Armenia and Caucasian Albania. Starting from the ninth and, particularly, the twelfth century during the reign of Queen Tamara (1184-1218 AD), Georgia became politically strong and had the primary role in propagating Christianity in the region. In the fourteenth-fifteenth centuries, few efforts were spared by Catholic missions from Venice and Genoa, and in the eighteenth century Protestant, Lutheran and Anglican churches sent their priests to the area, whose efforts, however, remained largely unsuccessful.

[21] See Shikhsaidov, 1984, p. 407; Lavrov, 1966, p. 83.

[22] See Shikhsaidov, 1957, vol. 3; Ataev, 1963; Dakhkilgov, 1991, story 176, p. 204.

[23] In 1404/5 the first *madrasah* was constructed, which suggests the existence of a considerable Muslim population in the city by that time.

[24] The first Muslim inscriptions in Qaytaq date back to 1422 AD. In the account of Afanasiy Nikitin, the town is described as a Muslim one, although another traveller of the same century, Barbado, claimed the existence among the Qaytaq of Christians of the Greek-Orthodox, Armenian and Catholic churches.

Ghazi-Ghumuqs, i.e. warriors for the sake of Islam. In the late fifteenth century, the Laks Islamised the people of Gidatl, which became one of the most important centres of Muslim learning and for centuries maintained strong links with Ghazi-Ghumuq. The Qarah, Tzunti and Archi peoples and some Avar *jama'ats*[25] also converted to Islam through Lak missionary activities, both peaceful and military. The process of the Islamisation of Daghestan was at least nominally completed by the late sixteenth century when the last Daghestani people, the Didoy, were converted to Islam by the missionary efforts of the Avar Muslims.[26]

Arab-Muslim learning in Daghestan[27]

By the sixteenth century Daghestan had become the major centre of Muslim learning in the area, where most of the local religious figures and clerics received their education. Many of the Daghestani *jama'ats* established an elaborate network of *madrasahs*, the most important of which were those in Ghazi-Ghumuq, Akusha, Qudutl, Khunzakh, Enderi, Tsakhur and Yaragh. The subjects studied were the Qur'an and Sunna, logic, law, mysticism and, particularly, the Arabic language, with much less stress laid on science and medicine.[28]

Once the Islamisation of the *jama'ats* in mountain Daghestan was complete, the domain of Arab-Muslim culture and learning expanded further to the north of Derbend. This expansion coincided with and was part of the wider process of Arabisation, which brought about the diffusion of the Arabic language and culture into the remote areas of the Muslim world (such as India, Malaysia, the Balkans) at the very time when the Arab countries themselves had finally lost their independence (the re-conquest of Grenada in 1492 by the Christians, the conquest of Egypt by the Ottomans in 1517, etc.).

One of the main channels of the influence of Arab-Muslim culture

[25] According to the local tradition, a certain man, Rutuya, was expelled from the village Hodota and settled in Ghazi-Ghumuq, where he converted to Islam. When the period of his exile ended, Rutuya returned to his native village as a devout Muslim. Not being able to convince his tribesmen to accept Islam, he invited the people of Ghazi-Ghumuq, Khunzakh and Gidatl, who spread Islam with sword and fire among the Avar, Bagulal and Tindi *jama'ats*.

[26] The Didoy people were under the strong political and cultural domination of the neighbouring Georgian Kakheti kingdom and at times were part of it. In 1469 a Georgian chronicler referred to them as pagan. By the end of the sixteenth century, due to the missionary activities of the Avar Muslims, the Didoy people became Islamised.

[27] The main sources used for this section in addition to the above mentioned are: Abdulaev, 1968; Gamzatov, 1990; Aytberov 1977; Aytberov, 1978-9; Barabanov, 1945; Genko, 1941; Krachkovskiy, 1960; Krachkovskiy, 1960(a); al-Shawqani, 1348 (1929/30); Saidov, 1963; Tagirova, 1988.

[28] See Gamzatov, 1990, pp. 211-46; Tagirova, 1988, pp. 136-8; Shikhsaidov, 1969, pp. 218-22.

in Daghestan was the Arabs who lived in the area. The first Arab settlers appeared in Daghestan at the time of the Arab military campaigns in the eighth century[29] when a considerable community was established in Derbend and its environs. The legacy of these settlers was felt up to the 1930s, when people in the village of Dar-Waq, 35km. to the west of Derbend claimed Arabic as their native language.[30]

Not all the Arabs in Daghestan were, however, the descendants of these original settlers; individual Arabs continued to settle in the area in the thirteenth-sixteenth centuries as well.[31] Most of these Arabs were well-educated scholars from Syria, Yemen etc. who gained positions of high prestige and influence in Daghestani *jama'ats*.[32] Individual Arabs continued to arrive in the eighteenth and nineteenth centuries.[33]

Another important channel of cultural exchange between Daghestani and Arab scholars was that of the Daghestani travellers in the Arab lands both on pilgrimage and for study at the leading centres of Muslim learning in the Hijaz, Syria, Egypt, Iraq and, especially, Yemen.[34]

The cultural links between Daghestan and the Arab world ensured the dominant role of the Arabic language in the Daghestani literary tradition. Not only were the local scholars copying various Arabic manuscripts, but they also created an indigenous Arabic literature of their

---

[29] According to al-Baladhuri, Maslama had settled 24,000 Syrian warriors at Bab al-Abwab, who lived in four quarters named Damascus, Homs, Kufa and al-Jazira. See Minorskiy, 1953, p. 19, n. 19. It is likely that the number of settlers was exaggerated, although it was undoubtedly quite significant.

[30] See Genko, 1941, p. 85.

[31] The theory that all Daghestani Arabs had been the descendants of the original settlers was dismissed by the epigraphic evidence: Lavrov, 1966; *idem.*, 1968; Shikhsaidov, 1984.

[32] Sheikh Mollah Yusuf from Mecca (d. early 14th century) settled in Muskur, see Genko, 1941, p. 93; Sheikh Mir Sulayman al-Baghdadi (d. 680 AH/1283 AD) settled in Targhu – see Shikhsaidov, 1969, p. 213; Sheikh Ahmad al-Yemeni (d. 1450/51 AD) before his settlement in Ghumuq had lectured at al-Azhar – see Aytberov, 1978-9, pp. 4-8.

[33] Gerber, 1760, pp. 307-8. For the evidence of the Caucasians who treated Arabic as their native language in the nineteenth century, see Bakikhanov, 1848; Zeydlits, 1871, pp. 46-67; Genko, 1941, pp. 88-9. In the nineteenth century Glinoetskiy produced some evidence according to which not only the Caucasians – mainly Circassians – had been traded as slaves in the Ottoman lands, but the wealthy Caucasians also brought back Arab slaves from the hajj. See Glinoetskiy, 1862, pp. 154-5; Genko, 1941, pp. 87-92.

[34] The links between the two countries went as far back as the fourteenth century, when a considerable Yemeni community existed in Ghumuq. In the seventeenth century a famous Daghestani scholar, Muhammad Ibn Musa al-Qudutli (d.1120/1708) went to study with a renowned Yemeni scholar and mujtahid Sayyid Salih al-Yemeni (d. 1047/1637), and made his ideas known to the local scholars, thus establishing a profound and long-lasting tradition which can be traced to the nineteenth century. See al-Shawqani, 1348 (1929/30 AD), p. 291; Krachkovskiy, 1960(a), pp. 574-84. In his bibliographical dictionary, al-Shawqani mentioned a Daghestani 'alim who travelled to Yemen in search of the works of Salih al-Yemeni. Al-Shawqani, 1348 (1929/30), p. 290.

own. By the nineteenth century Arabic had become the dominant language of culture[35] and correspondence between the Daghestani *jama'ats*.

The command of Arabic among the Daghestani scholars was very
high and those who met them were impressed by their mastery of the
language and knowledge of Muslim *'ulum*.[36] The seventeenth-century
Ottoman traveller, Evliya Celebi, praised the scholars of the Qumyq
village of Enderi which he described as 'an ancient city, the focus of
wisdom, the abode of poets and contented people', whose 'scholars
possess the wisdom of the Arabs and great knowledge.[37]

The prominent Yemeni scholar of the late eighteenth–early nineteenth
centuries, Ahmad al-Shawqani (1760-1834 AD) reflected:

I have not seen anyone equal to him [a Daghestani scholar] in expressiveness and
the use of the Arabic language in its totality. He indeed was an eloquent man. And
he had a good accent and his speech flowed pleasantly so that when I listened to
him I was utterly inspired.[38]

Persian was the second most widespread written language in Daghestan.
The degree of religious influence exercised by Shi'i Persia is much
more difficult to establish. For centuries Persia had claimed political
and cultural domination over the area,[39] but never reached the same
degree of influence as the Arabs. Shi'i Islam did not strike deep roots
anywhere in the area and apart from a small Shi'i community in southern
Daghestan, mainly in Derbend, the majority of Daghestani Muslims
remained Sunnis rigorously opposed to the Shi'ites.

[35] Aytberov, 1978-9, pp. 4-11. On the Arabic language in Daghestan, see al-Shawqani,
1348, pp. 290-1. Apart from creating original literature in Arabic, the Daghestanis
developed an elaborate system of signs to transcribe the sounds in the local languages
which did not exist in Arabic. See Barabanov, 1941, Introduction. The Arabic language
continued to play an important role as a medium of cultural exchange and official correspondence well into the twentieth century until it was prohibited by the Soviet authorities
in 1925, and since then was maintained only by the unofficial Muslim religious schools.

[36] Disciplines related to the study of Islam, such as the Qur'an and Sunna, Muslim
law, philosophy, mysticism, etc.

[37] Celebi, 1979, p. 115.

[38] al-Shawqani, 1348 (1929/30), pp. 290-1.

[39] These claims were particularly pronounced during the rule of the Shi'i Safavid dynasty
(1508-1736 AD), when the Kizilbashi sheikhs organised a number of unsuccessful military
campaigns into Derbend (1459, 1460, 1488 AD).

5

ISLAM AMONG THE VAYNAKH

Islamisation of the Vaynakh teips[1]

There is no agreement among scholars as to the timing of the 'decisive' Islamisation of the Chechen and Ingush tribes. Some are inclined to trace it back to the fifteenth century,[2] others claim that it was only in the course of the eighteenth century that Islam started to make any significant progress in the area.[3] Local traditions, however, refer the dissemination of Islam among the Chechen tribes to the time of the Arab conquests (eighth century), or to Timur's alleged campaigns into the Vaynakh lands in the end of the fourteenth century. It is best to regard such traditions as legendary rather than historical.[4]

The Islamisation of the Vaynakh tribes was a lengthy process which, most likely, started in the second half of the sixteenth century, when the first Chechen tribes of the Sunja, Aktash, Aqsay (Aqsakay) and Sulak valleys adopted Islam as their official religion.[5] The Islamisation of these tribes was associated with the political domination of the *shamkhalat* of Targhu and Ghazi-Ghumuq over the eastern part of lowland Chechnya, which dates back to the late sixteenth centuries.[6]

Local legends link Islamisation with the activities of the Qumyq missionaries, both peaceful and militant.[7] One such legend describes a certain Qumyq missionary called Termoal, who was

---

[1] The following material was used in the present chapter: the unpublished material from the *TsGADA*; published works by Akhriev, 1871; Avksentev, 1973; Dalgat, 1893; Dakhkil-gov, 1991; Grabovskiy, 1876; Genko, 1930; Krupnov, 1947; Krupnov, 1938; Krupnov, 1971; Laudaev, 1872; Miller, 1888; Pozhidaev, 1926; Shamilev, 1963; Shamilev, 1863(a); Shamilev, 1969(b); Shilling, 1931; Shilling, 1949; Vertepov 1892.

[2] Shamilev, 1963, pp. 98-100; Shilling, 1931, p. 99.

[3] See Makatov, 1965, pp. 9-12.

[4] There are legends about Abu Maslama and other Arab missionaries in Chechnya which certainly cannot be sustained by historic or archeological evidence. Pozhidaev, 1926 p. 17.

[5] In 1647 the chiefs of the Shibut peoples gave an oath on the Qur'an. *TsGADA*, fond Posol'skogo Prikaza, Kumykskie Dela, list 3; also in Gerber, 1760 pp. 42-3; Celebi, 1979, pp. 104-5.

[6] See Dalgat, 1893, p. 50; Krupnov, 1971, p. 98.

[7] Although legends and oral historical evidence should be treated with a certain degree

---

...an eloquent and cruel man. At a gathering of all the people he described in solemn words the omnipotence of the Muslim God, and in bright colours depicted Heaven awaiting the faithful. Carried away by the current of his speech, the Chechens submitted to him. With zealous followers at his side Termoal started to convert others by force, killing thousands of *deli mostaghoy* – God's adversaries. Many converted to Islam out of fear of him, but they never forgave him or forgot his cruelty.[8]

However, in most references the Chechen legends describe the proselytising activities of the missionaries as peaceful, with the Qumyq and Kabardian mullahs taking employment in various *tuqums* as shepherds in order to propagate Islam.[9]

Once firmly established in lowland Chechnya, it took a century and a half for Islam to reach the tribes of mountain and high-mountain Chechnya. Only by the second half of the eighteenth century had Islam become the official religion in virtually all the Chechen *tuqums*, although in 1770, during the military campaign of General Medem, the Russians noted the practice of 'a mixture of Christian and pagan rituals in the Upper Sunja areas'.[10]

The Islamisation of the Ingush started only in the second half of the eighteenth century.[11] Due to their geographical position on the main route between Georgia and southern Russia along the Daryal gorge, the Ingush tribes were, in particular, strongly drawn into the sphere of influence of Christian Georgia[12] and starting from the eighteenth century, Russia, which significantly hampered the process of their Islamisation.

The decisive phase of the Ingush conversion to Islam started only in the early nineteenth century and was not completed until the second half of the century, with the last Ingush, the Gvelety *tuqum*, converting to Islam in 1862.[13]

---

of scepticism, those relating to the Qumyq missions among the Chechen tribes appear to be reasonably accurate when examined within the context of the available written sources.

[8] Dakhkilgov, 1991, p. 128, story 64; Laudaev, 1872, pp. 64-5. Laudaev's version of the story ends with Termoal's decision to bury himself alive: 'He dug a grave and buried himself alive, saying: "Oh Muslims! you do not need me any longer but I will return when you need me again."' Up to the end of the nineteenth century people visited his grave in Ichkeria believing that he would return at the End of the World to bring the forgetful people back into the abode of the true faith. Compare with the theme of the Mahdi in the orthodox Islamic tradition.

[9] Avksentev, 1973, p. 13.

[10] Maksimov, 1893, p. 27.

[11] The first Muslim construction on the territory of present-day Ingushetiya, dating to 1406, is the mausoleum of Borga-Kash at Plievo near Nazran. In the fifteenth century, this territory, however, was still populated by the Kabardian rather than the Ingush, whose territory was confined to the high mountains. Thus, we cannot treat this construction as evidence of the early Islamisation of the Ingush, which did not start until the eighteenth century. See Lavrov, 1966, vol. I, pp. 215-16.

[12] Miller, 1893, pp. 112-13; Genko, 1930, pp. 728-3, Shamilev, 1963(a), p. 97.

[13] The local legends of conversion into Islam, see Dakhkilgov, 1991, pp. 200-4, stories

In 1770 a Russian traveller observed that the religious life of the Ingush people presented

...an incredible picture of complete religious chaos, in which beliefs of various epochs and religious systems are interwined in a most bizarre way. [...]Their religion is incredibly simple, yet it has clear signs of Christianity. They believe in one God whom they call Deli but they do not recognise any saints, celebrate Sunday not by a Christian ceremony but simply by taking a rest from work, have a long fast in the summer and a shorter one in the winter. They do not observe any [Christian] rituals at birth or death, they elect a man to slaughter sheep for sacrifice, who is called *tseysteg*, i.e. 'pure man' and who fulfils duties similar to those of a priest. The *tseysteg* maintains celibacy and lives in an old church high in the mountains. This church contains stone sculptures and many books which no one dares to read. At the same time the Ingush widely use Muslim names.[...][14]

Eleven years later, in 1781, another traveller observed pig-rearing among the Ingush which indicated that Islamisation had not advanced among them any further.[15]

In the Russo-Ingush treaty of 1810, the elders of the six *tuqums* representing the Ingush did not swear an oath on the Qur'an but rather 'in the name of the almighty heavenly god whom we take as our idol, the one who lives in the mountains and is called Gal-erda'.[16] Under the same treaty they took upon themselves not to allow effendis, mullahs and other persons of Muslim rank to preach among them and to prevent the building of mosques in their lands. This treaty, however, did not prevent the Ingush from forming alliances with the Kabardian and Chechen Muslims against the Russians.

Despite its geographical and cultural proximity, nowhere in the Vaynakh lands did Muslim and Arabic learning become as developed as in neighbouring Daghestan. With almost no *madrasahs* and very few well-educated scholars, knowledge of Islam and the Arabic language among the Vaynakh remained basic and was transmitted almost exclusively by visiting scholars from Daghestan and, more rarely, Kabarda.

Islam and pre-Islamic beliefs

As elsewhere in the North Caucasus, Islam had to combat both local pagan beliefs and Christianity. The influence of Christianity was at its strongest from the tenth to the thirteenth centuries when Georgia was the dominant political power in the area and inspired the spread of

---

171-4, 176.

[14] Guldenshtat, quoted from Genko, 1930, p. 74; for a description of Chechen and Ingush tuqums in the late eighteenth and early nineteenth centuries see Radde, 1880, book XI, issue 2, p. 246; K-n Bl., 1900, no. 10, pp. 33, 37.

[15] Genko, 1930, p. 744.

[16] The full text of this treaty in Shilling, 1949, p. 30; Dalgat, 1893, p. 52.

Christianity among various peoples of the central and eastern North Caucasus.[17] Later, the influence of both Georgia and Christianity declined, and by the time Islam was making headway in the area, paganism with some traces of degraded Christianity was the principal religious system of the Vaynakh tribes; and this continued to influence their religious life even after they had accepted Islam as their religion.

The Vaynakh pre-Islamic beliefs rested on an elaborate pantheon of various deities and the veneration of dead ancestors. The pre-eminent god in the Vaynakh pantheon was one-eyed Yalta – patron of wild animals and god of hunting.[18] Apart from Yalta there was Eter – the god of the dead and resurrection who had rule over time;[19] Seli – the god of fire who had a special place as patron of the domestic hearth and played the most important role in traditional mythology as the guarantor of the well-being and perpetuation of the family;[20] and Dela – the supreme god in the Vaynakh pantheon, father of all other gods, whose name was taken to mean Allah after Islamisation.[21]

Each tribe, village and *tuqum* had its patron – a deity or dead ancestor – whose small shrine, *elgits*, was built on the top of a rock close to the village.[22] The rocks, *yerda*, were also regarded as sacred with sacrifices being offered to them, especially at funerals. The Ingush had small silver idols of abstract form called *tsuv* (or *tsoum*), to which they prayed for rain, fertility and other blessings.[23]

Apart from various deities and venerated ancestors, the Vaynakh had an elaborate pantheon of good and evil spirits. Their forests were inhabited by forest creatures, *almas*, both male and female others lived in the water, mountains and sky. *Khi-Nana* (Mother of the Water), a kind and beautiful female spirit, sometimes pictured as a mermaid, lived in the pure mountain springs; *Moh-Nana* (Mother of Winds) and *Dartsa-Nana* (Mother of Snow-storms) lived on the high snow mountains; *Un-Nana* (Mother of Illnesses) lived among people. They had human emotions, were kind or evil, and could help or punish people for their deeds.

An example of the old beliefs that persisted is the legend about the emergence of the lake Galanchozh:

Once upon a time two women [mother and daughter] from the Akki [Akqqyn]

---

[17] Vertepov, 1903, p. 118; Bronevskiy, 1823, part I, p. 161; Shamilev, 1963(a), pp. 87-91; Butkov, 1869, pp. 270, 437-8.

[18] Akhriev, 1871, p. 258; Dakhkilgov, 1991, p. 167, story, 116.

[19] In which one can detect a clear Christian influence.

[20] Compare the sanctity of fire among the Zoroastrians.

[21] On various Vaynakh deities see Dalgat, 1893, pp. 90-113.

[22] For a description of *elgits*, see Dalgat, 1893 pp. 90-2; Vertepov, 1892, p. 115.

[23] Genko, 1930, p. 754, fn. 4.

tuqum came to wash dirty nappies in the crystal clean water of a lake not far from their village. Outraged, the spirit of water turned these women into stones as a punishment for polluting the water. The lake did not want to stay in the defiled place, so it turned itself into a strong and handsome bull and descended to the village of Galanchozh. People who lived there saw the bull, harnessed it and started ploughing the field. With the first furrow soil came out, with the second, water, and when the third furrow was ploughed more water gushed out and flooded the whole field, the bull disappearing into its waters. Since then Lake Galanchozh is believed to be sacred – no one is allowed to take its water or wash anything in it.[24]

A legend about the emergence of another lake, Qeyzen-am, on the other hand, clearly bears Biblical overtones and is likely to have appeared under the influence of Islam:

Once upon a time there was a village inhabited by people who were spoilt and badly behaved. Once an elderly man came to the village and asked for overnight shelter. No one would let him in but for a poor widow, who invited him to her house on the outskirts of the village and shared her frugal supper with him. In the morning the elderly man asked her to leave with him, saying that God wanted to punish the heartless people. She left with her guest and when she turned to have a last glance at her village, it was gone and there was emerald still water in the place where her village used to be.[25]

In the course of Islamisation many old beliefs were modified, especially the conceptions of the Other World, which are of particular importance in a system of beliefs. In the traditional pre-Islamic beliefs, the Other World was located beneath the earth, where the bodies of the Vaynakh ancestors descended after death. Their existence in the Other World was believed to be identical to the living: they were supposed to live in families and tribes, work and start and finish agricultural seasons at the same time as those on earth. However day and night were reversed: sunrise in This World was nightfall in the Other and *vice versa*.[26]

With the advent of Islam, the Other World was transformed into Heaven, to which the souls of the dead ascended along a long ladder (or chain) and entered wooden skeletons awaiting each of them. When a person was about to die, his wooden skeleton in Heaven would start to sway and as it swayed, flesh grew on it, so that the moment a person died his soul immediately ascended the ladder and entered the ready-made skeleton, taking the shape it would maintain after the Resurrection. This image was supposed to have nothing in common with the worldly appearance of a person but to correspond to his deeds on Earth – a beautiful skeleton awaiting the good, and an ugly one the bad.[27]

[24] Genko, 1930, pp. 102-3. The people who live close to the lake still do not wash or swim in it, although only very few remember the legend itself.

[25] Genko, 1930, p. 104.

[26] Dalgat, 1893, p. 60.

[27] Dakhkilgov, 1991, pp. 64-6.

The old myths explaining thunderstorms, earthquakes etc. also acquired Muslim colouring. Traditionally, thunderstorms were believed
to be produced by a blue bird, *Zehab*, flying above the rain clouds.
This myth was transformed into one in which thunder is produced by
Jabrail-malik (the angel Gabriel) chasing *Shaytan* (Satan) and waving
his sword around, thus producing a terrifying noise.

Jabrail also became responsible for earthquakes, which were seen
as God's reminder to the people forgetful of their faith. According to
legend, in the vicinity of Mecca there was a mountain Qap-lam (*Jabal
al-Qaf* – Arab.) from whose heart ran earthly veins throughout the entire
Earth. When people neglected God, *Jabrail-malik* would go into the
centre of that mountain where he would pull the veins of the earth thus
causing an earthquake in the place where people had forgotten God.[28]
Solar and lunar eclipses were also believed to be God's warnings to
those who corrupted faith and neglected their duties as Muslims.[29]

Other old beliefs persisted, but acquired a clearly Muslim character.
The Vaynakh animation of various objects, particularly rocks and mountains, found its reflection in the belief according to which all objects
submitted to One God are to be punished or rewarded on Judgement
Day. Hence the mountains covered with permanent snow had chosen
to suffer in This World in order to escape punishment in the Hereafter.

The Vaynakhs traditionally ascribed particular importance to the chain
on which they hung a copper pot above the hearth, which was considered
sacred. Many pre-Islamic rituals were centred around this chain: a bride
had to go three times around the home hearth and touch the chain,
while men coming home from a journey or going off to battle had to
touch the chain. After the advent of Islam these rituals were gradually
(although not completely) ousted, but the importance that the Vaynakh
ascribed to the chain persisted and acquired new meaning. Thus, the
Vaynakh came to believe that God had lowered the Qur'an down to
the Prophet on golden chains, and the dead ascended to heaven along
a chain-like ladder.

At the same time some Muslim beliefs were altered to accommodate
traditional Vaynakh notions. Thus, the Muslim conception of the Earth
being surrounded by mountains did not correspond to Vaynakh observations, and so they placed the mountains in the middle of the Earth.
This was explained within the creation story according to which God
first created the Earth three times larger that he wished to. To make it
smaller he squeezed it thus forming mountains in the middle.

Some pagan beliefs survived despite their obvious contradiction of
Islamic ones. This can be best illustrated by another Vaynakh myth
concerning the creation of the Earth. According to it, the Earth had

[28] Akhriev, 1871, p. 10.
[29] *Ibid.*, p. 11.

appeared prior to God and was shaped like an egg which rested on a board floating on the sea and was in eternal darkness.

A pagan-Christian synthesis prevailed among the Ingush tribes up to the second-half of the nineteenth century: old churches were used as holy places with religious rituals performed nearby;[30] crosses were applied as a cure for illness.[31] The practice of allowing four days delay in burial in case of an unexpected death was maintained under the pretext that the time was needed to enable relatives to attend the funeral.[32] *Elgits*, ancestors' shrines, were still regarded as sacred places, although they were frequented not so much as shrines but rather as places for people's gatherings.[33]

By the late eighteenth and early nineteenth centuries Islam among the Vaynakh was becoming the dominant religious system. In central and eastern lowland Chechnya Islam struck deeper roots and was more coherently adhered to, whereas in highland Chechnya and, particularly among the western Vaynakh (Ingush) tribes there reigned a religious syncretism which can best be described in the words of Shegren: 'The mullahs feel free to call upon Muslims when the bells ring, the Kist [Ingush] idol Gel-erda stands in peace in an old church built by Queen Tamara, which now lies abandoned.'[34]

---

[30] Pozhidaev, 1926, p. 517.

[31] Shamilev, 1963(a), pp. 91-2.

[32] This practice was a Christian anachronism, which by the second-half of the nineteenth century was abandoned by all Vaynakh societies. For a description of the funeral rituals among the Ingush, see Ahriev, 1871, pp. 67-72, 66; Grabovskiy, 1876, p. 248.

[33] Vertepov, 1892, pp. 114-5.

[34] Quoted from Miller, 1888, p. 3.

6

THE MUSLIM LEGAL SYSTEM AND THE JUDICIAL AUTHORITIES[1]

The degree of the Islamisation of the Daghestani *jama'ats* and Chechen *tuqums* by the nineteenth century could be seen through its reflection in their legal system and the balance between the *shari'a* and *'adat* legislature within it. It was a general practice to claim that 'almost all matters of civil law were settled on the basis of the *shari'a*, and criminal offences on the basis of the *'adat*".[2] This interpretation of the legal system in the North Caucasus does not, however, reflect the complexity of the situation or do justice to variations in the degree to which Islam had penetrated various areas. To do so one must establish the extent to which the traditional codes of law were influenced by the *shari'a* on the one hand, and how the local religious judges interpreted the *shari'a* on the other, for the traditional codes of *'adat* of some Daghestani communes 'were so heavily influenced by the *shari'a* that researchers all the time must ask themselves to what extent the *'adat* laws are the product of independent legal thought or a reflection of the *shari'a* law',[3] and at the same time examine the confines that the traditional laws imposed on the interpretation of the *shari'a*.

There are a number of fundamental differences between the Islamic and pre-Islamic tribal legal systems. The most important are, firstly, differentiation between the notions of personal and collective responsibility for a crime (one of the main characteristics of tribal society being the principle of shared responsibility – 'one for all and all for one' – while Islam introduced the notion of personal responsibility); secondly, differentiation between deliberate and accidental crimes and the establishment of different degrees of punishment for them, a concept which was wholly alien to the pre-Islamic tribal societies; thirdly, the concept of balance between the damage inflicted and the punishment;

---

[1] In addition to the works used for Chapters 2 and 3 the following sources have been used: Adaty Yuzhno-Dagestanskikh Obshchestv, 1975; Adaty Darginskikh Obshchestv, 1873; Adaty Kumykov, 1927; Berzhe, 1859; Dalgat, 1868; Khashaev, 1965; Kharuzin, 1888; Komarov, 1868; Komarov, 1873; Kovalevskiy, 1890, vols. 1-2; Laudaev, 1972; Leontovich, 1882-3; L'vov, 1870; Magomedov, 1957; Omarov, 1968; Tsadasa, 1958; Yaroshenko, 1898.

[2] Kovalevskiy, 1890 vol. 2, p. 127.

[3] *Ibid.*, p. 218.

and fourthly, legal procedure and the means of carrying out justice (i.e. judges, executive officers, type of oath etc.).

As a rule, the difference in the degree of Islamisation of the various Daghestani *jama'ats* and Vaynakh *tuqums* was reflected in the interpretation of each of these principles. Albeit with certain variations – each commune (*jama'at*) and *jama'at* association (*bo*) had their own code of laws – one can speak of the existence of two types of legal system in the nineteenth-century North-eastern Caucasus. In most Daghestani areas and in some Chechen lowland *tuqums* (particularly those bordering on the Qumyq lands), the legal system, and the codes of *'adat* were under a profound influence from the *shari'a*, while in the high-mountain Daghestan (e.g. Andi) and in most Vaynakh *tuqums*, the legal system had been Islamicised only superficially and remained largely based on the pre-Islamic value system.[4]

Starting with legal procedure and the means of dispensing justice, the difference between the two types of North Caucasian legal system was very obvious. Most of the Daghestani confederations had special religious and secular judges with well defined functions.[5] Both religious and secular judges were usually elected for a certain period, with the possibility of being re-elected an indefinite number of times. The *qadis*[6] were either elected from among the members of the *jama'at* they lived in, or were renowned for their religious learning (e.g. Tsakhur). In some *jama'ats*, the choice of a *qadi* was restricted to the members of one particular tribe or even family, but that was only the case when a *qadi* combined administrative and religious authority (e.g. Akusha).

The number of *qadis* in each commune and the prestige and power they exercised varied from one *jama'at* to another.[7] In Akusha, Rutul, Shinaz, Akhty and Khnov *qadis* rose to the rank of the supreme judicial authority and played the role of the supreme judge and head of the council of elders. In Tsakhur, Tabarsaran, Ghazi-Ghumuq, Targhu and regions where the supreme power was vested in a hereditary secular ruler, the *qadis* played a more traditional role as guarantors of the implementation of the shari'a and were held in extremely high regard, to the extent that all men, including the most respected elders, had to rise when a *qadi* (or *'alim*) approached, even if the latter was from another *jama'at*.[8]

One has to differentiate between the *qadi* as religious judge and as legal/administrative officer. As a religious judge, a *qadi* settled legal

---

4 Kovalevskiy, 1958, pp. 306-12.

5 Criminal offences were under the jurisdiction of the secular judges, while in matters of civil law the religious ones presided.

6 *Qadi* is a Muslim religious judge.

7 In Ghazi-Ghumuq, Targhu, Tabarsaran, Tsakhur there were up to six *qadis* each.

8 Kovalevskiy, 1890, vol. 2, pp. 152-60.

matters under the jurisdiction of the *shari'a*, while in those *jama'ats* where a *qadi* was a supreme legal authority (head of the *jama'at*, for example, Akusha) his activity and power were restricted by and legitimised in terms of local tradition. Thus, the chief *qadi* of Akusha 'exercised his power over all *jama'ats* within the confederation, settled law-suits on the basis of both *'adat* and the shari'a, declared wars, summoned the people's army, appointed commanders, concluded peace, etc.'[9]

Whatever the position of the *qadi*, he, as well as the mullahs, was integrated into the social structure and served the interests of a particular commune. In contrast, the *'ulama* (Muslim religious scholars) lived in various *jama'ats* and largely remained beyond the confines imposed by tribal or communal divides.

In the Vaynakh and high-mountain Daghestani communes there were few *qadis* and virtually no *'ulama*, the sole religious authority being the local mullahs, whose number rarely surpassed one per village. Most of the legal disputes were settled by the secular judges elected for each case by the two parties.[10]

The difference in prestige of *qadis* and mullahs in the Vaynakh and high-mountain Daghestani communes on the one hand and in other Daghestani areas on the other, was reflected in their financial position. *Waqf* property existed in all North Caucasian communes, but the distribution of the revenues from it differed from one area to another. In most Daghestani *jama'ats, waqf* property was twofold: part of it was distributed among the members of the commune who had to pay tax on it; the other part was held directly by the religious official (*qadis*, mullahs) and constituted the main source of their income. The tax and tributes that were paid by those who rented the *waqf* lands went partly to the religious officials and were partly distributed among the most needy members of the *jama'at*. This resulted in *qadis* forming a class of rich landowners, the most powerful of whom were the *qadis* of Ghazi-Ghumuq.

In contrast, all land constituting the *waqf* property in high-mountain Daghestan and in the Vaynakh communes was rented out and the income distributed among all people living in that particular commune. Similarly, while *zakat* formed an important source of income for the Daghestani religious figures, in the Vaynakh lands if paid at all, it was held by the council of elders, who apportioned it among the most needy members of the commune.[11]

With no fixed income, the religious officials in the Vaynakh and high-mountain Daghestani *tuqums* and *jama'ats* depended exclusively on the fees they charged for solving legal disputes and presents they

---

[9] Khashaev, 1961, p. 168.

[10] Leontovich, 1882-3, p. 149.

[11] *TsGADA*, fond 150, opis' 1, delo 4 list 11, 13.

were entitled to receive for officiating at funerals and weddings. Not surprisingly most of the Vaynakh and mountain Daghestani mullahs were extremely poor and enjoyed little respect.[12] Their rather pitiful condition was at least partly compensated for by the high prestige enjoyed by the Daghestani *qadis* and *'ulama*, whom the Vaynakh held in high esteem and often invited to mediate in their inter-tribal and inter-*tuqum* disputes.

Another difference between the *shari'a* and *'adat* lay in organisation of legal procedure. In the nineteenth-century North Caucasus there remained two types of oaths: the Muslim one taken on the Qur'an, and various traditional oaths.[13] In Daghestan, only the Muslim oath was generally accepted as valid. In Andi and the Vaynakh lands it was the traditional oaths on one's wife or on a dead ancestor that were commonly used.[14] Similarly, among the Vaynakh, witnessing was of greater importance than written evidence which, due to the low level of literacy, was accepted only after it was sworn on the traditional oath.[15] The number of witnesses varied and only in Daghestan corresponded to the shari'a requirements.[16]

The more profoundly Islamicised Avar, Gunib, Dargho, Ghazi-Ghumuq, Qumyq and southern Daghestani *jama'ats* interpreted criminal offence in terms close to those introduced by the *shari'a*,[17] and differentiated between deliberate and accidental crimes.[18] In all Avar and Didoy *jama'ats*, the code of *'adat* established personal responsibility for any type of crime;[19] in Ghazi-Ghumuq it was shared by one of the criminal's closest relatives;[20] in northern Tabarsaran by three close rela-

---

[12] Omarov, 1869, 1-70.

[13] Dalgat, 1929, p. 353; Kovalevskiy, 1890, vol. 2, pp. 127-8.

[14] Taking the oath 'on one's wife' meant that, if found guilty, the suspect had to divorce his wife. More dramatic still was an oath 'on the dog'. To swear this oath a suspect had to come to the house of a victim with a dog and kill it, saying that if he was guilty, the dog served as a sacrifice to his relatives. This was such a blasphemy that nobody dared to take this oath if guilty. Other oaths could be made in a sacred place – which could have been either pagan or formerly Christian – such as Thaba Erdy.

[15] See examples in Adaty Yuzhno-Dagestanskikh Obschestv, 1875, pp. 1-2.

[16] For examples see Kovalevskiy, 1890, vol. 2, p. 129.

[17] Adaty Yuzhno-Dagestanskikh Obschestv, 1875, pp. 4-7. In Samur accidental killing entailed 1/2 of *diyyat* (blood-money); in Qara-Qaytaq the owner of an animal who had caused harm was held responsible for negligence if similar incidents had occurred three times. In Gimrah the owner of an animal which had caused harm was to pay *diyyat* equal to an accidental crime. *Ibid.*, p. 49. Among the Darghins, killing or wounding in the course of self-defence did not entail any consequences, see Adaty Darginskikh Obschestv, 1873, p. 16.

[18] Adaty Yuzhno-Dagestanskikh Obshchestv, 1875, p. 49; Adaty Darginskikh Obshchhestv, 1873, p. 16.

[19] *Sbornik Adatov Avarskogo Naroda*, collected by Kalantarov in 1865, as quoted in Kovalevskiy, 1890. vol. 2, p. 223-4.

[20] *Sbornik Adatov Kazi-Kumukhskikh Obschestv* as quoted by Kovalevskiy, 1890, vol.

tives, in Upper Qaytaq seven, in Qara-Qaytaq four, in Untsuqul by the whole family[21] etc.[22] In almost all these communes, the appointment of an additional *kanly* (a person held responsible for a crime) was reduced to a mere formality – he had either to leave the village for forty days or pay the union penalty (the amount of which differed from one union to another).[23]

In contrast, the Andi and the Vaynakh codes of law did not draw any distinction between accidental and deliberate crimes and imposed shared responsibility for any misdeed on the whole family, tribe and, at times, even the *tuqum*.[24]

The difference between these two types of legal system was particularly important for those crimes that involved blood-revenge. Although, the *shari'a* recognises the legitimacy of blood-revenge, it prohibits taking revenge on any other than the killer himself and prefers the peaceful settlements of a dispute. Both the high-mountain Daghestanis and the Vaynakh treated the possibility of accepting blood money as a dishonour and humiliation. Only the pre-Islamic traditional ritual of a killer touching the breast of a victim's mother followed by his acceptance into the clan of a killed person could spare him from blood-revenge.[25] However, by the late eighteenth century, the ritual was very rarely applied, and with collective responsibility and no distinction being made between murder and manslaughter, long-lasting blood-feuds involving whole clans and tribes could lead to the mutual extermination of their entire male population.[26]

Even in the most profoundly Islamicised Daghestani *jama'ats*, certain spheres of life remained fully governed by local tradition. None of the Daghestani, let alone Vaynakh legal systems, had ever ventured to implement the *shari'a* in respect of theft. With constant land and property disputes, each of the *jama'ats* and *tuqums* practically encouraged appropriation of property by its members. Thus, the punishment for theft entailed mere compensation,[27] which was to be taken by the victim (alone or assisted by his family/tribe) from the thief, his relatives or other members of his commune.[28] This law contrasted sharply with the

---

2, p. 223.

[21] *Ibid.*

[22] Adaty Yuzhno-Daghestanskikh Obshchestv, 1875, pp. 23, 30, 42, 51, 63.

[23] *Ibid.*, pp. 20-4, 28-32, 33-6, 38-40, 42-3, 48-72.

[24] Kovalevskiy, 1890, vol. 2, p. 244.

[25] For more on this ritual see Laudaev, 1972, p. 59.

[26] See Leontovich, 1882-3, vol. 2, pp. 93, 148. The tradition of blood feuds persisted till modern times – the most violent period being the 1920s and '30s.

[27] See Kovalevskiy, 1890, vol. 2, pp. 293-5.

[28] This practice was generally known under the name of *ishkil*. See *idem.*, pp. 131-6. On laws concerning theft in the Chechen and Ingush tuqums see Yakovlev, 1992, pp.

punishment for stealing within one's tribe or *jama'at*, in which case the thief was expelled from the tribe or even killed.

Some matters that fell under the jurisdiction of a religious rather than secular judge, were not necessarily treated on the basis of the shari'a. Thus, although settled exclusively by the religious judges (mullahs, *qadis*), matters of inheritance were largely governed by the laws of *'adat*. In contradiction to the shari'a, particularly as interpreted in the Shafi'i *madhhab*, the North Caucasian judges did not distinguish between donation (*nazr*) and will (*wasiya*),[29] since the will was made orally and announced while the testator was still living. Moreover, the shari'a law according to which donation was free from all taxes and duties, debts, etc., led to abuses which in turn entailed disputes.[30]

In the high-mountain tribal unions, *'adat* fully governed matters of inheritance with a fixed share of property apportioned to all members of a family by laws which overrode all forms of will or donation according to the *shari'a*.[31]

Family life was the sphere most influenced by the *shari'a*. Marriage,[32] divorce[33] and burial[34] were observed in a traditional Muslim way. This, however, did not completely oust certain pre-Islamic practices. Thus, throughout the North Caucasus the tradition of *umykanie* (kidnapping) of a bride by a groom, persisted, although even in these cases, the marriage was considered to be valid only after approval by a religious official.[35]

Still, throughout the North Caucasus the local *'adat* continued to claim authority in matters of intermarriage. In Daghestan it was considered obligatory to marry within one's clan or tribe or at least *jama'at*.[36] In Vaynakh *tuqums*, marriage was prohibited between relatives up to

---

93-4; Leontovich, 1882-3, pp. 43-4, 115-25, 179-82.

[29] According to Muslim law, a donation can be of unlimited value, while a will can not exceed 1/3 of the total property value.

[30] On the difference between will and donation see Kovalevskiy, 1890, vol. 2, pp. 206-12.

[31] Sons of legal age shared equal rights for the property alongside their father and could at any time demand division of this property among them. Leontovich, 1882-3, pp. 96-111.

[32] For a description of a traditional wedding among the Avars, see L'vov, 1870, pp. 22-5; Yakovlev, 1992, pp. 44-50.

[33] In the case of divorce, the bride money, which under the influence of Islam was transformed into *maghar* (*kebin*), provided the woman with some financial support. Adaty Yuzhno-Dagestanskikh Obschestv, 1875, pp. 15, 32. On the laws concerning marriage among the Avars, see L'vov, 1870, pp. 31-2; on the Laks, see Omarov, 1869, pp. 16-21; on the Chechens, see Dalgat, 1868, p. 321.

[34] Grabovskiy, 1870, pp. 17-22; Akhriev, 1870, pp. 19-23.

[35] For a description of kidnapping, see L'vov, 1870, pp. 20-1; Leontovich, 1882-3, p. 98.

[36] Kovalevskiy, 1890, vol. 2, p. 143.

the seventh degree removed,[37] while at the same time in violation of the *shari'a*, intermarriage was allowed between a milk brother and sister.[38] Traditional Muslim polygamy, although allowed, was extremely rare in both Daghestani and Vaynakh lands and no form of temporary marriage as it existed among the Shi'i had ever been practised.

In contrast to the shari'a, Vaynakh women enjoyed the right to divorce their husbands on their own initiative – in which case the bride money remained with the family of her ex-husband.[39] Responsibility for adultery was equally shared between male and female parties and was kept as a family matter.[40] A husband (alone) had a right to kill his wife and her lover. He was not responsible for their blood if both of them were killed when caught in the act of adultery. Otherwise he was held responsible for the blood of both of them. The *'adat* continued to regulate relationships within one clan and tribe: it imposed a prohibition on leaving one's clan, regulated agricultural activities, etc.

Only the code of *'adat* in the Avar khanate introduced the concept of crime against religion. According to its rulings, each *jama'at* had to employ religious officials (*qadi*, mullah), and those communes that declined to follow it had to pay a fine of one sheep for each day that it did not employ a new *qadi* or mullah if the old one had departed or died. The neglect of religious duties such as fast, ablution or prayer by an individual also entailed severe punishment (penalty for such negligence included expropriation of property or expulsion from the *jama'at*).[41]

In most other *jama'ats* many of the religious obligations were often neglected. Hardly anywhere in the Caucasus was the prohibition of drinking alcohol and smoking adhered to. Besides, most of the Vaynakh never paid *zakat* which at best they substituted by *sadaqa*.

The certain degree of confusion that existed between the *shari'a* and *'adat* laws often resulted in manipulation of the laws and corruption. In the Vaynakh *tuqums* a verdict was accepted as final only if all judges reached an unanimous decision. This, however, was extremely rare as each party selected its own judges to defend its interests. Moreover, even if such a verdict was reached, the aggrieved party could appeal and demand a retrial or ignore it altogether, for with no executive authorities, the implementation of any decision remained largely arbitrary.[42]

---

[37] Dalgat, 1868, pp. 314, 318.

[38] *Idem.*, p. 316.

[39] Divorce seems not to have been a rarity among the Chechens, and widows and divorced women easily remarried. See Leontovich, 1882-3, p. 99.

[40] L'vov, 1870, p. 30.

[41] 'Kodeks Rustem Khana', in Khashaev (ed.), 1995.

[42] Leontovich, 1882-3, pp. 94-5.

7

SUFISM IN THE NORTH CAUCASUS[1]

Sufi ideas were known in the North Caucasus long before the nineteenth century. Southern Daghestan became an important centre of mysticism already in the eleventh century, when the area was visited by Sufi sheikhs, and the writings of various mystics, particularly those of al-Ghazali (d. 1111 AD) were studied and copied throughout southern Daghestan, particularly in Kubachi.[2] In fact, one of the earliest existing accounts of Sufi ideas, *Raihan al-Haqa'iq wa Bustan al-Daqa'iq*, was written in southern Daghestan by the local mystic Abu Bakr al-Derbendi.[3]

Sufi *khanaqas* (at least one of which was opened by 1150) and the Nizamiyye *madrasah*[4] in Tsakhur, which existed from the eleventh till the late thirteenth century (1295) became the centres of mystical learning.[5]

It is probable that the initial spread of Sufi ideas in southern Daghestan was associated with the rule of the Saljuq dynasty in neighbouring Persia (429-590 AH/ 1038-1194 AD), where Sufism became integrated into the fabric of Islamic social and communal life.[6]

Starting from the thirteenth century, the evidence of a Sufi presence in southern Daghestan declines. The title 'sheikh', which for the first time appeared in the epigraphic material of the twelfth century,[7] continued to be used in later inscription: Sheikh Mulla Yusuf (late thirteenth – early fourteenth century); Sheikh Mir Sulayman al-Baghdadi (d.680/1283); Sheikh Ahmad al-Yamani (1450/1). However, it seemed to have lost its purely mystical connotations.[8]

---

[1] The present chapter is based on the following sources: the material from the RF IIYaL, Mahachqala (Manuscript Collection of the Institute of Languages and Literature, Mahachqala, Daghestan), fond 3, opis' 1, delo 4; Celebi, 1973; Dubrovin, 1871, vol. 1, book 1; Lavrov, 1966; Lavrov, 1968; Makatov, 1965; Mamaev, 1970; Saidov, 1963; Shamilev, 1963(a); Shikhsaidov, 1984; Vertepov, 1914.

[2] Lavrov, 1966, pp. 63-4.

[3] Saidov, 1963; *RF IIYaL DAN*; fond 3, opis' 1, delo 94. The manuscript is being prepared for publication by A. Alikberov.

[4] Nizamiye *madrasahs* were so called after their founder Nizam al-Mulk, the wazir of Sultan Alp-Arslan (r. 1063-72 AD).

[5] Shikhsaidov, 1969.

[6] Malamud, 1994, pp. 427-42.

[7] Shikhsaidov, 1984, pp. 389-93.

[8] See the description of tombs in Shikhsaidov, 1884; Lavrov, 1966; Lavrov, 1968.

Despite the fact that there is little evidence to establish with any degree of certainty the existence of Sufi institutions in the fourteenth-eighteenth centuries in the North Caucasus, some data indicate a Sufi presence in the area. One piece of circumstantial evidence is the number of mausoleums (whether Sufi or not) which served as popular places of visitation. The proximity of and frequent contacts with Azerbaijan (particularly Shirwan[9] which had a deeply rooted mystical tradition), as well as the links between Daghestani and Central Asian Muslims who passed through Daghestan on route to Mecca, also must have at least acquainted the Daghestanis with Sufis from Central Asia and Azerbaijan.[10]

The presence of Central Asian Sufi sheikhs in Daghestan is confirmed in the record of the seventeenth-century Ottoman traveller Evliya Celebi, who recorded the existence of the mausoleums of Central Asian sheikhs – Al-Hajji Djam, Hajji Yasavi-Sultan, Hajji Abdallah Tashqandi – in the Qumyq fortress of Enderi.[11] The same author also provided the only existing evidence of the Naqshbandi *tekkes* in Daghestan prior to the nineteenth century: '...in the fortress of Koysu (near Enderi) there were seven *maktabas*, three *madrasahs* and two *tekkes* of the Naqshbandi dervishes'.[12] With no further evidence available, one can only speculate that the Naqshbandi brotherhood present in northern Daghestan was introduced by Central Asian Sufis and that it was the Naqshbandi order proper (rather than the Mujaddidiyya or some other sub order).

Among the Vaynakh, Islam from the very beginning was centred around holy men and was often referred to as being 'sheikhly Islam'.[13] One can easily detect a Sufi affiliation among the missionaries who preached Islam to the pagan mountain tribes. One of these missionaries was a Qumyq, Sultan Sheikh Mut, who before becoming a *shamkhal* in 1630, preached Islam in the mountains of Greater Chechnya. Up to the present day, the Chechens still refer to him as a sheikh and saint and revere the cave he lived in while in Ichkeria as a holy place.[14] Another missionary preacher to the Chechen tribes was a certain Bashkir, Sheikh Murad. Through his deep piety and wisdom, Sheikh Murad rose to the position of mediator among the highland Chechen tribes, who also regarded him as a holy man.

The local legends describe all missionaries as saints with supernatural powers such as the ability to predict the future, appear in remote places,

[9] E.g. the Junaid's unsuccessful campaigns against Derbend (1447-60 AD) stirred a certain degree of support among the Shi'i community of Derbend. See Neymatova, 1968, p. 112.
[10] Leskov, 1990.
[11] Celebi, 1973, p. 115.
[12] *Ibid.*, p. 117.
[13] Mamleev, Umarov and Shamilova, 1984.
[14] Dubrovin, 1871, vol. I, book 1, p. 621.

pray on a piece of felt floating on the water surface, etc.[15] One story of Sheikh Bersa, one of the first Chechen Muslims, is yet another illustration of this phenomenon. Bersa was fighting against the Muslims who were stealing sheep from the pagan Benoy *tuqum* to which his bride belonged. During one battle Bersa killed their leader, who exclaimed before dying: 'I pass my dagger and God's blessing to Bersa!' The same night the Divine Knowledge descended upon Bersa, who at once became a sheikh and in the morning found the dead man's dagger and a copy of the Qur'an which Bersa, who had never studied Arabic, could now miraculously read and understand. From that day Bersa became a pious Muslim and a zealous preacher of Islam.[16]

During his long and pious life, Bersa allegedly performed numerous miracles through which he converted many Chechens to Islam. One story describes how he converted his close friend, an elder from the *aul* of Guni, who was one of the strongest opponents of Islam. Having become a Muslim sheikh, Bersa arrived in the *aul* of Aghshpatoy, not far from Guni, to preach Islam among its people. The friend of Bersa from Guni took offence at his friend violating the tradition of hospitality and not coming to visit him. He reproached Bersa, who explained that however strong was his love for his friend, he could not keep friendship with an infidel and would even have to fight and kill him. He said that in his heart he felt the same love for him, but that their souls were separated by a barrier which his friend could only destroy by converting to Islam. After this appeal, Bersa's soft-hearted and loving friend converted to Islam. However, on returning home he could not resist eating his favourite pork dish and ordered his wife to cook it. When the meal was ready and he was about to eat it, Bersa miraculously appeared in his room reprimanding him for his behaviour. Impressed by his miraculous appearance and embarassed, Bersa's friend became a pious Muslim and never violated the *shari'a* again.[17] Both legends have strong mystical connotations, and suggest that the first Chechen Muslims were converted to Islam by Sufi sheikhs.

The legitimacy of religious authorities, including that of the Prophet Muhammad himself,[18] was interpreted by the Vaynakh in the context of their ability to perform miracles. In apparent contradiction to orthodox Islam, the Vaynakh mullahs maintained that the Prophet proved that he was a true Messenger of God by performing miracles. For instance there was the legend of Abu Jahl's conversion to Islam at the hands of the Prophet Muhammad, who demonstrated his Divine inspiration by performing three miracles: making the sun rise in the west and set

15 Laudaev, pp. 65-7; Dakhkilgov, 1991, p. 194, story 167 and p. 195, story 168.
16 Dakhkilgov, 1991, pp. 195-8, story 168.
17 *Ibid.*, pp. 194-5, story 167.
18 *Ibid.*, pp. 209-10, story 187.

in the east, stopping time to allow Abu Jahl's caravan to cover several week's journey in one day, and finding out the secrets of people in a distant land.[19]

These stories reveal distinct features about Islam in Chechnya: it was not so much disseminated by learned scholars and through Islamic institutions, but rather through divinely inspired holy men. However, there is hardly any evidence to claim that these holy men belonged to or established an elaborate Sufi network.

The Islamisation of Daghestan and the Vaynakh *teips* was a complex process which took over ten centuries to complete. Notwithstanding the complexity and length of the process, once it had been set in motion by the Arab conquests of the eighth century, Islamisation gathered its own momentum and began to develop and evolve according to the confines and particuliarities imposed by the local setting. Unlike the neighbouring North-western Caucasus, where Islamisation was conducted mainly by Ottoman missionaries and therefore was more formal – it followed the Hanafi *madhhab* and was based and centred around institutions (mosque, *madrasah*, mullahs, etc.) – in Daghestan and the Vaynakh lands the process of Islamisation was largely locally driven and employed formal and informal (holy men) means of propagation.

Daghestan, where Islamisation had a relatively profound effect, gradually became an important regional centre of Arab-Muslim scholarship and cultural tradition, closely linked to the Muslim world at large. In contrast, Islam in the high-mountain Vaynakh lands remained superficial and populist in character due to the lack of those well educated in religious matters. This, however, was largely compensated for by the influence and mediation of the Daghestani *qadis* and *'ulama* held in high regard by the Chechens, who resorted to their authority in religious matters. The Vaynakhs respected and almost venerated Daghestani scholars for their deep knowledge of Islam. Over time Daghestan became, for the Muslims of the North-eastern Caucasus, a means of self-identification and the whole area developed into a distinct enclave of Muslim tradition and culture which allowed for a variety of forms of expression of the Muslim faith.

As far as Sufism is concerned, one can confidently state that Sufi mystical ideas were widely disseminated throughout the North-eastern Caucasus. Moreover, although it is difficult to ascertain the existence of a coherent Sufi structure spanning the whole of the area, some Sufi brotherhoods (including the Naqshbandi order) were known to have a presence in northern Daghestan prior to the nineteenth century.

[19] *Ibid.*, p. 207, story 182.

Not only were Daghestani scholars coming to preach among the Vayunakh, but the latter also went to Daghestan to receive religious education at the Daghestani *Madrasahs*.

Part III
THE RUSSIAN EXPANSION AND THE BEGINNING OF THE RELIGIOUS REVIVAL

8

THE NORTH CAUCASUS AND FOREIGN POWERS: THE FIRST STAGE OF RUSSIAN EXPANSION IN THE AREA

The nineteenth century witnessed the culmination of the gradual process of increasing Russian involvement in the North Caucasus. Russia first appeared on the scene in the sixteenth century, when Ivan the Terrible conquered the khanate of Astrakhan (1556 AD) and came to rival Ottoman Turkey and Persia in their struggle for political domination over the area.[1] At that time the struggle was not about the annexation of its territory, but over control of trade and military communications.[2]

Apart from Russia, Iran and Ottoman Turkey the struggle also involved the Crimean khanate, the Shaybanis of Turkestan and the Great Noghay Horde. The Ottomans and the Crimean Tatars saw the North Caucasus as a key area in their struggle with Iran, while for the Shaybanis it could open a direct road from Bukhara to the heartland of Islam (Mecca and Medina) and link the western and eastern Turks.

With little interest in territorial gain, none of the rivals attempted to interfere in local affairs, but tried to ally themselves with the local peoples and their rulers. The latter learned how to manipulate the rival

---

[1] The present chapter is based on *TsGVIA*, fond VUA, Kollektsiya 482, dist 4; Belokurov, 1889; Smirnov, 1958; Zasedateleva, 1974; Kusheva, 1966; Yuzefovich, 1869; and Butkov, 1869, parts I, III.

[2] The Russians became particularly interested in the Caucasus as a route to the warm seas and Middle Eastern markets, after the notable journey of Afanasiy Nikitin, a Russian merchant of the late fifteenth century, who in 1475 was the first Russian to reach India via Tatarstan, Caucasus and Iran. Nikitin, 1986.

powers in their own interests. They accepted protectorates in order to ensure political support in local disputes, but should any threat to their sovereignty arise, manipulated the rivalry between them to preserve their independence.[3]

After their initial success the Russians were decisively defeated by the Ottomans and disappeared from the Caucasus for over a century.[4] The first round of Ottoman-Crimean competition with Moscow ended with the Russian defeat, but it was Safavid Iran which benefited from this struggle most and remained a dominant force in the area throughout the whole of the seventeenth century.

Russian political disengagement in the area was followed by the appearance of Russian peasant outlaws, Cossacks, who had fled from the Russian hinterland to escape serfdom.[5] The first Cossacks appeared in the late sixteenth-early seventeenth century and settled in the area at the mouth of the Terek river, and some time later established their settlements in the foothills along the Terek, thus wedging in between the Vaynakh and the Kabardian lands, from where they gradually moved further to the confluence of the Argun and Sunja rivers. The two groups of Cossacks subsequently became known as *Terskie* (the Terek) and *Grebenskie* (or *Grebentsy* from *greben'*, meaning 'crest' in Russian)[6] This new development proved to be significant in all later Russian conquests. For 'in the course of centuries [the Cossacks] added belt upon belt of fertile territory to their own possessions, and eventually to the Empire of the tsars'[7] because 'wherever Russian people would try to flee, even without any apparent political aim, the Russian state followed on their heels'.[8]

In the early eighteenth century during the reign of Peter the Great (r. 1684-1725) Russia once again appeared on the political scene of the North Caucasus. Having modernised the Russian army and secured Russia's possessions in Europe, Peter the Great organised a notorious Persian campaign (1722) which gained Russia the Caspian coastal lands and neighbouring provinces.[9] However, at that time the Russian tactics

---

3 For example, in 1601 the *shamkhal* of Targhu, the Khan of Ghazi-Ghumuq, the *utsmiy* of Qaytaq and Qarabudahkent *beks* formed an alliance with Russia and nominally accepted its protectorate. Only a few years later all the rulers dismissed the Russian claims over their domains and openly rebelled when the Russians tried to subdue them. On this period see documents in Materyaly Rossiiskogo Glavnogo Arhiva Miniserstva Inostrannyh Del (hereafter Materyaly...) in Belokurov, 1889, 1, pp. 1578-1613.

4 The seventeenth century was a time of permanent turbulence in the Russian hinterland, when priority was placed on the consolidation of the lands of Russia proper.

5 On the Cossacks in the Caucasus, see Kusheva, 1966; Popke, 1880; Zasedateleva, 1974.

6 Popke, 1880, Kusheva, 1966.

7 Baddeley, 1908, p. 5.

8 Popke, 1880, p. 25.

9 Yuzefovich, 1869, p. 187.

remained the same as before: to ensure the alliance of the local peoples and, if possible, establish fortified settlements.

In large part the Russians were successful: in 1718 the *shamkhal* of Targhu formed an alliance with the Russians. He was shortly followed by the *qadi* of Akusha, who nominally accepted a Russian Protectorate in 1723. To further their success, the Russians also set out in 1711 to fortify the Cossack settlements along the Terek and laid the foundations of the first Russian fortresses of St. Cross in 1722 and Kizlyar (Qidhlar) in 1735 in the Qumyq lowland.[10]

Alarmed by the foundation of military positions in their lands, the same rulers who had accepted the Russian protectorate, renounced it and in 1725 tried to destroy the St. Cross fortress. Although on this occasion the Russian soldiers not only managed to repulse the attack, but also capture the *shamkhal* and destroy his residence at Targhu,[11] only a few years later, in 1732-5, Russia lost its protectorate over the entire coastal area, which now fell under Persian protectorate, and in 1736 withdrew all its troops beyond the Terek.[12]

By that time, however, an important new development had become apparent. The Cossack settlements, hitherto viewed as a defensive possession, for the first time proved their utility as an offensive base. The Cossack military settlements now became fully integrated into and reinforced the Russian state.[13] Moreover, the victories of Peter the Great later gave Russia the pretext of re-claiming its 'legacy' in the area dating from the early seventeenth century, the time, they claimed, when Daghestan was 'adjoined' to the Russian Empire.

In the second-half of the eighteenth century, after the rise to power of Catherine the Great (r. 1762-96), the Russians resumed their military activities in the North Caucasus and now launched systematic offensives.

The main obstacles to the Russian advances in the Caucasus remained Ottoman Turkey and its ally, the Crimean khanate on the one hand and Persia on the other. The third-quarter of the eighteenth century was marked by numerous violent clashes between the Ottomans and Russians which mostly affected the north-western and to a lesser extent north-eastern Caucasus. In the course of these wars, Russia's dominance in the area was to become apparent. The first serious defeat of the Ottomans followed the first Russian-Turkish war of 1768-71 when the old Ottoman ally in the area, the Khan Girey of Crimea, was replaced by a new, openly pro-Russian one. This gave the Russians free access from the Sea of Azov into the Black Sea and a free hand in the western

---

[10] Smirnov, 1958, p. 67; *AKAK*, vol. I, p. x.

[11] *TsGVIA*, fond VUA, kollektsiya 482, list 4, Butkov, 1869, part I, p. 84 and part III, p. 37.

[12] Yuzefovich, 1869, p. 188.

[13] Potto, 1912, p. 27.

Caucasus.[14] A decade later in 1782 Russia finally annexed the Crimea, crushed the Noghay revolt and firmly established itself in the Kuban area.[15]

The Russians interpreted the annexation of the Crimean khanate as gaining protectorate over all the territories which had hitherto accepted the Crimean protectorate, which included all the tribes of the north-western Caucasus. This interpretation was disputed by the Ottomans and the struggle over the Caucasus between the two resumed.[16]

This centuries-long struggle between the rival powers now acquired distinctly new overtones. While the main motto of the Ottomans was to reduce rivalries, spread Islam, ensure order and promote trade',[17] the Russians now aimed at the establishment of strong military positions on the coast and at linking them overland to the territory under their control. Unlike previous centuries, the Russians now aspired to more than a merely political control over the area, but had pronounced interests over its territory.

The old Russian dream of constructing a fortified Caucasian line that they had already attempted to implement at the time of Peter the Great now began to be turned into practice. In 1863 they founded the Mozdok (Muzhlik) fortress in the Kabardian lands, which marked the beginning of the construction of the Caucasian military line. Within the next few decades the Ekaterinogradskaya fortress on the river Malka, Pavlovskaya on the river Kurah, Mariinskaya on the river Zolka, Georgievskaya on the river Podkumka and Alekseevskaya on the river Tomuz-lovka were constructed throughout the north-western Caucasus.

The establishment of the military garrisons was accompanied by the resettlement of Don and Volga Cossacks along the rivers Kuban and Terek and establishing their *stanitsas* (fortified settlements) further in the mountain areas,[18] which marked the beginning of the systematic Russian colonisation of the area.

The Russian settlements around Mozdok fortress were wedged into the territory used by the Kabardian tribes as seasonal pastures, and thus forced most of them to leave their traditional territories and retreat to the area beyond the Kuma and further into the mountains. The Russian authorities distributed the land thus acquired among the Cossacks and

---

14 The text of the Russian-Ottoman treaties of 1771 and 1774 are quoted in Butkov, 1869, vol. I, pp. 312-3.

15 On Russian advances in the western Caucasus, see Smirnov, 1958, pp. 84-135.

16 Now, as Russia became interested in eastern markets, particularly that of India, it tried to organise trade throughout the Caspian Sea.

17 As summarised by Paul Henze, 1992, pp. 76-7.

18 Throughout the eighteenth century all Volga and some Don Cossacks were resettled along the Caucasus military line. See *TsGVIA*, delo 482, sbornik 125, list 14.

Russian landlords from the Russian hinterland[19] at the expense of the local land users.

Although in the eighteenth century its policy in the north-eastern Caucasus was less advanced than in the western, Russia made a few advances in that area as well. In 1784 Vladikavkaz fortress, whose name translated from the Russian as 'Possess the Caucasus', was built in the western Vaynakh lands and clearly manifested Russian plans for the area. Shortly after the construction of the Vladikavkaz fortress, a Russian *guberniya* (province) was established in May 1785 with its centre in Ekaterinograd and Prince Potemkin as the *namestnik* (first vice-regent). A year later the *shamkhal* of Targhu, known in the Caucasus as the *wali* of Daghestan, accepted Russian protection.

At the same time Russian civil and military officials were granted the rights of local civil administration, which started to interfere directly in the internal affairs of the people. Notorious for constant abuses and bribery – the common evils of Russian administration – local officials forced the payment of numerous reparations, confiscated land and cattle from innocent people and violated the traditional principles of justice to the extent that in 1802 Tsar Paul I issued a special decree by which he tried to restrain the ardour of his Caucasian governor and reminded him that 'not by force alone can one subdue people. Try justice in winning their trust, tolerance in winning over their hearts.'[20] An appeal which remained largely unheeded.

Apart from other things, this decree also suggested that the renewal of traditional Russian policy in the area aimed at the co-optation of the local elite. Modelled partly on the Byzantine and partly on the Mongol traditions, co-optation of the elites has been a constant feature of Russian diplomacy in the Muslim world. It involved granting economic and political advantages to individuals, social groups and/or entire tribes as well as the delegation of power to the local ruler who became the representative of the Russian sovereign, and sought cultural and linguistic assimilation with or without conversion into Orthodox Christianity. It even went as far as forming marital strategy.[21]

In the eighteenth century the situation had changed. The hitherto semi-pagan tribes had by and large been converted to Islam (apart from some heathen Ingush tribes and the Christian Ossets), which made the Russian co-optation policy much more difficult. Moreover, having in the 1780s outplayed her traditional rivals and gained the upper hand in the power-struggle, the Russians now encountered a new force em-

---

[19] The biggest landlords from mainland Russia to acquire considerable land holding, in the north-western Caucasus in 1775-88 were Prince Vyazemskiy, Count Vorontsov, Count Chernyshov and Prince Potemkin-Bezborodko. See Butkov, 1869, p. 168.

[20] *Ibid.*, p. 225; *AKAK*, vol. II, pp. 123-4.

[21] Lemercier-Quelquejay, 1992, pp. 18-45.

bodied in Islam. The importance of this development first became apparent in 1785 when it was revealed in the first religious movement organised and led by a certain Sheikh Mansour.

9

SHEIKH MANSOUR AND THE BEGINNING OF THE MUSLIM REFORMIST MOVEMENT[1]

The North Caucasians responded to the growing Russian presence in the area in different ways. The peoples inhabiting the north-western areas resisted the Russian advances under the leadership of several secular leaders who closely co-operated with the Ottomans.[2] In the east, the anti-colonial struggle came to be expressed in terms of a broader religious movement under the auspices of Islam. Usually associated with the Naqshbandi imams, this tendency first became embodied in the movement led by a Chechen from the village of Aldy, Ushurma (Ucherman in the Russian sources),[3] generally known as Sheikh or Imam Mansour.[4]

Popular memory in the North Caucasus has preserved his image as the first Naqshbandi imam, a claim which was later upheld by virtually all scholars who studied the North Caucasian Muslim resistance.[5] Although one has to recognise that the Naqshbandi credentials of Sheikh

---

[1] I have based my research of the present chapter on the Russian archives: *TsGVIA*, fond 52 (Knyazya G.A. Potemkina-Tavricheskogo); *TsGVIA*, delo 350; *TsGADA*, razdel VII, delo 2777; *TsGADA*, razdel XIII. The secondary sources used are as follows: Akhmadov, 1991; Bennigsen, 1964; Butkov, 1869; Dzhevdet-Pasha, 1888; Dubrovin 1886, vol. 1, 2; Farfarovskiy, 1914; Farfarovskiy, 1914(a); Gapurov, 1988; Kakhovskiy, 1786; Khizriev, 1977; Korol'kov, 1914; Krupnov, 1971; M., 1884; Potemkin, 1785; Potto, 1897, vol. 1; Prozritelev, 1912; Rumyantsev, 1859; Savinov, 1852; Sheripov, 1927; Skitskiy, 1932; Smirnov, 1950; Tereshchenko, 1856; Vinogradov, 1934; Yudin, 1914.

[2] On Circassian resistance see, Henze, 1992, pp. 62-112.

[3] Report on Sheikh Mansour's Interrogation by Taynaya Komissiya of 28 July 1791, in *TsGADA*, razdel XXIII, chast' 10, list 9-18.

[4] In Russian literature there are many fantastic and colourful stories about his origin. Thus, Rumyantsev, 1859, claimed that he was born in Orienburg. Lavrov 1904; Potto, vol. I, 1897; Prozritelev, 1912; Vinogradov, 1934 – all uncritically borrowed from the author of *Avantyurist XVIII veka*, 1884, the version according to which Sheikh Mansour was a Catholic priest Jean Batist Boetti. This version was first expressed by Professor Ottino in *Fantula de la Domenica* in 1881. He claimed to have unearthed a series of letters allegedly written by Mansour to his father and kept in the State Archive of Turin.

[5] Both Russian and Soviet scholars as well as Bennigsen recognised Mansour as a Naqshbandi sheikh. However, in the course of my research I found no direct evidence to substantiate this claim. Thus, although this idea must not be disregarded completely, I would like to suggest a more cautious approach.

Mansour are less than certain, he was the first Naqshbandi leader who combined the national struggle with the religious one and as such can be seen as first in the line of North Caucasian imams.

Accounts of his appearance state that he was so tall that in a crowd it looked as if he was mounted on a horse;[6] he was wrapped in a green shawl under which he wore a costume of many colours 'such as no one has ever seen before'[7], with a turban on his *papakh*; eloquent, brave and with strong will and resourceful wit, able to command trust and respect,[8] Sheikh Mansour 'dropped as it were from the clouds a full-grown warrior, preacher and prophet'.[9]

Indeed, his life and preaching are surrounded by mystery and are frequently described in terms reminiscent of the Prophet Muhammad and later Naqshbandi imams. Not much is known about his early life. Born in the 1760s[10] in a poor family of the Chechen *uzden* (free men of a common origin)[11] he claimed to have had no formal education[12] and in his youth earned his living as a shepherd.[13]

In his own words he led an 'ordinary life of stealing, robbing and participating in blood feuds'[14] when he suddenly awoke to the Divine Truth and realised that the life that he and his compatriots were leading was full of sin and in contradiction to Muslim law.[15]

The time and the manner in which he turned to religious preaching remain obscure. The Russians first heard about him in 1785 when Major-General P.S. Potemkin submitted the following report to the vice-governor of the Caucasus, Prince G.A. Potemkin: 'On the opposite bank of the river Sunja in the village of Aldy a prophet has appeared and started to preach. He has submitted superstitious and ignorant people to his will

---

6 *AKAK*, vol. XII, p. 1403.

7 *TsGADA*, Arkhiv Komendanta Kizlyara, svyazka 284, zakaz 3 as quoted in Skitskiy, 1932, p. 119; Akhmadov, 1991, p. 88.

8 Dubrovin, 1886, vol. 1, p. 87.

9 Baddely, 1908, p. 47.

10 *TsGADA*, razdel XXIII, chast' 10, list 9-18; Bennigsen dated his birth to the early 1770s. Bennigsen, 1964, p. 159.

11 Terechshenko, 1856, p. 52.

12 As stated during the interrogation by the Taynaya Komissiya, see *TsGADA*, razdel VII, delo 2777, list 9-30. However, in the Russian archives there are a number of his letters written in Arabic with Mansour's seal affixed to them. Thus, one can either consider his claims to have no religious education to be false, or suppose that the letters were written by one of his more educated associates on his behalf. In light of the independent evidence unearthed by A. Bennigsen in the Ottoman archives, the latter version seems more plausible. Bennigsen, 1964, p. 183.

13 *TsGADA*, razdel VII, delo 2777, list 9-18.

14 *Ibid.*

15 *Ibid.*

by claiming to have had a revelation.'[16]

In fact Mansour's religious awakening dates back to the early 1780s[17] and there are several stories which account for it. According to Mansour himself, he first started to see visions in the solitude of the Chechen mountains where he spent many days as a shepherd.[18] 'While I, Imam Mansour, was a shepherd, I saw the Prophet Muhammad in my dream and he told me that it was I, Imam Mansour, who had to return [the people] to the true path and Muhammad's prophecy – and there are no other prophets apart from him and there is only one *mahdi* to come.'[19]

According to another version, Mansour saw a vision in his dream in which two horsemen miraculously appeared in his yard and, addressing him as an imam, said that God Almighty and His Prophet grieved at seeing the mountain peoples negligent of the Divine Law and had chosen Mansour to turn them back to Islam, in which he would be assisted by God and His Prophet. On awakening, Mansour went into seclusion for three days, during which he fasted and prayed[20] and only then revealed his vision first to his brothers and then to other people.[21]

One of the independent observers gave the following account of his first public appearance:

After two painful nights during which his relatives tried to prevent him from preaching, [....] Sheikh Mansour came up to the village mosque and called upon everyone to pray. From the roof of the mosque, he addressed the people who flocked up to the mosque in great numbers, exhorting them to abandon their evil deeds, put aside enmity and fighting against each other and be reconciled, stop drinking vodka and wine, give alms and follow the Muslim law. Having finished his speech he returned home with the people following him, ordered two sheep to be slaughtered and he immediately distributed the meat among all those present. Thus, ended the first day. On the second day he took one of his two bulls and went to a cemetery, walked around it three times, returned back home, slaughtered the bull and gave half of the meat to the poor and the other half to the students at the madrasah. From that day onwards rumours about him spread all around and people started to bring him livestock which he slaughtered and gave out as alms, feeding on the rest himself with his family.[22]

In preaching forgiveness in blood disputes Mansour persuaded his mother

---

[16] *TsGADA*, razd. XXIII, delo 13 chast' 10, list 143-4; also quoted by Smirnov, 1950, p. 35; Bennigsen, 1964, p. 159.

[17] *Ibid.*, p. 162.

[18] *TsGADA*, razdel VII, delo 2777, list 9-18.

[19] *TsGVIA*, fond 52, opis' 1/194, delo 366, chast' 2, list 274.

[20] According to yet another version, he died and was resurrected after three days. *TsGADA*, razdel XXIII delo 13, chast' 10, list 133-8; also in Smirnov, 1950, p. 25.

[21] Dubrovin, 1886, vol. II, p. 89.

[22] 'Pokazaniya Tatarina Ali Soltana iz Bolshikh Atagov ot 8 marta 1785 g.', *TsGVIA*, fond 52, opis' 1/194, delo 350, chast' 5, list 8-10 ob.

and other relatives to forgive their blood enemies which made a deep impression on his compatriots.[23] The rumours about his piety started to spread throughout the area and in 1783 he was proclaimed a sheikh and an imam[24] and took the name Mansour.[25] Moreover, when following people's demands to produce 'a real miracle', two severe earthquakes – on 12-13 February and on 4 March 1785 – struck Chechnya; many saw them as a special sign from God and believed that Mansour was indeed sent by God and His Prophet to save them.[26]

The reaction of the Muslim clergy towards Mansour's claims to be an Imam was more mixed. Some supported him (among the most respectful of his supporters were the *qadis* Umar Hajji from Shali, Noghay Mirza Hajji, Bisultan Hajji and Hambe Hajji),[27] others (such as the *qadis* and mullahs of Tabarsaran) denounced him as a 'humble shepherd' and 'an impostor' who had no right to instruct them or others.[28]

Although at the end of his life Mansour claimed that he never declared himself a prophet 'but could not prevent people from seeing [him] as such, since [his] ideas and lifestyle seemed a miracle to them',[29] he did not hesitate to promise miracles[30] and called upon people throughout the North Caucasus to come to visit him to witness them.[31] Moreover, to encourage what could be a difficult and dangerous journey across the line of the Russian fortifications, he declared that a visit to him across the Russian line was accepted by God as a Hajj to Mecca.

Rumours about his alleged ability to perform miracles such as predicting the future, seeing hidden things, appearing in more than one place at once and praying on felt carpet floating on water, spread throughout the area, and numerous visitors including mullahs, *qadis, 'ulama* and other respected people such as the Qumyq ruler from the Buynaq *jama'at* and the son of the *utsmiy* of Qaytaq[32] came to see 'the new prophet'.

---

[23] *TsGVIA*, fond 52, opis' 1/194, delo 350, chast' 5, list 8-10 ob.

[24] *TsGADA*, razdel VII, delo 2777, list 19-33. Some Russian/Soviet scholars claimed that Mansour was declared a sheikh in 1784, see Akhmadov, 1991, p. 92.

[25] Mansour in Arabic means victorious.

[26] The earthquake being interpreted in accordance to the belief that Jabrail malik caused it in order to remind people of God and restore their belief. On this belief see Chapter 5.

[27] Smirnov, 1950, p. 24, as quoted from *TsGADA*, razdel XXIII chast' 15, list 151; chast 18, list 259 – Pokazaniya Brata Mansoura, Etta.

[28] *TsGVIA*, fond 52 opis' 1/194, delo 350, part II, list 53.

[29] *TsGADA*, razdel VII, delo 2777, list 9-18.

[30] 'Rapport ot leytenanta Babushkina Kommendantu Kreposti Kizlyar ot 6 Marta 1785 g.', *TsGVIA*, delo 350, chast' 4, list 34-34 ob.; chast' 5 list 7-7 ob.

[31] In 1784 he sent his first envoy to the people of the Kuban area and in 1785 appealed for support to the rulers of Daghestan. Doc. 941 from the Hatti-Humayun archive in Istanbul as quoted in Bennigsen, 1964, p. 183.

[32] *Arkhiv Checheno-Ingushskogo Kraevedcheskogo Muzeya*, opis' 2, svyazka 3, papka 7, list 23, as quoted in Akhmadov, 1991, pp. 109-11.

The people of Salataw, Qumyq and Chirkah *jama'ats* accepted him as a sheikh and imam[33] and 'with each hour Mansour was gaining strength, his teaching was losing its purely religious character until it gradually acquired explicitly political overtones'.[34]

From the very beginning Mansour preached the need to restore Muslim law and spiritual values as a necessary prerequisite to a successful war against the Russians in which only the true believers would be assisted by God.[35] Although the Russians were the ultimate enemy, Mansour forbade his followers from entering into any conflicts with the Russian troops 'until I start my quarrel with Russia. [...] With God's help my troops will take over and conquer other peoples. But meanwhile you must be patient.'[36] Thus, in his aspiration firmly to establish Islam in the area, he declared *ghazavat* against the pagan and semi-pagan Ingush and Christian Ossets, by first sending his emissaries to them,[37] and later in June 1785 organising two military campaigns against them.[38] The ultimate aim of these campaigns was not so much to put them under the imam's rule as to convert them to Islam.

Seen in historical perspective, this was a logical continuation of a general process of Islamisation in the central Caucasus which spread from eastern coastal Daghestan westwards. This time it had, however, two new important characteristics. For the first time in history Islamisation was carried out by a Vaynakh (Chechen) rather than a Daghestani preacher, and it occurred in a broader context of general confrontation between the world of Islam and the increasingly domineering Christian powers.

The context in which sheikh Mansour set out to further Islam among the North Caucasian peoples was novel. From the second-half of the eighteenth century, the religious struggle for the semi-pagan mountain tribes attained explicitly political overtones. In 1774 the Russians established a special committee in Vladikavkaz whose aim was 'to propagate Christianity among the the Ossets and the Ingush',[39] and to establish Christian schools among them. At the same time, the Russian authorities demanded

[33] Yudin, 1914, p. 218.

[34] Dubrovin, 1886, vol. II, pp. 100-1.

[35] In his appeals Mansour promised that God would make him and his followers invulnerable to the Russian bullets and at the same time make their daggers stretch by a few metres so that with each stroke one faithful man could engage ten infidels. *TsGVIA*, fond 52 opis' 1/194, delo 350, chast' 5, list 9-9 ob., 10-10 ob.

[36] *TsGVIA*, fond 52 opis' 1/194, delo 350, chast' 6 list 36. The letter was written in Arabic and addressed to the Kabardian Hajjis.

[37] *TsGVIA*, fond 52, opis' 1/194, delo 366, part 2, list 274. Letter sent to the Ingush and the Ossets, written in Arabic.

[38] Butkov, 1869, part 3, p. 171.

[39] *Ibid.*, p. 268.

that the Ingush forbid 'effendis, mullahs and other persons of Muslim religious rank to preach among them [...] and to build mosques in their land'.[40]

In this environment, Mansour's efforts to reinforce Islam and Islamicise the Ingush and the Ossets were seen by the Russians as a challenge to their authority in the area. With increasing alarm they tried to hamper Mansour's growing popularity by distributing proclamations against him[41] and ordered people under the Russian protectorate to sever all their links with Mansour and his followers.[42] At the same time they brought additional troops into the area, reinforced all the fortresses and Cossack *stanitsas*,[43] and prohibited the north Caucasians from travelling in the territory between the mountains and Kizlyar without special written permission issued by the Russian authorities.[44]

Instead of achieving the results desired by the Russians, these measures only served to alienate further the local people, who saw the Russian orders as a direct violation of their rights.

Military confrontation

Failing to stop Mansour from gaining strength and popularity among the North Caucasians, the Russians staged a military campaign against him in July 1775. Designed as a typical punitive expedition, the campaign was to destroy Mansour's base in the village of Aldy and capture him and his supporters. Although the Russians did not anticipate any serious resistance, they sent over 3,000 Russian soldiers and officers on the expedition, who were to teach the rebel a decisive lesson.[45]

The first disappointment came when, having stormed and entered the village of Aldy, the Russians found it virtually abandoned with no sign of Mansour or his supporters. Disappointed, they set fire to all the houses in the village and made sure that Mansour's house was completely destroyed.[46]

As far as Mansour and his people were concerned the main battle was yet to come. Hiding in the forest-covered mountains, they surrounded

---

[40] Dalgat, 1893, p. 52.

[41] *TsGVIA*, fond 52, opis' 1/194, delo 350, chast' 5, list 71, chast' 7, list 4.

[42] *TsGVIA*, fond, 52, opis' 1/194, delo 350, part 6, list 32, *Arkhiv Checheno-Ingushskogo Kraevedcheskogo Muzeya*, opis' 2, svyazka 3, papka 7, list 6, as quoted in Akhmadov, 1991, p. 146.

[43] *Ibid.*, chast' 5, list 71 and chast' 7, list 4.

[44] *Ibid.*, chast' 5, list 5-50b. 'Rapport Astrakhanskogo Gubernatora Statskogo Sovetnika Zhukova na Imya General-Porutchika P.S. Potemkina ot 26 Marta 1785 g.', also quoted in Akhmadov, 1991, p. 112.

[45] *Ibid.*, chast' 7, list 20b.-3, 'Kopiya Prikaza General-Leytenanta Leonteva na Imya Polkovnika Pierri ot 3 Iyulya 1785 g.', no. 19 also quoted in Akhmadov, 1991, p. 118.

[46] Korol'kov, 1914, p. 412.

the village unnoticed by the enemy and when the Russians set off on their return march, they suddenly ambushed them, destroying at least half of the Russian force with the rest fleeing in panic across the Sunja river where many were drowned.[47]

Even the Russians had to admit the devastating consequences of their defeat and that 'this unfortunate occurrence not only upset the situation in the area but also gave the Chechens ground for further exploits.'[48] The extent to which this remark was true is highlighted by the suggestion of a historian that 'the great revolt of the Naqshbandis in the nineteenth century was possible only as a direct consequence of the unheard victory of the *va-nu-pied* (ragamuffins) who had destroyed the column of Peirri in the Chechen forests.'[49]

Uneducated shepherd as he was, Mansour fully appreciated the importance of his victory and how to capitalise on it. Thus, he immediately sent letters to all North Caucasian *jama'ats* in which he described his success and the shameful flight of the Russians as a miracle produced by him with assistance from God. His own accounts of the event quickly became embroidered with many fantastic stories in which Mansour was presented as a holy man and miracle-worker,[50] so that the people of the North Caucasus became convinced that Mansour had indeed been chosen by God to free them from the oppression and injustice of the Infidels.

In this situation Mansour made several attempts to reorganise the life of the mountain peoples. He put an obligation on each mosque to mobilise from two to ten people and demanded 60 kopecks from each household to support the army during the military campaigns. At the same time Mansour form military alliances with the rulers of Aqsay, Enderi and some Kabardian princes, and by the end of July 1785, his 'army' numbered up to 12,000 men[51] massed from among the Chechens, Kabardians, Qumyq, Avar, Noghay and Circassians.[52]

He tried to further the *shari'a*, as much as he understood it.[53] It was

---

[47] *TsGVIA*, fond 52, opis' 1/194, delo 350, part 11, list 25-25 ob. 'Rapport General-Leytenanta Potemkina knyazyu Potemkinu P.S. ot 8 Noyabrya 1785 g.'?

[48] *Ibid.*, part 7, list 53-53 ob. 'Rapport Knyazya Potemkina Ekaterine'.

[49] Bennigsen, 1964, p. 187.

[50] Such stories maintained that Mansour could transform a handful of earth into bullets and that the Russian weapons were harmless to the Muslims fighting with Mansour. See Sheripov, 1927, p. 153.

[51] *TsGVIA*, fond 52, opis' 1/194, delo 350, chast' 9, list 39; chast' 8, list 4-4ob.

[52] Although the *shamkhal* of Targhu and the Avar khan did not support Mansour and remained loyal to the Russians, they could not prevent their people from crossing over to Mansour and joining the ranks of his followers. Akhmadov, 1991, p. 146, n. 2; also see al-Qarakhi, 1929, pp. 104-5.

[53] According to Dubrovin, Mansour made the men who had not been circumcised undergo the operation, and forbade drinking and smoking among his followers. Dubrovin, 1886, vol. 2, pp. 105.

also at that time that Mansour fabricated a seal similar to the one used by the Ottoman governors with which he affixed his letters and verdicts.[54]

Reluctant as Mansour initially had been to start the military confrontation with the Russians, once it was opened he took the offensive and in August 1785 set up a raid against one of the most important Russian centres in the area, Kizlyar.[55] However, once outside his native Chechnya and lacking the protection of the mountain forests, Mansour's capacity to 'produce miracles' declined and he had to retreat before overwhelming Russian military might.[56] This as well as several further military defeats[57] revealed the shortcomings of Mansour's movement. All military fortunes were interpreted by the north Caucasians as miracles. The defeats on the other hand deprived Mansour of his claims of Divine assistance and considerably undermined people's belief in him. At the same time, through bribes and threats, the Russians won back the allegiance of the Qumyq and Kabardian rulers[58] and restored peace. Thus, while in September 1785 the whole of the Caucasus from the Black Sea to the Caspian Sea coast was caught up in a series of disturbances, by December Mansour had lost the greater part of his followers, and most local rulers, including the elders of Mansour's native village of Aldy, had appealed for forgiveness and had sworn an oath of allegiance to the Russians.[59] The last to leave Mansour were the Kabardians.[60]

It appears from the Russian sources, that Mansour himself tried to negotiate his submission to the Russians and in October 1785 sent his brother Etta to Major-General Potemkin with an offer of surrender on the condition that the Russians would allow him to stay in the Caucasus and preach Islam so that he 'could prevent the north Caucasians from evil deeds'.[61]

One can only speculate how events in the Caucasus would have developed had the Russians been prepared to negotiate and accommodate Islam in their North Caucasian policy. But, as it was, they deemed anything short of decisive and complete victory over Mansour as not worthy of Russia's status as a great power and treated any possibility

---

54 Smirnov, 1950, p. 46.

55 Situated at the cross-roads between southern Russia, Daghestan and the North Caucasus, Kizlyar was crucial in linking the Caucasian fortified line with Astrakhan and the Russian hinterland and as such was the true centre of Russian might in the North Caucasus both in political and economic terms (although the Russian official administrative centre was Ekaterinodar, present-day Krasnodar).

56 On Mansour's campaign against Kizlyar, see Akhmadov, 1991, pp. 149-56.

57 *Ibid.*, pp. 156-94.

58 *TsGVIA*, fond 52, opis' 1/194, chast' 7, list 4-4ob., list 50-50ob.

59 Akhmadov, 1991, p. 184.

60 Smirnov, 1950, p. 49.

61 Akhmadov, 1991, p. 192.

of negotiations with the 'shameless impostor' as a humiliation to the Empire. At the same time they came to see Islam and the Muslim religious leaders as the main enemies of and major threat to Russian domination in the area (the attitude which with some modifications, shaped Russian and later Soviet policy towards Islam).

Thus, Major-General Potemkin ignored Mansour's appeal, which he believed to be a sign of the imam's weakness and desparation, convinced that it was a matter of days before he would catch him and teach all the people of the North Caucasus a lesson. This, however, proved to be premature and it took the Russians five more years to capture Mansour and over half-a-century to bring the North Caucasus under their rule.

Despite repeated Russian attempts to catch him, Mansour in early 1787 managed to escape unharmed into the western Caucasus, where he soon rose to a position of rare influence and authority.[62] His military endeavours are beyond the scope of the present work and it is sufficient to say that for three years he led the Circassians in the North-western Caucasus in anti-Russian resistance, until at last they were overpowered by Russian military might[63] and had to surrender. The last refuge of Sheikh Mansour was in the Ottoman fortress of Anapa, destroyed in July 1791, and there he was finally captured.[64]

Transported with special care to St Petersburg, Mansour was sentenced by the Empress to life imprisonment in the Shlisselburg fortress, where on 13 April 1794, 'in the afternoon, shortly after 1 p.m. [Mansour] died of his illness'. Three days later, on 16 April 1794, he was buried 'as instructed on the Preobrazhenskaya hill'.[65]

The memory of Mansour long outlived the man himself. It was his religious rather than military achievements which were of greater importance both to him and his followers. Moreover, although he was more successful in the north-western Caucasus, it was in the east, especially in Chechnya, where he left a lasting legacy. Up to his last days in Anapa he continued sending letters and appeals to the eastern Caucasus. The last letter sent shortly before his captivity was to his native Chechnya in which he urged his countrymen 'to purify their hearts from evil, follow the righteous path according to God's laws, fight what is harmful and illegal',[66] and promised to return with reinforcements to drive the Russians out of the area.

Perhaps it was this letter followed by his suffering in Russian captivity

---

[62] On Mansour's military and religious activities among the Circassians see *ibid.*, pp. 222-56.

[63] Determined to crush the Circassian resistance, the Russians even brought in forces from the Russian-Ottoman front which was newly opened on 9 September 1787.

[64] Dubrovin, 1886, p. 275; Korolkov, 1914, pp. 414-5.

[65] *TsGADA*, razdel VII, delo 2777, list 44.

[66] Sheripov, 1927, p. 157.

that convinced the Chechens of his sanctity. No stories about Mansour's death in Russia could shake the Chechens' belief that he had miraculously escaped and would return and liberate them from the Russian yoke, any doubt of his return was considered as the worst sacrilege and blasphemy.[67]

The North Caucasians' vivid memories of Mansour, his preaching and military activities prepared the ground for the later Naqshbandi imams who saw themselves as his disciples. Indeed, Mansour's religious preaching and the pattern of his life bear strong Sufi connotations[68] and as such are reminiscent of the nineteenth-century Naqsbhandi leaders. The mode of his religious awakening, the source of his authority based on the claim of Divine inspiration and the ability to perform miracles are features common to many Sufi sheikhs. Moreover, some who met the imam described him as one who had 'devoted himself to the life of a dervish'.[69] Bennigsen suggested that Mansour could have been inducted into the Naqshbandi brotherhood by two pilgrims (from Bukhara and from the Qumyq lands), who had allegedly met and had a lengthy conversation with him on their way to the *hajj* via the North Caucasus.[70]

Mansour himself never mentioned the name of the brotherhood, nor did he try to establish a Sufi network in the area. With 'sheikhly' Islam wide-spread in the Vaynakh lands and Sufi ideas floating widely throughout the area, his resemblance to the Sufi patterns is hardly surprising. Moreover, his image and the context of his preaching were likely to have been enhanced in the later period under the influence of the Naqshbandi imams of the nineteenth century. Thus, it seems that whether Mansour was a Naqshbandi or not is likely to remain an open question.

Mansour left a long-lasting legacy in the North Caucasus. His activities to a certain extent shaped Russian tactics and policy in the area, and it must be taken as more than pure coincidence that the establishment of the Caucasian vice-regency as a military rather than civil administration coincided with the beginning of Mansour's activities and could have been due to the need to meet the challenge posed by him and his supporters.

Furthermore, Mansour's movement revealed general tendencies which later manifested themselves once again in the activities of the nineteenth-century North Caucasian imams. It was he who first applied the guerilla

---

[67] *Ibid.*, p. 152.

[68] Particularly interesting is the story of Mansour having a dugout in his yard, where he retreated for fast and prayer. This account bears a remarkable resemblance to the Naqshbandi practice of *khalwa*, i.e. forty days' seclusion accompanied by prayer and fasting. Skitskiy, 1932 p. 119.

[69] As described by two hajjis from Bukhara and the Qumyq lands, see Bennigsen, 1964, pp. 177-8.

[70] *Ibid.* p. 163.

tactics of retreating in the face of the Russian offensive and then attacking the retreating Russian forces, which later became the most typical strategy of Caucasian warfare. Even his failures revealed the general pitfalls of Caucasian warfare: his defeats on the plain were suffered by Shamil in almost the same place half-a-century later.

Greatest significance, however, must be attributed to his efforts to cross the tribal and ethnic confines and unite the mountain peoples under the auspices of a broader religious movement.

He failed it is true, in his endeavour to unite them [the mountain peoples] against a common enemy, but he it was who first taught [the peoples of the North Caucasus] that in religious reform lay one chance of preserving their cherished liberty and independence and therefore laid foundation for future union and for the great movement which under the name of *Muridism* was, in the coming century to set at naught year after year, decade after decade the whole might of Russia.[71]

71 Baddeley, 1908, pp. 47-8.

10

THE RUSSIAN MILITARY CAMPAIGNS
AND ANNEXATION OF
THE NORTH CAUCASUS

In the early nineteenth century Russia continued its expansion into the area. In 1805-6 most khanates of northern Azerbaijan were added to the Russian Empire, and in the first decade of the century the *utsmiy* of Qaytaq, the *shamkhal* of Targhu, the khan of Derbend, the *qadi* and the *maysum* of Tabarsaran and the khan of Kurah accepted Russian protectorate.

At the same time Russia gained the upper hand in the struggle with Persia. The treaty of Gulistan signed between the two powers in 1813 recognised Russia's claims over the North Caucasus. The treaty consolidated Russia's position as the major power in the area and confirmed its aspiration that the whole of the North Caucasus be adjoined to the Empire.

This task was assigned to General A.P. Ermolov, who enjoyed the full confidence and backing of Tsar Alexander I.[1] In 1816 Ermolov was appointed governor and chief administrator of Georgia and the Caucasus, commander-in-chief of the Separate Georgian Corps and ambassador extraordinaire to the court of the Persian shah, Fath Ali Shah.[2] He shared the Emperor's views that:

The existence of independent or semi-independent states or communities of any description, whether Christian, Musulman or Pagan, in the mountains or in the plain, was incompatible with the dignity and the honour of his Master [the Russian tsar], the safety and welfare of his subjects.[3]

To incorporate the North Caucasus into the Russian Empire Ermolov applied the so-called 'siege policy'.[4] Using the Caucasian fortified line

---

[1] On his arrival in the Caucasus, Ermolov was assigned the task of evading a promise given by Alexander I to Fath Ali Shah to restore to him part of the territories acquired by Russia in the treaty of Gulistan, a task which Ermolov fulfilled completely. Potto, 1887-8, vol. II, part I, p. 14.

[2] His vast powers and the special protection he enjoyed from the Emperor won Ermolov the title of Proconsul of the Caucasus. Gammer, 1994, p. 29.

[3] Baddeley, 1908, p. 99.

[4] On the 'siege policy,' see Gammer, 1992, pp. 45-9.

as the first parallel, he started construction of a second parallel which consisted of the Sunja and the Sulak (or Qumyq) lines. At the same time he resolved to wage persistent military campaigns against the local rulers who tried to resist the Russian advances.

First Ermolov forced the khan of Mekhtuli to flee into the mountains and in 1818 abolished the khanate. He transferred some of its *jama'ats* to the jurisdiction of the *shamkhal* of Targhu, the only Daghestani ruler who at that time remained loyal to the Russians. The rest of the former khanate's lands were adjoined directly to the Russian Empire.

In 1819 the Avar ruler Ahmad Khan was also defeated and deposed.[5] Shortly after defeating Ahmad Khan, the Russians stormed the residence of the *utsmiy* of Qaytaq. The *utsmiy* fled, his domain was abolished and annexed to the Empire.[6] This allowed Ermolov to deal with the powerful confederation of Akusha. Defeated at the battle of Lavashi, the people of Akusha, who 'had taken pride for three-quarters of a century in the memory of their defeat of Nadir Shah, bowed to the Russian yoke'.[7] The Russians replaced the elderly *qadi* of Akusha, who had resisted the Russians with one who was their 'friend in the full meaning of the word'.[8] Finally in 1820 Ghazi-Ghumuq was added to the list of Russian conquests, followed by the voluntary submission of Kubachi.

Thus, Ermolov by the early 1820s, had brought the larger part of Daghestan under submission. Apart from the western areas of Inner Daghestan, which had so far retained their freedom and were described by the Russians as *vol'nye* (independent, free),[9] the rest of Daghestan, including the Qumyq and Samur *jama'ats*, Tabarsaran, Ghazi-Ghumuq and Kurah were treated by the Russian authorities as *pokornye* (submissive) and *mirnye* (peaceable). Ermolov believed that the complete and permanent conquest of the whole of the North-eastern Caucasus was now merely a matter of a few years.

The aged Lieutenant-General Mekhti, renowned for his devotion to us was administering the domain of *shamkhalate*. Sultan Ahmad Khan of the Avars, our main enterprising enemy, died, leaving his three under-aged children and widow, the cunning Pahu-Bike, who governed in Avaria [the Avar khanate] and tried to assist the claims of our government. The domain of Mekhtuli, was given after the death of the traitor Hasan Khan, to his son, who came to Ermolov to express his

---

[5] Ramazanov and Hadzhiev (eds), 1959, pp. 31-2,; Grunberg and Bushuev (eds), 1940, p. 121.

[6] Ramazanov and Hadzhiev (eds), 1959, p. 31.

[7] Baddeley, 1908, p. 134.

[8] Dubrovin, 1871-88, vol. X, p. 12, Khashaev, 1965, pp. 50, 56.

[9] Six *jama'ats* within the Qaytaq association were independent, while two others were subject to the Russians.

full and complete submission [*pokornost'*]. The troublesome *utsmiy* of Qaytaq, who used to disturb the peace was replaced by the well intentioned *naib* Amir-Hamza. The khanates of Ghazi-Ghumuq and Kurah which had been subdued already in 1820 kept their loyalty to the rule of colonel Usman Khan. The *sultan* of Ilisu, Ahmad [...] distinguished himself by his zeal and faithfulness to Russia. Independent communes nestling in the inaccessible mountains did not attempt any hostile activities. Moreover, the most powerful of them, the Akusha and Andalal confederations, had recognised the Russian protectorate, the Salataw and Aukh were dependent on the princes of Andrey [Enderi] submitted by us; some people of Gumbet paid tribute to the *beks* of Arghanay. Only the Chechens did not obey our *pristavs* [bailiffs] and at times were in open rebellion.[10]

The Russian policy of colonisation

Having achieved the submission of a large part of Daghestan, Ermolov started to reorganise the administration in the area. The first and most important step in fulfilling this aim was the co-optation of the local political elite. Already at the beginning of the nineteenth century the Russian authorities attempted to turn the local rulers into Russian subjects. They allotted them a permanent salary for their 'loyal service to the Russian tsar',[11] gave them titles[12] and requested a certain number of armed men to be put forward to serve under Russian command. Prior to Ermolov's appointment to the Caucasus, the agreements between Russia and the local rulers were little more than treaties of alliance. The North Caucasians remained free, did not have to pay any taxes and duties and were merely obliged to acknowledge the Russian protectorate over them and remain loyal during wartime. A special decree issued by the Tsar in May 1800 advised the military administration in the eastern Caucasus not to interfere in the domestic life of the mountain peoples and to treat them as being in 'vassalage dependence' (*vassalnaya zavisimost'*) rather than in 'citizenship' (*poddanstvo*).[13]

The situation started to change when in 1812 the Chief Directorate (*Glavnoe Upravlenie*) had been established in Derbend. At the same time Count Tsitsianov, its first director, imposed certain taxes and duties over all the *jama'ats* which had recognised the Russian protectorate. Although the traditional rulers were allowed to keep their titles, their rights became restricted and the Russian administration imposed its control over the process of their election or succession.[14] To keep local

10 *TsGVIA*, fond VUA, delo 655, list 2-21.

11 Khashaev, 1961, p. 38.

12 The *shamkhal* of Targhu, for example, held the title of Councillor and received a salary worth 6,000 silver rubles per annum, the *utsmiy* of Qaytaq received 2,000 silver roubles per annum, the *qadi* of Tabarsaran and the *maysum* of Tabarsaran each received 1,500 silver rubles per year. See Khashaev, 1961, p. 38.

13 Butkov, 1869, vol. 2, p. 562.

14 See Khashaev, 1965, p. 38; Khashaev 1969, pp. 38, 70.

rulers in subordination, they dissolved some political formations and replaced them with new ones, gave loyal rulers land that belonged to *jama'ats* outside their jurisdiction,[15] or in case of insubordination, deprived them of the land that lawfully belonged to them. Furthermore, they controlled all their links with other North Caucasian communes and with the outside world.

Ermolov stepped up this policy. He limited the number of people allowed to attend *jama'at* gatherings from all male members of a *jama'at* to one representative per household. The head of the council of elders, who had traditionally been elected by the whole *jama'at* was now made accountable to the Russian administration, without whose authorisation his election was deemed illegal.[16] Furthermore, the Russian administration appropriated communal land into the treasury under the pretext that it did not belong to anyone, and forced people to pay tax and duties on it.[17] He also imposed control over communications between various North Caucasian peoples as well as their links with foreign powers and greatly restricted freedom of travel and trade.[18]

Trying to resist these drastic measures that greatly disrupted the traditional way of life in the area, the people of the North Caucasus staged a number of armed rebellions. These, however, were brutally suppressed. Guided by his vain conviction that 'gentleness in the eyes of the Asiatics was a sign of weakness',[19] Ermolov saw terror as the only method appropriate in respect of the North Caucasians.[20] In his own words he claimed that he 'desire[d] that the terror of my name should guard our frontiers more patently than chains of fortresses, that my word should be for the natives a law more inevitable than death'.[21] Thus, he engaged in a series of devastating punitive expeditions during which executions were carried out on a massive scale and whole villages punished for the fault of just one or a few of its people.[22]

---

[15] For example a certain Hamza Bek and his brother received under their jurisdiction the *jama'ats* which had never recognised their authority. *AKAK*, vol. VI, part II doc. no. 146; also Khashaev, 1961, p. 64. The domain of the *shamkhal*, who on many occasions had proven his loyalty to the Russians, was enlarged at the expense of the *jama'ats* of the Avar and the Mekhtuli khanates. See Khashaev, 1969, pp. 37-8.

[16] Ermolov's decree of 23 December 1819, as qouted in Khashaev, 1961, p. 168; Esadze, 1907, p. 178.

[17] Khashaev, 1961, p. 128.

[18] *Ibid.*, p. 116; *AKAK*, vol. VI, part II, pp. 26-39. On the importance of Daghestani trade see Khashaev, 1961, pp. 113-25.

[19] As quoted in Baddeley, 1908, p. 97.

[20] This view was shared by the majority of the Russian officers (and in fact still forms the governing doctrine of the Russian army), 'the whole art of which, in the words of an Austrian diplomat, is in the use of violence.' As quoted in Gammer, 1994, p. 34.

[21] As quoted in *ibid.*, 1992, p. 47.

[22] For more on Ermolov's policy see, pp. 40-1; 1994, pp. 29-38.

Ermolov believed that these expeditions had once and for all put an end to any attempts on the part of the North Caucasian anti-Russian resistance. He was convinced that 'under his firm hand the bowed head of subdued and submissive people could not possibly rise again'.[23] In 1820 he reported to the Emperor:

The subjugation of Daghestan [...] is now complete and this country, proud, warlike and hitherto unconquered, has fallen at the sacred feet of Your Imperial Majesty.[24]

The developments which occurred in the coming years were to prove him wrong.

In the second half of the eighteenth century the traditional power-struggle between the Ottomans, the Persians and the Russians over the Caucasus reached a new stage, with Russia now distinctly interested not merely in gaining political control over the area but in incorporating the whole of its territory into the Empire.

The convenience of Russia's geographical position combined with her clear military and political advantages ensured that she emerged as the winning side in this struggle and dislodged her Muslim opponents from direct involvement in the area. This left the local peoples on their own in their struggle with one of the major European powers of the time.

In this environment a new tendency crystallised, and Islam emerged as the major political force capable of crossing tribal and ethnic divides and uniting various peoples in a broad anti-colonial struggle. Formulated by Sheikh or Imam Mansour, who combined an appeal for religious reforms and armed resistance, the new movement first emerged in the central areas of the North Caucasus from where it gradually spread into the eastern and western areas.

It was hardly a coincidence that it was Chechnya that produced a leader and a movement which advocated a pan-Caucasian military-political alliance in the face of Russia's growing ambitions. The Chechens became exposed to Russian policy only in the late eighteenth century and were quick to react to the challenge. Their readiness to mount resistance was intensified in the absence of ruling elites or princely dynasties whereby Russia lacked the levers of influence by which to manipulate local political entities to its own advantage (as was the case in lowland areas of Daghestan and the western Caucasus).

However, having risen to the challenge, Mansour soon discovered a lack of enthusiasm among his fellow Chechens and mountain Daghes-

---

[23] Volkonskiy, 1886, vol. X, p. 19.
[24] As quoted in Baddeley, 1908, p. 138.

tanis, which was largely due to the fact that the latter had not yet been subjected to the turbulent effects of Russian colonial policy. Even those who whole-heartedly supported Mansour's appeal to fight against Russia were reluctant to join his military campaigns outside their own locality. Furthermore, despite a strong ideological attraction to the Islamic dimension of the new movement, it was largely driven by the strength of Mansour's personality and lacked any coherent infrastructure.

It was from northern Daghestan and the western Caucasus where the full consequences of falling into the Russian imperial domain had become apparent, that Mansour drew most of his support and following. However, while the people in the western North Caucasus saw him mainly as a military leader whose importance ceased once the resistance was crushed and its leader captured, in Chechnya and Daghestan, Mansour left a long-lasting legacy as a religious reformer who set a precedent by appealing to Islamic ideology as a force overriding the ethnic and tribal factions inherent in the region.

Mansour's ideas became imbedded in the collective memory of the local peoples and when the Russian determination to conquer the Northeastern Caucasus and bring it into submission gathered full momentum, it was only a matter of time and relevant political force for a new wave of resistance to develop. This time, however, strong leadership was to be coupled with an equally powerful institution.

Of all Islamic institutions of the time, the Sufi organisation, informal and 'populist' in its nature, was best equipped to rise to a position of influence and power in the nineteenth-century North Caucasus. Among the Sufi orders, the Naqshbandiyya, in particular, possessed an elaborate doctrine and political experience which not only offered an answer to the problems that overwhelmed the North Caucasian peoples, but also provided both the structure and leadership to tackle them.

Part IV. ORIGINS AND DEVELOPMENT OF THE NAQSHBANDIYYA-MUJADDIDIYYA-KHALIDIYYA: DOCTRINE AND PRACTICES

11

THE FORMATION OF THE MAIN PRINCIPLES OF THE NAQSHBANDI TARIQA[1]

The Sufi *tariqa*[2] which was introduced into the North Caucasus in the nineteenth century bears the name of Baha al-Din Naqshband who lived in the fourteenth century in Bukhara (b. 1318 – d. 1389 AD). However, neither the Naqshbandi tradition nor the scholarly–historical one regard Baha al-Din as the real founder of the order. Any Sufi adept, sees *tasawwuf* (Sufism in Arabic) as coeval with Islam itself and traces its origins back to the Prophet Muhammad. The latter is seen in the Sufi tradition not only as a recipient and expositor of Divine Revelation, but as the Supreme Guide on the Path to God and the first link in his *silsila*.[3] The importance of a *silsila* lies precisely in its role as 'a means of tracing one's way back to the Prophet, of gaining access, in a certain

---

[1] The research on the general history of Sufism and the formation of the Naqshbandi order is based on the following sources: al-Khani, 1308 AH; Algar, 1975; Algar, 1976; Algar, 1985; Algar, 1985(a); Brown, 1986; Burkhart, 1990; Dewasse, 1993; Gellner, 1969; Habib, 1962; Habib, 1969; Nasr, 1991; Nicholson, 1923; Nickolson, 1963; Popovic, 1968; Schimmel, 1975; Shushud, 1983; Scholem, 1955; Trimmingham, 1971.

[2] *Tariqa* literally means 'path, road [to God]'. The Sufi *tariqas* are not sects and the closest analogy (although not fully accurate) in the Christian world are the monastic Catholic orders. Thus, I translate the word *tariqa* as an order or a brotherhood.

[3] Silsila in Sufi terminology means the chain of transmitters of the divine message.

fashion, to that auspicious age which it is the purpose of the Sufi to relive'.[4]

Early Islam (as indeed any other monotheistic religion) placed a great emphasis on asceticism and the virtue of unworldliness.[5] However, the underlying philosophy of the early Muslim ascetics differed dramatically from that of the later mystics. The basis of early asceticism in Islam was fear of the Day of Judgement which came with realisation of the uniqueness of God. The overwhelming consciousness of sin combined with a fear of Hell, so vividly painted in the Qur'an, drove the early mystics (or rather ascetics) to seek salvation in flight from the World. In essence, however, they were not much different from other Muslims, both following a common aim, namely winning salvation in the Other World. Only gradually did the ascetic movement start to develop towards mysticism with the driving force behind ascetic practices being not so much the fear of God as the desire to cross the abyss between human existence and the Divinity and achieve union with God through following a special path of utmost devotion. Unlike the ascetics, mystics were concerned not so much with their salvation as with gaining an insight into the Divine Reality.[6]

Thus, being 'a definite stage in historical development of religion',[7] mysticism crystallised only in the third century of the Muslim era (eighth-ninth century AD). It was also at that time that the lines of mystical affiliation were drawn, expository literature written and technical vocabulary elaborated. However, it was not until several centuries later that the final institutionalisation of Sufism was completed.[8]

This lengthy crystallisation of the Sufi tradition, far from undermining the importance of the scholarly study of the *silsila* of the *tariqa*, strengthens it, for different stages of the development of the *tariqa* are clearly reflected in its *silsila*.

Although each *tariqa* carefully preserves its *silsila*, there are considerable gaps of several generations between the links. For the Sufi adepts this gap simply means that the initiation of one sheikh by another was carried out through the *ruhaniyya* (spiritual being) of a dead sheikh

[4] Algar, 1976, p. 127.

[5] Note for example the obligations for self-discipline such as the five obligatory prayers a day, the additional recommended prayers, fasting during the month of Ramadan etc. The Prophet Muhammad himself is credited with preaching during the day-time and praying the larger part of the night in the seclusion of his home mosque.

[6] Driven by what has been defined in Sufi literature as Love for the Absolute, the mystics saw their greatest reward not in salvation but in the mercy or love of God, of which salvation can only be a sign.

[7] Scholem, 1974, pp. 7-8.

[8] On the early history of Sufism see Trimmingham, 1971, pp. 1-30.

rather then physical contact.[9] For a historian these early links point to the interrelation of various traditions as well as highlighting the points which are of primal importance for the followers of a *tariqa*.

The early Naqshbandi silsila

The Naqshbandis divide the early history of their *tariqa* into several sub-periods.[10] The first is called *siddiqiyya* after Abu Bakr al-Siddiq, who became generally accepted as the first link in the Naqshbandi *silsila* after the Prophet.[11] Bakri origin came to signify the particular 'orthodox' character of the Naqshbandi *tariqa* and set it apart from the rest of the Sufi orders, almost all of which trace their *silsilas* through Ali ibn Abu Talib. It is also to the Bakri link that the Naqshbandis ascribe their distinctive methods of *dhikr*[12] – the silent *dhikr* (*al-dhikr al-khafi*) and the *dhikr* of the heart (*al-dhikr al-qalbi*), for it is maintained that the Prophet had instructed Abu Bakr in this type of *dhikr* when they were hiding in a cave during the *hijra* (exodus from Mecca to Medina which took place in 622 AD).

The next period in the Naqshbandi development is associated with Abu Yazid al-Bistami (d. 879 AD) after whom the *tariqa* was called *tayfuriyya* – Tayfur being a sobriquet of al-Bistami. Regarded by scholars of Sufism as the forefather of the so-called 'intoxicated' Sufism 'immoderate in the language of pantheism',[13] al-Bistami's connection appears at first sight to contradict the 'orthodox' character of the Naqshbandi brotherhood.[14] However, it is precisely this link that establishes the Naqshbandi order as belonging to the Iranian Sufi tradition,[15] which is traced to al-Bistami.

9 Algar, 1974, pp. 130-1; Schimmel, 1975, p. 105.

10 As regards the early history of the *tariqa*, there are three distinct *silsilas* preserved in the Naqshbandi historiography. Al-Khani, 1308, p. 6. The full description of all of them is, however, beyond the scope of the present and I will discuss the one which became generally accepted in the Mujaddidiyya-Khalidiyya suborder. For the detailed description of the Naqshbandi *silslas*, see *ibid.*, the first *silsila*, pp. 10-73, the second, pp. 73-87, the third pp. 87–98.

11 There are also some Naqshbandi branches which trace their *silsila* through Ali ibn Abu Talib. see Algar, 1972, pp. 191-3; al-Khani, 1308, p. 6.

12 *Dhikr* literally means remembrance or recollection. In Sufi practice it implies a certain ritual of individual or communal prayer aimed at the remembrance and glorification of God.

13 See Arberry, 1950, p. 54.

14 However, other early 'less orthodox' Naqshbandi *silsilas* which trace the initiation through 'Ali, name as the second link not al-Bistami, but Junayd al-Baghdadi (d. 910 AD), generally regarded as the founder of the 'moderate' Sufi tradition.

15 The Iranian Sufi tradition tended to express greater individualism, divergent tendencies and heterodox doctrines and practices. On the different Sufi traditions, see Trimmingham, 1971 p. 54. Naqshbandiyya first rooted among the Persian-speaking Muslims of Central

The Iranian character of the Naqshbandi order is further emphasised by the next link in its *silsila*, which goes directly from Abu Yazid al-Bistami to Abu al-Hasan al-Kharaqani (d. 425 AH/1033 AD),[16] one of the most prominent figures in medieval Persian (Central Asian) Sufism. Also, the characteristic (although not unique)[17] Naqshbandi *uwaysi* tradition[18] of achieving initiation through the *ruhaniyya* (spiritual being) of a dead sheikh is related to this Iranian link.

From Abu al-Hasan al-Kharaqani the Naqshbandi *nisba*[19] passed through Abu al-Qasim al-Jurjani and Abu Ali al-Farmadhi (d. 447 AH/1055 AD),[20] to *Khawaja* Yusuf al-Hamadani (440-536 AH/1048-1141 AD).[21] One of the great Central Asian Sufi masters, generally known as *khawajakan* (or *khawajagan*), al-Hamadani is the first sheikh in the Naqshbandi *silsila* whose name is not a patronym common to many Sufi orders but is associated only with the closely related Naqshbandiyya and Yasawiyya orders.[22]

However, it was not until a century later that the main characteristics of the Naqshbandi brotherhood became finally crystallised. This process was completed by and is associated with Abd al-Khaliq al-Ghujduwani (d. 1220 AD)[23] who formulated the main spiritual principles of the *tariqa*. These principles were formulated in Persian and are always quoted in that language:[24]

Asia and despite later dispersion throughout the Muslim world, and particularly among the Turks, never fully lost its Iranian character.

[16] Al-Khani, 1308 AH, p. 109.

[17] This tradition goes back to al-Uwaysi al-Yemeni who lived at the time of the Prophet Muhammad but never met him and is believed to have converted to Islam through spiritual initiation.

[18] An *uwaysi* is a mystic who has attained illumination ouside the regular mystical path without any mediation or guidance of a living sheikh, but through the spiritual being of a sheikh. This concept was based on the belief that saints (the friends of God) do not die. The *uwaysi* tradition is so called after Uways al-Qarani, who allegedly lived in Yemen and was 'initiated' into Islam by the spiritual being of the Prophet Muhammad, although the two never met. For more on Uways and *uwaysi* tradition, see Schimmel, 1975, pp. 28-9, 105-6.

[19] *Nisba* can be translated as lineage, from the Arabic *nasaba* – to attribute, to link, to derive from. In a Sufi context, it means the initiatory affiliation with a particular Sufi tradition.

[20] With this link all three different *silsilas* merge. Al-Khani, 1308 AH, p. 71.

[21] In Central Asia the title *khawaja* (master in Persian) was applied to great scholars as well as to men of noble origin. See Shushud, 1983, p. 2.

[22] *Ibid.*, p. 7.

[23] Al-Khani, 1308, p. 8.

[24] Formulation of the principles was peculiar to the Central Asian Sufis. Algar, 1985, p. 9, also see Mole, 1963, pp. 15-22.

Yad Kard[25] (remembrance): The *salik* (one who follows the spiritual path) must constantly remember and mention God both orally and silently by *ism al-dhat* (the name of God itself) and by *nafi wa-l-ithbat* (by saying *la ilaha illa allah* – there is no other god but God alone).

Baz Gasht (returning): The *salik* must constantly restrain his thoughts from distractions by repeating the phrase: '*Allahu anta maqsudi wa ridhak matlubi*' (O God, You are my goal and Your satisfaction is my aspiration).

Nigah Dasht (attentiveness): Concentrating on the phrase of *nafi wa-l-ithbat (la ilaha illa allah)* during *dhikr* and ensuring that no stray thoughts or desires disturb the *salik* from remembering God.

Yad Dasht (recollection): Keeping one's heart in the Presence of God by holding one's breath.

Hosh Dar Dam (conscious breathing): The *salik* must remember God with every breath he takes. This is considered to be one of the most important requirements in the Naqshbandi *tariqa*, for in the words of Baha al-Din Naqshbandi, this *tariqa* is built on breathing.[26]

Safar Dar Watan (journey homeward): The *salik* must travel from the world of mankind towards the world of God, ascending higher and higher with every stage. It also implies that only after a Sufi has achieved perfection should he go travelling.

Nazar Dar Qadam (watching the feet): The *salik* must look down at his feet while walking so that sight does not put a veil over his heart and distract him from his main goal.[27]

Khalwat Dar Anjuman (solitude in the crowd): This fundamental principles of the Naqshbandi order is generally interpreted as the necessity of combining intense outward activity with inward devotion and tranquillity following the example of the Prophet Muhammad, who preferred the crowd to solitude and said: 'a *mu'min* [true believer] who mixes with people and calmly tolerates for their sake is better than a *mu'min* who does not mix with people.'[28] However, al-Ghujduwani himself gave a different meaning to this principle. According to him a *salik* must 'not get involved in other people's affairs, nor frequent the company of kings and princes, must avoid the crowd and preserve [his] own solitude.'[29]

These principles were not unique, but put together laid the foundation for the specific character and spiritual method of the Naqshbandi *tariqa*.

---

25 The description of all these principles is based on al-Khani, 1308 AH, pp. 113-14; Shushud, 1983, pp. 24-7.

26 Al-Khani, 1308 AH, p. 114.

27 Shushud described it simply as: 'Direct yourself constantly towards your goal.' Shushud, 1983, p. 25.

28 Al-Khani, 1308 AH, p. 115.

29 As quoted in Shushud, 1983, p. 26.

Al-Ghujduwani also promoted the practice of silent *dhikr* to a paramount principle of the Naqshbandi *tariqa*. Before him, the sheikhs of the Naqshbandi *silsila* including al-Hamadani, had practised both silent and vocal *dhikr*. Appealing to his experience with Khidr (the legendary immortal prophet, the patron and the highest source of mystical inspiration of the Sufis[30]) who had allegedly instructed him in the way to practise *al-dhikr al-khafi* (silent of secret *dhikr*),[31] al-Ghujduwani stated a clear preference for the silent *dhikr*. At the same time, he had some reservations about the common usage of music and dancing during the vocal *dhikr* and is quoted as saying: 'Do not engage too often in sacred music and dance, for over-indulgence in this is fatal to the life of the heart. But do not reject the sacred dance for many are attached to it.'[32] The last reservation allowed Ghujduwani's successors to return to the vocal *dhikr* which is used by some Naqshbandi adepts up to the present day.[33]

Baha al-Din al-Naqshband and the final crystallisation of the tariqa[34]

The *tariqa* attained its distinctive character and final name[35] during the life-time of *Khawaja* Baha al-Din al-Naqshband[36] (717-791 AH / 1317-1389 AD). Despite the exceptionally high esteem in which Baha al-Din is held by the followers of the *tariqa*, not much is known about him.[37]

[30] Khidr is usually associated with the mysterious companion of Moses as mentioned in Sura 18. For more on Khidr, see Schimmel, 1975, pp. 103-4.

[31] According to Muslim tradition, Khidr made al-Ghujduwani perform *dhikr* plunged into the water and saying in his heart the phrase *nafi wa-l-ithbat*. During this *dhikr* Ghujduwani allegedly experienced *fath* (opening of a soul) and *jadhba qayumiya* (ever-lasting gravitation towards God) as never before, and from then on performed the silent *dhikr* exclusively. See al-Khani, 1308, p. 111.

[32] Shushud, 1983, p. 24.

[33] The practice of vocal *dhikr* was maintained by al-Ghujduwani's *khalifa* Sheikh Ali Ramitani, known as Sheikh Azizan. In the beginning of the century some Central Asian Naqshbandis continued to preform vocal *dhikr*. Sitnyakovskiy, 1900, p. 50. I myself have watched the vocal *dhikr* performed by the Chechen Naqshbandis.

[34] In addition to the above-mentioned sources, see Gordelevskiy, 1962; Khanykoff, 1843, Kolosenko, 1887; Shubin, 1892; Sitnyakovskiy, 1900.

[35] In some Naqshbandi sources, the explanation of the name of the order is on a completely different basic and claims that at the Creation, God attributed Adam some of the divine *sifat* (features, qualities). Since then mankind bears the impression (*naqsh*) of some features of the essence of God which appeared with Adam. The majority of people have erased part of this imprint by *sifat haywaniyya* (animal features) and only the chosen few who followed the righteous path made that imprint (*naqsh*) perfect.

[36] The sobriquet Naqshband means 'he who fixes in the heart the impression of the Divine Name', Algar, 1985, p. 12.

[37] In Naqshbandi sources, Baha al-Din is presented as a humble *murid*, ill-treated both by his master and his master's other followers – al-Khani, 1308, p. 129 – while in the

He is reputed to have been a humble and pious man, who finally established the silent *dhikr* as the normative practice of the Naqshbandis and formulated three additional principles of the *tariqa*:

Wuquf Zamani (awareness of time): The *salik* must check how he spends his time and how well he concentrates his attention during the silent *dhikr*.

Wuquf Qalbi (concentration [presence] of the heart): According to one interpretation, the *salik* must examine his heart to make sure that it is in the state of *muraqaba* (surveillance) or *mushahada* (perception of God). This principle is almost identical to that of *yad dasht* (recollection).[38]

Wuquf Adadi (awareness of number): The *salik* must be aware of how many times he has performed *dhikr* (although Baha al-Din stressed that it was not the number that counts, but rather *al-wuquf al-qalbi* (concentration [presence] of the heart [on God]).[39]

During Baha al-Din's lifetime the Naqshbandi *tariqa* gained one of its most characteristic features, namely a strong relative to other Sufi orders, involvement in political affairs. This development coincided with and can be explained by the introduction of a new, Turkish dimension into the order.[40] Prior to Baha al-Din, the sheikhs of the Naqshbandi *silsila* were mainly active among the Persian-speaking urban population, and only starting with Baha al-Din[41] did they become more closely associated with the Central Asian rulers.[42]

The increasing involvement of the Sufi sheikhs in worldly affairs was a two-way process. On the one hand, the Timurids after Khan Sharuh (r. 1405-1447 AD) drew legitimacy for their rule from Islam and claimed the rank of Caliph of all Muslims and Sultan of Islam, and, conversely the Central Asian Sufis declared that rulers were made responsible by God for the well-being of the Muslim *umma* and as

---

non-Naqshbandi ones there is only passing reference to him – Algar, 1985, p. 129.

[38] On those principles see al-Khani, 1308 AH, pp. 111-18; Shushud, 1983, pp. 15-27; Trimmingham, 1971, pp. 203-4.

[39] Shushud, 1983, p. 26.

[40] Baha-al-Din's search for a Sufi master led him first to the 'Turkish' Yasawi Sheikh Khalil, who initiated him into the Yasawiyya *tariqa*. Gordelevskiy, 1964, p. 379.

[41] Algar, 1985, p. 10; al-Khani, 1308 AH, p. 129.

[42] In the turbulent times of the Mongol conquests in Central Asia, the Sufi brotherhoods became of paramount importance in both maintaining Islam among the Muslims of the area and Islamicising the pagan (shamanistic) Turkic conquerors. The more flexible Sufi framework made Islam more accessible to the Turkic nomads, for it allowed them to translate tribal loyalties into those interpreted in terms of tribal alliance to a particular Sufi sheikh. Moreover, the functions performed by a Sufi sheikh as a mediator between mankind and the Divinity resembled those of a traditional Turkic shaman (pagan priest and witchdoctor) which made the transition to Islam easier.

such were obliged to uphold and safeguard the shari'a of which they claimed to be the main interpreters.

Political activisation of the Naqshbandi tariqa[43]

By the mid-fifteenth century the Sufi sheikhs of Central Asia had become extremely influential, and their spiritual prestige and religious authority had translated into political and economic power. In this environment, the Naqshbandi *tariqa* was rapidly expanding,[44] and reached its peak during the third generation successor of Baha al-Din, Sheikh or *Khawaja* Ubaydallah Ahrar (1404-90).[45]

Khawaja Ubaydallah Ahrar was the first Naqshbandi *sheikh* to become directly involved in politics as well as to enjoy unique economic and social powers. In 1431 he established himself as a chief Sufi sheikh in Tashkand (Tashkent) and used his influence over the Uzbek tribes to assist the future Khan, Abu Said, in his struggle for power. Once the struggle was over and Abu Said had become established as a khan, Ubaydallah Ahrar moved with him to the new capital Samarkand and, due to his unique spiritual authority over the khan, 'became a virtual ruler of Transoxiana'[46] and its largest and richest landlord.[47] *Khawaja* Ahrar drew legitimation for his direct involvement in political affairs by the claim to have been endowed with a special mission to protect the Muslims from evil and oppression by reinforcing the *shari'a*[48] through trafficking with kings and conquering their souls for the purpose of the Muslim cause.

He was the first Naqshbandi sheikh to bring the shari'a from the individual to the political level[49] and canonise the interpretation of al-

---

[43] This subsection is based on al-Khani, 1308 AH; Algar, 1985(a); Bartold, 1964; Boldyrev, 1985; Bregel, 1991; Canfield, 1991; Checovich, 1974; Gross, 1985; Khanykoff, 1843; Kolosenko, 1883; Shubin, 1892; Sitnyakovskiy, 1900.

[44] By the mid-fifteenth century Baha al-Din was accepted as a patron saint of Bukhara. A large complex including mosques, several *khanaqas* and *madrasahs* was built around his tomb, which became one of the most famous places of pilgrimage.

[45] On Khawaja Ahrar, see al-Khani, 1308 AH, pp. 156-74; Bartold, 1964, pp. 156-74; Bartold, 'Ulugbek i Khodzha Akhrar', unpublished paper from *Arkhiv AN SSSR*, fond 68, opis' 1, no. 47, list 40-1; Boldyrev, 1985; Chekovich, 1974; Gross, 1985.

[46] Algar, 1976, p. 138.

[47] Gross, 1985; Barthold 1963, vol. II; Chechovich, 1974; Boldyrev, 1985.

[48] Among other orders of Khawaja Ahrar to reinforce the Shari'a was the final abolition of the traditional Mongolian non-Muslim tax, *tamga*.

[49] Ahrar's fundamental interpretations of the shari'a, which led him to forbid music, dancing and poetry, was contrasted by the liberal Naqshbandi tradition upheld in Khorasan, particularly in Herat, by Abd al-Rahman Jami (1414-92). Like Ahrar, Abd al-Rahman Jami also enjoyed exceptional prestige and influence over rulers in Khorasan, but his interpretation of the shari'a was completely different from that of Ahrar. On Jami and his policies see Algar, 1985, p. 19; Bartold, 1964, p. 174; al-Khani, 1308, p. 166.

Ghujduwani's principle of *khalwat dar anjuman* as the necessity of combining worldly and spiritual activities. Ubaydallah Ahrar established the Naqshbandi *tariqa* as most influential in Central Asia[50] closely associated with the local rulers.[51] Furthermore, his numerous *khalifas* insured its wide diffusion throughout the Muslim world and turned the *tariqa* into one of the most widespread Sufi orders.[52]

[50] His tomb became one of the most impressive and frequently visited mausoleums. Several visits to it were considered by the Naqshbandis of Central Asia to equal the hajj to Mecca. The mausoleum itself imitated the Qa'ba. For a description of the tomb, see Gordelevskiy, 1962, pp. 370-1; Khanykoff, 1843, pp. 94-5; Kolosenko, 1887, pp. 44-7; Shubin, 1892, pp. 110-18; Sitnyakovskiy, 1900, pp. 49-56.

[51] In the late eighteenth century a Naqshbandi sheikh Shah Murad (d. 1801 AD), who claimed spiritual descent from Ubaydallah Ahrar, became the head of the emirate of Bukhara. Seeing himself as a deputy of God on earth, he upheld policies similar to those of Ubaydallah Ahrar, reinforced strict implementation of the *shari'a* in its fundamental interpretation, and was notorious for his overt hostility towards the Shi'i and non-Muslims. See Gordelevskiy, 1962, p. 382. The combination of direct political rule with the position of a Naqshbandi sheikh was even more frequent in Eastern Turkestan. See Algar, 1985, p. 128. After the Russian conquest of Central Asia in the mid-nineteenth century the Naqshbandi *tariqa*, although having acquired a new character, continued to exercise major influence over the Muslims of Central Asia. In the early 1970s the Naqshbandiyya was still an order 'in full vigour and exercised a great influence upon society'. Ishans (Sufi sheikhs), on account of their aura of mysticism, enjoyed a high degree of popular esteem. 'Their rivals are the interpreters of holy scriptures, but...the native of Central Asia is more easily imposed upon by magic then by books.' Vambéry, 1971, p. 10.

[52] Travelling alongside traders, the Naqshbandis penetrated the areas populated by the Volga Tatars and played a most important role in furthering Islam among them. At the same time it transmitted the Central Asian model of the organisation of the Muslim clergy to the Volga Tatars. Ubaydallah Ahrar's khalifas also introduced the brotherhood into the Ottoman lands and Iran. Algar, 1985(a), p. 139.

12

THE DEVELOPMENT OF NAQSHBANDI PRINCIPLES AND THE FORMATION OF THE MUJADDIDI SUBORDER[1]

The political aspect of the Naqshbandi doctrine developed further in India, where its dissemination was associated with the establishment of the Moghul dynasty (1526-1858). Of Central Asian origin, the Moghul emperors and many members of the ruling elite had connections with the Naqshbandi order: a fact that ensured its special position in India. By the late eighteenth century those Naqshbandi centres which encompassed the Central Asian emigrees had started to decline,[2] however the branch founded by a local Indian sheikh was active within the reformed Naqshbandi tradition. This order became known as the Naqshbandiyya-Mujaddidiyya, after its founder Sheikh Ahmad Sirhindi al-Faruqi (971-1034/1564-1624),[3] who was generally known under the sobriquet of *Mujaddid*.[4]

Sheikh Ahmad Sirhindi was born into an Indian Muslim family of long scholarly tradition which claimed descent to the third rightly guided caliph, Umar al-Faruq (hence Sheikh Ahmad's sobriquet al-Faruqi).[5] Deeply rooted in Indian soil, he transformed the image of a Naqshbandi sheikh into one more suited to the Indian environment, and in so doing caused certain modifications to the character of the *tariqa*.

From the early days of his spiritual career in the closing years of the rule of Jalal al-Din Akbar (936-1014 AH / 1556-1605 AD), one of

---

[1] This chapter is based on the following sources: al-Khani, 1308; Adams, 1985; Ahmad, 1964; Ahmad, 1969; Algar, 1985; Algar, 1985(a); Ansari, 1986; Digby, 1985; Faruqi, 1977; Friedman, 1971; Fusfield, 1981; Nizami, 1965; Rizvi, 1965; Rizvi, 1975; Rizvi, 1985; Robinson, 1991; Schimmel, 1973; Troll, 1928.

[2] For more on the traditional Naqshbandis in India, see Digby, 1985, pp. 167-207.

[3] On Sirhindi see Damrel, 1985; Digby, 1985; Faruqi, 1977; Friedman, 1971; Friedman 1985; Fusfeld, 1981; Rizvi, 1975; Schimmel, 1973.

[4] Sirhindi was considered to be *mujaddid alf al-thani*, the renovator of faith in the second [Muslim] millennium. On the concept of *mujaddid* and *tajdid* see below.

[5] Sheikh Ahmad's father was a learned scholar and associated with the Suhrawardiyya, Chishtiyya and Qadiriyya *tariqas*. He was the first to introduce his son to formal and mystical knowledge. Later Sheikh Ahmad studied at Sialkot and Agra, the main centres of Islamic scholarship of the Moghul empire.

the most enlightened and liberal Moghul emperors, Sirhindi expressed his deep concern with the state of Islam in the Muslim *umma*. In accordance with Muslim eschatological tradition, he believed it only natural that with almost 1,000 years separating contemporary Muslims from the Prophet, a general decline in religion and morality had occurred. However, unlike many of his contemporaries, Sirhindi did not see it as an irreversible process, but argued that it could be reversed through the restoration of the basic tenets of Islam – the Sunna and the *shari'a* – in their original purity. This, he explained, could only be attained through realising the inner meaning of laws of the *shari'a*.

However, according to Sirhindi not only were the *'ulama* incapable of capturing the essence of God's knowledge, but the Sufi Sheikhs too. This knowledge, he argued, could be inspired only through Divine intervention; as had happened in pre-Islamic times when God relayed His message through a chosen one, He would maintain the link with mankind through His special envoys in the Muslim era. To resolve the apparent contradiction with one of the basic principles of orthodox Islam – that the Prophet Muhammad was the last in the line of prophets – Sirhindi argued that unlike the pre-Islamic prophets who had been sent by God to establish His Law, after 'the most perfect shari'a' had been installed by 'the last and the best of all the prophets,'[6] the task of a chosen one was not to announce a new Law but to revive the existing one and purify it of non-Islamic ideas and practices. The new status for such a chosen one was hence not that of prophet but of *mujaddid* – renovator of the faith.[7]

According to Sirhindi, at the end of each century God would send such a renovator, and at the end of each millennium an extraordinary one.[8] Although Sirhindi never directly claimed the title of a *mujaddid* for himself, he explicitly identified himself as such and his descendants always referred to him as *mujaddid alf al-thani* – renovator of the second millennium.[9]

In pursuing the renovation of the faith, Sirhindi emphasised the necessity of strict adherence to the 'normative example of the Prophet' (Sunna) and his *shari'a*, whose importance he ranked above any kind of mystical experience.[10] However, his concern with the shari'a was of a particular Sufi character: he was not so much interested in legal injunctions as in

---

6 In orthodox Muslim tradition, the Prophet Muhammad is seen as the last and the most perfect of all prophets, the seal of prophethood.

7 Friedman, 1971, pp. 13-33.

8 In justifying his claims, Sirhindi appealed to the hadith according to which on the eve of every century God would sen a man who will renew the *din* (*faith*). Sunna, Abu Daud, II, p. 518, as quoted in al-Khani, 1308 AH, p. 181.

9 Friedman, 1971, p. 104.

10 Nizami, 1965, pp. 41-52.

theoretical discussion of the concept of *shari'a* in the light of a contemporary Sufi outlook.[11] He analysed the shari'a in a characteristically Sufi way, drawing a clear distinction between its *zahir* (outwardly) and *batin* (inwardly) dimensions (in other words, the *sura* [form] and *haqiqa* [essence]). In Sirhindi's view a true Muslim, whether an advanced mystic or a humble believer, was obliged to comply with the *shari'a* and seek to understand its inner essence. The shari'a and *haqiqa* were for Sirhindi two expressions of the same reality unattainable without following one of the righteous Sufi paths,[12] for he believed that a *tariqa* was a servant of the *shari'a*, and its service was essential to make the shari'a complete.[13] As to mystical experience, Sirhindi claimed that only when the mystical knowledge of a *salik* coincided with the *shari'a* and he stopped seeing any contradiction between the two, had he attained true knowledge of God, for as long as the slightest contradiction between the two remained, *haqiqa* was not fully attained.[14]

Sirhindi's emphasis on orthodoxy had yet another effect on the Naqshbandi doctrine. The influential and sizeable Shi'i community on the Subcontinent was perceived by many Sunnis as a real danger. Thus, many Indian Sunnis, Sheikh Ahmad included, became deeply involved

[11] It is hardly surprising that such an attempt should have been made in the Indian environment, where Sufism faced a great challenge in Hindu mysticism and had to take special care to resolve its differences with the orthodox Muslim outlook. The integration of Muslim religious law and mysticism goes back to the advent of Sufism in the Subcontinent – from the eleventh century onwards. Despite the emphasis laid by the majority of Sufi orders there on the *shari'a*, some elements of yogic asceticism were infiltrated into the practices of individual Sufis. See Ahmad, 1969, pp. 131-3.

[12] It is only natural that Sirhindi viewed the Naqshbandi *tariqa* as the best and the closest path to God.

[13] Sirhindi saw the shari'a and *haqiqa* as the same in essence. Out of the two the former was superior for, while the shari'a was *ijmal* (whole), the *haqiqa* was *tafasil* (details), the shari'a – *istidlal* (influence), *haqiqa* – *kashf* (illumination), the shari'a – *gaib* (transcendental), *haqiqa* – *shahada* (witnessing), etc. al-Khani, 1308, p. 190; Friedman, 1971, p. 60.

[14] These ideas were expressed by Sirhindi in his doctrine on *wahdat al-shuhud* (the Unity of Witnessing) which claimed that after the period of initial spiritual intoxication associated with attaining the understanding of *wahdat al-wujud* (the Unity of Being) comes the higher stage of *al-sahw al-thani, al-sahw al-jami* second or complete sobriety. By introducing the concept of *wahdat al-shuhud*, Sirhindi tried to reconcile the classical Sufi ideas of Ibn al-Arabi, with the more 'sober' views. It is, however, very difficult to draw a distinction between 'Ibn al-Arabi's doctrine on *wahdat al-wujud* and that of Sirhindi. Ibn al-Arabi seems to have distinguished *wujud* as belonging to God, and *shuhud* as belonging to a Man. According to him God is present everywhere and finds Himself in all things, while Man only witnesses His presence. For more on Ibn al-Arabi's ideas on *wujud* see Chittick, 1989, pp. 6-8; on *shuhud* and *wahdat al-shuhud*, pp. 225-31; on *wahdat al-wujud*, pp. 79-81. On Sirhindi's teaching as regards to *wahdat al-wujud* and *wahdat al-shuhud* see al-Khani, 1308 AH, pp. 180, 190; Friedman, 1971, pp. 24, 66-8.

in passionate anti-Shi'i polemics.[15] As a result, to emphasise the orthodox character of the Naqshbandi order Sirhindi came to lay stress on its 'Bakri' origin,[16] which for the first time was accepted and emphasised.[17] From that point, anti-Shi'i hostility became a common feature of the Naqshbandi adepts.[18]

Like his Transoxianian predecessors Sheikh Ahmad saw his task as providing spiritual guidance to the Muslim rulers. However, unlike them he did not seek direct involvement in politics, but rather tried to influence the Moghul emperors through a network of high-ranking adepts within the army and administration.[19]

Sirhindi always referred to the Naqshbandi order as 'an ideal path',[20] but he believed that even it had not escaped the general state of spiritual decline and sought to purify the Naqshbandi *nisba*. He prohibited the practice of establishing a spiritual link with a dead sheikh common to the Central Asian Sufis and thus put an end to the Naqshbandi *uwaysi* tradition. Instead, he emphasised the importance of *suhba* (keeping the company of a living sheikh)[21] and of *rabita* (the spiritual bond between a *murid* and his sheikh),[22] which in his view was essential in allowing a *murid* to proceed along the mystical path.

Another practice denounced by Sheikh Ahmad as a sinful innovation was that of ecstatic dancing (*raqs*) and singing (*sama'a*). Common to most Indian Sufis and accepted even by the *'ulama* as a non-harmful innovation, this practice was outlawed by Sirhindi who claimed that even 'good innovations' destroy some part of the *shari'a* and thus divert

---

15 One of the first treatises composed by Sirhindi even before he entered the Naqshbandi *tariqa* was directed against the Shi'i.

16 I.e., on the fact that the Naqshbandi tradition was passed from the Prophet Muhammad through Abu Bakr rather than 'Ali. See above.

17 Sirhindi argued that the Naqshbandi *tariqa* was superior to all other Sufi orders due to its Bakri link.

18 Sirhindi's third son and successor, Muhammad al-Ma'sum became one of the strongest advocates of the necessity to reduce the Shi'i presence at the Moghul court; Mirza Janjanan, one of the outstanding Naqshbandi sheikhs of the seventeenth century generally known for his humble and generous character, fought vigorously against the Shi'i; and 'Abd al-Aziz Dihlawi, the eighteenth-century Naqshbandi sheikh, composed a detailed refutation of the Shi'i which became required reading in the Naqshbandiya-Mujaddididiyya *tariqa*. See Schimmel, 1980, p. 160.

19 Sirhindi maintained a vast correspondence with a number of Moghul court high officials upon whom he tried to impress his views on the state of Islam and the importance of the strict following of the shari'a. See Friedman, 1971; Ansari, 1986.

20 Sirhindi stated that the Naqshbandi *nisba* would be preserved till the end of the world and that the Mahdi would belong to it. Al-Khani, 1308 AH, p. 182.

21 This practice, although present in many other Sufi *tariqas*, became a particular feature of the Naqshbandi doctrine.

22 For more on the practices of *suhba* and *rabita*, see Abu-Manneh, 1985, pp. 289-302; Ter Haar, 1985, pp. 311-21.

a *salik* form God.[23] By prohibiting music and dancing during *dhikr*, Sirhindi stressed the importance of the silent *dhikr*.[24] At the same time he condemned the practice of seclusion for forty days during the initiation period (*'arba'in*) adopted by some Naqshbandis, which he saw as a violation of Ghujduwani's principle of *khalwa dar anjuman* – solitude within society.

In his thinking, Sirhindi to a certain extent resolved the contradictions between Sufism and the *shari'a* along theoretical lines and further emphasised the 'orthodox' character of the Naqshbandi order, which became generally recognised as a bastion of orthodoxy in Muslim India.[25]

Furthermore, Sirhindi and his spiritual progeny earned for the Naqshbandiyya a reputation as an 'intellectual' *tariqa*. Unlike the Transoxianian Naqshbandi sheikhs who had taken pride in a lack of formal learning which they saw as a sign of special mystical insight and divine grace, the Indian Naqshbandis emphasised the importance of formal learning as a means of attaining a deep knowledge of the *shari'a*. Having himself received an excellent education,[26] Sirhindi urged his disciples to perfect their learning – especially in Sunna and *fiqh*. Subsequently, many of his followers became renowned authorities on the Qur'an, *hadith* and *shari'a*,[27] and the Mujaddidi branch of the Naqshbandi *tariqa* gained a reputation for scholarly and intellectual excellence.

This 'intellectual' image of the *tariqa* was furthered by the fact that the Indian Naqshbandis were reluctant to settle in rural areas with an almost exclusively non-Muslim population, and thus the Naqshbandiyya-Mujaddidiyya became largely an 'urban' *tariqa*.

Finally, in the Indian environment it was possible for Sufi adepts to belong to more than one brotherhood. Tradition ascribes to Sirhindi

---

[23] Al-Khani, 1308, p. 183.

[24] Although Sirhindi accepted that vocal *dhikr* accompanied by mystical singing and dance could in fact be useful to those at a lower level of spiritual journey, who 'were still on the stage of *tajalliyyat dhatiyya*' (revelations through attributes and names) once a *murid* overcame the stage of stagnation and reached the state of *hal* and attained *tajalliyyat dhatiyya* (revelations of God Himself) he must concentrate on more advanced silent *dhikr*. Al-Khani, 1308, p. 189. A similar line was later taken by the North Caucasian Naqshbandis.

[25] Nizami claimed that Sheikh Ahmad Sirhindi was a main inspirer of Aurangzeb's (1658-1707) shari'a-reinforcing reforms. For the counter arguments see Friedman 1971, pp. 77-85.

[26] Sirhindi received his education at the best centres of Muslim learning of contemporary India. He studied logic, philosophy and theology at Sialkot with a renowned scholar of the rational disciplines Kamal Kashmiri (d. 1608 AD); hadith with the author of a commentary on *Sahih al-Bukhari*, Sayyid Ya'qub Sarfi (d. 1594 AD). After completing his education he was accepted at the leading centres of scholarship in Agra, the contemporary capital of the empire. See Ansari, 1986, pp. 11-13.

[27] For example Janjanan and Abdallah Dihlawi. On these see al-Khani, 1308 AH, pp. 193-221.

a saying that the 'Mujaddidiyya *tariqa* feeds itself from four seas –
Naqshbandiyya, Qadiriyya, Chishtiyya and Suhrawardiyya, of which
the Naqshbandi *nisba* is the highest'.[28]

Ahmad al-Sirhindi bestowed on the Naqshbandiyya-Mujaddidiyya a
universal pan-Muslim character and outlook according to which its
sheikhs were entrusted with a special mission. As such, the suborder
became firmly established both on the Subcontinent[29] and worldwide.
Its Indian *khanaqas*, particularly the one in Delhi, became major Muslim
mystical centres that drew seekers of divine inspiration from throughout
the Muslim world.

[28] *Ibid.*, p. 213.
[29] At the time of Janjanan the Naqshbandiya-Mujaddidiyya became established in no
less than fifty *khanaqas*.

13

THE FORMATION OF THE NAQSHBANDIYYA-MUJADDIDIYYA-KHALIDIYYA SUBORDER[1]

It was in eighteenth-century Turkey that the Naqshbandi *tariqa* finally acquired the form in which it was introduced into the North Caucasus. The development of its new characteristics was associated with an Ottoman sheikh, Diya al-Din Khalid al-Shahrazuri al-Kurdamiri (1779-1827 AD), who gave his name to a new branch, known after him as Khalidiyya.

Diya al-Din Khalid was born in 1193 AH/1779 AD in Qaradah (Karadah), a town in Shahrazur district, five miles away from Sulaymaniya in the Baban province of Kurdistan. His father belonged to the Jaf tribe, which claimed descent from the caliph Uthman.[2] In his early years Khalid received a good traditional education, first at his father's court and later in Sulaymaniya, the Baban capital, and other renowned teaching centres of Kurdistan,[3] after which he established himself as a teacher at a *madrasah* in Sulaymaniya.

According to the predominant pattern of the time, 'the most educated Muslims who took their religion seriously interpreted it within the framework created by the great masters of spiritual life and many adhered to one or other of the brotherhoods founded by them or in their names'.[4] Although reduced to a mere formality by some Muslims, the search for an appropriate well-established sheikh and a suitable Sufi tradition which could accommodate one's particular views was vital for the pursuit of a successful religious career.

In seventeenth-century Kurdistan the most widely spread Sufi brother-

---

[1] This chapter is based on the following sources: Al-Khani, 1308 AH, pp. 224-59; Algar, 1985; Aglar, 1985(a); Abu-Manneh, 1971; Abu-Manneh, 1982/84; Abu-Manneh, 1985; Bruinessen, 1985; Bruinessen, 1992; Hakim 1985; Hourani, 1981; Jong, 1978; Mardin, 1989; Sahib, 1334; Ibn Sulayman, 1313. I am extremely grateful to Dr Abu-Manneh for providing me with a copy of Sahib's and Sulayman's treatises.

[2] On Khalid see Algar, 1985; Aglar, 1985(a); Abu-Manneh, 1985; Abu-Manneh, 1982/84; Hourani, 1981; al-Khani, 1308 pp. 224-59.

[3] He studied logic in Kawa and Harid, and mathematics, geometry and astronomy in Istanj. Al-Khani, 1308, p. 224.

[4] Hourani, 1981, p. 76.

hood was the Qadiriyya, and the two most powerful Kurdish clans – the Barzanji (or Barzani) and Sayyid Nehri (both of whom claimed their descent from Abd al-Qadir Gilani, the founder of the *tariqa*) – virtually monopolised political and spiritual power.[5] The Naqshbandis were represented in Kurdistan mainly by foreign, primarily Central Asian, sheikhs[6] and at that time could hardly compete with the Qadiriyya in terms of diffusion and influence.

However, for reasons of his own,[7] Khalid did not seek initiation into a Sufi brotherhood in Kurdistan but rather set off on the *hajj* in the hope of finding spiritual inspiration in the holy land of Islam. This was a common practice at the time, for initiation into a *tariqa* at the hands of a sheikh living in the Muslim holy cities could bestow special legitimacy in the eyes of other Muslims.

During his *hajj*, Sheikh Khalid formally accepted initiation into the Qadiri order at the hands of a fellow countryman. But he failed to find a 'perfect sheikh' in Mecca[8] and returned home still lacking a strong affiliation with any Sufi *tariqa*. The Khalidi sources interpret Khalid's failure to associate himself with any Sufi order during the *hajj* as Divine Providence which was to lead him to India to Sheikh Waliullah Dihlawi.[9] In 1223 AH/1809 AD, inspired by Mirza Rahmullah 'Azimabadi, a Mujaddidi sheikh and a disciple of Sheikh Dihlawi, Diya al-Din Khalid set

---

[5] They provided the *'ulama* and the Qadiri sheikhs, presided over all weekly ritual meetings for *dhikr* and *maulid* and through their religious prestige had acquired extensive political influence and vast material wealth. Bruinessen, 1992; Hourani, 1981.

[6] Kurdistan, situated on the *hajj* route of the Central Asian and Azeri Muslims, had accumulated a considerable presence of Central Asian Naqshbandi sheikhs, while the Naqshbandis of Kurdish origin tended to go to the Ottoman lands. Bruinessen, 1985, pp. 341-59.

[7] Khalid's decision not to seek initiation into the Qadiri order in Kurdistan could have been influenced by the rivalry between the members of his own Jaf tribe and the Barzanji family, in whose hands the sheikhhood of the Qadiri *tariqa* was concentrated. Alternatively the strictly stratified *tariqa* in which the sheikhhood remained within either the Barzanji or Sayyid Nehri families, could give but little room for the fulfilment of the strong religious and political aspirations of intelligent and ambitious Khalid. Outsiders to these families were at times appointed as *khalifas* but almost never became sheikhs in their own right. It can also be suggested that some of the heterodox practices of the Kurdish Sufis could have contradicted Khalid's own views on the necessity of strict orthodoxy.

[8] The Khalidi sources preserved the story about Khalid's stay in Mecca. According to this, he once saw a man who turned his back on the Qa'ba and faced Khalid instead. In his heart Khalid condemned the man for what he saw as a blasphemy, but did not show his contempt. However, the man turned to him and asked Khalid what the reasons were for his disapproval and remarked that the worth of God's servants was far greater than that of the Qa'ba and hence it seemed more appropriate to him to face Khalid rather than the shrine. Impressed by his mode of reasoning, Khalid asked to accept him as a *murid*. The man refused and told him to go to seek illumination in India. Al-Khani, 1308 AH, p. 225; Algar, 1985, p. 29.

[9] On Dihlawi, see Abu-Manneh, 1982/4, p. 4; Troll, 1928, pp. 171, 174.

off for India, where he finally found himself a 'perfect sheikh' in Waliallah Dihlawi and accepted the Naqshbandi-Mujaddidi *tariqa* from him.[10]

Not much is known about Khalid's stay in Delhi apart from the fact
that he was initiated into the *tariqa* directly by Sheikh Waliallah Dihlawi,
who after a year's training granted him the licence to initiate his own
pupils (*ijaza*) and full and absolute successorship (*khalifa tamma mut-
laqa*),[11] which confirmed Khalid as a sheikh in his own right and allowed
him to initiate followers into the Naqshbandi-Mujaddidi, Qadiri, Suh-
rawardi, Qubrawi and Chishti *tariqas*.[12]

On his return to Sulaymaniya in 1226 AH/1811 AH, Khalid established
himself as an independent sheikh in his own right and soon gained a
popular following with many seeing him as a miracle worker who could
foresee the future, protect people from harm and establish contact with
the spirits of the dead. Not surprisingly his growing popularity alarmed
the members of both the Barzanji and Sayyid Nehri clans whose religious
and political influence was associated with the Qadiri order and was
now threatened. After a number of clashes with the Barzanji clan, Khalid
was forced to leave Sulaymaniya and move to Baghdad. It was during
his stay there that the new character of the Naqshbandi-Mujaddidi order
started to take shape and became known after him as the Khalidiyya.[13]

Khalid's elaboration of the Mujaddidi doctrine

From his early years Sheikh Khalid had been alert to the general decline
of Muslim political vigour and the growing intervention of the European
powers in the Muslim world.[14] This feeling of imminent religious and
political catastrophe had been further reinforced during Khalid's visit
to India, which by that time had largely lost its independence and fallen

---

[10] For Khalid's trip to India and the manner in which he was allegedly Divinely inspired
to go to Waliallah Dihlawi, see al-Khani, 1308 AH, pp. 226-9.

[11] In the Naqshbandi *tariqa* there are several terms which describe the ordaining of a
disciple as a *khalifa*. See al-Khani, 1308 AH, p. 229; Abu-Manneh, 1982/84, p. 5.

[12] In the eighteenth century such a short period of training was extremely rare and it
usually took decades of training and close association with a Sufi sheikh to attain the
rank which Khalid achieved in less than a year. The Khalidi sources provide little explanation as to this and give only a brief account of Khalid's stay in Delhi. They claim
that in less than five months he attained 'the secret knowledge' and became one of the
'ahl al-hudhur' (those present with God) and half-a-year later was ordained as Waliallah's
khalifa. While in Delhi, Khalid associated himself with another Naqshbandi sheikh, Abd
al-'Aziz al-Hanafi al-Naqshbandi, who was a renowned authority on the Sunna and the
Qur'an. Al-Khani, 1308 AH, pp. 229-30.

[13] In Baghdad the followers of Sheikh Khalid 'agreed to call it as from him Khalidiyya'.
Quoted from Abu-Manneh, 1985, p. 291.

[14] Although not as strong as in other parts of the Muslim world, the European presence
in Khalid's native Kurdistan in the second-half of the eighteenth century became noticeable
through the increasingly open Christian missionary activities and the expansion of European
commerce.

under British control. Furthermore, on his return to Kurdistan, Khalid found that the Ottoman Empire, though still independent, had suffered a series of defeats at the hands of the Europeans.

In this environment, Khalid revived Sirhindi's belief that the political weakness of the Muslim *umma* was caused by a general neglect of the *shari'a* and the corruption of true Islam.[15] Referring back to early Islamic history, when the *shari'a* was truly observed, *jihad* undertaken and Muslims victorious, he believed that to regain their former inner strength and international prestige Muslims had to return to a strict observance of rules as laid down in the Qur'an and sunna and restore the *shari'a* as the only law acceptable in Muslim lands.

However, unlike his spiritual predecessor, Sheikh Ahmad Sirhindi, who had treated the *shari'a* in the framework of the traditional Sufi triad of *shari'a-tariqa-haqiqa*, for Khalid the *shari'a* was simply an integral part of Muslim society and he discussed it almost exclusively within its *fiqhi* (legal) dimension. For him the *shari'a* was the main constituent part of Muslim society and sole guarantor of its independence from the rule of foreign infidels. Khalid rarely discussed the inner aspects of following the mystical path of devotion to God, and his writings imply that to obtain the goals of the *tariqa* one needs only to immerse oneself comprehensively in the *shari'a*, with the Naqshbandi path amounting solely to an obligation 'to hold firmly to the exalted *shari'a* and to revive the Sunna'.[16] Khalid saw his own mission not so much in the inner purification of the soul as in the restoration of the supremacy of the *shari'a* and the sunna.

According to Khalid, following of the *shari'a* by Muslim individuals was not enough to re-establish the Muslim *umma* on the righteous path or even to achieve individual salvation, which he believed was not possible under an unjust and non-Islamic rule. For both individual Muslims and the Muslim community at large to return to virtue, they had to be governed by a ruler who assumed the *shari'a* as the legal foundation for all his deeds and orders, since Khalid maintained that 'the monarch is to the state what the heart is to the body, if the heart remains pure so does the body'.[17]

Thus, Sheikh Khalid came to see the Sultan as guarantor of the vitality of the whole Muslim community and maintained that it was the duty

15 Khalid seems to have placed special emphasis on the shari'a from the early years of his career. Furthermore, one can speculate as to what extent his travelling through the Hijaz, at the time when the Wahhabis had just established their rule in the holy cities of Islam had shaped his views on the shari'a and Muslim orthodoxy. On comparison between Khalid's teaching and the Wahhabi ideology, see Hourani, 1981, p. 82; Algar, 1985, pp. 30-1. Abu-Manneh suggested that the attitude of Khalid towards the Wahhabis was less than favourable. Abu-Manneh, 1982/4, p. 3.

16 Sahib, 1334 (1915), p. 79, also quoted in Abu-Manneh, 1982/4, p. 13.

17 *Ibid.*, p. 255, also quoted in Abu-Manneh, 1982/4, p. 14.

of each Muslim to obey the Sultan's orders, as long as they did not contradict the *shari'a*.[18] This last prerequisite was to be guaranteed by the watchfulness of the Muslim religious authorities and hence Khalid maintained that the task of a righteous sheikh was to instill virtue into those in power.[19] With this objective in mind he recruited many members of the high-ranking *'ulama* and sent his *khalifas* to spread the *tariqa* to Istanbul and other centres of the Ottoman Empire.

The development of new characteristics of the Khalidiyya

To ensure the rapid expansion of his *tariqa*, Khalid needed a large number of deputies, something difficult to achieve following the traditional way of training novices. In medieval times, when the *tariqa* was a closed, elitist organisation and initiation and training as an adept were only open to a few the process was slow and lengthy. Now with different aims in mind Khalid set out to reform the very method of initiation and training of a Sufi adept.

First he revised the Naqshbandi practice of *suhba* – the traditional means to transform a Naqshbandi novice into a fully-fledged sheikh through the association of a *murid* with his sheikh who instructed him in the rituals of the order and led him along the lengthy spiritual path to God. Khalid acknowledged *suhba* as 'the first among the paths leading to the knowledge of God'[20] but interpreted it in a somewhat different way.[21]

A Khalidi novice received his initial training not from the sheikh himself, but from one of Khalid's deputies. This period was usually quite short (not more than several months) and upon completion was followed by forty days in seclusion. In those forty days the training of a *murid* was given the final touch either by Sheikh Khalid himself or by one of his most trusted deputies. Known as *khalwa arba'iniyya* (forty days seclusion) or *riyada arba'iniyya* (forty days retreat), this practice was a certain deviation from the Naqshbandi tradition, since most Naqshbandi sheikhs followed Ghujduwani's advice 'to close the door of *khalwa* and open the door of *suhba*', and denounced this practice as a harmful innovation.

It was the mode of initiation of a novice, however, rather than Khalid's restoration of the practice of *khalwa*, that was in the main rejected by his opponents. Even more radical was Khalid's re-interpretation of the practice of *rabita* (the link between the *murid* and his sheikh). This

---

[18] *Ibid.*, p. 109, also quoted in Abu-Manneh, 1982/4, p. 14.

[19] In this he once again followed the footsteps of Ahmad Sirhindi, both of them seeking to influence the rulers through their teaching rather than exercise direct power in the fashion of Ubaydallah Ahrar.

[20] Abu-Manneh, 1985, p. 291.

[21] On Khalid's interpretation of *suhba* and *rabita* see Abu-Manneh, 1985, pp. 289-301.

brought about numerous accusations of heresy even from some of his own followers.[22]

The practice of *rabita* in the Naqshbandi tradition was understood as the absorbtion of a *murid* by his sheikh and as such was seen as a complementary, although not obligatory, part of *suhba* as was practised with one's immediate sheikh. In striking contrast with the Naqshbandi tradition, Khalid not only made it obligatory, but completely divorced it from that of *suhba*. He instructed that all those initiated into the sub-order should undertake *rabita* exclusively with him, regardless of whether he was training them personally or they were trained by his *khalifas* (which implied that even after his death, the followers of the Khalidi sub-order were to enter *rabita* directly with him).[23]

Such an interpretation of *rabita* clearly aimed at reinforcing the highly centralised character of the order, and among other things implied that none of the deputies ordained by Khalid was given the rank of sheikh in his own right, but was merely regarded as an intermediary between Khalid and the numerous followers of the *tariqa*.[24]

Despite opposition and criticism, it was largely through the application of his new methods that Khalid succeeded in making his order one of the most rapidly growing *tariqas* in the Ottoman lands. Khalid's followers and Khalidi lodges quickly became well established in Kurdistan, Iraq and Syria, although the initial stage of the establishment of the Khalidiyya in Istanbul was not altogether successful.

Despite the high esteem in which Khalid held the Sultan as the main guarantor of the independence and well-being of all Muslims – esteem which he demonstrated by ordering his followers to 'urge the high and low to pray for the Caliph of the Muslims, the commander of the faithful', and to end the *dhikr* by praying a *du'a* for the safety of the Sultan' – [25] Sultan Mahmud II was apprehensive about this new 'sect' with pronounced political ambitions, while other well established Sufi sheikhs viewed the new suborder with hostility. In early 1820 a number of Khalid's *khalifas* were sent into exile from Istanbul,[26] and Khalid himself

---

22 Among those who had initially objected to this was Sheikh Isma'il al-Shirwani, the sheikh responsible for the introduction of the Naqshbandiyya-Khalidiyya into the North Caucasus. For more on the opposition to Khalid's interpretation of *rabita*, see Abu-Manneh, 1985, pp. 297-302.

23 The practice of establishing a link with a dead sheikh relates closely to the early Sufi *uwaysi* tradition. However, in the environment of the nineteenth century, it appeared most controversial and seen as the manifestation of *shirk* (pantheism).

24 It is interesting to compare this practice with that of Barzanji and Nagris, who also kept the sheikhhood within their family and prevented their *khalifas* from attaining full successorship.

25 Abu-Manneh, 1971, p. 33.

26 The Sultan's suspicion of Khalid and his followers found reflection even in Khalidi sources. Al-Khani, 1308 AH, p. 231.

was accused of pursuing private political ambitions hostile to the Sublime Porte[27] and forced to leave Baghdad.[28]

In 1236/1820 Khalid moved to Damascus, a Naqshbandi centre from the late fifteenth century, where his name had already been made famous by his *khalifas*.[29] Invited to the city by Sheikh Husain Effendi, the Mufti of Damascus,[30] Khalid was well received by the city's dignitaries and the *'ulama*, while the al-Ghazzi, the great Damascene family, took him under their protection.[31] Khalid's house, in a Kurdish quarter of the city, became a popular place frequented both by commoners and notables, who attended the *dhikrs* held by him.[32]

The Khalidiyya after Khalid

The position of the *tariqa* was considerably undermined by the untimely death of Sheikh Khalid and many of his closest *khalifas* from plague in 1827.[33] Despite his attempts to ensure the strictly-centralised character of his *tariqa*, soon after his death[34] the order was left without a central leadership and the *tariqa* split into two rival lodges. One was led by

---

[27] The Pasha of Baghdad launched an investigation following numerous reports from Khalid's enemies who had declared him an infidel with political aspirations hostile to the Sublime Porte. The investigation cleared him of all accusations, partly due to the Pasha's own sympathies towards Khalid. However, the Ottoman officials in Istanbul remained suspicious of Khalid and his followers.

[28] The Naqshbandi sources remain silent on the issue of Khalid's departure from Baghdad, the only account of which was given by Mr Rich, a British resident in Baghdad. 'This morning the great Sheikh Khaled (Khalid-AZ) ran away... The cause of his flight is variously reported. Some say he had formed a design of establishing a new sect and making himself temporal as well as spiritual lord of the country. Of course a great deal more is laid to his charge than he was really guilty of. All the regular Ulama and Shaikhs with Sheikh Ma'aroof at their head, hated Sheikh Khaled, who as long as his power lasted, threw them into the background.' Quoted from Hourani, 1981, p. 84.

[29] Two of Khalid's *khalifas* – Muhammad ibn Sulayman al-Irbili and Ahmad Katib al-Irbili – had settled in Damascus a couple of years earlier and prepared the ground for the spread of the Khalidi sub-order.

[30] Sheikh Hussein Effendi was himself a Naqshbandi from the famous Muradi family, the first Mujaddidi sheikhly family in Syria.

[31] Khalid married the sister of the head of the family. See Abu-Manneh, 1982/4, p. 8.

[32] Among the most outstanding Khalidi recruits were Makki Zadeh Mustafa Emin, the Sheikh al-Islam, and Kececi Zadeh Izzaet Mollah, an outstanding poet and the *qadi* of Istanbul. See Abu-Manneh, 1982/4, pp. 14, 24; Algar, 1985(a), p. 140.

[33] His burial place in the Salihiya district of Damascus has become one of the favourite places for visitation of the Naqshbandi-Khalidi adepts on their way to and from the hajj. There is an adjoining *zawwiya*, where Khalidi adepts perform *dhikr* on the first Monday of each Muslim month before *salat al-fajr* (dawn prayer). See Algar, 1985, p. 29.

[34] Shortly before his death Sheikh Khalid wrote a letter to his followers in which he discussed the matters of succession and instructed that after his death supremacy within the *tariqa* should pass to his children 'as soon as they become worthy of it'. Al-Khani, 1308 AH, p. 248.

Khalid's younger brother Mahmud al-Sahib and the other by Muhammad al-Khani, the son and grandson respectively of two of Khalid's foremost disciples. No leading figure, however, was recognised beyond Syria, and the order that had been constructed by Khalid as the most centralised of the *tariqas* swiftly became one of the most decentralised Sufi orders.

Furthermore, relations between the Naqshbandi-Mujaddidi-Khalidi *tariqa* and the central Ottoman authorities also underwent revision. Formerly financially independent of the central government and sustained through voluntary contributions, soon after Khalid's death the *tariqa* was endowed with a monthly stipend bestowed by the state which placed the Khalidiyya, like many other Sufi orders, under state control.[35]

The latter shortcomings notwithstanding Khalid had succeeded in turning his order into one of the most widely spread and influential Sufi *tariqas*. Diffused throughout the Ottoman lands with lodges in Anatolia,[36] Rumelia, Hijaz and Palestine[37] alongside long–established ones in Syria, Iraq and Kurdistan,[38] it soon extended its influence over more remote areas of the Muslim world.[39]

The success of Khalid's teaching and the rapid spread of his sub-order must be seen in the light of the political situation at the time. Growing alarm over the influence of European Christian powers in the Muslim world and their military confrontation increased the sense of Muslim identity and made clear the necessity for change. It was also in this context that the idea of the *shari'a* as the basis upon which the Muslim community could and should be regenerated grew in importance.

35 For more on Khalidiyya and Ottoman officials see Abu-Manneh, 1982/4, pp. 18-28.

36 In Anatolia, the Khalidi sub-order had fully replaced other Naqshbandi lodges. Many Naqshbandi sheikhs renewed their initiation into the Naqshbandi order through Khalid's *khalifas*.

37 Khalid's deputies established their lodge in Jerusalem, which came to enjoy a strong position. Many local Muslim dignitaries including the mufti of Jerusalem became members of the Naqshbandiyya-Mujaddidiyya-Khalidiyya. Abu-Manneh, 1982/84, p. 11.

38 In Kurdistan, within a few decades the Khalidiyya expanded to such an extent that it became synonymous with the Naqshbandiyya itself – all Naqshbandis now tracing their spiritual descent from Sheikh Khalid. Several members of the Barzanji family also joined the *tariqa* and, alongside with the formerly flourishing Qadiriyya, it became the second most important order in the area. Bruinessen, 1985, pp. 337-9.

In a familiar pattern, religious authority bred wealth, and social and political power, and many Kurdish authorities started to base their legitimacy on their association with Khalid and his *tariqa*. The spiritual heirs of Sheikh Khalid altered his doctrine significantly and, as the Qadiri sheikhs had done before them, they became centres around which the local population consolidated in their opposition to the central government – each movement of discontent looking up to them for leadership. The importance of the Naqshbandi sheikhs grew further when the Ottoman authorities, in order to impose central control, undermined the power of hereditary rulers, thus leaving Sufi sheikhs as the main focus of political activity.

39 The Indonesian Archipelago, Egypt, Central Asia, Afghanistan, North Caucasus to name but a few. See Algar, 1985, pp. 37-43.

Thus, the Khalidi *tariqa* became closely associated with the Ottoman elite who came to share Khalid's concern with the restoration of the *shari'a* and Sunna as the only guarantors of the inner strength and independence of the Muslim *umma*.[40] At the same time, the Naqshbandi-Mujaddidi-Khalidi *tariqa*, with its doctrine based on the necessity of restoring the ideal model of the early caliphate and of closely following the shari'a and reviving the Sunna, provided an ideology as well as a ready-made organisational framework for the resistance struggle of various Muslim peoples against growing Western domination.

Islamic mysticism arose as an attempt to restore the spiritual link between God and mankind and fill the void between the Divine Essence and Worldly Reality which had emerged after the death of the Prophet Muhammad, the last prophet in the orthodox Muslim tradition. Conceived as a movement of mystics and philosophers, whose principle preoccupation was the search for Divine Knowledge and Inspiration, Sufism gradually evolved into a broader phenomenon spread throughout the Muslim world, and became embodied in the institution of Sufi *tariqas*.

The evolution of philosophical mysticism into Sufi brotherhoods led to the crystallisation of the fundamental principles of the *tariqas* and laid the foundation for their doctrine and practices. These principles were regarded by the followers of a given brotherhood as universal and sacred, although each generation offered its own interpretation of them.

Thus, the thirteen fundamental principles of the Naqshbandi creed, already formulated by the fifteenth century, gave rise to the core characteristics of the *tariqa*, which shaped the mainstream Naqshbandi brotherhood. One of its central tenets was a strict adherence to the shari'a – both for ordinary Muslims and Sufi adepts. Seen as the necessary prerequisite to ascending the mystical path to God, the strict following of the shari'a at any stage of spiritual development became an integral part of the Naqshbandi doctrine.

The second most important principle of the Naqshbandi doctrine was that of *khalwa dar anjuman* (solitude within the crowd), the predominant interpretation of which implied the active involvement of a Sufi sheikh in the political and religious life of the Muslim *umma*. According to this principle, a Naqshbandi sheikh was responsible for

---

[40] Sultan Selim III and Mahmud II carried out reforms which, on the one hand aimed at technical and military modernisation of the state and, on the other, tried to promote strengthening of Islamic values and institutions. In his DPhil thesis, Abu Manneh suggested that the inspiration of these reforms can be, at least partly, attributed to Naqshbandi-Khalidi influence. Abu-Manneh, 1971, p. 169.

correct interpretation of the shari'a and the Muslim community's compliance with its rules.

The idea of a Sufi (Naqshbandi) sheikh as the sole guardian of the shari'a and purveyor of its true meaning was elevated in the Naqshbandiyya-Mujaddidiyya-Khalidiyya to a level of utmost importance. First Sheikh Ahmad Sirhindi expanded the concept that a Sufi sheikh could become a recipient of Divine Inspiration in a fashion similar to the pre-Islamic prophets. Through his doctrine of *tajdid* (renovation of faith), Sirhindi provided the theoretical justification for his claims of divine prophetic inspiration and hence re-opened the gateway to direct communication with God (rather than the traditional Sufi unity with God).

The importance of the *shari'a* for the Muslim community at large and Naqshbandi adepts in particular was further stressed in the Naqshbani-Khalidi sub-order, which maintained the importance of the *shari'a* as the sole guarantor of the inner strength and international prestige of the Muslim community. However, in the atmosphere of the increasing weakness of Muslim rulers *vis-à-vis* European powers at the onset of the era of European domination in the Muslim world, emphasis was laid on preserving and reinvigorating the *shari'a* in its *fiqhi* (legalistic) rather than mystical dimension.

In essence one can argue that, at this stage, the Naqshbandi order became more of a political movement than a purely mystical *tariqa*. Furthermore, the combination of the rigid and hierarchical structure of Sufi lodges with an appeal to restore universal Muslim values, turned the Naqshbandi order into a formidable political force capable of organising and providing leadership for anti-colonial movements.

Part V. INTRODUCTION OF THE NAQSHBANDIYYA-MUJADDIDIYYA-KHALIDIYYA TO THE NORTH CAUCASUS: THE FORMATIVE PERIOD

14

INTRODUCTION OF THE NAQSHBANDI ORDER TO DAGHESTAN[1]

Sheikh Isma'il al-Shirwani[2]

According to Naqshbandi sources the Naqshbandiyya-Mujaddidiyya-Khalidiyya *tariqa* spread to the North Caucasus from neighbouring Azerbaijan. It was introduced by Sheikh Isma'il al-Shirwani al-Kurdamiri,[3] one of the early *khalifas* of Sheikh Khalid.[4]

Sheikh Isma'il al-Shirwani enjoyed unique popularity in Azerbaijan and by the late 1810s was accepted as the *qutb* (pole) of the Naqshbandi *tariqa*, with his followers addressing him as '*Maulana*', a title reserved solely for Sheikh Khalid himself.[5] This went against Khalid's policy of not granting any of his *khalifas* the full and complete *ijaza*. Khalid's resentment of the prominent position of one of his *khalifas* further increased when Sheikh Isma'il al-Shirwani, in contradiction to Khalid's instructions concerning the practice of *rabita*, instructed his *murids* to exercise it by linking themselves directly with him and not with Sheikh

---

[1] The main sources for this chapter are Bodenshtadt, 1855; Dubrovin, 1891; Mahmudbekov, 1898; Neverovskiy, 1847(a); R-v, 1859; Sahib, 1334; Tsudaqari, 1904; Volkonskiy, 1886.

[2] On Sheikh Isma'il al-Shirwani, see Abu-Manneh, 1985, pp. 295-6, 302; Bodenshtadt, 1855, pp. 131-42; Mahmudbekov, 1898, pp. 21-3; Sahib, 1334 (1915/16) pp. 174-7.

[3] He was born in Kurdamir in northern Azerbaijan.

[4] Mahmudbekov, 1989, p. 22. On Sufi tradition in Shirwan, see *idem.*, pp. 14-40.

[5] *Ibid.*, pp. 22-3.

100

Khalid. The latter saw it as the worst kind of insubordination and threatened to denounce Isma'il al-Shirwani and expel him from the *tariqa*. This conflict very nearly resulted in the creation of a new independent sub-order, but Sheikh Isma'il withdrew his instructions on *rabita* and complied with Khalid's demands. This preserved the bond between him and his followers and the Naqshbandiyya-Mujaddidiyya- Khalidiyya.[6]

Apart from this act of insubordination, the ideas upheld and propagated by Sheikh Isma'il al-Shirwani appear to have been closely associated with the Khalidiyya teaching. He shared Khalid's concern over the spiritual and political decline of the Muslim *umma* which, viewed within the reality of the nineteenth-century Caucasus, was closely linked with Russian expansion. Isma'il al-Shirwani taught that the obligation of a Sufi sheikh to restore the true virtues of Islam was far more important than the search for spiritual purification and individual service to God:

Pilgrimage to the holy places is a praiseworthy deed, but the holy war is far more sublime than that. One step taken by a believer against his enemy is better than a long trip to a holy place, and each word uttered by a preacher to reassure a *ghazi* [warrior for Islam] is better than a prayer to God.[7]

In pursuing his aim to restore 'true Islam', Isma'il al-Shirwani discarded the traditional Naqshbandi hostility towards the Shi'i Muslims and urged 'the devoted children of the Prophet' to unite and overcome enmity to each other. He claimed that in a revelation received by him from God he saw

[....] the sons of Iran and Rumelia[8] sitting peacefully and conversing.[...] Suddenly a huge army of ugly soldiers started to descend from the mountains, and conquered our villages[...] all Muslims were killed and their beautiful mosques destroyed.[9]

Surprising as it may seem, this conciliatory tone expressed by a Naqshbandi sheikh towards the Shi'i was natural enough in the circumstances of the nineteenth-century Caucasus, especially in Azerbaijan with its predominantly Shi'i population, where all Muslims faced great danger from the Russian 'infidels'. Furthermore, Sheikh Isma'il al-Shirwani had himself been a Shi'i before his initiation into the Naqshbandiyya-Khalidiyya.[10]

---

6 Sahib, 1334 (1915/6), pp. 174-7; Abu-Manneh, 1985, p. 296. For the English translation of Khalid's letter to Isma'il al-Shirwani, see in *idem.*, p. 302.

7 As quoted in Bodenshtadt, 1855, p. 140.

8 Persians and Turks who symbolise in this story the Shi'i and Sunnis.

9 Khass Muhammad as quoted in Bodenshtadt, 1855, p. 138.

10 In the story about Isma'il al-Shirwani's revelation which he told to Muhammad al-Yaraghi, he claimed that the revelation had occured to him during his *hajj* to the tomb of Hussain, which is a pilgrimage mainly undertaken by the Shi'i. For the account of the story, see Bodenshtadt, 1855, p. 133.

The first steps of the Naqshbandiyya-Mujaddidiyya-Khalidiyya in Daghestan

The fame of Sheikh Isma'il al-Shirwani brought him many followers from not only Shirwan, but also Central Asia, the Volga Basin and Afghanistan.[11] Among others came a certain Khass Muhammad – according to some sources from Bukhara,[12] others from Shirwan[13] – who was to play a crucial role in the diffusion of the *tariqa* in neighbouring Daghestan. All sources agree that Khass Muhammad was the first Khalidi to introduce the *tariqa* into Daghestan, although they provide varying details of the way it took place. According to Sheikh Ilyas al-Tsudaqari, the late-nineteenth-century Daghestani Naqshbandi sheikh, it was Sheikh Isma'il al-Shirwani who initiated the meeting between his student, Khass Muhammad, and the Daghestani *'alim* who later became the first Naqshbandi sheikh in the North Caucasus.

Once Sheikh Isma'il al-Shirwani looked at Daghestan with his heart and saw it submerged in darkness. Only in Kurah did he see a glimmer of light and that was the light of Muhammad al-Yaraghi, the *'alim*, teacher and *faqih*. [Sheikh Isma'il al-Shirwani] sent two of his *murids* – Khass Muhammad al-Shirwani and someone else – to study *'ilm* from him [Muhammad al-Yaraghi] and instructed them that when [Muhammad al-Yaraghi] asked them with whom had they studied *'ilm* before, to tell them that they were the students of Sheikh Isma'il al-Kurdamiri [al-Shirwani].

So they did[...] and when one day, he [Muhammad al-Yaraghi] asked them from whom had they attained their knowledge, they said that they were the students of Sheikh Isma'il al-Kurdamiri. [On hearing this] Muhammad al-Yaraghi became frightened. He jumped up, saying: 'Who am I to give lessons to the students of Isma'il al-Kurdamiri' and began praising him and took Khass Muhammad as his sheikh and accepted the *tariqa* from him and entered the *silsila*.[14]

The Daghestani sheikh mentioned in the passage, Muhammad al-Yaraghi, was a famous *'alim* who lived and taught in the village of Yaragh, in the Kurah khanate. Even Russian authors present him as an honest, direct and virtuous man with a striking saintly appearance.[15]

Tall, with his eyes swollen because of his many sleepless nights spent in constant prayer, he had a short grey beard that edged around his dark, thin and expressive face. Gentleness and kindness in his features revealed a scholar, ascetic and mullah in him, the rank confirmed by his green turban.[16] He spoke in a low voice barely

---

[11] Mahmudbekov, 1898, p. 22; Sahib, 1334 (1915/6), pp. 174-5.

[12] Bodenshtadt, 1855, p. 126; Neverovskiy, 1847(a), p. 1.

[13] Tsudaqari, 1904, p. 12.

[14] *Ibid.*

[15] Volkonskiy, 1886, p. 21; R-v, 1859, p. 113.

[16] North Caucasians who held religious rank usually put a green band around their *papakha*, described by Russian sources as a turban.

distinguishable in silence. Because of his intelligence and learning he was accepted as the leading scholar in Daghestan while his rank of the chief *qadi* provided him with the means to live in comfort.[17]

His fame as a learned scholar brought Muhammad al-Yaraghi numerous students from both Daghestan and neighbouring countries among whom came Khass Muhammad. According to another version, Khass Muhammad first came to Sheikh Muhammad al-Yaraghi in 1813/14, long before he met Isma'il al-Shirwani and became associated with the Naqshbandi order. Due to his inquisitive and quick mind Khass Muhammad soon became one of Muhammad al-Yaraghi's favourite students and stayed with him for several years. However, not satisfied in his search for Divine knowledge, Khass Muhammad decided to continue his studies in Bukhara; it was on his way there in the early 1820s that he first heard about Sheikh Isma'il al-Shirwani and went to visit him. Deeply impressed by the saintliness and wisdom of Isma'il al-Shirwani, Khass Muhammad gave up his plans of going to Bukhara. Instead, he accepted the *tariqa* from Sheikh Isma'il al-Shirwani and stayed at his *khanaqa*.[18] His training continued for a whole year, after which he decided, apparently with the encouragement of Sheikh al-Shirwani himself, to return to Kurah to his first teacher 'to express [his] gratitude and to share the fruits of his knowledge [with him]'.[19]

Surprised at the unexpected appearance of his favourite student whom he believed to have been far away, Muhammad al-Yaraghi allegedly saw in his sudden arrival a divine sign. His amazement further increased when, to his questions about Khass Muhammad's travels and what he had learned during his absence, the latter answered by reproaching him for 'following the letter of the *shari'a*, while its spirit escapes you'.[20] He told him about Sheikh Isma'il al-Shirwani, who made him 'see the lightning striking in the clouds, which turned all my former knowledge into a field fertilised by the Divine Spirit out of which grew a beautiful flower of knowledge'.[21]

Impressed by this story, Muhammad al-Yaraghi asked his former student to initiate him into the *tariqa*. According to some sources Khass Muhammad did so,[22] while others maintain that he refused, saying that only Sheikh Isma'il al-Shirwani was fit to be Muhammad al-Yaraghi's

---

[17] Quoted from R-v, 1859, p. 113. Similar accounts see in Volkonskiy, 1886, pp. 6-7; Neverovskiy, 1847(a), p. 1.

[18] Bodenshtadt, 1855, pp. 126-30; Volkonskiy, 1886, pp. 7-8.

[19] Bodenshtadt, 1855, p. 129.

[20] Mahmudbekov, 1898, p. 23.

[21] As quoted in Bodenshtadt, 1855, p. 130.

[22] Tsudaqari, 1904, p. 12.

murshid.[23] Whatever the truth, shortly after Khass Muhammad's arrival in Kurah, Muhammad al-Yaraghi and several other Daghestani mullahs set off to Shirwan to visit the famous *murshid*.

Muhammad al-Yaraghi's meeting with Sheikh Isma'il al-Shirwani.

Led by Khass Muhammad, Muhammad al-Yaraghi and his companions arrived in Kurdamir, where, like so many visitors, they were impressed by the spiritual insight of the great sheikh. The story of the first meeting between the Daghestani *'ulama* and Sheikh Isma'il al-Shirwani reveals that far from being a rigid legalist, as many Khalidi followers are some-times depicted, Sheikh Isma'il al-Shirwani upheld the Sufi spirit by following the inner meaning of the shari'a rather than its literal pronoun-cements.

According to this story, when Muhammad al-Yaraghi and his com-panions entered the court of Sheikh Isma'il's house, they saw the famous *murshid* cutting young branches from a mulberry tree – an activity strictly forbidden in the Qur'an. They tried not to show their astonishment but Sheikh Isma'il al-Shirwani turned to them and no sooner had his guests uttered the words of greeting than he spoke up explaining that he was cutting the young branches to feed his silkworms. The silkworms provided the sole income for him and his family, and he added that no harm was done to the trees which would not dry out but grow only with greater vigour. Sheikh Isma'il explained that in forbidding his followers to cut the young branches, the Prophet had referred only to Arabia and similar places where such trees were rare, and thus needed extra protec-tion. 'I however, act in close accordance with the spirit of God and His Prophet, for I take care of my family and do not harm anyone.'[24] Impressed by his reasoning, Sheikh Muhammad al-Yaraghi approached him and kissed his hands, all the others following his example.[25]

Muhammad al-Yaraghi stayed in Shirwan for no more than a few weeks, after which Isma'il al-Shirwani ordained him as a sheikh in his own right and appointed him as a *murshid* of the Naqshbandiyya-Mujaddidiyya-Khalidiyya in the North Caucasus.[26] This was an extremely

---

[23] Bodenshtadt, 1855, p. 130. Mahmudbekov also upholds that Khass Muhammad refused to initiate his teacher into the *tariqa* and insisted that he should go to a 'more worthy' sheikh, i.e. Isma'il al-Shirwani. Mahmudbekov, 1898, p. 23.

[24] As quoted in Bodenshtadt, 1855, p. 132.

[25] For the full story, see *ibid.*, pp. 131-2; Mahmudbekov, 1898, p. 24.

[26] It was partly after that visit and the subsequent events in Daghestan that the Russians became alerted to the political character of al-Shirwani's teaching. They imprisoned and sent into exile most of his followers. Sheikh Isma'il al-Shirwani himself escaped arrest through the protection of the Shirwani high officials. Soon, however, he was forced to leave for Ottoman Turkey, where he died. Mahmudbekov, 1898, p. 23.

short period for initiation and training even by Khalidi standards. This short period of their association seems to suggest that Muhammad al-Yaraghi could have been previously initiated into the *tariqa* by Khass Muhammad and that Isma'il al-Shirwani merely put the finishing touches on his spiritual education. This would have followed the traditional practices of Khalid and his close *khalifas* who met adepts personally only at the very last stage of their training.

Furthermore, the accounts of the discussions held between Ismai'l al-Shirwani and Muhammad al-Yaraghi describe them as those of equals, with Isma'il al-Shirwani showing as much respect to his guest and new disciple as the latter displayed towards the famous sheikh. This is, perhaps, hardly surprising if we take into account that by the time the meeting took place (some time in the early 1820s) Muhammad al-Yaraghi was in his mid-fifties with a well established reputation as a learned scholar and *qadi*.

The focal point of these discussions appears to have been not so much the Naqshbandi techniques of spiritual purification as the state of Islam in the Caucasus and the Muslim *umma* at large, and urgent need to restore the shari'a. On parting, Muhammad al-Yaraghi promised his *murshid* to do his best to strengthen the *shari'a* among the North Caucasian Muslims and to return them to the righteous path:

The seeds of your words – Muhammad al-Yaraghi allegedly told his sheikh at parting – have produced shoots in my heart and as long as God gives strength to my old hands and eloquence to my tongue, I must and will start a great work.[27]

Muhammad al-Yaraghi's appeals in Daghestan

On his return to Kurah, Muhammad al-Yaraghi at first continued his preaching at the local mosque and his work as a local *qadi*. He did all he could to attract more people to the right path – his way of life became more secluded and pious, he was more generous with alms and charitable meals. People did not fail to notice the change that had occurred in the famous *'alim* after his return from Shirwan and rumours started to spread about the Divine Revelation that Muhammad al-Yaraghi had received during his stay in Kurdamir. These rumours set the scene for the launch of Muhammad al-Yaraghi's teaching.

One day after his regular preaching Muhammad al-Yaraghi addressed the gathering with a speech in which he described himself as 'the greatest sinner of all mankind' and asked people for forgiveness.

Only now, due to the grace of God my eyes have been opened and I can see the source of the eternal Truth pouring forth, sparkling like diamonds. All my former deeds lie as a heavy burden on my soul. I made use of the fruits of your fields, I became rich through your wealth, but it is not fitting for a *qadi* to receive taxes

---

[27] As quoted in Bodenshtadt, 1855, p. 141.

[*zakat*]. A *qadi* must carry out his duties his only reward being from God. Now I weep over my sins and only want to redeem them and to attain forgiveness. Take my property, it is now yours, distribute it amongst yourselves, for I want to return to you everything I owe.[28]

This speech made a deep impression on his listeners and confirmed peoples' belief that he possessed Divine Revelation. They rejected his offerings and threatened to punish anyone who tried to take anything belonging to him. They urged Muhammad al-Yaraghi to reveal his secret knowledge to them.

Answering their pleas, Muhammad al-Yaraghi called upon them to follow his example and offer their repentance for all their misdeeds and sins. In his speech he gave a menacing portrayal of the punishment that awaited those who did not turn to the righteous path:[29]

Beware! Soon the day will come when you will not be saved either by your treasures, your friends or your children. Only those who come to God's presence with a clear heart and a clear conscience will be let into the abode of the faithful.[...] And all the sinners will see Hell, this gloomy dwelling of the *munafiqun* [hypocrites] and they will be asked 'Have you not met people who showed you the road to salvation?' and they will say, 'Yes, we have, but we did not believe their words.'[30]

To achieve salvation according to Muhammad al-Yaraghi, the Muslims had to follow the shari'a and denounce all worldly pleasures, wealth, family, etc.[31]

Drive away lewdness, mortify passions by fasting and abstention. Do not drink wine, this produce of the devil, do not follow the examples set by the infidels, who smoke pipes but weep in repentance, swear that you will never commit sins again.[32]

Even individual piety was not enough to achieve salvation:

As long as we remain under the supremacy of the infidels we are covered with shame. The prayers of slaves are not heard in Heaven.[...] All your ablutions, prayers and pilgrimages to Mecca, your repentance and sacrifices, all your holy deeds are invalid as long as the Muscovites supervise your life. Moreover, even your marriages and children are illegal as long as the Muscovites rule over you.

---

[28] As quoted in *ibid.*, pp. 161-2.

[29] Unfortunately there are no written accounts of this or any other of Muhammad al-Yaraghi's speeches. Thus, given that we have no other indigenous source which could shed light on his way of thinking and the reasoning behind his initiating Naqshbandi political activity in Daghestan, I find it justifiable to provide lengthy and detailed quotations from the available accounts, of which that written by Bodenshtadt is, perhaps, of foremost importance as it is based on local sources.

[30] As quoted in Dubrovin, 1891, p. 20.

[31] *Ibid.*, p. 19.

[32] *Ibid.*, p. 20

So how can you serve God if you are serving the Russians?[33]

Muhammad al-Yaraghi's preaching implicitly encouraged defiance of Russian rule. However, despite his decreeing a *ghazavat* against the 'infidels' and 'apostates', who deny the shari'a, the holy war was to be undertaken only after the Muslims had purified their souls and come to follow the rules laid down by the shari'a, and as a reward for their righteous behaviour.

Go to the mosques, weep and pray in repentance, shake dreams from your eyes and God will forgive you and restore you to the righteous path and arm you for great deeds.[34]

Then [after purification of their souls] Almighty God will reinforce you for the battle against the infields. Azrail[35] will fly over the Russian troops, their bayonets and cannons will not be dangerous to you and you will learn that God has more power than any earthly tsar.[36]

You must be ready when the hour comes and you are called to battle. God will give me a sign when this day has arrived and I will tell you. Meanwhile, pray and weep.[37]

The words of Muhammad al-Yaraghi fell onto fertile ground and soon the whole of Daghestan was filled with stories about the 'new prophet' and 'saint'. Mosques 'became filled with grown up men and teenagers, who offered their sincere repentance and expressed their wishes to start a new life'.[38]

At the same time, Muhammad al-Yaraghi appealed to other Daghestani mullahs and *qadis* to recognise their sins, accusing them of having acted illegally by appropriating part of the *zakat* and taking payment for fulfilling their religious duties.[39] Some of the *'ulama* indeed accepted the Naqshbandi order, others denounced it on the grounds that it was an innovation (*bid'a*) or because of its dangerous political overtones.

---

[33] As quoted in Bodenshtadt, 1885, pp. 161-2.

[34] As quoted in *ibid.*, pp. 162-3.

[35] Azrail is the angel of death in Islam.

[36] Dubrovin, 1891, p. 20.

[37] Bodnshtadt, 1855, p. 62.

[38] Dubrovin, 1891, p. 21.

[39] 'Prushanovskiy, Obschiy Vzglyad na Prichiny i Posledstviya Besporyadkov v Dagestane', in *TsGVIA*, VUA, delo 6430, list 342-3 ob.

15

'SPIRITUAL' NAQSHBANDIYYA AND ITS DOCTRINE[1]

The philosophical and mystical dimensions of the *tariqa* remained the concern of a much smaller number of Naqshbandi adepts who chose to pursue the path leading to Divine Knowledge. However, they became crucial in the establishment of the Naqshbandi network and formed the Naqshbandi elite which wielded great influence over the Muslims of the North Caucasus.

The main role in developing and laying out the Naqshbandi doctrine and practices belonged to Sheikh Jamal al-Din al-Ghazi-Ghumuqi, who personified the mystical Sufi trend in the North Caucasian Naqshbandiyya.

Jamal al-Din al-Ghazi-Ghumuqi

From a well-established family of Daghestani sayyids,[2] Jamal al-Din received a good religious education and held the rank of mullah. However, his main occupation prior to his initiation into the Naqshbandi order was not as a Muslim official but as a secretary to Aslan Khan, the khan of Kurah and Ghazi-Ghumuq, who 'liked him and for his loyalty and good service granted [Jamal al-Din] three villages in the Kurah khanate, which had to pay tribute to him'.[3] Thus, through his close association with one of the most powerful Daghestani rulers and through his considerable wealth, Jamal al-Din enjoyed a comfortable living and had little interest in religious affairs. When he heard about the new teaching preached by Muhammad al-Yaraghi, Jamal al-Din 'recovered

---

[1] This chapter is largely based on the work of Jamal al-Din al-Ghazi-Ghumuqi, *Adab al-Murdiya fi al-Tariqa al-Naqshbandiyya*. The work was published in 1905, but never fully translated. A partial and inaccurate translation was published in *SSKG*, 1869. vol. II, pp. 1-21. I have made a full translation of this work, which I intend to publish in the near future with annotation. Other important sources for the present chapter are al-Thughuri, 1907 and al-Tsudaqari, 1904, which I have also translated. None of these have been studied or translated even partially before.

[2] The alleged descendants of the Prophet Muhammad.

[3] Seyid Abdurahman (Sayyid Abd al-Rahman), 1869, p. 2.

from his secular oblivion and turned to God with full repentance'.[4] He renounced all his wealth and went to see the *murshid*.

After his initiation into the order and a short period of training, in 1824 Muhammad al-Yaraghi granted Jamal al-Din the title of sheikh in his own right as well as the rank of *murshid* with the right and obligation to initiate his own adepts into the *tariqa*.[5]

Back at Ghazi-Ghumuq, Jamal al-Din established himself as a *murshid* second only to Muhammad al-Yaraghi. His house became one of the most important Naqshbandi lodges in Daghestan. Unlike Muhammad al-Yaraghi, Jamal al-Din, rather than criticising the spiritual degradation of the Muslim *umma* as a whole, pursued individual purification. He trained his students in traditional Sufi fashion: a number of years study of both traditional Muslim *'ulum* and Sufi doctrine and practices. Moreover, Jamal al-Din tried to distance himself from politics, spending his time in prayer and mystical exercise as well as in the spiritual education of his numerous *murids*.[6]

To all the prominent mystics and ordinary *murids* of mystical inclination, Jamal al-Din soon became a pillar of Sufi knowledge in the Caucasus and the ultimate teacher at whose hands they received insight into the true meaning of the *tariqa*. Furthermore, since Muhammad al-Yaraghi did not leave any writings related to Naqshbandiyya or Sufism,[7] Jamal al-Din was the first North Caucasian Naqshbandi sheikh to compose a treatise on Naqshbandi doctrine and practices (*al-Adab al-Murdhiyya fi al-Tariqa al-Naqshbandiyya*). This is the only source of its kind and, as such, is crucial for the understanding of the way the Naqshbandi *tariqa* was practised in early nineteenth-century North Caucasus.

Jamal al-Din's elucidation of the meaning of the tariqa

Jamal-al-Din's understanding of the Naqshbandi *tariqa* was similar to that of Sheikh Khalid. Both saw it first and foremost as

[....] a complete adherence to the Book [Qur'an] and the Sunna, the correction of faith in accordance with the decision of the Sunni authorities[...] precision in following the shari'a, avoidance of innovations and of what is forbidden.[8]

---

4 *Ibid.*

5 Al-Tsudaqari, 1906, p. 13.

6 Among the latter were Ghazi Muhammad and Shamil, the first and the third Daghestani imams.

7 The only writing of Muhammad al-Yaraghi which I have found during my field work in Daghestan is a poem on Arabic language and grammar, Athar Muhammad al-Yaraghi, 1910.

8 Jamal al-Din, 1905, pp. 26-7.

Furthermore, it was precisely in the 'orthodox' character of the Naqshbandi order that, according to Jamal al-Din, its main virtue lay:

The Naqshbandi *tariqa* is the most exalted and the best one since it has retained
its original basis [*asl*] without additions and reductions [and has upheld] the way
of the Companions and the Prophet and [is] free from the innovations [*bid'a*] which
were introduced by some Sufi sheikhs, such as the loud dhikr, listening [to music
– *sama*] and dancing which did not exist at the time of the Prophet or the righteous
caliphs.[9]

To Jamal al-Din, as to many of his predecessors, the *tariqa* and the
shari'a were intertwined aspects of Islam.[10] Thus, he maintained that
'following one of the righteous *tariqas* which goes back to the Prophet
Muhammad...and...the association with one of the Sufi sheikhs'[11] were
essential for both Sufi adepts and ordinary Muslims, who otherwise
would not be able to understand and hence implement the shari'a properly,
without which they would be unable to achieve Salvation and enter
Paradise.[12]

If you look at yourself in a just and compassionate way, you will realise that your
need of *tauba* [repentance which is associated with the initiation into a Sufi *tariqa*]
is stronger than your need of food, drink and shelter, for only through repentance
does a servant of God escape from Hell on Judgement Day.[13]

However, while affirming the necessity for each Muslim to adhere to
a Sufi path, Jamal al-Din recognised the difference in the ultimate aims
of an ordinary Muslim and a Sufi – that of the former being to achieve
Salvation and enter Paradise, while the latter aspired to achieve

[....] the Presence of God [*hadrat allah*][14] when a servant becomes unveiled as if
he is sitting in front of his Lord and sees Him and becomes aware of Him. And
whilst a servant maintains his witnessing [of God-*shuhud*][15] he becomes one who
keeps God's company [sits with God-*jalis allah*] in His special Presence [*hadratihi
al-khassa*].[16]

---

[9] Jamal al-Din, 1905, pp. 2-3.

[10] See Chapter 9 on Ahmad al-Sirhindi's views on the *tariqa* and the shari'a.

[11] Jamal al-Din, 1905, pp. 2-3.

[12] *Ibid.*, p. 15.

[13] *Ibid.*, p. 20.

[14] *Hadrat Allah* can be explained as the domain in which God is to be found or perceived.
The concept was introduced by Ibn al-Arabi, who believed that in the last analysis there
is but a single Divine Presence (*al-hadra al-illahiyya*) which comprehends everything
that exists. Chittick, 1989, p. 5.

[15] Nowhere in his writing does Jamal al-Din talk about *wujud*. Thus, it seems that he
had adopted a Mujaddidi interpretation of Ibn al-Arabi's concept of *wahdat al-wujud*,
which replaced it with the doctrine of *wahdat al-shuhud*.

[16] Jamal al-Din, 1905, p. 34. Elucidating the meaning of the Divine Presence (*hadra*)
Jamal al-Din adds that one must 'understand that *hadra* does not mean any particular

Hence, an ordinary Muslim and a Sufi differed in the way they worshipped God. While for the former it was enough to adopt sincere repentance (*tauba*), and follow the shari'a under the guidance of a Sufi sheikh, for a *salik* (the one who travels along the mystical path) this was not enough.

All sheikhs agree that through his worship a servant will gain the reward and enter Paradise, but he cannot come into the presence of God [*hadhrat allah*] without adhering to the ethics of the *tariqa [sahabuhu bi-l-adab]*.[17]

Among the latter *Tauba, dhikr, rabita*, and *suhba* formed the core of the Naqshbandi path.

Tauba. The first stage of initiation was *tauba* – repentance.

Tauba means return to God and when one embarks on it [begins the course of spiritual training] one starts his return to God moving from what is unworthy [*madhmum*] to what is praiseworthy [*mahmud*] in the shari'a. [*Tauba*] requires remorse for offences against the shari'a, the abandonment [of these offences] and a firm commitment to avoid them in future. And if *tauba* concerns the violation of the rights of other people, then it is necessary to remove the injustice and be reconciled with them.[...] In *tauba* God's servant escapes from Hell on Judgement day.[...]
Tauba has precedents [*muqaddamat*], signs ['*alamat*] and results [*thamarat*]. The precedents are the vigilance of the heart over ignorance, man's awareness of what is harmful for him[...] and fear of God's punishment. The signs are renouncing friends and associates[...] love of solitude, brevity in speech, indifference to what does not concern oneself [the *murid*], zeal in performing rituals, constant *dhikr*[...] sorrow, tears and [...] prayers for God's forgiveness day and night. And the results are[...] numerous because of God's forgiveness day and night. And the results are[...] numerous because of God's greatness and His generosity towards His servant.[...]
Travelling [along the Sufi path – *suluk*] has the aim of reaching God and that does not happen without *tauba*.[18]

Tauba was the first step taken by a novice at his initiation into the *tariqa*. It was performed in the presence of a sheikh who henceforward took a novice as his *murid*. At the same time the sheikh swore an oath to instruct (*talqin*) the novice in Divine Knowledge to the best of his

---

place in the Heavens or on Earth...for there is no place that can hold God, since He is greater and larger than any place'. Jamal al-Din, 1905, p. 34. He, however, does not give any detailed discriptions of various aspects or forms of *hadra* which are to be found in the writings of some Sufi followers of Ibn al-Arabi, e.g. Qunawi, who distinguished 'Five Divine Presences' or five domains in which God is to be found. For more on *hadra*, see Chittick, 1989, pp. 4-6.

17 Jamal al-Din, 1905, p. 33.

18 *Ibid.*, pp. 6-7, 15-16, 20.

ability, while the *murid* promised to follow and obey his sheikh in deed and thought. This is how the procedure is described by Jamal al-Din:

The *murid* places himself in a clean area in front of the sheikh, and puts his hand into the hand of the sheikh while the latter utters: 'This is an oath to God [*ahd allah*] sworn by you and me on the Qur'an and Sunna that you should neither commit great sins nor persist in the lesser ones. And if something of this sort happens you must be quick to repent [*tauba*] and rid yourself of the sin. You must tenaciously follow your duties [*wajibat*] and display zeal in the additional prayers [*nawafil al-'ibadat*]; work with determination; avoid concessions [*rakhsa*] and innovations [*bid'a*]. We are brothers in God and the one who is rescued on the Day of Judgement will lend a hand to his brother. We are the followers of Khawaja Baha' al-Din al-Naqshband Muhammad al-Bukhari.'

Then they ask the Sheikh [Khawaja Baha al-Din] to mediate for their sins and the rules they have broken[...] saying: '*Astaghfir allah alladhi la ilaha illa huwa al-hayy al-qayyum wa atubu ilayhi*'[19] three times each.

Then the sheikh asks for a blessing [*tabarruk*] by reciting a Sura from the Qur'an: 'Those, who pledge allegiance to you, do pledge it to God...' Then sheikh and *murid* put their hands on their knees and close their eyes and then a sheikh invokes in his heart the Name of God, his own name and his intention to give instruction [*talqin*] and teaching (*ta'lim*) to a *murid*. He does this three times. Then a *murid* utters to himself his intention to take *talqin* and both the sheikh and the *murid* raise their hands in prayer [*du'a*], the sheikh reads the prayer and the *murid* says '*amin*'. After the prayer they stroke their hands and faces. Then the *murid* kisses the sheikh's knee, stands up, asks the sheikh's permission to leave, and thereafter does what the sheikh orders him to do.[20]

Following the ritual, the novice went into seclusion (*khalwa*) for forty days, which in the North Caucasus were usually spent in a special pit dug out in the yard of the sheikh's or the *murid's* house. During this period, the *murid* could not see anyone and had to go through all stages of repentance, and purify his heart and soul from sins and delusions.[21]

Dhikr. Jamal al-Din saw *dhikr* as one of the most characteristic features of the Naqshbandi *tariqa* and the essential part in the spiritual journey of a *salik* towards God:

[Dhikr] is a frequent repetition of God's name by heart and tongue...it is a constant obligation [of *murids*...] and the shortest way to God and a measurement of the [*murid's* degree of] connection [with God] (*wusla*), [for...] all the praiseworthy qualities come from *al-Madhkur* [the remembered one, i.e. God] and *dhikr* is the origin of all such features... and it lifts the evil which prevents [a *salik*] from

---

[19] Translated as: 'I ask the pardon of God who is the only deity, everlasting and eternal and I turn to God in repentance.'

[20] Jamal al-Din, 1905, pp. 28-9.

[21] On the disgraceful morals which should be purified at the first stages of the spiritual journey, see *ibid.*, pp. 20-6.

entering the Presence of God (*hadrat allah*) and when this veil is lifted...he attains the degrees [*maqamat*]...until he reaches the degree of perfection [*kamal*].'[22]

Well in line with the Naqshbandi doctrine, Jamal al-Din stressed the priority of a *dhikr* of the heart (*al-dhikr al-qalbi*) or the silent *dhikr* (*al-dhikr al-khafi*) over the *dhikr* of the tongue (*al-dhikr al-lisani*).

The silent *dhikr* is the most sublime form of veneration of God...the *dhikr* of the heart (*al-dhikr al-qalbi*) is a witnessing [of God] (*shuhud*) and [it leads to the] Presence of God (*hudur*) and closeness to Him (*qurba*).[23]

However, Jamal al-Din did not forbid or deny the validity of vocal *dhikr*, which, he saw as a lower stage of the Naqshbandi path suitable for a *salik* who had not yet achieved the state of 'the presence of heart (with God)' (*al-wuquf al-qalbi*).[24]

Rabita. Even more important than *dhikr* according to Jamal al-Din was the practice of *rabita.* On a *murid's* way to God, *rabita* enabled him to transcend the veils between him and the Divine Presence.

He [*murid*] imagines the appearance of the *murshid's* spirituality and deeply penetrates with his sight into the fore part of the sheikh's heart (*nasiyat al-sheikh*) and with his [i.e. the *murid's*] heart he borrows from it [the heart of the sheikh] and that observance and imagining is the noble *rabita.*[25]

Despite Sheikh Khalid's insistence on instructing all *murids* of his sub-order to practise *rabita* by linking with his own image, this doctrine had apparently been abandoned by the North Caucasian Naqshbandis, who restored *rabita* directly with one's immediate sheikh.[26] They did, however, accept the validity of *rabita* practised through the spirituality (*ruhaniyya*) of a deceased sheikh, especially that of Baha al-Din al-Naqshband himself.[27]

[....] There are two types of *rabita.* The first one is exercised in the presence of a sheikh and the way to perform it is for a *murid* to turn with his 'essential love' [*mahabba dhatiyya*] towards the heart of his sheikh by greeting [the heart of his

22 *Ibid.*, pp. 30-1.

23 *Ibid.*, p. 32.

24 On the way to perform the silent *dhikir* (*al-dhikr al-khafi*) and the *dhikr* of the heart (*al-dhikr al-qalibi*) see, Chapter 7, pp. 39-55. On the vocal *dhikr* (*al-dhikr al-lisani*) see Chapter 9, pp. 58-64.

25 *Ibid.*, p. 42.

26 In none of the sources which I have studied do the authors mention Khalid as a person with whom a *murid* should link while practicing *rabita.* Some point to the fact that once a *murid* reached the rank of a sheikh in his own right he was allowed to take his own *murids* who would practise *rabita* with him. Dubrovin, KS, XII, p. 62.

27 Usually the 'spirituality of a dead sheikh' seems to imply that of Baha al-Din al-Naqshband.

sheikh] and losing himself in it, so that all his characteristics dissolve in those of the sheikh.

The second type of *rabita* is performed in the absence of the sheikh and involves a *murid's* imagining the appearance [*sura*] of his sheikh, turning to his spirituality [*ruhaniyya*] and keeping directed towards it until divine gravitation [*jadhba*][28] occurs.[...]

To achieve *rabita* with a deceased sheikh, a *murid* must rid himself of all material links [associations – *'alaqat 'unsuriyya*], free his inner world from all physical constrains (*quyud tabi'iyya*) strip his heart of [worldly] knowledge and thoughts, then imagine the spirituality of the deceased sheikh as a light devoid of any sensual qualities. [A *murid* must] keep this light in his heart until the spiritual flow (*faid*) or exhalation (*hal*) [29] overcomes him.[...][30]

Furthermore, in his treatise Jamal al-Din indicates the usefulness of practising *rabita* with a deceased sheikh, especially if it happens at the latter's grave.[31] By doing so he revived the *Uwaysi* tradition which had been abandoned by Khalid and his close associates who saw it as the worst kind of religious innovation. At the same time he diminished the importance of *rabita* as ascribed to it by Khalid by suggesting that only those who were unable to receive the spiritual flow (*faid*) from God without the mediation of a deceased or a living sheikh should practise *rabita*. Anyone who succeeded in witnessing the Divine Presence (*mushahada*) should stop practising *rabita*, otherwise he 'would prefer the stage of the veil [*maqam*[32] *al-hijab*] to the stage of witnessing [God] [*maqam al-shuhud*]'

Suhba. At the same time, Jamal al-Din restored the primary importance of *suhba* with a living sheikh for successfully following the Sufi path – the essence of the Naqshbandi *tariqa* in the words of Baha al-Din.[33]

That is because God has established a custom according to which the unveiling of the secrets of His Name occurs only through the instruction of the Prophet and his deputies. And if someone who performs *dhikr* invokes the name of God by the entire range of *dhikrs* but without the instruction of a sheikh, he will not reach...the

[28] The Sufi believed that if God wishes and chooses a person for His special grace, the chosen one can be exalted in one single spiritual experience into a state of ecstacy and Union with God through *jadhba*, the Divine Gravitation or the Divine Attraction. Chittick, 1989, p. 383, n. 12; Schimmel, 1975, p. 105.

[29] *Hal* is also translated as state. Unlike *maqam* (degree, station) which can be attained by a mystic through persistent exercise, *hal* is 'something that descends from God into a man's heart, without his being able to repel it when it comes, or to attract it when it goes, by his own effort'. Quoted from Schimmel, 1975, p. 99.

[30] Jamal al-Din, 1905, pp. 34-8.

[31] *Ibid.*, p. 38.

[32] *Maqam* can be translated as a lasting stage in the mystical spiritual journey which a man reaches through persistent spiritual exercise.

[33] *Ibid.*, p. 64.

degree of perfection [*martaba al-kama*] unless he is instructed by a *murshid*. That which a *salik* finds in *suhba* with a perfect sheikh in one second he will not find by reading one thousand books or in a thousand-years-long exercise, for a perfect sheikh...leads a *murid* upwards to the degree of *mushahada* [witnessing of God] which is impossible to reach in any other way than through *suhba*.[34]

To benefit from the association with a sheikh, a *murid* had to follow the 'ethics of *suhba*': love and sincerity and the attention of one's heart and thoughts, submission and modesty, affection and attentiveness, and good faith...'[35]

[....] and he [the *murid*] should...always be loyal to his sheikh even if [the sheikh] humiliates or insults him in the presence of his companions, and should never contradict his sheikh even if he appears to be contradicting the shari'a and if [a *murid*] cannot understand his words, [he must] say ' he knows better'...and never say 'No' to [the sheikh]...but believe that he is one of God's saints and [as such] is protected from fallacy, and believe that he is the best of all sheikhs and his *tariqa* is the best one. [...]And only he who follows these ethics (morals) will benefit from *suhba* that leads him towards God, otherwise *suhba* will turn him to hatred and will lead him astray."[36]

The principle of the utmost loyalty and submission to one's sheikh served to sanctify the bond between the *murid* and his sheikh. The obligation to uphold this bond referred not only to those following the mystical path, but also 'common adepts' of the *tariqa*, who by adopting *tauba* in the presence of a sheikh put themselves under his full authority.[37]

---

[34] *Ibid.*, pp. 32-3.

[35] *Ibid.*, p. 64.

[36] *Ibid.*, p. 69.

[37] The tradition laid down by Jamal al-Din was upheld by the future North Caucasian Naqshbandis. Al-Tsudaqari later expressed similar views on the *rabita, suhba*, the necessity to uphold the Sunna and the shari'a, etc. Tsudaqari, 1906, pp. 27-8, 33, 36-7, 48.

16

'POLITICAL' NAQSHBANDIYYA[1]

The majority of those who accepted the teaching of Muhammad al-Yaraghi were attracted primarily by its political connotations. Having sworn *tauba* and accepted Muhammad al-Yaraghi as their sheikh and chief *murshid*, his followers went back to their villages to propagate the new teaching and to set an example of 'a truly Muslim way of life'. For the majority of such *murids* following the *tariqa* amounted to the strict implementation of the *shari'a* which they perceived as the way out of the moral and political decline that pervaded the North Caucasus.

Despite Muhammad al-Yaraghi's orders 'to submit and give *amanats* (hostages) to the Russians as long as they are stronger than we are...[until] one of the mighty rulers of the East in the glory of the Qur'an subdues the Russians, at which time we should rise against them and declare *ghazavat*',[2] the people in the khanate of Kurah made themselves wooden swords and waved them around shouting: 'Muslims, *ghazavat*! Muslims, *ghazavat*!' This battle-cry, started by the Naqshbandi adepts in Yaragh, was taken up by those in other Kurah villages and from there spread all over Daghestan like ripples on water.[3]

The Russians once alerted to the new movement and its overtly political overtones, tried to stop it. Warned of the dangers of Muhammad al-Yaraghi's preaching by Sayyid al-Harakani, Ermolov on his way through Kurah in March 1824 summoned its ruler, Aslan Khan and ordered him to see that the anti-Russian propaganda was brought to an end. Following his orders, Aslan Khan called Muhammad al-Yaraghi and some of the mullahs close to him to Qasim-kent, where he enquired about Muhammad al-Yaraghi's new teaching. He reminded him of the might of the Russian tsar and the misfortunes that could befall the people of Daghestan if they adopted his rebellious ideas.[4] Muhammad al-Yaraghi replied that he was aware of the Russian strength, but that

---

[1] The sources for this chapter largely coincide with those of Chapter 14.

[2] Volkonskiy, 1886, p. 28.

[3] For the accounts on such *murids*, see Bodenshtadt, 1855, p. 165; Neverovskiy, 1847(a), pp. 7-8; R-v, 1898, p. 114; Volkonskiy, 1886, vol. X, p. 29.

[4] Bodenshtadt, 1855, p. 166.

nobody was more powerful than God, Who had inspired him and his followers.

My aspirations rise to God, and from God I receive my instruction. My aim is His glorification. We wandered in darkness, we forgot the source of truth, our aspirations were sinful and our deeds criminal. The torch which was lit in the Prophet by God Almighty Himself died out and the temple of faith lay in ruins. And I came to fill the gap between us and Salvation, and to restore the temple of faith. I shall light up the torch and bring those who went astray back to the truth. Thus I shall continue my efforts for the glory of God alone.[5]

Aslan Khan responded to Muhammad al-Yaraghi by saying that he would not impede this effort, but he demanded an explanation as to why his armed *murids* travelled from one *aul* to another and gathered in the forests and gorges, turning their faces to the East and calling out their war-cries against the Russians. Muhammad al-Yaraghi answered:

'My *murids* are only the executors of the Supreme Will. Although they have reached a high degree of knowledge and, following my example, direct all their thoughts and aspirations towards investigating the might and greatness of God, and although they submit themselves to His will, worshipping Him directly without any human mediation, yet they fear your punishment and do not realise what they are doing. They wander in a dream state, which precedes full knowledge and therefore they are innocent of what they are doing. But it seems to me that their deeds clearly indicate what we all should do. And I would like to advise you, O Khan, to renounce your worldly vanity and desires, and instead of governing people you should obey God, for otherwise you will find no happiness and greatness in the Hereafter. We must all follow the path that leads us to the Other World and we will never be able to find this path unless we follow the *tariqa* in which the Supreme orders of the Almighty God are recorded.'
    'I do follow his path as the Holy Book instructs me' retorted Aslan Khan 'You are wrong, O Khan,' replied Muhammad al-Yaraghi. 'How can you possibly follow the path of the faithful and at the same time be the infidel's slave?'[6]

Outraged by this remark, Aslan Khan slapped Muhammad al-Yaraghi, and ordered all the other mullahs to dance in the manner of whirling dervishes for a whole hour until his anger faded away and he became ashamed of his reaction.

It was the truth of Muhammad al-Yaraghi's remarks that hurt him most, but he was not yet prepared to sacrifice his career and join the new movement. Instead, he apologised to Muhammad al-Yaraghi and urged him in the interests of both of them to calm down his *murids* and to forbid them to agitate the people by calling them to rebel. Otherwise Aslan Khan would be forced to commit an awful sin and arrest the great *'alim* and hand him over to the Russians, to prevent the Russians

---

5 *Ibid.*, p. 167.
6 As quoted in *ibid.*, p. 168.

from taking his land and inheritance and exiling him and his family.[7]

'Do not join us,' replied Muhammad al-Yaraghi, 'but do not act against us either. If you do not wish your subjects to accept the new teaching, at least let the other peoples of Daghestan be free in their deeds and faith. Stay outwardly friendly to the Russians – it will be safe for you and useful to us. Soon a bloody war will break out between us and the infidels, but that will by no means harm you. If we win we shall protect you and your land, if the enemy triumphs they will be favourable to you as their old ally and grant you distinctions and honour.'[8]

Having achieved this reconciliation they parted. Aslan Khan promised to follow the advice of Muhammad al-Yaraghi and gave him rich presents as a sign of his goodwill.[9] Back in Yaragh, Muhammad al-Yaraghi addressed his followers with a long speech in which he forbade them to carry swords and call openly for *ghazavat*, but promised that an hour would come when he would summon them to battle.

Muhammad al-Yaraghi's appeal to the people from the free *jama'ats* which lay outside Russian control was somewhat different. When a new party of mullahs and *'ulama'* arrived from the free *jama'ats* of Avaria, Tabarsaran and Ghazi-Ghumuq, he informed them of his recent meeting with Aslan Khan, who, he said, was fearful of taking any action against the Russians. He then appealed to them:

'Your visit, Oh, people of Avaria and Tabarsaran who can carry weapons, came as a sign from Heaven. In the name of the Prophet, I order you to return to your country, assemble the people of your tribes, teach them my doctrine and call them to a holy war against the hated Muscovites. We must rid ourselves of the oppressors and the state of slavery...if we adhere to our faith in God and His Prophet we need not fear anyone and their threats. I tell you what you must convey to your people on my behalf.[10]

Thus, the Naqshbandiyya-Mujaddidiyya-Khalidiyya whose roots were first planted in the area under Russian control, gradually shifted to the free Daghestani *jama'ats*, where it found its most ardent supporters. These *jama'ats* were gradually covered with a network of semi-clandestine Naqshbandi lodges.

The time of agitation in the mountains and gorges of Daghestan had come, the new clandestine societies spread everywhere and the number of fanatical followers of *muridism* had increased. The sense of tense anticipation of the call to war for the sake of freedom and Islam was growing every moment.[11]

Convinced that the movement was identical with its leader and that by

[7] *Ibid.*, p. 169.

[8] As quoted in *ibid.*, p. 170.

[9] This meeting is also described with some variations in Volkonskiy, 1886, pp. 26-7; Neverovskiy, 1847(a), pp. 8-9. A shorter account in R-v, 1898, p. 114.

[10] As quoted in Bodenshtadt, 1855, p. 172.

[11] *Ibid.*, p. 174.

removing the leader they would halt its development, the Russians in early 1825 ordered Aslan Khan to arrest Muhammad al-Yaraghi. The *murshid* allowed himself to be arrested without showing any resistance but escaped on the road to Tiflis, apparently not without the collusion of Aslan Khan, as the Russians correctly suspected. The *murshid* was promptly provided with refuge by the people of Tabarsaran from where he continued his preaching.[12]

Jamal al-Din, after a number of heated arguments with Aslan Khan during which the latter demanded that Jamal al-Din should stop accepting students and spreading the *tariqa*, left Ghazi-Ghumuq and settled in Tsudaqar (Tsudakhar).

Satisfied with the disappearance from the scene of both Naqshbandi leaders, the Russian authorities did not pursue their anti-Naqshbandi measures any further. This withdrawal allowed the order to plant deep roots in the North Caucasus with many Naqshbandi lodges being established throughout the area. Besides, Russian attention was diverted from Daghestan to Chechnya, where the new teaching was being put to the test as the driving force behind a major uprising in 1825-6.

The establishment of the Naqshbandi order in the North Caucasus was part of a broader process of dissemination of the Naqshbandiyya-Mujaddidiyya-Khalidiyya throughout the Muslim world. Sheikh Khalid's ideas, according to which Muslims could recapture their former glory and resist the encroachment of the Western powers in their lands through the strict implementation of the *shari'a*, appealed not only to the mystically inclined *tariqa* adepts but also to ordinary Muslims seeking a way out of the spiritual and political crisis. This general appeal, combined with the special techniques of initiation and spiritual upbringing introduced by Sheikh Khalid, allowed the order to recruit a considerable number of adepts in a relatively short time.

The Naqshbandi order took root in the North Caucasus at the time when the area was experiencing political and social collapse as a result of Russia's continuous efforts to bring it under submission. The desperate attempts of various North Caucasian political entities to resist the expansion of the Russian empire did no more than temporarily frustrate Russian military efforts. The traditional secular and religious authorities failed to offer any viable answer to the Russian challenge, and each new military failure added to the atmosphere of resignation and acceptance of the inevitability of their loss of independence.

In this environment the Naqshbandi order emerged as a force which transcended local limitations and offered people an ideology capable of uniting the various tribes of the North Caucasus into a broad movement.

12 R-v, 1898, p. 115; Bodenshtadt, 1855, p. 175.

The Naqshbandis preached a clear and comprehensible message according to which the decline of North Caucasian (or indeed any Muslim) society was due to the people's corruption of the 'true spirit' of Islam and their failure to adhere strictly to the *shari'a*, the restoration of which as the ultimate system of law was the only way out of the crisis. However, according to the Naqshbandis a true understanding of the *shari'a* was impossible without the spiritual guidance of a Sufi (or to be more precise Naqshbandi) sheikh.

For the first time in the North Caucasus (although not elsewhere in the Muslim world) the Naqshbandiyya introduced the notion that for every true believer – mystic or not – it was necessary to adhere to a Sufi *tariqa* and place oneself under the guidance of a Sufi sheikh. They emphasised ideas of a loyalty and allegiance owed to God and His mediator and thus affirmed the special character of the sheikh-*murid* relationship.

The appeal of the Naqshbandi order was twofold. Exceptionally, it combined the values of the asceticism of early Islam with those of developed philosophical mysticism. While it urged ordinary Muslims to practise restraint reminiscent of asceticism, for those who chose the mystical path it provided guidance in achieving unity with God. By doing so the Naqshbandi order not only introduced a new ideology but also bred its own leaders from among those who devoted themselves to the pursuit of Divine Knowledge and whose legitimacy was considered to be derived directly from God.

Initially the 'political and 'mystical' trends within the Naqshbandi order seemed to develop along different paths, but within a few years they merged and reinforced each other, so that the order provided the structure, leadership and ideology for a viable religious-political movement.

Part VI. THE FIRST
NAQSHBANDI IMAMS AND THE
BEGINNING OF GHAZAVAT

17

DIFFUSION OF NAQSHBANDI IDEAS IN CHECHNYA: THE GREATER CHECHNYA REVOLT (1825-6)[1]

News of Naqshbandi teachings quickly spread from Daghestan to Chechnya. Many ordinary people, but mullahs especially, went to Kurah to meet Muhammad al-Yaraghi and listen to his preaching. Some accepted the *tariqa* from him while others returned without any formal association with the order, but inspired nonetheless by its message.[2] Once back in Chechnya they spread reports of Muhammad al-Yaraghi and his teaching, which in the process became somewhat transformed to suit local circumstances. Among the less-educated and more-prejudiced Chechens the image of Muhammad al-Yaraghi was similar to that of Sheikh Mansour, whose memory still dominated the religious consciousness of the Chechen people. Rumours started to circulate that a new imam was about to appear in the Caucasus, who would make the Russian cannons and bayonets harmless to the true believers and would lead people into battle against the Russians under Divine protection, and so expel the enemy from the Muslim lands.

It was the political rather than the spiritual message that captured people's imagination and soon revealed itself in a particular trend. In early January 1822 one of the most respected Chechen mullahs, Abd

---

[1] This chapter is based on the following sources: unpublished archival documents in *TsGVIA*, fond. 428; Published documents in *AKAK*; Ramazanov and Khadzhiev (eds), 1959; Ermolov, 1865; Ermolov, Dibich and Paskevich, 1872; Kolosov, 1991; Potto, 1901-4, vol. III, part I; Volkonskiy, 1886-7, vols X-XI; Serov, 1927.

[2] The majority of those who adopted *tauba* and entered the *tariqa* received only a short training during which they were introduced mainly to the 'political' rather than philosophical tenets of the Naqshbandi teaching.

al-Qadir, the *qadi* of Germenchuk[3] urged people to unite in the name of Islam in anti-Russian resistance. Abd al-Qadir's summons to actions roused 'all [*tuqums*] from Aqsay up to Assa, the Chechens abandoned their homes and went into the mountains' in preparation for the uprising. However, the expedition organised and led by Grekov defeated the revolt in its early stages. Two large villages – Shali and Malye Ataghi – were destroyed and Abd al-Qadir was mortally wounded by a Russian shell.

The religious feelings of the Chechen people were further stirred up when a plague epidemic broke out in the winter of 1822-3. It was interpreted by many Chechen mullahs and *qadis* as a sign that God was punishing the Muslims for the corruption of Islam and forgetfulness of their religious duties. This combination of a religious movement and anti-Russian feelings culminated in the major Chechen revolt of 1825-6.[4]

The revolt took place primarily in Greater Chechnya (and hence became known as the Greater Chechnya revolt), but it also drew many Chechens from Lesser Chechnya, as well as the Ingush, Kabardians, Aqsay Qumyqs, Ossets and a few hundred Daghestanis into the military actions.[5]

Although, the ultimate leader of the revolt was a secular Chechen leader, Beybulat Taymi (Taymiev or Taymazov in Russian translation, Taymazoghly in Turkish), it was Naqshbandi teaching that provided the ideological drive behind it.

Musulman fanaticism [i.e. the Naqshbandi teaching – A.Z.], which was aroused in Daghestan by his [Ermolov's] conquests, but driven, temporarily, to concealment through fear of his cannon and bayonets, found a ready outlet in Tchetchnia [Chechnya – A.Z.], and focused there all the hatred and discontent that had long been gathering head among the forest dwellers.[6]

Furthermore, the revolt played a crucial role in transforming Chechen society which consisted of small 'republics'

[....]connected only by language and religion...Although they often united to resist us [the Russians], their alliances...dissolved as quickly as they had been formed. Full and complete unity among the Chechens which was to last until the 1850s, appeared only in 1825, due to religious teaching, and became further strengthened in the 1830s by the same teaching and specific political circumstances.[7]

---

[3] On Abd al-Qadir see Potto, 1901-4, vol. III, part I, p. 303; Kolosov, 1991, p. 50. Unfortunately there is little information available on him and we do not even know whether he had any association with the Naqshbandi *tariqa* or not.

[4] Ermolov, 1868, p. 162.

[5] On the Greater Chechnya revolt, see *TsGVIA*, fond 482, delo 152, list 19-42; *AKAK*, vol. VI, part I, pp. 508-16; Ramazanov and Khadzhiev (eds), 1959, pp. 53-5; Pogodin, 1863, pp. 179-80, 182-4; Potto, 1901-4, vol. III, part II, pp. 207-28; Kolosov, 1991; Baddeley, 1908, pp. 148-53; Gammer, 1994, pp. 36-7.

[6] Baddeley, 1908, p. 147.

[7] Volkonskiy, 1886, vol. X, pp. 37-8.

Although these factors were important in its original motivation, the real reasons for the outbreak of the revolt must be sought elsewhere.

The Russians, be it noted, assigned religious fanaticism as the primary cause of this and all similar outbreaks; but in truth it was only secondary. It was in the role of invaders, oppressors, conquerors – or, to use the current euphemism, civilisers – that excited such bitter resentment...The Ghazavat would never have been preached in the Caucasus had the Russians been peaceful and friendly neighbours.[8]

Russian policy

Ermolov commenced implementation of his 'siege policy' in the Chechen lands as part of his general plans to subjugate the Caucasus with its 'bold and dangerous people'.[9] In 1818 he built the first fortress of the Sunja and Sulaq (Qumyq) lines. Named Groznaya (Russian for menacing), it was designed to drive the Chechen tribes away from the plain and restrict them to the mountains.[10]

In 1819 the Russians built a second fortress, Vnezapnaya (Russian for sudden) on the Aqtash river opposite Enderi in the area where Chechnya borders Daghestan to bar the way between high mountain Daghestan and Chechnya.[11] This was followed by the construction in 1821 of Burnaya (Russian for stormy) fortress near Targhu at the point where the North Caucasian mountains come down to the Caspian Sea.

The policy of establishing fortified garrisons was accompanied by a corresponding land policy. Ermolov believed that only by depriving the Chechens of agricultural land and pastures could they be forced into submission.[12]

The enemy is absolutely dependent on his crops – wrote Ermolov – let the standing corn be destroyed each autumn as it ripens and in five years they will be starved into submission.[13]

At the same time his policy was to ensure that the newly-acquired lands were resettled with loyal Cossacks, who would form a wedge between the troublesome Chechen and Qumyq tribes and secure Russian military communications.[14] The gradual occupation of hostile territory by means of forts and Cossack settlements was designed to bring about the gradual exhaustion of the mountain peoples.

8 Baddeley, 1908, p. 147.

9 *AKAK*, vol. VI, part. II, p. 498.

10 On the construction of Groznaya and the events which accompanied it, see Baddeley, 1908, pp. 106-22.

11 On the construction of Vnezapnaya, see *ibid.*, pp. 123-83.

12 *AKAK*, vol. VI, part II, p. 498.

13 As quoted in Baddeley, 1908, pp. 121-2.

14 See *ibid.*, pp. 106-7; Gammer, 1994, pp. 30-1; Ramazanov and Khadzhiev(eds), 1959, p. 25; Potto, 1901-4, vol. II, p. 83.

In 1818 Ermolov set up the system of *pristavstvo* (bailiffs). They were appointed by the Russian military administration from among the Russian military officers and the local militia. The *pristavs* were accountable only to Russians and had to comply with Russian law. The application of the Russian legal system based on serfdom, totally inadequate in the socio-economic reality of the North Caucasus, led to disruption of the traditional way of life. To uphold the imposed laws, the bailiffs had to rely exclusively on Russian military support and as such became virtual outlaws in their *tuqums.*

Ermolov built his policy on the traditional Russian premise that 'fear and greed are the two mainsprings of everything that takes place here'.[15] The construction of the second Caucasian fortification line was accompanied by regular Russian punitive expeditions, during which whole villages were destroyed and their inhabitants, including men, women and children, slaughtered.[16] At first sight these tactics might seem to have been immediately effective, but they failed in the long run.

It is a most pregnant fact that Ermolov prepared the way for Shamil...by his ruthless methods [he] aroused that fierce spirit of fanaticism and independence which alone made political union possible amongst the turbulent tribesmen of Daghestan and Tchetchnia [Chechnya].[17]

The limited application by Ermolov of traditional Russian policy aimed at the co-opting of the local elite also failed to produce any positive results. With no traditional hereditary elite, Ermolov failed to create a buffer between the Russians and the local peoples (as was the case in Daghestan).

The extent to which Russian carrot and stick policy failed to subdue the North Caucasus, especially Chechnya, was clearly revealed in the Greater Chechnya revolt of 1825-6. Organised within the Naqshbandi ideological framework it was led by a traditional Chechen secular leader, Beybulat Taymi.

Beybulat Taymi[18]

Beybulat Taymi was born in 1779[19] to the family of a Chechen craftsman in the village of Bilty (close to Nozhay-yurt) in the Biltoy *teip* of the Nohchmahkoy *tuqum.*[20] By his courage and daring raids against the

[15] Titsianov to the Emperor, as quoted in Baddeley, 1908, p. 65; also see Gammer, 1994, p. 35.

[16] For a description of some of these campaigns, see Baddeley, 1908, pp. 130-2 as quoted from Potto; Volkonskiy, 1886, vol. X, pp. 40-1; Dubrovin, 1890-3, vol. VI, p. 302.

[17] Baddeley, 1908, p. 138.

[18] On Beybulat see Kolosov, 1991; Serov, 1927, pp. 125-39; Volkonskiy, 1886, vol. X pp. 42-220.

[19] Serov, 1927, p. 127; Kolosov, 1991, p. 7.

[20] Kolosov, 1991, p. 7-8. According to Potto, Beybulat was born in Geldegen village near Shali in a rich family. Potto, 1901-4, vol. III, part. I, p. 299.

Russian and Cossack settlements,[21] as well as his qualities as a statesmen, Beybulat rose to a prominent position of an elder well-known both among the Chechens and among the Russian Caucasian administration.

His importance was recognised even by Ermolov, who met Beybulat shortly after his arrival to the Caucasus in 1816, treated him 'with special care'[22] and offered him the rank of lieutenant with a regular salary in the hope that winning Beybulat to the Russian side would ensure peace in the whole of Chechnya.[23] Beybulat accepted the rank and salary, although his service had more symbolic meaning and amounted to little more than abstaining from active participation in anti-Russian military activities.[24]

The truce between Beybulat and the Russians was short lived. Following the construction of Groznaya and Russian punitive expeditions against the Chechen villages, Beybulat escaped into the mountains and assumed the leadership of numerous Chechen raids across the Russian military line.

However daring these raids were, they had little chance of success against the stronger, better organised and better equipped Russian army. In 1822 Beybulat once again entered into negotiations with the Russian Command to solicit the renewal of peace. This time he met Major-General N.V. Grekov,[25] the head of the left flank of the Caucasian line. 'Heart and soul devoted to carrying out Ermolov's policy and orders',[26] Grekov was notorious among the Chechens for his cruelty, brutality and vanity. He treated the Chechens with the utmost contempt and 'in his speech as well as in official papers had no other name for them than rascals, and [called] any of their representatives either robber or cheat'.[27] His treatment of Beybulat was no different. Offended and humiliated by a cold and rude welcome received from Grekov on his arrival in Groznaya, Beybulat left the Russian fortress with no reconciliation achieved.

Russian historians have tended to see this incident as the sole reason for the future uprising led by Beybulat.

Who would have thought that this trivial incident could become the basis and the

---

[21] On Beybulat's early raids across the Russian military line, see Kolosov, 1991, pp. 9-11; *AKAK*, vol. I, p. 752; Serov, 1927, p. 128.

[22] Potto, 1901-4, vol. III, part I, p. 299.

[23] See, for example, *AKAK*, vol. IV, p. 905.

[24] Especially after the foundation of Groznaya fortress, when Beybulat escaped into the mountains and led numerous raids against the Russians. For more on the anti-Russian activities of Beybulat, see Potto, 1901-4, vol. III, part I, p. 350; *TsGVIA*, fond 482, delo 152, list 3-14, 127-8.

[25] On his biography, see Volkonskiy, 1886, vol. X, pp. 42-3.

[26] Baddeley, 1908, p. 147.

[27] Volkonskiy, 1886, vol. X, p. 44. The translation is based on Gammer, 1994, pp. 35-6.

origin of our war with the Chechens which for so many years exhausted our means and forces.[28]

Hardly a 'sole' or even a 'major' reason for the uprising, the meeting between Grekov and Beybulat is indicative of the treatment the local people, even the most influential of them, received from the Russian military administration. It is this treatment coupled with other manifestations of Russian policy that in the end accounted for the Chechen resistance.

The ideological premises of the revolt

Soon after his ill-fated meeting with Grekov, Beybulat went to Kurah, to visit Muhammad al-Yaraghi.[29] It is not clear whether Beybulat sought to be initiated into the Naqshbandi order or not, but he apparently invited one of the Daghestan Naqshbandi adepts, Mullah Muhammad al-Quduqli, to come to Chechnya.[30] The latter arrived in Chechnya shortly afterwards and settled in Mayurtup village,[31] where he established himself as a pious and learned scholar.

The mullah behaved like an important, well established [man], he prayed constantly and soon earned the respect of all citizens in the *aul*, who...started to follow him everywhere.[...] Soon the mullah became accepted [by the Chechens] and started to visit the mosque [regularly]. Little by little the people heard such truths from the Qur'an as they had never heard before...while the mullah himself inspired pious reverence.[32]

Muhammad al-Quduqli was the first Daghestani Naqshbandi to settle in Chechnya and although we do not have any direct mention of him recruiting adepts into the *tariqa* it seems likely that he contributed to the establishment of the Naqshbandi network there.[33]

The fame of Muhammad al-Quduqli quickly spread far beyond Mayurtup and many visitors from the neighbouring villages came to see and hear him. His message was in essence similar to that preached by Muhammad al-Yaraghi but in Chechnya it acquired some local colouring. Unlike the chief *murshid*, Muhammad al-Quduqli – now generally known as Muhammad al-Mayurtupi – promised the appearance of Imam Haris who would 'win back from the Russians all the lands which belonged to

---

[28] *Ibid.*, pp. 44-5.

[29] *Ibid.*, p. 46.

[30] Potto, 1901-4, vol. III, part I, p. 316; Volkonskiy, 1886, vol. X, p. 47.

[31] After which he became generally known in Russian historiography as Muhammad Mayurtupskiy, i.e. Muhammad from Mayurtup.

[32] Volkonskiy, 1886, vol. X, p. 47.

[33] The Chechen Naqshbandis trace their lineage through the sheikhs who arrived to the area in the early 1830s and were associated with Ghazi Muhammad, the first Daghestani imam. See below.

the Muslims and denounce the hateful rule of the *gyaurs* [infidels]. Meanwhile true believers were to pray while awaiting the arrival of this prophet at any time and then rebel at his first call.'[34] Reminiscent of the stories of the expected return of Imam Mansour, these appeals were readily accepted by the Chechens.

The rumours started to spread that the Prophet Muhammad himself had sent the Chechens an imam to liberate them from Russian rule. Stories were told throughout Chechnya that the imam could fly on his *burka* (sheepskin cloak), walk above the trees, be below grass, walk over the water as if it was ground; that he cast spells on the Russian bayonets and cannons which, if they fired at all, would bring no harm to the true believers, and only the sinful Chechens, i.e. those who did not believe in the imam's holiness, would be harmed by them.[35]

By the summer of 1824 the whole of Chechnya was aroused, and numerous crowds arrived in Mayurtup in order to witness the appearance of the imam. Most Chechen mullahs took the side of Muhammad al-Quduqli and repeated his preaching to the people in their *tuqums* urging them to prepare for the appearance of the imam. The scene was set for the appearance of an imam and one day after a communal prayer Muhammad al-Quduqli announced that he had seen a vision. In it, he had been instructed to gather forty-five of the most pious men, slaughter a red bull and two black sheep, after which the imam would appear. The following day the most respected of the Chechen elders and mullahs met in a clearing in the Mayurtup forest near the village and after a long prayer slaughtered the animals. Indeed, in the dusk of the descending evening a man in white clothes appeared and without uttering a word stood in front of the amazed gathering. When the elders and mullahs resumed praying, the new imam 'miraculously' disappeared. Muhammad al-Quduqli addressed the gathering with a speech in which he announced that the imam had appeared only due to his prayers, and in order to assure the people of the truth of his words – and that he would return 'when the time comes to expel the Russians'.[36]

The mysterious imam was a Chechen mullah Howk [Avko or Auk in the Russian translation] from the Germenchuk village (the same village as Abd al-Qadir). The available sources do not reveal a great deal about him.[37] However, it seems safe to assume that he was one of the first

34 Volkonskiy, 1886, vol. X, p. 47.

35 Dubrovin, 1890-1, vol. VI, p. 524; Volkonskiy, 1886, vol. X, pp. 49-51.

36 Potto, 1901-4, vol. III, part I, pp. 316-18; Volkonskiy, 1886, vol. X, pp. 51-2.

37 Some authors refer to him as 'God's fool'. See, e.g. Volkonskiy, 1886, vol. X, p. 73. Other authors claim that he was a respected mullah, (Musaev as quoted in Kolosov, 1991, p. 69). Yet others refer to him as a member of a 'dervish Tulik sect, who was unlikely to be a supporter of the establishment of the shari'a'. See Kolosov, 1991, p. 69. The author, however, does not give the source of this information, which is highly doubtful.

Chechen Naqshbandi adepts, for in the coming years he acted as a
lieutenant of the Daghestani Naqshbandi imams.[38] Furthermore, the very
mode of Howk's actions reveal a common Naqshbandi pattern. He went
into seclusion, fasted and prayed asking God to reveal His will to him.
After secluding himself for a few days, Howk announced that he had
a Divine Revelation and that his decisions were inspired by God.[39]

Following his first appearance as an imam in the Mayurtup forest,
Howk disappears from the political scene for some time and we next
hear of him only in the context of the military campaigns of the winter
of 1825-6. The man who became the ideological leader of the Chechen
revolt at the time it started in May 1825 was not Howk, but Muhammad
al-Quduqli himself.[40]

In May 1825, having secured the alliance of most *tuqums* in Greater
Chechnya, some support of the Avar, Andi and Aukh *jama'ats* and
won over few Ingush and Kabardian leaders, Beybulat called for people
to come and witness the appearance of the imam. On 24 May 1825
numerous crowds gathered in Mayurtup in anticipation of a miracle.

From the early morning the whole of Mayurtup was crowded with thousands of
people...agitated and awaiting a miracle [they] surrounded the mosque, the win-
dows and doors of which were locked. From inside the mosque the gathering could
just catch the sound of a prayer being sung...then suddenly the singing stopped,
the doors burst wide open with a loud sound and a solemn procession came out.
Here was the future imam, Mullah Muhammad dressed all in the white with a
green turban on his head, accompanied by other mullahs and *qadis*. Beybulat
followed them under three banners with a party of his followers closing the
procession.[41]

The gathering followed the procession until they reached the very place
in the Mayurtup forest where a year earlier Howk had appeared as
imam. There, Muhammad al-Quduqli al-Mayurtupi stepped forward and
announced that he had had a revelation in which God had appointed
him as imam. People were startled but Beybulat came forward and
assured the gathering that he had personally seen the sign of God's
blessing Muhammad al-Quduqli, and gave an oath on the Qur'an that
his words were true.

A few days later, on 29 May 1825 the Chechen elders and mullahs

---

[38] Howk acted as a lieutenant of Ghazi Muhammad, the first Daghestani imam, as well
as assisting Ghazi Muhammad's emissars in Chechnya. See Volkonskiy, 1888, vol. X,
p. 61; Kolosov, 1991, pp. 140-1.

[39] Volkonskiy, 1886, vol. X, p. 197. Though, this account refers to a later period in
Howk's activities in 1826.

[40] This is one of the least clear episodes in the whole history of the Chechen uprising
with almost no information available to elucidate relations between Howk, Muhammad
al-Quduqli and Beybulat.

[41] Potto, 1901-4, vol. III, part I, pp. 322-3.

as well as the Naqshbandi sheikhs from Daghestan, among whom, allegedly, was Muhammad al-Yaraghi himself, held another meeting.[42]

According to a description given in Russian sources, the meeting started with Beybulat's speech in which he appealed to the gathering to 'stop enmity amongst themselves, change their way of life, follow the shari'a, stop stealing and unite against the Russians' and assured them that 'God had sent them an imam who would purify people from their sins and free them from their enemies'.[43] Following Beybulat, a Daghestani *'alim* (allegedly Muhammad al-Yaraghi) appealed to the gathering in support of Muhammad al-Quduqli's claim to the imam's title and called the people to unite under his banner.[44]

The majority of the Chechen elders present at the meeting recognised Muhammad al-Quduqli al-Mayurtupi as an imam and accepted Beybulat as the military leader. As a token of their loyalty they elected *turqkhs*[45] who were made directly responsible to Muhammad al-Quduqli and Beybulat. The *turqkhs* were elected from among the most respected members of the *tuqums* as supervisors of people's behaviour and to guarantee that they followed the shari'a.[46]

The *turqkhs*, initially made responsible to the leaders of the revolt, in the end turned out to be protectors of the people in their *tuqums*. For when the interests of the supreme leaders clashed with those of the people, the *turqkhs* denounced their authority and Beybulat had to resort to persuasion or even force.[47] His methods were not always successful and his leadership was accepted only as he commanded the general respect of the people.

Despite these pitfalls *turqkhs* formed the first semi-centralised institution through which Beybulat and Muhammad al-Quduqli could channel their authority and unite various Chechen *tuqums* for common action. Furthermore, the *turqkhs* formed the nucleus of Beybulat's people's guard, which was the first attempt to create a regular army.

The Russian military administration received regular and generally accurate information on the developments which were taking place in Chechnya. Convinced however that the severe punishment which was often inflicted on insubordinate villages would prevent any further anti-Russian uprising,[48] both Grekov and Ermolov disregarded the information

---

[42] Volkonskiy, 1886, vol. X, p. 75-6.

[43] *Ibid.*, p. 78.

[44] *Idem.*

[45] The *turqkh* in Chechen *tuqums* traditionally played the role of public crier (Daghestani equivalent of a *ma'dhun*). Later, with the establishment of a comprehensive Sufi network, the name *turqkh* came to mean *khalifa*, a head of a village or a quarter Sufi organisation.

[46] Volkonskiy, 1886, vol. X, pp. 79-80.

[47] Kolosov, 1991, p. 87.

[48] For the reports on the events in Chechnya sent by Musa Khosaev to Grekov and the

as implausible and insignificant. The local people saw in the Russian inaction the manifestation of Divine interference, which had blinded the Russians and protected Beybulat and the imams.[49] The people came to believe that the imam's spells had already started to work and that those who joined him would not even have to fight the Russian army, which would be expelled from the Caucasus by the imam's prayers alone.

The beginning of the Greater Chechnya revolt[50]

In early July 1825 Beybulat, with 2,000 armed followers, arrived in Greater Chechnya. There he was accepted by the two large Chechen villages – Shali and Ataghi – which had up till then recognised the Russian rule. Alerted by the news, Grekov undertook a march towards Ataghi village. However, Beybulat avoided direct clashes with the Russians and retreated into the mountains before Grekov entered the village. Having failed to find Beybulat in Ataghi, Grekov once again misinterpreted Beybulat's actions as a sign that the Chechens had been cowed into submission and would not dare to oppose the Russians again. Thus, he did not attempt to pursue Beybulat and his army and contented himself with taking a renewed oath of loyalty to the tsar from the people of Ataghi.[51]

Rather than serving as a warning signal, as Grekov intended his campaign to be, it confirmed people in their superstitious belief that the imam and his party were protected by God who had once again diverted any danger from them and prevented the Russians from pursuing and destroying them. This belief was further strengthened by the decisive success of Beybulat in storming and destroying the Russian garrison of a significant Russian fortification at Amir Hajji-yurt on the night of 7-8 July 1825.[52]

The devastating blow dealt by Beybulat to the Russians at Amir Hajji-yurt finally alerted the latter to the full potential of the revolt. The Russians themselves recognised that their awareness had come too late to stop the revolt from spreading. In his report Ermolov complained that this failure 'multiplied greatly the number of Beybulat's supporters and those who believed in the false prophet [i.e. Muhammad al-Mayurtupi

---

attitude of the latter towards them, see Volkonskiy, 1886, vol. X, pp. 66-7, 71, 80-9.

[49] According to some sources, Beybulat and Muhammad al-Mayurtupi were joined by Howk as a second imam, who accompanied them in Lesser Chechnya. *Ibid.*, p. 86.

[50] On the military history of the Chechen revolt, see *AKAK*, vol. VI, part I, pp. 508-16; Potto, 1901-4, vol. III, part 2, pp. 207-28; Volkonskiy, 1886, vol X, pp. 52-220; Kolosov, 1991, pp. 66-104.

[51] See Potto, 1901-4, vol. II, part II, pp. 324-6.

[52] *Ibid.*, pp. 329-30; Volkonskiy, 1886, vol. X, p. 101-4; *TsGVIA*, fond 482, delo 152, list 19.

– A. Z.]'[53] while Grekov grieved that 'this most unhappy and unexpected event [i.e. the Russian defeat at Amir Adji Yurt – A. Z.] changed the whole course of events'.[54]

The results of Beybulat's success were quick to follow. By July 1825 the number of his followers had increased to 4,000 and, apart from the Chechens from both Lesser and Greater Chechnya, included some Avar, Qumyq, Ingush and even Osset followers.

On 16 July 1825 Beybulat laid siege to another Russian fort at Gerzel-*aul*, which was relieved only after Grekov and Lisanevich[55] brought in a considerable force.[56] To 'punish' the rebels, Lisanevich summoned 318 elders to Gerzel-*aul*. When they arrived on 18 July 1825, he addressed them in a humiliating speech in which he insulted and abused them in their own language.

Having finished his speech, Lisanevich started to call out the elders one by one, ordering his guards to seize their daggers. Surrendering one's dagger was seen in the Caucasus as the worst kind of humiliation to a man's honour and while the first two elders allowed themselves to be disarmed, the third, a certain Mullah Uchar Hajji, refused to do so. Outraged, Grekov struck the man in the face and ordered one of his soldiers to disarm him. However, no sooner had the latter approached than Uchar Hajji stabbed first Lisanevich and then Grekov and several other Russian officers before falling dead under the Russian bullets.[57]

This triggered hand-to-hand fighting, in the course of which almost the entire delegation of the Aqsay elders was slaughtered.[58] However, the Russians could hardly claim a victory. In this incident both Grekov and Lisanevich were killed, the first died instantly, the second shortly afterwards, thus leaving the Caucasian line leaderless.

The party which benefited from the incident at Gerzel-*aul* most was that of Beybulat. Summoned by the Aqsay people he returned as a victor and destroyed the houses of those known for their collaboration with the Russians.[59]

On hearing the news, Ermolov mobilised all available resources from both the North Caucasus and Transcaucasus and arrived in Chechnya

53 Potto, 1901-4, vol. III, part II, p. 330.

54 *Ibid.*

55 Lisanevich was Grekov's immediate superior and the commander of the Caucasian line.

56 On the siege of Gerzel-*aul* see *TsGVIA*, fond 482, delo 152, list 2-4; Volkonskiy, 1886, vol. X, pp. 113-16, Potto, 1901-4, vol. III, part II, pp. 330-1.

57 Volkonskiy, 1886, vol. X, pp. 117-18.

58 *TsGVIA*, fond 482, delo 152, list 27-28; Volkonskiy, 1886, vol. X, pp. 117-18; Potto, 1901-4, vol. III, part II, pp. 355-6.

59 In his campaign to Aqsay, Beybulat was accompanied by both Muhammad al-Quduqli and Howk. However, it is not clear in what capacity Howk participated in the campaign and what the relationship was between him and Muhammad al-Quduqli.

to lead in person the Russian campaign against Beybulat and his supporters.[60] It took him a whole year of enormous efforts to quell the Chechen
revolt, during which Ermolov 'punished rebellious Chechens, burning
their villages, destroying their forests, beating them in skirmishes that
never developed into battles, and occasionally even seeking to win them
over by an unwonted display of clemency'.[61] However, it appears that
the revolt died out in the second-half of 1826 not so much because of
Ermolov's persistent campaigns, but due to the mounting conflicts between its leaders which caused it to collapse from within.

In 1825 during Beybulat's campaign against Gerzel-*aul*, he was accompanied both by Howk and Muhammad al-Quduqli. We have little
information on the relationship between the two, but apparently it brought
about certain tensions in the leadership. In August 1825 the conflict between
Beybulat and 'his' two imams on how best to conduct the revolt first
became apparent.[62] This tension further increased after a number of
Russian victories considerably undermined the unity of the leadership
of the revolt and all those who took part in it.[63]

Towards the end of 1826 the revolt was finally broken by its internal
contradictions and by military effort. 'To outward appearance his
[Ermolov's] success was complete. There was once more peace on the
Line, and for a time no more was heard of the Ghazavat.'[64]

Closer examination, however, reveals that this was not the 'decisive'
victory the Russians needed to prevent the anti-Russian movement from
spreading. Not one of the leaders of the revolt was captured: Beybulat
left Chechnya until times improved;[65] both Muhammad al-Quduqli and
Howk stayed in Chechnya and continued their religious preaching. Furthermore, as the first test of the utility of Naqshbandi ideology in the
anti-Russian resistance, the Chechen revolt set an example and inspired
the activation of 'political' Naqshbandiyya in neighbouring Daghestan.

The aftermath

No sooner had the Greater Chechnya revolt died out than the Russians
were presented with a new challenge. On 31 July 1826 Abbas Mirza

[60] Ermolov's task was made all the more difficult due to the renewed disturbances in
Kabarda and northern Tabarsaran.

[61] Baddeley, 1908, p. 153.

[62] According to Kolosov, Beybulat insisted that all the people should leave their houses
and escape into the mountains, to fight the Russians from there, while both Muhammad
al-Mayurtupi and Howk supported the demands of the people to stay in their villages
and fight the Russians only when the latter advance against them. Kolosov, 1991,
p. 78.

[63] Potto, 1901-4, vol. III, part II, p. 340.

[64] Baddeley, 1908, p. 153.

[65] He returned in 1829, but did not participate in any further military actions.

(the Qajar ruler) crossed the border established between Russia and Persia by the treaty of Gulistan in 1813 and started a new Russo-Persian war. This coincided with the unexpected death of Alexander I and the succession to the throne of Nicholas I. The changes in St. Petersburg were immediately felt in the Caucasus. Having lost in Alexander I his imperial protector and fallen out of favour with Nicholas I, Ermolov was replaced by Count (later Prince) Paskevich,[66] the protégé of the new emperor,[67] and left the Caucasus on 9 April 1827.

Not unexpectedly, the new commander laid all the blame for the Russian failures in the Caucasus on the tactics of his predecessor and tried to disengage from them. Having settled the dispute with Persia by signing the Peace Treaty of Turkmanchay 1828,[68] Paskevich set out to revise Russian policy in the area.[69] First he had to acquaint himself with the area and its people, of which he knew but little. While Paskevich occupied himself with this task, the North Caucasus remained remarkably calm with neither the Russians nor the mountain peoples attempting any serious military actions. This, however, was merely the calm before the storm, which broke out in 1830.

In Chechnya the Naqshbandiyya first spread in early 1820s in the form of ideas rather than as an institution. Despite the large number of sympathisers who readily accepted the political message of the Naqshbandi teaching, the order only institutionalised its popular following by establishing lodges and recruiting *murids* almost a decade later. The lack of established centres of Muslim learning and of well-educated Muslim clerics who had been the main vehicles for the Naqshbandiyya's proliferation in Daghestan accounted for most of this time-lag. Notwithstanding the lack of institutional support, it was in Chechnya that the forcefulness of the Naqshbandiyya's political appeal was revealed to its full extent for the first time.

The Great Chechnya revolt had been brewing for a number of years before it finally broke out in 1825. The significance of this uprising lay in the fact that the individual and spontaneous attacks by various Chechen war parties against the Russian military lines eventually turned into an all-out war between the majority of the Chechen tribes and the

---

[66] On his bibliography and activities in the Caucasus, see Shcherbakov, 1888-1904, vols II-III.

[67] Paskevich first arrived in the Caucasus to take command of the forces at the front. Paskevich's powers duplicated those of Ermolov and after half-a-year of intrigues and quarrels, Ermolov wrote the Emperor a letter in which he tendered his resignation. In fact, even before the letter arrived in St. Petersburg, Nicholas I gave his instructions concerning Ermolov's resignation. Volkonskiy, 1887, vol. XI, pp. 7-9, 14-20, 51-3.

[68] The treaty of Turkmanchay established the borders between the two countries which have remained largely unaltered up to the present day.

[69] On Paskevich and his strategy in the North Caucasus, see Gammer, 1992, pp. 49-50, 54.

Russian troops. This transformation was made possible largely by the ideological motivation and blessing provided by the Naqshbandiyya.

However, the brotherhood's involvement in the uprising was mostly symbolic for it was confined to providing an additional but by no means the most important source of legitimation for its leaders. The limits of Naqshbandi influence and that of Islam as a universally acceptable source of legitimacy and power were graphically revealed in the supremacy of the traditional secular leader, Beybulat, over the imams. Furthermore, the lack of developed Naqshbandi institutions resulted in the emergence of two religious leaders. The poorly educated Howk represented 'popular' Islam and rose to the rank of imam on the back of his alleged ability to perform miracles and to receive inspiration directly from God. Muhammad al-Quduqli owed his status to his reputation as a learned Daghestani scholar and to his Naqshbandi affiliation and training. Despite the growing influence of Islam as an important source of legitimacy, both imams had to be endorsed by the traditional tribal institution of the council of elders in order to be accepted by the Chechens at large.

Beybulat was the first Chechen leader to perceive the need to introduce some degree of centralisation and to attempt to achieve it by appointing *turqkhs* as agents of the 'central authority'. Although significant as a reflection of a centralising tendency that began to emerge in the region, Beybulat's efforts had limited success. On the one hand, his and the imams' leadership credentials were closely linked to the outcome of their military campaigns. On the other hand, when conflict arose between central authority and various tribes and regions, the *turqkhs* tended to side with their respective clans and tribes to the detriment of the leaders of the revolt.

Beybulat's movement was a transitional phenomenon that combined the traditional forms of political activity and the newly emerging pattern of mass, popular religious movement. However, the upsurge of religious sentiment inspired by Naqshbandi teaching had yet to be translated into the necessary institutional allegiances for it to be able to overcome fragmentation and regionalism and to support a rising trend towards centralisation. Only when the Naqshbandiyya established itself as a network of lodges and devoted *tariqa* followers did it become possible for this tendency to materialise.

18

GHAZI MUHAMMAD: THE FIRST DAGHESTANI IMAM AND THE BEGINNING OF GHAZAVAT[1]

In the few years during which Russian attention was diverted from Daghestan – first by Chechnya and later by the renewed hostilities with Persia and Ottoman Turkey – the Naqshbandi order put down deep roots in the area and developed an elaborate network of *tariqa* adepts and clients.[2]

With the emigration of Muhammad al-Yaraghi, and some time later, Jamal al-Din al-Ghazi-Ghumuqi from the khanate of Kurah and Ghazi-Ghumuq, the centre of Naqshbandi activities shifted from the Russian-controlled territories to the independent rural communes of mountain Daghestan, which had largely remained outside Russian control. In the late 1820s Gimrah village in the Koysubu (otherwise knows as Hindal) *jama'at* confederation emerged as one of the most important Naqshbandi centres of Inner Daghestan.

The establishment of Gimrah as an important Naqshbandi centre was linked to the activities of Mullah Muhammad, generally known as Ghazi Muhammad (Kazi Mulla in the Russian sources). Ghazi Muhammad transformed the Naqshbandi order in the North Caucasus by bridging the gap between the 'political' and 'spiritual' Naqshbandiyya and merging the two into a religious-political movement that dominated the North Caucasus for over thirty years.

---

[1] This chapter is based on the following sources: unpublished documents in *RF IIYaL Dag*, fond 7; *TsGVIA*, fond VUA; *TsGA GSSR*, fond, 1987; published documents in *AKAK*; Ramazanov and Khadzhiev (eds) 1959; al-Qarakhi, 1946, pp. 36-56; Hajji Ali, 1873, pp. 11-12; Zamir Ali, 1990; Genichutlinskiy (Genichutli), 1992, pp. 57-66; Grezhegorzhevskiy, 1842, no. XI, pp. 508-15; Dubrovin, 1890, no. 10, pp. 197-240; 'Dva Imama ili Istreblenie Doma Avarskogo', 1915, no. 1, pp. 116-46; Okolnichiy, 1859, No. 1; Prushanovskiy, 1847, pp. 22-39; Prushanovskiy, 1902; Przhevlatskiy, 1864, pp. 155-78; T., 'Vospominaniya o Kavkaze i Gruzii,' 1869; Dubrovin, 1891, no.3; Neverovskiy, 1847(a), pp. 1-36.

[2] The Naqshbandi clients are those who accept formal affiliation with the *tariqa* but, unlike adepts, they did not pursue religious education or follow the mystical path. Their initiation was limited to adopting *tauba* and accepting the patronage of one of the Naqshbandi sheikhs.

Ghazi-Muhammad: his life and education

Ghazi Muhammad ibn Isma'il al-Gimrawi was born some time in the early 1790s[3] in the village of Gimrah.[4] At the age of ten he was sent to Karanay village in the *shamkhalat* to study Arabic and the Qur'an and; once his initial training was complete, he visited other Daghestani centres of learning. There, in the established pattern of the time, he studied with various Daghestani *'ulama*. One of Ghazi Muhammad's teachers who left a deep impression on him was Sayyid al-Harakani, the chief *qadi* of Harakan and one of the most respected and prominent *'alims* in Daghestan. Allegedly Ghazi Muhammad was at first suspicious of the Naqshbandis and their teaching due to his teacher's hostility towards the order. However, he could not resist the temptation to see the famous Naqshbandi sheikhs and some time in 1825 went to Ghazi-Ghumuq.

It has been said that he intended to conceal his identity and only listen to Jamal al-Din's preaching, without initiation into the order. However he was so impressed by the sanctity and knowledge of the sheikh, that he accepted the *tariqa* and brought one of his close friends, Shamil, who was later to became the most famous Daghestani imam, to his *murshid*.

The story of Ghazi Muhammad's meeting with Jamal al-Din as preserved in the Naqshbandi sources is presented as a miracle during which the future imam became awakened to the spiritual Sufi path by the greatness and sanctity of his sheikh.

Ghazi Muhammad wanted first to try [Jamal al-Din] and discover whether he was indeed a sheikh who could gain insight into secrets as [people] ascribed to him. With this aim he went to Kumukh [Ghazi-Ghumuq] with a companion of his and when he approached [the house of Jamal al-Din] told his companion to enter [the house] first and lagged behind. Then he entered a secluded room [of Jamal al-Din]...he sat silently by the door to discover whether [Jamal al-Din] indeed could recognise the name and kin of someone completely unknown to him. When Ghazi Muhammad took his seat at the door, [Jamal al-Din] said: '*Salam 'aleikum*, Ghazi Muhammad, take a seat close to me, that seat [by the door – A.Z.] is not befitting for you.' Surprised Ghazi Muhammad asked him 'How do you know that I am Ghazi Muhammad? You did not know me before and you did not hear of me before.' 'Is it not said in the Book "Beware of the insight of a devoted slave: he looks through [things] by Divine light." Or do you doubt that I am a devoted

---

[3] The dates mentioned in most of the sources are 1793 and 1795, see, for example, Okolnichiy, 1859, no. 1, p. 115; *RF IIYaL*, fond 7, opis' 1, delo 236, list 31. Other authors place his birth in a much earlier period. Hajji Ali claimed that at the time of his death in 1832 Ghazi Muhammad was aged seventy-five, which dates his birth back to 1757. Hajji Ali, 1990, pp. 11-12. This version, however, seems much less plausible than the first.

[4] Unfortunately nothing is known about his natal family. It is likely that it was a common family of the Avar uzden.

slave?'[...] Then Ghazi Muhammad came to [Jamal al-Din] for the second time with Shamil and they accepted the *tariqa* from him.[5]

From a suspicious opponent of the Naqshbandis, Ghazi Muhammad in a short span of time became transformed into one of the order's most devoted followers, who fully devoted himself to the pursuit of the Sufi path, 'left all people and engaged in self-purification, ate but little, exceeded in fasting and hardly spoke [to anyone]'.[6]

On completing his religious training at the hands of Jamal al-Din al-Ghazi-Ghumuqi, Ghazi Muhammad was taken by his teacher to Muhammad al-Yaraghi.[7] In prevalent Khalidi fashion the latter gave the final training to Ghazi Muhammad and granted him the title of sheikh with the right and obligation to initiate *murids* into the *tariqa*.[8] Furthermore, Muhammad al-Yaraghi married Ghazi Muhammad to his daughter as a sign of his particular favour. The Naqshbandi tradition maintains that Muhammad al-Yaraghi was so impressed with the knowledge and piety of Ghazi Muhammad that he praised him as the one whose 'vision penetrates the future and everything reveals itself to him except only for the circumstances of the (God's) throne (*al-'arsh*)'.[9]

In early 1827 following his meeting with Muhammad al-Yaraghi, Ghazi Muhammad returned to his native Gimrah, where he established himself as a sheikh in his own right and started to take up *murids*, who practised *rabita* with him.[10]

The fame of Ghazi Muhammad spread quickly throughout his native Koysubu *jama'at* confederation, and beyond, and won him the respect of both common people and established religious authorities. According to the Naqshbandi sources he was generally seen as a 'saint' who had reached the heights of spiritual knowledge. Thus, a respected *'alim*, Hajji al-Uruti, allegedly said that, 'If I and Ghazi Muhammad lived before the Prophet Muhammad, I would have said that he [Ghazi Muhammad] was a prophet'.[11] According to yet another story preserved by the Naqshbandi tradition, a certain sheikh who lived near the Prophet's

---

5 Abdurakhman (Sayyid Abdurahman), 1869, pp. 3-4.

6 Genichutlinskiy (Genichutli), 1992, p. 60.

7 According to Genichutlinskiy, 1992, p. 60, Ghazi Muhammad received his training from Muhammad al-Yaraghi. This version, however, does not agree with all other available sources which clearly point to Jamal al-Din as Ghazi Muhammad's sheikh and *murshid*. The reference to Muhammad al-Yaraghi can, perhaps, be explained by the final stage of spiritual training that Ghazi Muhammad received from him.

8 Zamir Ali, 1990, p. 35.

9 al-Qarakhi, 1946, p. 51.

10 See Volkonskiy, 1888, vol. XII, p. 62.

11 Genichutlinskiy (Genichutli), 1992, p. 59.

grave in Madina, saw in a dream Ghazi Muhammad sitting next to the Prophet Muhammad.[12]

Promoted to a rank immediately below the prophet, Ghazi Muhammad was referred to by most of his followers as *mujaddid al-din* (renovator of the faith). Although there is no elaboration in the North Caucasian Naqshbandi literature on the concept of *tajdid* and *mujaddid*, it clearly bears strong resemblance to the tradition laid down by Ahmad al-Sirhindi.[13]

Teaching of Ghazi Muhammad[14]

In his teaching Ghazi Muhammad combined the individual need to purify the soul with the Khalidi doctrine according to which one cannot attain salvation in an unjust society governed by any legislation other than the *shari'a*.

In the atmosphere that prevailed in the nineteenth-century North Caucasus when 'different Daghestani rulers, whether out of weakness of character, despair or other reasons became engrossed in drinking, gambling and in some cases, debauchery',[15] Ghazi Muhammad saw the *shari'a* as the only guarantee against the corrosion of North Caucasian society by Russian colonial rule. From the early days of his sheikhdom, Ghazi Muhammad was preoccupied with the state of Islam and the Muslim *umma* in the North Caucasus and saw his main task as ensuring the implementation of the *shari'a* in both the public and private life of the mountain peoples.

He ascribed the North Caucasian peoples' loss of independence not to Russian military might but to corruption of the *shari'a* laws which had plunged Daghestan into a state of religious decline and internal discord. In this light he called upon Muslims to replace the traditional *'adat* system with *shari'a*-based legislation.

Be aware that in recent times people have been governed [according to] the customs [*'adat*] of their ancestors. They promoted them to the rank of religious obligation and preferred them to the Qur'an and Sunna. And by not renouncing the former [i.e. the customs] they [the people] renounced the latter [i.e. the Qur'an and Sunna]... I swear by God this straying from the righteous path is most obvious and their blasphemy has been revealed. They preferred their ancestors to God and this is similar to what has happened to other communities [*umam*] and [their behaviour] resembles the vanity of those who had perished [in disbelief] because

---

[12] al-Qarakhi, 1946, p. 51.

[13] See Chapter 9 above.

[14] This section is based largely on the manuscript by Ghazi Muhammad, *Bahir al-Burhan li-'Irtidat 'Urafa Daghestan* (hereafter, *Bahir al-Burhan...*), copy from the *RF IIYaL*, Mahachqala.

[15] Gammer, 1994, pp. 41-2.

of their worship of the Calf[16] and the Cross[17] and the Messiah.[18]

Applying the Khalidi teaching that the righteousness of the Muslim community lies in the hands of its rulers, Ghazi Muhammad laid the main blame for the internal decline and political weakness of the North Caucasian Muslim community on the local secular and religious authorities – elders, *qadis*, mullahs and *'ulama* – whom he accused of self-interest and held responsible for the internal disarray in the North Caucasus.

In this [i.e. blasphemy] [the people] are supported by those whom they call 'learned men', who not only support but lead them in this [blasphemy]... Those who have reached a position of leadership and pre-eminence...boast as if they were the greatest of all the kings and there is no other way for them to leadership except by skilfully imposing the customary law (*'urf*). [And they rule the following way], two people lodge their claims with them and they both try hard to observe the conditions of the legal procedure according to their incessant and insufficiently supported customary law (*'urf*. And...they declare as innocent or guilty whomever they want – and often heated quarrels and disputes occur between them and they shout at each other...and part without reaching a solution. Then they meet for a second and third time...for a year or two and it goes endlessly... And one [judge] takes bribes from one party and another one from the other party, or sometimes one and the same judge takes bribes from both of them. And both sides believe that they have won the case. And when someone tells them to end this...and refers to God's revelation and to His Prophet, they ridicule him and mock him...,' and say, 'If we follow God's revelation and His Prophet...the way of life will go out of control'. And this disaster has already spread among all people of Daghestan.[19]

He denounced authority based on local tradition and established the *shari'a* as the sole source of the legitimation of ruler.

Those who do not govern according to the *shari'a* are indeed infidels [*kafirun*]...and sinners [*dhalimun*]...and [they are] godless [*fasiqun*]. And if [people] are to be governed by God's revelation they should not follow their [i.e. the traditional authorities'] sectarian inclinations. Beware of them, or they will turn you astray from God's revelation.[20]

Ghazi Muhammad introduced a fundamentalist understanding of the shari'a and its implementation. Among other things, he wished the fixed fine for stealing to be replaced by physical punishment. This he hoped would significantly limit the most common offences such as robbing

---

[16] In which he refers to the Jews who worshipped the Golden Calf and angered God.

[17] By which Ghazi Muhammad seems to imply the traditional Muslim view that the Christians had corrupted monotheism by venerating the Cross and treating Jesus as a living God.

[18] Ghazi-Muhammad, *Bahir al-Burhan*... pp. 1, 3.

[19] *Ibid.*, pp. 1-2.

[20] *Ibid.*, p. 4.

and stealing,[21] which led to the lengthy blood feuds involving whole clans, villages and *jama'ats.*

To prevent the erosion of Islamic values and the corruption of society by alien Russian rule, Ghazi Muhammad demanded that the people should know at least the basics of their faith and threatened to punish all those whom he found not knowing *al-Fatiha* (the first Sura of the Qur'an), *al-Tashahhud* (the formula of witnessing that there is no deity but God) and the compulsory prayers. To reinforce Islamic morals, Ghazi Muhammad demanded that people stop drinking, forbade music and dancing as well as any other public events during which men and women could mix together and obliged women to cover their faces in the streets.[22]

The teaching of Ghazi Muhammad sparked a lot of controversy. On the one hand, his challenging of centuries-long traditions and his questioning of the very legitimacy of the local secular and religious authorities incited bitter opposition from them. The latter formed a powerful camp, which included Hasan Muhammad, the chief *qadi* of his native Gimrah and Sayyid al-Harakani, his former teacher and mentor.

Among the most ardent adversaries of the Naqshbandi order was Sayyid al-Harakani, an elderly *'alim* and respected *qadi* of the powerful confederation of Akusha. One of the most learned *'ulama* in Daghestan. Sayyid al-Harakani accused Naqshbandis of creating a sectarian movement which, he argued, violated the laws of Sunni Islam.[23]

It seems, however, that the main reason for Sayyid al-Harakani's denunciation of the Naqshbandi order was its explicitly anti-Russian ideology. Having once advocated military resistance to Russian rule (1811), Sayyid al-Harakani later became convinced that any resistance to the Russians was futile and, as such, only harmful to the North Caucasian peoples. Thus, he established close links with Russian officials and became one of their most loyal supporters whom Ermolov praised as 'a sensible and fully trustworthy man'.[24] In return, Ermolov provided him with the title of a Russian officer and a good salary.[25] Sayyid al-Harakani kept his alliance with the Russians throughout the troublesome years to come and was the first to warn them of the danger presented by the new teaching.

On the other hand, in an atmosphere of despair and disillusionment, when the prestige and legitimacy of the traditional local authorities had

---

[21] On legislation on stealing property from a different society, see Chapter 6.

[22] al-Qarakhi, 1941, p. 40.

[23] Many Daghestani scholars were profoundly influenced by the ideas of Sayyid al-Yemeni, who was a strong opponent of Sufism. On Sayyid al-Yemeni's teaching in Daghestan, see Krachkovskiy, 1960.

[24] Volkonskiy, 1886, p. 26.

[25] Pogodin, 1863, p. 363.

been compromised by their association with the Russians and their failure to preserve the much cherished independence and traditional way of life, the Naqshbandi views that strict adherence to Islam could save them from 'slavery' in This World and win salvation in the Hereafter, were accepted by many North Caucasian Muslims as a divinely-inspired revelation.

Consolidation of power

The fame of Ghazi Muhammad grew rapidly and soon the people of Gimrah, other Koysubu villages, and the neighbouring Aukh and Salataw communities accepted him as their spiritual leader. Building on this success Ghazi Muhammad, accompanied by a group of his most loyal *murids*, went to Chirkah, a large, rich village on the Qumyq plain.[26] At a communal gathering, he addressed the people of Chirkah in a passionate speech, in which he reminded them of the horrors of the Day of Judgement and reproached them for their corruption of faith and un-Islamic behaviour. He urged the people of Chirkah to establish the shari'a and declare *ghazavat*.[27]

However, Ghazi Muhammad's call for *ghazavat* did not imply an immediate revolt or any anti-Russian action. Rather it was declared against those local rulers whom he held responsible for corrupting the Muslim faith. As to the relationship with the Russians, he preached the necessity of *ghazavat* against them in principle only, at least for the time being, the main obligation at that moment being repentance, acceptance of the *shari'a* and adoption of the 'truly Muslim' way of life.

The people of Chirkah accepted Ghazi Muhammad as the supreme spiritual authority, promised to cease internal disputes, stealing and drinking, and as a proof of their firm intentions, publicly destroyed all their stores of wine and spirits.[28]

This success gave Ghazi Muhammad an important base in the Qumyq lands from where his fame spread rapidly throughout the plain, and in 1829 reached Mehti Khan, the elderly *shamkhal* of Targhu who was commonly accepted as the *vali* of Daghestan.[29] The position of Mehti Khan had been significantly undermined partly by his close association with the Russians, partly by his notoriously dissolute way of life, so

[26] Dubrovin, 1890, no. 10, p. 14.

[27] The record of his public appeals, as related in the secondary sources, bears a striking similiarity to the preaching of Muhammad al-Yaraghi. In fact some Russian authors attribute one and the same speech to both of them. This is, however, hardly surprising since the two men preached similar messages.

[28] Ghazi Muhammad's visit to Chirkah is described in Bodenshtadt, 1855, p. 184; al-Qarakhi, 1946, p. 38; Dubrovin, 1891, no. 3, p. 14; Neverovskiy, 1847 (a), pp. 13-14; Prushanovskiy, 1902, p. 12; Yuryev, in *TsGVIA*, fond VUA, delo 6550, list 2-21.

[29] Volkonskiy, 1887, vol. XI, pp. 146-9.

that by 1828 many important villages, such as Erpeli, Karanay, Kazanis-cha, Buynaks and Yangi-yurt, had denounced his authority altogether.[30] Thus, he decided to invite Ghazi Muhammad to come to the *shamkhalat*, probably in the hope that association with the popular religious leader of his time would restore his lost prestige.[31] Thus, in 1829 he sent Ghazi Muhammad a letter in which he invited him to come to his capital at Piri-*aul*.

I heard you are prophesying. If that is true, come and teach me and my people the holy shari'a. And fear God if you reject my invitation. On the Judgement Day I shall point to you as the one who is responsible for my negligence.[32]

Ghazi Muhammad readily agreed and soon arrived at Piri-*aul*.[33] There he had a lengthy discussion with Mehti Khan during which he passionately spoke about the decline of faith in Daghestani and the importance of the *shari'a*. Not to arouse suspicion in Mehti Khan, who was known for his loyalty towards the Russians, Ghazi Muhammad allegedly made no mention of *ghazavat* as one of the main obligations of the *shari'a*. Mehti Khan, satisfied that the sole aim of Ghazi Muhammad was to restore morals, asked him to stay in his domain and teach his subjects the 'true spirit of Islam'.[34]

This gave Ghazi Muhammad a unique opportunity to preach and spread his teaching in the lands under direct Russian control. Moreover, soon after Ghazi Muhammad's arrival in Piri-*aul*, Mehti Khan died on his way back from one of his regular visits to St. Petersburg, and Ghazi Muhammad was left free to preach in the *shamkhalat* without any constraints.

The first villages to accept Ghazi Muhammad as the foremost religious authority in their lands were the two large *auls* of the Greater and Lesser Kazanischa. Shortly afterwards other villages in the *shamkhalat* followed suit. From the Qumyq plain, the fame of Ghazi Muhammad reached the Chechen lands. The Qaytaq and Tabarsaran where Naqshbandi positions

[30] On the situation in the *shamkhalat* in 1828-9, see *AKAK*, vol. VII, pp. 509-10.

[31] The very fact that the *shamkhal* decided to invite Ghazi Muhammad to his court serves as a clear indication that at least at that point in his religious activity, the main message of Ghazi Muhammad was that of religious purification, rather than anti-Russian hostilities.

[32] As quoted from *TsGA GSSR*, fond, 1987, opis' 1, delo 323, list 13 ob. A similar account is in Neverovskiy, 1847(a), p. 14; Dubrovin, 1890, no. 10, p. 17.

[33] Some sources claim that Ghazi Muhammad came to Piri-*aul* on his own initiative. When he entered the *shamkhal*'s residence he ordered him to turn to the shari'a. Other sources claim that the *shamkhal* had sent Ghazi Muhammad several invitations before he agreed to come and did so only after his *murshid* Jamal al-Din reproached him for refusing his duty of instructing rulers onto the righteous path. Al-Qarakhi, 1946, pp. 38-9.

[34] For the account of the conversation, see *TsGA GSSR*, fond 1087, opis' 1, delo 323, list 14-14 ob.

were strong also recognised him and by late 1829 Ghazi Muhammad was accepted as supreme religious authority by the *jama'ats* along the rivers Andi and Avar Koysu, in Gumbet and Andi, the larger part of the *shamkhalat*, Koysubu and Salataw.[35]

His eloquence and the power of his words, combined with deep knowledge, made his listeners receive his teaching with enthusiasm, so that people gradually got used to the rules of the *shari'a* and stopped noticing the harshness of its demands, the men gradually gave up smoking and stopped drinking, women covered up and the young people started to behave well and stopped singing, apart from the hymn *'la ilaha illa allahu*,[36] as not befitting a true Muslim.[37]

The rise to power of the first Daghestani imam

In this atmosphere, at the end of 1829 Ghazi Muhammad summoned the Naqshbandi *qadis* and mullahs to a gathering at Gimrah. Addressing the gathering Ghazi Muhammad declared that the time had come to start a decisive campaign to insure the implementation of the *shari'a*.[38] At the same time Ghazi Muhammad declared *ghazavat* an integral part of the shari'a and the Naqshbandi *tariqa*, and promoted it to a religious obligation, more important than the *hajj*.[39]

Although Ghazi Muhammad's interpretation of the *ghazavat* still did not imply the necessity of instigating a direct confrontation with the Russians, but aimed rather at those local authorities whom he accused of the corruption of 'truly Muslim' values, many saw the declaration of *ghazavat* as dangerous and tried to oppose it. Among those Naqshbandis who were opposed to the idea was his own *murshid* Jamal al-Din al-Ghazi Ghumuqi.

Now you work to spread the *shari'a* – he warned him – and your task is to strengthen it. The Daghestanis do not reject the shari'a, moreover, they come asking you to establish it in their lands, you are well accepted and listened to. [...] If you start a war, clashes will occur among Muslims, people would think that you aspired to power and look at you with suspicion.[40]

Furthermore, Jamal al-Din opposed the very idea of direct Sufi involvement in politics, and wrote that even if the common people were prepared to fight 'let them lead the *ghazavat*, but the head and preacher of the *tariqa* should not do so'.[41]

35 *Ibid.*, list 15-15 ob., list 16 ob.
36 The formula of a *dhikr* chanted by the North Caucasian Naqshbandi adepts.
37 *Ibid.*, list 13.
38 Genichutlinskiy, 1992, p. 60.
39 Dubrovin, 1891, no. 5, p. 202; Volkonskiy, 1888, vol. XII, p. 76. Shamil's account quoted in Dnevnik Runovskogo, part II, list 115-7; Smirnov, 1963, p. 172.
40 Zamir Ali, 1990, p. 35.
41 *AKAK*, vol. XII, p. 1496.

One of the most important reasons behind Jamal al-Din's reluctance to accept Ghazi Muhammad's call for *ghazavat* was his fear that it would arouse Russian suspicions and destroy the *tariqa* and its adepts.

There were many learned men who were fully aware of the necessity of *ghazavat*, but did not do anything since they believed it was impossible. Indeed, the Qur'an itself forbids a war against a superior enemy.[42]

If you gathered an army they [the Russians] would...start an offensive against Daghestan. Do not hurry, do not act like the one who beats a beehive with his stick, raising a swarm of bees, do not disturb the Russians – otherwise they will sting Daghestan. If you fail to resist them they will destroy the Daghestani villages, destroy faith, capture men, humiliate women and children and then turn our people into soldiers. God save us from this evil.[43]

To overcome the opposition of his sheikh, Ghazi Muhammad went to Muhammad al-Yaraghi,[44] who was more sympathetic to the idea of political action. The chief *murshid* of Daghestan blessed Ghazi Muhammad for *ghazavat* and confirmed him in his title of imam. At the same time he wrote a letter to Jamal al-Din in which he asked him to stop putting obstacles in the way of Ghazi Muhammad. 'One can find many *murshids* living in seclusion, but a good military and civil leader [imam] is very rare.'[45]

The support of Muhammad al-Yaraghi changed the balance of power in favour of Ghazi Muhammad. The strict discipline of a Sufi order ensured that any internal opposition was silenced. Following the recognition of Ghazi Muhammad by the chief *murshid* of Daghestan, Jamal al-Din and other Naqshbandi sheikhs in Daghestan and Chechnya[46] accepted Ghazi Muhammad as their imam and supported his activities.[47]

In early 1830 at a second Naqshbandi gathering Ghazi Muhammad was accepted by all Naqshbandi representatives as imam and the *ghazavat* was officially declared.[48]

---

[42] *Idem.*

[43] Zamir Ali, 1990, p. 35.

[44] The meeting took place in Kurah, where Muhammad al-Yaraghi had returned in 1826 at the invitation of Aslan Khan.

[45] Dnevnik Runovskogo, chast' 2, list 122.

[46] These included Howk and Muhammad al-Quduqli, who from that time onwards acted as the imam's lieutenants. Dubrovin, 1891, no.4, p. 8.

[47] After Jamal al-Din lifted his prohibition on *ghazavat*, Shamil, who hitherto had to abstain from supporting Ghazi Muhammad took Ghazi Muhammad's side and joined in the *ghazavat*. Runovskiy Diary, chast' 2, list 122; Volkonskiy, 1888, vol. XII, pp. 9-10; Ramazanov and Khadzhiev (eds), 1959, pp. 412-3, doc. no. 22.

[48] It was also then that Ghazi Muhammad acquired the title Ghazi.

The beginning of the ghazavat

Having won the support of the internal Naqshbandi opposition, Ghazi Muhammad had to meet yet another challenge presented by the non-Naqshbandi religious authorities. Led by Sayyid al-Harakani, who denounced both the order and its teaching, this opposition was outside the Naqshbandi framework and had to be overcome by Ghazi Muhammad in person. He first tried to do so by winning his former teacher over to his side. Thus, he wrote Sayyid al-Harakani a letter in which he urged him to accept the *tariqa* and join their efforts in spreading the *shari'a* throughout the North Caucasus: go to Jamal al-Din, accept the *tariqa* from him, enter into our deeds, help us to establish the *shari'a* in Daghestan and we will make you the first among us.[49]

However, Sayyid al-Harakani sharply rejected his offer, saying that he had no political ambition and could not abandon the beliefs he had held during his long and contemplative life.[50] Moreover, he accused Ghazi Muhammad of violating the spirit of the shari'a by calling people for *ghazavat* against a far stronger enemy. Insulted by his answer, Ghazi Muhammad broke all the links which bound him to his former master and from that time onwards turned from a loyal student into a most dangerous opponent.

Thus, Ghazi Muhammad's first military action was aimed against Sayyid al-Harakani. In January 1830, shortly after his election as imam, accompanied by a group of armed *murids* who formed the nucleus of his army, Ghazi Muhammad stormed and entered Harakan. He seized the house of Sayyid al-Harakani who was absent from the village, publicly destroyed the supplies of wine found there and set the house on fire.[51] He then took over thirty hostages from among the most respected families of Harakan, thus forcing the people to recognise his authority and uphold the shari'a in their land.[52]

Sayyid al-Harakani stayed at the court of Aslan Khan of Kurah and Ghazi Ghumuq, whom he was visiting at the time, thus leaving Ghazi Muhammad as the highest spiritual authority in Inner Daghestan. Following his victory at Harakan, Ghazi Muhammad initiated a new campaign against

---

[49] Zamir Ali, 1990, p. 34.

[50] Dubrovin, 1891, no. 3, p. 18. According to another version, Ghazi Muhammad visited Sayyid al-Harakani to make this offer and had a long conversation with him. *TsGA, GSSR*, fond 1087, opis' 1, delo 323, list 17 – 18 ob.

[51] Allegedly the rich manuscript collection of the famous *'alim* was distroyed by fire. Dubrovin, 1890, no. 10, p. 27; Bodenshtadt, 1855, p. 188. However, this is not substantiated by the local Daghestani sources. See al-Qarakhi, 1946, p. 41. It is more likely that it was seized by Ghazi Muhammad and his supporters. Allegedly some manuscripts from al-Harakani's collection were seen in the rich library of Shamil.

[52] On the campaign of Ghazi Muhammad against Harakan, apart from the above mentioned works see *TsGA GSSR*, fond 1087, opis' 1, delo 323, list 20-21; Ramazanov and Khadzhiev (eds), 1959, pp. 62-5; Volkonskiy, 1887, vol. XI, pp. 153-8.

those Qumyq and Avar *jama'ats* which still did not recognise his authority.

His campaign bore a clearly militant character, and Ghazi Muhammad did not hesitate to apply force where he found it necessary:

> He reached the *vilayat* of Bagulal, gave orders and prohibitions to its people. He beat the qadi of Mehelty, and subdued the people [of this village]...the village of Gagal resisted him and several of his supporters and few people [who came with him] from Mehelty and other villages were killed, and many people of Andalal were killed. [As a result] the people of Andalal were defeated, humiliated and became resigned to carry out all Ghazi Muhammad's orders and prohibitions.[53]
> [....]and one *jama'at* after another went along the path of the shari'a, either of their own free will or yielding to superior force.[54]

By February 1830 Ghazi Muhammad had won most of the Andi and Bagulal *jama'ats* to his side. Now the only political entity in the Avar lands which remained outside his control was the Avar khanate. In mid-February, Ghazi Muhammad arrived in Andi from where he entered into negotiations with Pahu Bike, the widow of Ahmad Khan[55] and regent of the khanate.

The Khunzakh campaign and its aftermath[56]

In her policy Pahu Bike seems to have been guided by her intention to secure for her sons the title of khan and regain the part of the Avar khanate which, after the defeat of Ahmad Khan in 1819, had been added by the Russians to the khanate of Mehtuli.[57] Both these aims, she believed, could only be achieved with Russian approval.[58] At the same time, she had to recognise the strength of Ghazi Muhammad, who had by mid-February 1830 become a powerful religious and military leader and enjoyed considerable support among the religious authorities in the Avar khanate.

Following Ghazi Muhammad's appeals to the people of the Avar khanate, Pahu Bike summoned a special gathering of Avar notables and religious officials to discuss their future actions. Those assembled expressed their wish to join the imam and install the *shari'a* in the

---

[53] Al-Qarakhi, 1946, pp. 41-2.

[54] *Ibid.*, p. 38.

[55] Ahmad Khan had been expelled by Ermolov in 1819. See Chapter 10, above.

[56] *TsGA GSSR*, fond 1087, opis' 1, delo 323, list 22-7; al-Qarakhi, 1946, pp. 42-3; *AKAK*, vol. VII, p. 515, doc. no. 468; Ramazanov and Khadzhiev (eds), 1959, pp. 66-7; Bushuev, 1939, pp. 202-13.

[57] On the events of 1818-9, see Volkonskiy, 1886, vol. X, pp. 11-12; Dubrovin, 1871-88, vol. VI, pp. 339, 346-7, 356.

[58] Most Russian authors present her as loyal to the Russians, albeit for her own self-interests. Potto, 1901-4, vol. III, part 1, pp. 158-61; Volkonskiy, 1887, vol. XI, pp. 160-72.

khanate.[59] However, Pahu Bike was engaged in a delicate political game that attempted to reach a compromise without alienating either the Russians or Ghazi Muhammad. She sent Ghazi Muhammad a letter in which she offered Bulach Khan, her youngest son, as an *amanat* to Ghazi Muhammad, to prove her good intentions towards him and his cause, but refused to let him into Khunzakh. Ghazi Muhammad, sure of the support of the people of Khunzakh and determined to bring it under his control, refused the offer. He entered the khanate and laid siege to Khunzakh. If he had been successful, the whole of Inner Daghestan would have come under his authority, but events were to unfold in a somewhat different way.

The people of Khunzakh were sympathetic to the imam's cause, but when confronted with a military challenge, they employed all their resources and fought with such vigour and determination that they gained a decisive victory over the imam's far superior forces.[60] Defeated, Ghazi Muhammad had on 24 February 1830 to leave the khanate and retreat to his native Gimrah.

Ghazi Muhammad's campaign against Khunzakh seriously alerted the Russian military administration for the first time.[61] Shortly after the Khunzakh campaign Count Paskevich wrote to Chernyshev, the Russian Minister of War: 'Undoubtedly the aim of Ghazi Muhammad is to separate all Daghestani tribes from us and unite all Muslim mountain peoples under one single theocratic rule.'[62]

Even though they were now alerted to the potential danger presented by the new powerful leader, the Russians lacked accurate information on Ghazi Muhammad – his aims, plans and supporters – and their reaction was slow and confused.

The first Russian encounter with Ghazi Muhammad

In early March 1830 Paskevich sent his *protégé*, Major Ivan Karganov to Daghestan to gather more information and on the basis of his intelligence

---

[59] Dubrovin, 1890, no. 10, pp. 30-1; Volkonskiy, 1887, vol. XI, pp. 123-4.

[60] Ghazi Muhammad's army numbered up to 3,000 men according to some sources – Volkonskiy, 1887, vol. XI, p. 164; Dubrovin, 1890, no. 10, pp. 32-3; 8,000 according to others – Neverovskiy, 1847(a), p. 18; Bodenshtadt, 1855, p. 191.

[61] This was partly due to Pahu Bike's efforts to present Ghazi Muhammad's attempt to take Khunzakh as a clear manifestation of his plans to draw most of Daghestan out of Russian control. By doing so, she presented her victory over the imam's forces as a service she had done for the Russians and requested a reward – confirmation of Nutsal Khan, her eldest son in his title of an Avar khan, and return under his authority the part of the Avar khanate which had been annexed by Ermolov to the khanate of Mehtuli in 1819. The Russians sent Pahu Bike a reward but rejected all her other demands. Volkonskiy, 1887, vol. XI, p. 160.

[62] Dubrovin, 1891, no. 3, p. 38; Volkonskiy, 1887, vol. XI, p. 2.

advise the Russian command what course of action to pursue with Ghazi Muhammad.[63]

The Field-Marshal could not make sense of the mass of contradictory data and in order to solve this impossible situation sent to Daghestan...Major Karganov, with a secret mission to find out the true state of events and, should he find it necessary, seize Kazi Mulla [Ghazi Muhammad] with whose elimination he believed all the troubles would stop. This was the first measure undertaken by the Russian authorities...to explain the phenomenon of *muridizm*, which was a mystery to them.[64]

Entrusted with freedom of action and enjoying the unequivocal support of Count Paskevich, Karganov represented the worst type of Russian officer and even among his brother officers was notorious for his greed and lack of any moral principles – for which he was nicknamed 'Van'ka Cain'.[65] His appointment to Daghestan, rather than solving the Russian's problems there, confused matters even more. Even Russian historians saw 'the criminal activities of Karganov' as 'one of the main reasons for the rapid spread of *muridizm* on the [Qumyq] plain'.[66]

Driven by greed and self-interest Karganov, within a short space of time, succeeded in alienating even those local rulers most loyal to the Russians, and brought the Daghestanis in both the *shamkhalat* and the khanate of Mehtuli to the brink of revolt.[67] As to resolving the Russian problem with Ghazi Muhammad, he not only failed, but actually assisted the imam to gain more strength and support.

Ghazi Muhammad after Khunzakh

Immediately following his defeat at Khunzakh, Ghazi Muhammad and his followers lost many of their supporters. The people of Gumbet, for example, denounced Sheikh Shamil, the imam's deputy who had led them into the attack against Khunzakh. Humiliated, his sword confiscated and the turban torn off his head, Shamil was nearly killed by his former supporters. He was saved only by the mediation of Nur Muhammad, a respected *qadi* from Ihnov,[68] but he was forced to leave Gumbet and join Ghazi Muhammad in Gimrah. Even in Gimrah, the prestige and popularity of Ghazi Muhammad dropped and people started to accuse him of fomenting feuds among the people of Daghestan.

---

[63] *AKAK*, vol. VII, pp. 514-15, doc. no. 467; Dubrovin, 1891, no. 3, pp. 187-202.

[64] *TsGA GSSR*, fond 1087, opis' 1, delo 323, list 39 ob.

[65] Van'ka – diminitive from Ivan (John), Cain as in the Bible. *TsGA GSSR*, fond 1087, opis' 1, delo 323, list 40-2.

[66] *TsGA GSSR*, fond 1087, opis' 1, delo 323, list 50.

[67] On Karganov's activities, see Bushuev, 1939, pp. 213-19, Volkonskiy, 1888, vol. XII, pp. 43-59.

[68] Al-Qarakhi, 1946, p. 43; *TsGA GSSR*, fond 1087, opis' 1, delo 323, list 26-26 ob.

The anti-Naqshbandi opposition raised their heads. Sayyid al-Harakani returned to his native village, and the people approached him with their regrets and promises never to listen to Ghazi Muhammad or any other Naqshbandi again.[69] Most other *jama'ats* which had hitherto recognised Ghazi Muhammad as their leader, sent their representatives to the Russian headquarters to express their loyalty and submission to the tsar.[70]

It seemed that the old pattern of direct connection between the military success and religious prestige of a North Caucasian leader had prevailed once again. This time, however, the situation was different because legitimation for Ghazi Muhammad was based mainly on his religious prestige and standing as a Sufi sheikh.

Defeated and largely abandoned by his supporters, Ghazi Muhammad alongside Shamil and Doudil Muhammad, the *qadi* from Erpeli, settled 'in an isolated mud-hut at the outskirts of Gimrah...spending time in prayer and fasting, apparently uninterested in any [political] events'.[71] This pious behaviour considerably improved people's attitude towards Ghazi Muhammad, who became restored in their eyes as primarily a religious figure. Several weeks after his return to Gimrah from Khunzakh, he invited people to come to Untsukul to attend his sermon. On 27 February 1830 Ghazi Muhammad addressed the gathering with a speech in which he compared his defeat at Khunzakh with that suffered by the Prophet Muhammad at the battle of Badr in 625 AD. He claimed that God had punished the people at Khunzakh for their poor faith and hesitancy:

Our failure at Khunzakh occurred because, although we belong to the followers of the true *tariqa*, we not only doubt it but even the *shari'a* itself. O, my people, those who desire to follow the righteous *tariqa* should not be afraid of death, for Heaven with beautiful houris awaits each of us. Give *tauba* and beg God to forgive your sins.[72]

Although many important *jama'ats* did not send their representatives to the meeting, the news of Ghazi Muhammad's speech spread rapidly throughout the area and made a deep impression on the people. The effect of this appeal was further increased by the occurrence of one of the worst earthquakes experienced in the North Caucasus, which shook Daghestan and Chechnya at the end of February-beginning of March 1830.

---

69 *TsGA GSSR*, fond 1087, opis' 1, delo 323, list 34; Volkonskiy, 1888, vol. XII, p. 3.

70 Volkonskiy, 1888, vol. XII, pp. 3-4, 10-2.

71 *TsGA GSSR*, fond 1087, opis' 1, delo 323, list 35 ob. The same story is quoted in Volkonskiy, 1888, vol. XII, p. 3.

72 Quoted in *ibid.*, p. 5.

According to eye-witnesses one could hardly imagine anything more terrifying: on the whole territory between Khunzakh and the village of Enderi on the Qumyq plain, the earth was moving, large cracks were forming, houses were falling to the ground, people were losing their lives, even animals were overcome by panic.[73]

All the people saw the earthquake as a Divine Sign and, both Ghazi Muhammad on the one hand and the Russians and their allies on the other, tried to give it the interpretation which benefited their policy. Thus, the Russians and the mullahs loyal to them interpreted it as the sign of God's anger at the military hostilities of the North Caucasians against the Russians. Baron Rozen, the newly appointed commander of the Left Flank, sent numerous proclamations in which he claimed that the earthquake was God's punishment for the Daghestanis' failure to keep their oaths given to the Russian government on the holy Qur'an.[74]

For his part, Ghazi Muhammad and other Naqshbandis explained the event as God's punishment for the people's disbelief and failure to live according to God-given laws.[75] They claimed that only by sincere repentance and through turning to the righteous path could the people earn God's forgiveness, and urged them to accept the *tariqa* and follow the *shari'a*. Not surprisingly, the latter explanation was viewed by the local people as much more credible and soon the balance of power once again shifted in favour of the Naqshbandis.[76]

The Russians unwittingly boosted Ghazi Muhammad's popularity by several political and military blunders. Convinced that after the defeat at Khunzakh, Ghazi Muhammad had no real power, they treated him correspondingly. Shortly after his arrival in Jengutay, the capital of the khanate of Mehtuli, Karganov sent Ghazi Muhammad a letter calling on him to surrender to the Russian tsar. In this letter he drew heavily on the religious argumentation of Ghazi Muhammad's local adversaries and accused him of unlawful and un-Islamic activities. Ghazi Muhammad did not hurry to enter into negotiations with the Russian officer, whose reputation in the North Caucasus had been most tarnished. When he did finally reply to Karganov's letter a month later, he expressed his surprise at the 'unprovoked Russian enmity' towards him and asked for a special pass to allow him pilgrimage to Mecca.[77] Convinced that Ghazi Muhammad had decided to leave the area because he lacked any support, Karganov set up the necessary arrangements to provide

---

[73] *TsGA GSSR*, fond 1087, opis' 1, delo 323, list 34, ob.-35.

[74] *Ibid.*, list 35 ob.-36; Volkonskiy, 1888, vol. XII, p. 18.

[75] *TsGA GSSR*, fond 1087, opis' 1, delo 323, list 35 ob.

[76] Even Musa Khasaev, the oldest and the most devoted Russian ally among the Daghestani dignitaries, had accepted Ghazi Muhammad's interpretation of the earthquake. He left Russian service and spent all his time at home praying and fasting.

[77] From the time of Ermolov, North Caucasians were not allowed to travel abroad without special permission issued by the local Russian military authorities.

Ghazi Muhammad with the pass to Mecca and undertook no further actions.[78]

Meanwhile, the position of Ghazi Muhammad grew stronger, and Karganov had to recognise that he had been grossly mistaken as to the imam's plans. Disappointed and desperate, he gave orders to capture the imam dead or alive and tried to organise his assassination. However, this plan went dramatically wrong. The first assassin hired by Karganov openly joined Ghazi Muhammad,[79] and the other two missed while trying to shoot him after the Friday prayer.[80] Thus, instead of removing Ghazi Muhammad from the political scene, these two incidents boosted his popularity and convinced the people that he was protected by God.

After these failures, Karganov made further attempts to check the spread of the Naqshbandi ideology. First he ordered the capture of Muhammad al-Yaraghi[81] and when the latter escaped and took refuge in the upper Tabarsaran, Karganov entered into negotiations with Jamal al-Din. The latter refused to undertake any actions against Ghazi Muhammad, under the pretext that he had no authority over the imam and was in no position to criticise him or his policy.[82]

In reality Jamal al-Din under the influence of the chief *murshid* of Daghestan, changed his attitude towards *ghazavat* and Ghazi Muhammad's activities. From outright opposition at first, followed by tactical support, Jamal al-Din now actively supported Ghazi Muhammad. In March 1830 the two of them issued a number of joint appeals and proclamations.[83]

These failures made Karganov review his tactics and resume the traditional Russian policy of indiscriminate punishment of whole villages. 'He came to realise the necessity of bringing to account the whole population of Koysubu, since the troublesome Gimrah, one of the largest Koysubu villages, was the home village of Ghazi Muhammad and a cradle of his teaching.'[84]

Following Karganov's advice, Count Paskevich decided that it was time to implement his so-called 'one-blow approach'.[85] In May 1830 he ordered Baron Rozen to 'enter the mountains and march across them in all directions',[86] thereby bringing all people into submission. The

---

78 *TsGA GSSR*, fond 1087, opis' 1, delo 323, list 42 ob.-43.

79 *Ibid.*, list 43-3ob.

80 *Ibid.*, list 49-9 ob.

81 *Ibid.*, list 44; Dubrovin, 1891, no. 3, pp. 191-3.

82 *Ibid.*, list, 46.

83 Volkonskiy, 1888, vol. XII, p. 7.

84 *TsGA GSSR*, fond 1087, opis' 1, delo 323, list 44 ob.

85 On his tactics, see Dubrovin, 1891, no. 3, pp. 177-85; Gammer, 1992, pp. 49-54.

86 Dubrovin, 1891, no. 3, p. 185.

campaign, however, was executed with such confusion and incompetence that it brought about completely opposite results.[87]

First, the Russians destroyed the villages of Kazanischa, Erpeli and Karanay, which had already broken their forced alliance with Ghazi Muhammad and renewed their oath of submission to the Russian Empire.[88] Then, for reasons which are still unclear, the Russian column under Rozen's command stopped short of Gimrah, without any battle seized the livestock belonging to the Koysubu *jama'ats* and retreated.[89]

Enraged by the loss of their herds and at the same time perceiving Rozen's decision not to enter into battle with them as a sign of Russian weakness, the Koysubu people were determined to fight back. Immediately following Rozen's campaign they called a *jama'at* gathering at which they discussed the question of opening anti-Russian hostilities straight away but decided first to seek alliance with the Avars of the khanate.[90]

The people of Kazanischa, Erpeli and Karanay on the other hand, tried to stop the unprovoked 'punishment' by seeking mediation with the Russians through the newly appointed *shamkhal* of Targhu. The latter, however, proved to be wholly incapable of any independent role and demonstrated the complete degradation of those who had been formerly the most powerful rulers in Daghestan.

The result of Rozen's campaign was to alienate the whole of Daghestan. Even in Khunzakh, where Pahu Bike tried to profess loyalty to the tsar, a powerful anti-Russian party was formed. Lead by Ali Bek, the mentor and guardian of Nutsal Khan (the eldest son of Pahu Bike), this party advocated joint military actions with the Koysubu people under the overall command of Ghazi Muhammad.[91]

Ghazi Muhammad's military activities

One of the side-effects of Rozen's campaign was to strengthen Ghazi Muhammad's popularity. The Russian decision not to have any military clashes with him nor to enter Gimrah was seen as a manifestation of

---

[87] On Rozen's campaign, see Dubrovin, 1891, No. 4, pp. 9-13; Yuryev, in *TsGVIA, VUA*, delo 6550, list, 11-2; *TsGA GSSR*, fond 1087, opis' 1, delo 323, list 50-3 ob.; Volkonskiy, 1887, vol. XI, pp. 167-82.

[88] *TsGA GSSR*, fond 1087, opis' 1, delo 323, list 46-8.

[89] Gammer suggests that Rozen decided not to storm Gimrah, because he considered his force too weak. Gammer, 1994, p. 52. Another theory which accounts for Rozen's decision was his conviction that the area was on the verge of being fully pacified and there was no need to shed Russian blood, simple "preventive" measures such as driving the herds away being more than sufficient. On the situation in the area see *TsGA GSSR*, fond 1087, opis' 1, delo 323, list 45-7.

[90] *Ibid.*, list, 47.

[91] *Ibid.*, list 42 ob.

God's protection extended over Ghazi Muhammad and his followers, whose destruction, as all knew, was the main aim of the Russian campaign. Following Rozen's retreat, Ghazi Muhammad issued an appeal in which he declared:

The hour of liberation has come. God has declared His will and called upon His people to start the struggle against the infidels. Many miracles and signs have been revealed to reassure the believers and encourage the hesitant ones and faint-hearted. A large army of the enemy has been struck by God's anger and without taking a single stroke of sword they retreated [reference to the Russian campaign against Gimrah -A. Z.]. His second army was defeated at Chunkeskent and now more strength is needed to complete the task. God calls all those who accept Islam as a true faith to fight against the infidels in order to recover the pearl of freedom from the dirt of slavery. Those who do not use the opportune moment sent by God Himself will never have it again and eternal slavery will be their destiny.[92]

This was the first direct call for *ghazavat* against the Russians and it is from this point perhaps that the Caucasian War should be considered to have begun.

During the next two years (1831-2), the imam invaded the Qumyq plain, looted the Russian fortress of Kizlyar, besieged Burnaya, Vnezapnaya and Derbend, and threatened Groznaya and Vladikavkaz.[93]

Later Russian historians attributed Ghazi Muhammad's success to the shortage of Russian human and military resources, which in 1831 were withdrawn to quell the revolt in Poland and neighbouring areas.[94] While being a possible explanation of fleeting military success under the first imam, this could hardly account for such long-lasting resistance, which required the full mobilisation of the human and military potential of the mighty Russian Empire for almost half-a-century. Rather the explanation of Ghazi Muhammad's success as well as that of his followers is to be sought in their strategy and tactics which united the various peoples of the North Caucasus for a common purpose. The most crucial factor ensuring the co-ordination of their military and political efforts was provided by the Naqshbandi network, and it is the way Ghazi Muhammad utilised it for the purpose of the resistance that largely accounts for his success.

Ghazi Muhammad's domestic policy

The establishment of Ghazi Muhammad's authority in various remote areas of the North Caucasus was closely associated with the traditional Naqshbandi practice of dispatching deputies and establishing lodges.

---

[92] Bodenshtandt, 1855, p. 195.

[93] Gammer, 1994, pp. 52-9.

[94] In May the Emperor ordered units from the Caucasus to be sent to the Western Front and transfered Paskevich to command the military in Poland.

Centred around the local mosques or in the purpose-built mud-houses on the outskirts of villages, these lodges served as the focal points for recruiting new adepts into the *tariqa* and for the mobilisation of people for *ghazavat*. For the first time in the North Caucasus these lodges went beyond their religious function and engaged in political and military activities. The high degree of centralisation in the Sufi order ensured that all Naqshbandi sheikhs at these lodges acted in strict accordance with the policy of Ghazi Muhammad and served as the vehicles for the implementation of his plans in remote areas, which otherwise would have remained outside his reach. At the same time the authority of the local sheikhs was to a considerable extent legitimised by their association with the imam, with whom they claimed to have spiritual links that enabled them to inform him of all the developments in their lands and receive instructions from him.[95]

Thus Ghazi Muhammad's military achievements were preceded and consolidated by the activities of his emissaries and deputies. The latter were at different times active in various areas of the North Caucasus, including the Chechen, Ingush and Noghay lands.[96] Military success played an important role in extending the authority of Ghazi Muhammad, which at the time of his greatest power in 1831 extended over the larger part of Chechnya and Daghestan including Tabarsaran, Qaytaq, Terkem, Ghazi-Ghumuq, most *jama'ats* of Inner Daghestan,[97] Greater Chechnya and the remote Jaro-Belokany *jama'ats* in southern Daghestan. In 1831 the latter staged a revolt under the leadership of Ghazi Muhammad's deputies.[98] At the same time his success gave a great impetus to the Naqshbandi cause, and the Naqshbandi order struck deep roots in the lands which had at various periods been brought under the imam's control.

The establishment of the Naqshbandi network in Chechnya

It was largely due to the efforts of Ghazi Muhammad and his deputies that Chechnya became an important centre of Naqshbandi activities

---

[95] Dubrovin, 1891, no. 4, p. 8; No. 5, p. 205; Volkonskiy, 1888, vol. XII, p. 62.

[96] Ghazi Muhammad's emissaries gained some influence even among the remote Qarabulaq and Ingush tribes who, in solidarity with the imam, mobilised 500 armed men in 1831 and interrupted Russian communications along the military highway passing through their lands. Bodenshtadt, 1855, pp. 202-3.

[97] The only areas of Inner Daghestan which remained outside the imam's reach were the Avar khanate and the powerful confederation of Dargho, which, led by the *qadi* of Akusha appointed by Ermolov, refused him entry into their lands. Volkonskiy, 1887, vol. XI, pp. 155, 165-6; Dubrovin, 1891, no. 3, p. 28.

[98] An important role in leading the Jar people in revolt was played by Hamza Bek – the second imam of the North Caucasus, who was captured during the operation and released only due to the mediation of Aslan Khan of Ghazi-Ghumuq. On the revolt, see Dubrovin, 1891, no. 4, pp. 19-23; no. 5, pp. 197-8.

closely connected with Daghestan. From the beginning of Ghazi Muhammad's activities as imam, Howk and Muhammad al-Quduqli (the two imams of the Greater Chechnya revolt) accepted his authority and resumed their religious activities as his deputies.

Shortly after the earthquake in early March 1830 which devastated a considerable part of lowland Chechnya, a delegation of Chechen mullahs led by Howk arrived in Gimrah. They assured Ghazi Muhammad that the people were ready to follow him and invited him to come to Chechnya. Ghazi Muhammad accepted the invitation and sent a written appeal to the Chechens in which he urged the people to accept the shari'a and prepare themselves for a 'decisive' battle, and he promised to come to Chechnya the following summer with 'a huge army' nobody could resist.[99]

At the same time he dispatched several of his other most trusted deputies. Sheikh Mustafa, a respected *qadi* from Germenchuk was active among the people of Aukh, Qachqalyq and other lowland Chechen *tuqums*;[100] Sheikh Hajji Yahya preached on the right bank of Sunja from where his message spread over the area between Sunja and Terek. More important still was 'Abdallah al-Ashilty, who arrived in Chechnya in May 1830[101] and settled in the Bayan village of Greater Chechnya.

He arrived during the celebration of *kurban* ['*id al-adha* – festival of sacrifice A. Z.]...came to the mosque and gave a solemn sermon at a huge gathering of people who came to see him from all neighbouring villages.[...] By his eloquence and the unusual body movements of a dervish he captured the hearts of the listeners...[the people] put on white turbans and unanimously announced him to be a saint and themselves to be his humble followers.[102]

Having won the acknowledgement of the Chechens in Bayan and neighbouring villages, Abdallah tried to ensure the implementation of Ghazi Muhammad's policy. He sent appeals throughout Greater Chechnya in which he urged people to accept the shari'a as the obligation placed on them by God through Ghazi Muhammad and his deputies.

He forbade drinking and smoking...demanded that one out of ten men should be educated enough to preach the shari'a and that every tenth household in Ichkeria [Greater Chechnya] should send one armed man with provisions and wearing a white turban [as a sign of being Ghazi Muhammad's follower]. Any household which did not fulfil this obligation was to pay a fine of one bull.[103]

---

[99] *TsGA GSSR*, fond 1087, opis' 1, delo 323, list 37; Volkonskiy, 1888, vol. XII, p. 24.

[100] On Mustafa al-Germenchuki, see *Ibid.*, pp. 20-2.

[101] It is through these two sheikhs that most of the Chechen Naqshbandis trace their spiritual geneology.

[102] *Ibid.*, pp. 61-2.

[103] *Ibid.*, p. 62.

The success of the imam's cause in Chechnya was finally assured during the promised visit of Ghazi Muhammad to Chechnya in the summer of 1830. The imam started his visit from the most militant and *tariqa*-oriented Benoy *tuqum*, and from there travelled throughout mountain Chechnya.[104] 'From Benoy, Ghazi Muhammad proceeded accompanied by shooting in the air and chanting of '*la ilaha illa allah*' to Kishen-Aukh and then to Zandaq. Everywhere he went he preached the shari'a, executed justice, exacted punishments and impressed everyone by his righteousness[105] so that most *tuqums* in Greater Chechnya accepted him as their imam and military-religious leader. This ensured him the broad participation of Chechen armed men in most of his military campaigns of 1831-2.[106]

The decline of Ghazi Muhammad's military power

In late 1831 the Russians brought in a considerable force and started a general offensive against Chechnya and Daghestan during which they gradually brought Tabarsaran, Qaytaq, Chirkah, Salataw and most Koysubu villages back under their control.[107]

For some time Ghazi Muhammad divided his time between his native Gimrah and the Chechen lands, which alone stood loyal to him. However, in early 1832 their support also started to crumble. Following the Russian punitive expeditions the Chechens asked Ghazi Muhammad to leave. In a desperate attempt to bring them back under his control Ghazi Muhammad executed a number of people whom he held responsible for accepting Russian citizenship. This, however, proved to be counterproductive and alienated the Chechens who now submitted to the Russians, paid tributes and handed over *amanats*.[108]

Deprived of almost all support, Ghazi Muhammad in early July 1832 entered into negotiations with the Russians through Aslan Khan of Kurah and Ghazi-Ghumuq. The negotiations failed. Ghazi Muhammad offered a truce on the condition that the Russian authorities would permit him to stay in the area and allow the people of Daghestan to uphold the *shari'a*.[109] The Russians, however, had come to regard the *shari'a* as a major obstacle to the establishment of their full control over the area, and they tried to reinforce traditional and, wherever possible, Russian legislation. Furthermore, any idea of fair negotiations with the local

---

[104] Dubrovin, 1891, no. 4, pp. 195-6; 1891, no. 5, p. 200; Volkonskiy, 1888, vol. XII, pp. 72-4.

[105] Dubrovin, 1891, no. 5, p. 200.

[106] Volkonskiy, 1889, vol. XIII, pp. 159-74, 177.

[107] Neverovskiy, 1847(a), p. 29.

[108] *Ibid.*, pp. 28-35.

[109] *AKAK*, vol. VIII, pp. 557-8, 695; Volkonskiy, 1889, vol. XIII, pp. 337-8, 343-7.

Martyrs' cemetery in Gimrah, Daghestan.

Mausoleum of the first imam, Ghazi Muhammad, Gimrah.

The site of Ghazi Muhammad's death, Gimrah.

The tombstone of
Ghazi Muhammad.

leaders, whom they saw as nothing more than rebels and bandits, was seen by the Russian command as a humiliation for the mighty Russian Empire. They believed that the only appropriate tone was to act from a position of force and they demanded Ghazi Muhammad's full and unconditional surrender. With these apparent contradictions, the negotiations had little chance of success and ended almost as soon as they had begun.[110]

The battle of Gimrah and Ghazi Muhammad's death

In September 1832 a force of 10,000 men led by Baron Rozen, who had replaced Paskevich as the chief commander of the Caucasus,[111] crossed Greater and Lesser Chechnya and brought it into full submission. This allowed the Russians to consolidate all their efforts against the imam and so they did.

On 17 October 1832 the Russian detachment swooped down on Gimrah from the side of the mountains.[112] Abandoned by most of his supporters, with only 600 armed men at his side, Ghazi Muhammad lost the battle at Gimrah and alongside a dozen of his *murids*, including Sheikh Shamil, found shelter in a small house outside the village. The house was quickly surrounded by the Russian soldiers who started to climb the roof and pierce it with their bayonets. With no chance of escape the only option open to the defenders was surrender. However, to the amazement and admiration even of their enemies, they refused to do so.[113]

Ghazi Muhammad prayed asking God to forgive his sins, and constantly repeating the *shahada* (*la ilaha illa Allah*), bared his sword and leaped from the house. He fell on the Russian bayonets and died instantly. The second to leap from the house was Shamil. In a huge jump he landed beyond the first line of soldiers, stabbed the first and second soldier who rushed towards him, but was wounded seriously by the third, who stabbed him with his bayonet right through his chest. With incredible effort, Shamil pulled the bayonet from his chest and ran away. The Russians hesitated to shoot at him for fear of wounding one of their own – Shamil was in-between the two lines of Russian soldiers – and they only threw stones at him, one of which broke Shamil's shoulder-blade. By that time, however, Shamil was already far away

---

110 *AKAK*, vol. VIII, pp. 695, 557-8, doc. no. 589, 438, 439.

111 He replaced Paskevich in 1831 when the latter was called to subdue the uprising in Poland.

112 This was a daring enterprise. To approach Gimrah from the mountainside they had to go across the snow-covered mountains with only a narrow and slippery path running above the deep gorges.

113 Bodenshtadt, 1855, p. 208.

and the Russians did not pursue him, certain that he was mortally wounded.[114]

Indeed, Shamil soon collapsed due to loss of blood. Fortunately, he was not the only one to escape. Another *murid* had jumped after Shamil and, following him step by step, remained unharmed. With his help, Shamil reached a safe place where he spent several months until he fully recovered.

The campaign which had started over two years before with the first march of Baron Rozen against Ghazi Muhammad in May 1830 was finally over, its aims achieved – Gimrah captured, Ghazi Muhammad dead, the North-eastern Caucasus seemingly subdued. To enhance the Russian success, a proclamation was issued to all Daghestani and Chechen people in which the Russians boasted of their victory and threatened with severe punishment[115] anyone who would dare to oppose them again.

To reinforce their message, they put the body of Ghazi Muhammad on display. This, however, proved to be a grievous miscalculation. The body, which was found several days after the battle, did not even start to decompose. Furthermore, it was found in a striking posture – with one hand the imam held his beard as if he was about to pray while the other pointed to heaven. The set features on his face had such a peaceful and happy expression, it was as if he had died not on the Russian bayonets but in a wonderful dream.[116]

Seeing the imam's body in such a posture made a deep impression on the people of Gimrah. They now became convinced that Ghazi Muhammad was indeed a saint who had prayed calling for battle and fought with prayer, who had sealed his preaching with his own blood and died as a messenger of God – pointing even in death to where they all should aspire. The faith that had weakened during the final year of Ghazi Muhammad's life was revived by his very death – people reproached themselves and repented for abandoning such a great saint at that crucial moment of his life.

Ghazi Muhammad, the first of the three Naqshbandi imams, asserted the pattern of leadership which for the first time combined the credentials of a Sufi sheikh with a military-political leader. Being a Sufi sheikh who had reached the highest degree of Divine Knowledge and assumed the title of imam whose primary responsibility was to provide guidance

[114] For a description of the battle, see al-Qarakhi, 1941, pp. 53-7, Bodenshtadt, 1855, pp. 208-9; Genichutlinskiy, 1992, pp. 64-6, Krovyakov, 1990, pp. 22-3.

[115] For the full text of the proclamation, see Bodenshtadt, 1855, p. 211.

[116] Ghazi Muhammad was buried by the Russians in Targhu. In the time of the imamate of Shamil, Ghazi Muhammad's body was brought to Gimrah. It was buried in the local cemetery where his *ziyarat* with a small wooden chapel became a place for pilgrimage and is much venerated up till the present day.

on matters of Islamic propriety and the *shari'a* for the rulers of Daghestan, he managed to overcome the bridge between the 'spiritual' and 'political' Naqshbandiyya and combine the resources of both trends in his quest for power.

By asserting the supremacy of God and His Prophet in all matters of law and government, Ghazi Muhammad challenged the traditional institutions of power and the entire set of laws and customs that governed North Caucasian society, and introduced an alternative system of values. This transformed him and the Naqshbandi order into the main source of legitimacy as the sole conveyors and guarantors of the 'true meaning of the *shari'a*'.

Ghazi Muhammad transformed the relationship between the ruler and his subjects. Whereby the political standing of the former depended almost entirely on his military force and his expertise in traditional legislation, under the new arrangement, the imam for the first time could afford to suffer defeat on the battleground without significantly impairing his popularity. Furthermore, he transcended local limitations and for the first time succeeded in mobilising the Chechens for a large-scale military campaign carried out outside their *tuqums*.

Finally, the first imam established a strong Naqshbandi presence throughout Chechnya and Daghestan and laid the foundation for a future theocratic state. In his drive for the unification of various *tuqums* and *jama'ats* under the Naqshbandi's aegis, he deployed the Naqshbandi order's structure and personnel.

In hindsight, Ghazi Muhammad's main achievement as the first imam was to consolidate the Naqshbandi position in areas which, although influenced by its teaching, had no established Naqshbandi infrastructure (for instance, in Chechnya).

19

HAMZA BEK: THE SECOND NAQSHBANDI IMAM[1]

After Ghazi Muhammad's death the Russians were convinced that they had seen the end of the Naqshbandi cause. The whole of the North-eastern Caucasus was subdued, many of the militant Naqshbandi *murids* had been killed, and those left alive turned to the spiritual rather than the political tenets of the *tariqa*. Shamil, once recovered from his wounds and back in Gimrah, tried to restore the *shari'a* and improve the 'fallen morals' of the people, but was still too weak to take up Ghazi Muhammad's cause.[2] For several months the North Caucasus was quiet, but beneath this apparent peace the new leadership was crystallising, and in 1833 one of Ghazi Muhammad's former deputies, Hamza Bek, was accepted as the new imam.

Hamza Bek: biography

Hamza (Gamzat in Russian) ibn Ali al-Iskander[3] Bek was born in 1789 in Hutsal (New Gotsatl),[4] one of the largest villages of the Avar khanate. His father al-Iskander Bek belonged to a side branch of the family of the Avar khans and enjoyed the respect of the people in Hutsal and had close relations with the Avar khans.[5]

In 1801, at twelve years of age, Hamza was sent to Chokh village in the Avar Andalal *jama'at* where he studied the Qur'an and Arabic

---

[1] The present chapter is based on the following sources: documents published in *AKAK*; Ramazanov and Khadzhiev (eds), 1959; the works of al-Qarakhi, 1946; Hajji Ali, 1990; Drozdov, 1899; Grzhegorzhevskiy, 1875, no. 3; Kuzanov, 1861, no. 3; Neverovskiy, 1848; R-v, 1859; Volkonskiy, 1899, vol. XX.

[2] Al-Qarakhi, 1946, pp. 57-60.

[3] The accounts of Hamza's biography are taken from R-v, 1859, no. 34, pp. 117-19; no. 35, pp. 123-5; 'Kratkiy Ocherk Zhizni Gamzat Beka Sostavlenny po Svedeniyam Maklacha, syna Chohskogo Zhitelia Gazi, u kotorogo v Detstve Zhil Gamzat bek' (manuscript from the RF IIYaL, Mahachqala). A shorter version was published in 1911, *Kavkazskiy Sbornik* 1911, vol. XXXI, pp. 1-30 under the title 'Gamzat bek, 2oy imam Chechni i Dagestana'.

[4] Eighteen miles from Khunzakh.

[5] He was at the side of Ahmad Khan when the latter fought the Russians in 1818-9 and, after the khan was deposed by Ermolov, maintained friendly relations with his family. R-v, 1859, p. 117.

with Muhammad Effendi, one of the most learned mullahs in the Avar lands. According to his contemporaries, Hamza was a good student but preferred physical activities to reading and spent all his free time shooting and horse riding. He spent twelve years in Chokh and after the death of his teacher went to Khunzakh. There Pahu Bike, the widow of Aslan Khan gave him a warm welcome, allowed him to stay at the khans' palace and arranged for his further education with Nur Muhammad, the chief *qadi* of the Avar khanate.

Several years later Hamza Bek returned to Hutsal. Despite his religious education, he did not take any religious office and with no particular occupation led a carefree life, indulging in drinking and entertainment. All this changed dramatically when Hamza Bek met Ghazi Muhammad some time in the late 1820s and accepted the *tariqa* from him. However, it seems that he was not so much interested in the spiritual-mystical dimension of the *tariqa*[6] as in its political teaching and particularly in its call for *ghazavat*.[7] Unlike both the first and the third North Caucasian imams, Hamza Bek did not achieve the rank of a Sufi sheikh and had no Sufi *murids*[8] of his own. However, being extremely courageous, Hamza Bek demonstrated a natural military prowess which won him the trust and respect of both Ghazi Muhammad and his followers. Actively involved in most of the imam's military campaigns,[9] Hamza Bek quickly rose to a prominent position as one of the imam's most trusted deputies,[10] so that on one occasion at least they issued and co-signed a joint declaration.[11]

Hamza Bek was among those few who stayed with Ghazi Muhammad until the latter's death,[12] but he did not participate in the last battle at Gimrah. Sent by the imam to bring in reinforcements, Hamza Bek arrived with several hundred armed men when the battle had already

[6] Which can, perhaps, explain why he had not sought training from more established and advanced Sufi sheikhs such as Muhammad al-Yaraghi and Jamal al-Din al-Ghazi-Ghumuqi and joined the Naqshbandis only when they started to rally actively for *ghazavat*.

[7] Before he joined the Naqshbandis, Hamza participated in anti-Russian activities in 1826. Volkonskiy, 1887, vol. XI, pp. 34, 136. It has been suggested that Hamza was among those who had encouraged Ghazi Muhammad to start the *ghazavat*. Gammer, 1994, p. 60.

[8] In the North Caucasus there were two types of *murids* – the *tariqa murids* and the imam's or *naib's murids*. See below, Chapter 22.

[9] In 1830 during one of the *murid's* first campaigns, in the lands of the Jaro-Belokany *jama'at* confederation of southern Daghestan, Hamza was arrested, sent to Tiflis and only released by the Russians at the mediation of Aslan Khan of Ghazi-Ghumuq. See *AKAK*, vol. VIII, pp. 581-4; Dubrovin, 1871-88, vol. XIV, pp. 165, 180, 195; vol. XVII, p. 361.

[10] On the close relations between the two, see, for example, *ibid.*, vol. IX, pp. 34, 136.

[11] Declaration of Ghazi Muhammad and Hamza Bek to the People of Daghestan, January 1831, as quoted in Ramazanov and Khadzhiev (eds), 1959, pp. 87-8, doc. no. 49.

[12] Volkonskiy, 1897, vol. XVIII, p. 361.

begun. Seeing the overwhelming superiority of the Russian forces, Hamza did not join the defenders and watched the battle from afar.[13]

The election of the second imam

On learning that Ghazi Muhammad was dead, Hamza acted as his natural successor. He prayed, then appeared to be asleep and on waking up announced that he had had a prophetic dream in which he had seen Ghazi Muhammad in heaven surrounded by beautiful *houris*.

Each of you – he announced – can join him if you follow his example, uphold the shari'a and fight the *ghazavat*.[...] Do you know that Ghazi Muhammad did not abandon us and will act alongside us against the infidels if we do not abandon *ghazavat* and will follow his teaching? We shall not see him, but he will terrify our enemy during battles by appearing on his white horse, dressed in green and surrounded by all those *murids* who were killed with him. Ghazi Muhammad will cut into the ranks of the Russian soldiers, his sword will be fatal to the infidels and horrified they will find their only solution in retreat.[14]

However, Hamza made a decisive claim over the imamate only in early 1833. He sent numerous appeals to the Daghestani mullahs and elders affiliated with the Naqshbandi order. In these appeals he invited them to attend a gathering in the Koradakh village during which he promised to make an important announcement.

When people arrived and gathered at the Koradakh mosque, Hamza Bek made his solemn appearance. Dressed all in white and surrounded by numerous armed followers he entered the mosque and after the afternoon prayer addressed the gathering. In his speech he appealed to the legacy of Ghazi Muhammad, whom he claimed to have been seeing in his prophetic dreams. Once again he claimed that Ghazi Muhammad would support the people in their struggle against the infidels, but that since in this struggle people could not be left without a living imam, Ghazi Muhammad had appointed him as his successor.[15]

In spite of his bravery and military talent, Hamza was not an obvious choice for the new imam. His claim was weakened by the fact that he had not completed his spiritual training and also by his failure to come to the rescue of Ghazi Muhammad at his greatest hour of need. This, however, was compensated for by the support Hamza Bek received

---

[13] R-v, 1859, no. 34, p. 118, *AKAK*, vol. VIII, pp. 558-67, 695-6.

[14] Quoted in R-v, 1859, no. 34, p. 118.

[15] *Idem.*; al-Qarakhi, 1946, p. 61; Hajji Ali, 1873, p. 8; Volkonskiy, 1899, vol. XX, pp. 131-2. The accounts of his speech seem to suggest that Hamza Bek claimed to have been appointed as Ghazi Muhammad's successor by the *ruhaniyya* (spiritual being) of the deceased imam. In this respect the North Caucasian Naqshbandi doctrine permitting the practice of *rabita* and achieving unification with the spirituality of a deceased sheikh proved to be useful for gaining legitimacy of the imam's worldly powers.

from the mother of Ghazi Muhammad and from Muhammad al-Yaraghi, the chief *murshid* of Daghestan.

Following Hamza Bek's self-declaration as an imam, Muhammad al-Yaraghi, who had been allegedly present at the Koradakh gathering, confirmed him in this title, thus providing him with the vital religious legitimation.[16] Following his decision, the mother of Ghazi Muhammad sent him a letter in which she also recognised him as her son's successor and transferred the imam's treasury to him.[17]

On hearing of Muhammad al-Yaraghi's confirmation of Hamza Bek as an imam, Shamil, who allegedly was not present at the meeting due to his wounds, issued an appeal in which he urged his supporters to recognise the authority of 'whoever becomes a leader, so that the people of Daghestan would not be like dogs who squabble over a bone which can be stolen by the infidels'.[18] The tone of his appeal seems to suggest that Shamil was more than reluctant to recognise Hamza Bek's authority, but the strict Naqshbandi hierarchy ensured that once Hamza Bek was acknowledged by Muhammad al-Yaraghi, the rest followed his example. Thus, among others, Shamil joined Hamza Bek as his close ally and supporter.[19]

The undertakings of the new imam

It took Hamza Bek almost another year to gain prestige among the North Caucasian peoples and restore their confidence in the Naqshbandi cause.

At the beginning his [the new imam's] authority was acknowledged only by Hutsal, Ashilta and Gimrah, Tiliq and Mohokh.[...] He employed all possible efforts to convince people [of other places] to accept his authority and to establish a proper administration. But they did not recognise his rule and declared war on him.[20]

While trying to win the support of the mountain peoples, Hamza entered into negotiation with the Russians. Giving the Russians his assurance that it was not in his plans to fight them, Hamza Bek offered them peace on conditions similar to those of Ghazi Muhammad, i.e. that they would allow him to stay in the area and propagate the shari'a.[21] However,

16 Magomedov, 1991, p. 55.

17 R-v, 1859, no. 34, p. 118.

18 Chichagova, 1889, p. 32. It seems that both Muhammad al-Yaraghi and Shamil were influenced in their decision to recognise Hamza Bek not so much by the latter's virtues, as by the understanding that the swift appointment of a new imam was crucial to prevent the *ghazavat* from collapsing.

19 *AKAK*, vol. VIII, pp. 585-6, 695-9.

20 Muhammad al-Qarakhi, as quoted in Gammer, 1994, p. 61.

21 For the translation of the correspondence between Hamza and the Russian authorities,

as with Ghazi Muhammad, the Russians found these terms unacceptable and Hamza's conditions unreasonable[22] and instead offered him terms of 'full and complete' surrender promising as 'a sign of special Russian mercy to allow him to go to Mecca'.[23] With no chance of success, the negotiations continued for some time, during which Hamza tried to win time and bring various North Caucasian communities under his control. By the time the negotiations finally collapsed,[24] Hamza Bek's position had already been considerably consolidated.

Unpleasantly disappointed in their hope of seeing the last of Naqshbandi activities with the death of Ghazi Muhammad, the Russian command first ordered Hamza Bek's assassination[25] and later tried to foster the anti-Hamza Bek coalition of the Daghestani rulers.[26] Such efforts were unsuccessful, however, and in October 1833 Hamza Bek scored his first significant military victory over the people of Girgil (Gergebil), who were assisted by the khan of Mehtuli, the *shamkhal* of Targhu and the powerful *jama'at* confederation of Akusha.[27]

Further reinforced by this victory, Hamza Bek established control over the Avar Andalal and Bagulal *jama'ats*, which left the Avar khanate surrounded by the imam's forces from three sides. A confrontation between the Naqshbandis and the Avar rulers once again seemed inevitable.

In the spring of 1834 Hamza took up residence in his native Hotsal, situated eighteen miles from Khunzakh, and from there started his propaganda campaign against the Avar rulers. He accused the family of the Avar khans of behaving unlawfully by accepting Russian rule and maintaining peace with them and called the people to unite and fight them in the name of God and His shari'a.[28]

Having mobilised an army of 15,000, Hamza Bek at the beginning of August 1834 approached Khunzakh and laid siege to it. Deprived

---

see Volkonskiy, 1899, vol. XX, pp. 132-4.

[22] This attitude is clearly stated in almost all historiographies of the Caucasian War by pre-Revolutionary Russian historians. Only radical liberals such as Dobrolyubov actually placed the blame for the Caucasian War upon the tyrannical methods of subjugation of the Caucasian peoples exercised by the Russian commanders in the North Caucasus.

[23] See the correspondence, as quoted in Volonskiy, 1899, vol. XX, pp. 132-4.

[24] The negotiations were brought to an end when answering the Russian request to hand over his son as an *amanat*, Hamza demanded that in this case the *shamkhal's* son should be given to him as an *amanat* in exchange. Annoyed at the tone of his negotiations, Rozen remarked sharply that 'the word of a Russian commander should be enough for him'. Volkonskiy, 1899, vol. XX, p. 134, as quoted in Gammer, 1994, p. 61.

[25] *AKAK*, vol. VIII, pp. 569-72, doc. no. 449, 451, 453; Bodenshtadt, 1855, p. 216; Ramazanov and Khadzhiev (eds), 1959, pp. 130-1.

[26] *AKAK*, vol. VIII, pp. 573-4, doc. no. 457, 458.

[27] Gammer, 1994, p. 62.

[28] R-v, 1859, no. 34, p. 119.

of water and food supplies and surrounded by the enemy the people of Khunzakh continued their resistance. However, the elderly Pahu Bike, who only several years earlier had stood firm against Ghazi Muhammad and by her courage inspired her people's victory over him, now gave in to Hamza's demands to hold negotiations and sent her youngest son, Bulach Khan, to him as an *amanat*. Refusing the imam entry into Khunzakh, she promised to establish the shari'a under the guidance of one of his deputies and offered secret assistance in all his anti- Russian plans, reminding him of the time when Hamza's father and her own husband, Aslan Khan, were fighting the Russians side by side. However, she pleaded with him not to make her stand openly against the Russians, 'for the reasons the imam himself knew too well'.[29]

Hamza Bek replied through his negotiators that he was ready to recognise Nutsal Khan (Pahu Bike's oldest son) as the khan of Avaria if the latter accepted the *tariqa* and assumed leadership in the *ghazavat*, and demanded that the young khan should come forward to his camp for direct negotiations.[30] By that time Pahu Bike had already sent Umma Khan, her second son, sixteen years of age, to Hamza Bek, and Nutsal Khan was the only one left. Despite his reluctance to go, Pahu Bike, trustful of her distant relative whose father was a close friend of her late husband and who himself had spent some time in her house as a young man, accused her son of cowardice and persuaded him to go to the imam to negotiate with him.

On 25 August 1834 Nutsal Khan arrived in Hamza's camp, where he was met by the imam with due respect. Hamza Bek assured Abu Nutsal Khan of his loyalty and repeated his invitation to accept the *tariqa* and assume the leadership in *ghazavat*. Upon acceptance of those terms Hamza Bek offered to place his army under the khan's command and act as his assistant and loyal subject.[31] However, as soon as Hamza left the tent of Abu Nutsal and Umma Khan, shooting started in which both khans were killed.[32]

Most of the Russian sources maintain that from the very beginning Hamza lured the young khans into his residence intending to slaughter them and deprive the khanate of its rulers. However, both the local chronicler[33] and the immediate report of the Russian commander[34] present

---

[29] Bodenshtadt, 1855, p. 219.

[30] R-v, 1859, no. 34, p. 119; no. 36, pp. 123-4; Hajji Ali, 1873, p. 8; Genichutlinskiy, 1992, pp. 67-8; Bodenshtadt, 1855, pp. 217-20.

[31] R-v, 1859, no. 36, p. 124.

[32] *Ibid.*, no. 34, p. 117, Bodenshtadt, 1855, pp. 220-2; *Smert' Khanshi Pahu Bike*, 1911, p. 33.

[33] Al-Qarakhi, 1946, p. 64-5.

[34] A report from Rozen to Chernyshev of 9 August 1834, as quoted in *AKAK*, vol. VIII, pp. 584-5, doc. no. 468.

the killing not as intentional, but rather as brought about by Hamza's *kanly*, who came to the imam's camp in the khan's suite.[35] Even if the killing of the khans was accidental Hamza Bek did not seem to regret it. He entered Khunzakh as a conqueror, took up residence in the khan's palace and ordered the killing of Pahu Bike and all other members of the family of the Avar khans,[36] sparing only the widow of Abu Nutsal Khan because of her pregnancy.[37]

Shortly afterwards Surkhay, a distant relative of the Avar khans, arrived in Khunzakh. Through his service to the Russians Surkhay had gained the title of khan and Russian military rank. Now, with the khans' dynasty extinguished, he hoped to ascend to the throne by offering his loyalty to Hamza Bek. It was not, however, in the imam's plans to replace the former khan with a new one and after a mocking welcome, in which he accused Surkhay of neglecting his duties in avenging his cousins, the imam ordered him beheaded.[38]

With all his rivals annihilated, Hamza himself took the place of the Avar khans. Although not claiming the title of khan, he took the Avar capital as his main residence, settled in the khan's palace and appropriated the treasury. This met with strong disapproval from many of his close followers including Shamil who approached the imam and advised him to leave Khunzakh.

As from now, it would be best for you if you stay at your home in Hutsal in humble repentance and contemplation. And I shall carry out your business and take care of it in my country, as much as Sayyid al-Ihali in his, Ghazi al-Kartli in his, Kibit Muhammad in his, and Abd al-Rahman al-Qarakhi in his.[39]

Shamil himself, as well as most of the other imam's deputies, left Khunzakh, but Hamza Bek neglected the warnings, dispersed his forces and remained in the Avar capital. This vanity proved to be his greatest mistake and eventually cost him his life.

---

[35] According to this version, one of Hamza's *murids* recognised among Nutsal's *nukers* a certain Buga who had killed Hamza's cousin. He told the imam about it and Hamza approached Abu Nutsal Khan with a request to hand Buga over to him. The Khan gave his permission to arrest Buga, but when the *murids* came for him, the Khan's *nukers* refused to hand him over. This started the fatal shooting in which both Nutsal Khan and Umma Khan were killed.

[36] Al-Qarakhi, 1946, p. 66; Bodenshtadt, 1955, p. 223; Chichagova, 1889, p. 36; Genichut-linskiy, 1992, pp. 70-1; R-v, 1859, no. 36, p. 124. Only Bulach Khan, the youngest son of Pahu Bike, who had been given out as an *amanat* some time earlier and kept in Hutsatl outlived his family, as well as Hamza Bek himself. He was later killed (thrown into a mountain river and drowned) at the orders of Shamil. Al-Qarakhi, 1946, p. 132.

[37] According the *'adat*, the killing of a pregnant woman was one of the worst crimes and the one responsible for it was dishonoured and held double *kanly*.

[38] Bodenshtadt, 1855, pp. 223-5.

[39] Al-Qarakhi, 1946, p. 65.

The death of the second imam

The killing of the Avar ruling family shocked not only the common people of Khunzakh, but also some of Hamza's own followers and caused a split in their ranks. Some kept their loyalty to the imam, others held him responsible for the blood of the slain khans and sought to avenge the crime.

Itim Muhammad, a guardian of the dead khans and the father of two of Hamza Bek's *murids*, urged his sons, Usman and Hajji Murad, to avenge the killing of the khans, one of whom, Umma Khan, had also been a milk brother of Hajji Murad. The day chosen for Hamza's assassination was Friday, 19 September 1834. Hamza Bek was warned by one of his loyal *murids* about the conspiracy against him but did not take the threat seriously. Only when he entered the mosque and saw Usman and Hajji Murad in their *burkas* did he realise that the danger was real. It was already too late. Usman pulled out his pistol and fired at Hamza. This triggered an exchange of shots between Hamza's guards and the people of Khunzakh during which Hamza was killed. His *murids* retreated to the Khunzakh fortress and, when they tried to escape, the people led by Hajji Murad set fire to it. Most of Hamza's supporters were killed and those who survived the fire and the fighting fled from Khunzakh.[40] Thus ended Hamza's short rule. For three days Hamza's body remained on the square by the mosque and was buried only four days later.[41]

In the aftermath of the killing and expulsion of the *murids* from the Avar capital, the people of Khunzakh elected Hajji Murad as their new ruler. To defend the khanate from the *murdis* Hajji Murad accepted Russian citizenship and appealed to the Russian command for assistance. The latter readily accepted Hajji Murad and brought in considerable forces, which gave them direct control over one of the most powerful Daghestani principalities in the very heart of the remote Avar mountains. At the same time they appointed Aslan Khan of Ghazi-Ghumuq as the new khan of Avaria, although Hajji Murad continued to remain a *de facto* ruler of the khanate.[42]

Hamza Bek's short spell in power as the second imam confirmed the importance of religious legitimacy in claiming authority over the North

[40] R-v, 1859, no. 36, p. 124. For a description of the killing of Hamza Bek see in 'Zapiska sostavlennaya iz Rasskazov i Pokazaniy Hadji Murata, po prikazaniyu glavkoma Loris Melikovym', manuscript in RF IIYaL, Mahachqala, list 2-3; Bodenstadt, 1855, pp. 228-30.

[41] His grave is still preserved in Khunzakh and although not as popular as the mausoleum of the first and the third imams, is still visited by the local people.

[42] After his death in 1836, Aslan Khan was replaced by his sucessor, Nutsal Khan of Ghazi-Ghumuq. However, both the first and the second rulers showed little interest in the khanate's internal affairs and it was Hajji Murad who *de facto* ruled in the khanate.

Caucasian peoples. Despite his association with the Avar ruling house, he tried to distance himself from the latter and promote his Naqshbandi credentials. Moreover, he was accepted by the people of Daghestan and Chechnya only in the capacity of imam, while his relationship with the Avar khans always cast doubt on his efforts to bring free Daghestani *jama'ats* under his control and these were interpreted in the mould of the traditional expansionist policy of the Avar rulers.

Ironically, it was Hamza Bek who eliminated the dynasty of the Avar khans altogether. By doing so he changed the traditional balance of power in the North Caucasus in that it removed the most powerful local force capable of resisting the spread of the imams' authority and deprived the Russians of their most important allies. At the same time, following Hajji Murad's invitation, the Russians gained access to the heart of Daghestan, which made the direct confrontation between them and the Naqshbandi warriors inevitable and, one can argue, cleared the way for the creation of the North Caucasian imamate.

Part VII. SHAMIL: THE THIRD IMAM OF THE NORTH CAUCASUS

20

THE NAQSHBANDI TARIQA AFTER THE ASSASSINATION OF HAMZA BEK; THE RISE OF THE THIRD IMAM

The assassination of Hamza Bek and many of his followers at Khunzakh and the events that had preceded it considerably undermined the Naqshbandi position in the area. Most of the Daghestani *jama'ats* denounced the authority of Hamza's deputies and sent their representatives to the Russian command to express their loyalty to the Russian tsar.[1]

Furthermore, the split in the ranks of the Naqshbandi leaders resulted in the creation of several rival parties competing for the title of imam. The most powerful contestants were Sheikh Shamil, Tashou Hajji al-Enderi and Qibid Muhammad al-Tilitli, Akhberdy Muhammad and Sayyid al-Ihali.[2] Rivalry for the leadership was not a new phenomenon, but after the death of Muhammad al-Yaraghi, the chief *murshid* of Daghestan,[3] there was no central authority able to stop internal disputes by supporting one of the candidates, as he had done in the case of the first and second imams. Whoever was to become the new leader would by his own endeavours have to both overcome internal discord and regain the respect and trust of the people outside the Naqshbandi brotherhood. This proved to be a lengthy process which lasted for several years

---

[1] This mood of submissiveness to the Russians was reinforced by several campaigns of Kluki von Klugenau undertaken in 1834 into Girmrah, Akusha and Hutsal. See *AKAK*, vol. VIII, pp. 588-94 doc. no. 477, 478, 479, 481, 482, 484; Gammer, 1994, pp. 72-3; Grzhegorzhevskiy, 1875, no. 3, pp. 547-9; Drozdov, 1899, vol. XX, pp. 255-62.

[2] Al-Qarakhi, 1946, p. 65.

[3] Muhammad al-Yaraghi died in 1834 in Tabarsaran, where his grave became a popular place of pilgrimage.

and was finally completed only with the consolidation of power in the hands of Sheikh Shamil.

Sheikh Shamil[4]

Shamil was born in 1797 in Girmrah, to the family of Dengaw Muhammad, an ordinary *uzden* and Pahu Mecedu – the daughter of a branch of the ruling Ghazi-Ghumuq family.[5] He received a solid religious education, first in the Gimrah and later in Untsukul (Ansal), where he studied Arabic grammar, the Qur'an, *tafsir*,[6] logic, philosophy and law. He was a thoughtful student who took his studies seriously and combined them with strenuous physical exercise. Thus, in his early youth he won the respect of his fellow students both as a promising scholar and an outstanding athlete, who even by mountain standards was recognised as a superior horseman and a master of sword and dagger.

From his early childhood he developed a close friendship with Ghazi Muhammad who was four or five years his senior and who commanded the respect of his younger friend. It was he who in 1824 brought Shamil to Jamal al-Din al-Ghazi Ghumuqi.[7] Shamil entered the *tariqa* and spent a number of years at his house studying Sufi practices and other *'ulum* with the famous sheikh, finishing his spiritual education at the same time as Ghazi Muhammad. Along with Ghazi Muhammad, Shamil went to Muhammad al-Yaraghi who put the final touches on his spiritual training. The latter nominated Shamil as sheikh in his own right, but unlike Ghazi Muhammad, who went and established his own lodge in Gimrah, Shamil stayed with Jamal al-Din.[8]

The traditional *murid-murshid* relationship between Shamil and Jamal al-Din was reinforced by the close personal links between the two. Throughout his life Shamil kept his loyalty and obedience towards his sheikh, who 'alone commanded his full and complete respect and trust'.[9] Jamal al-Din favoured him more than any other student and arranged a marriage between Shamil and one of his daughters.

---

[4] The main sources for Shamil's biography and early activities used here are: unpublished documents from *TsGA GSSR*, fond 1087; al-Qarakhi, 1946; Hajji Ali, 1873 (1992); Baratov, 1909-10; Bodenshtadt, 1855; Drozdov, 1899; Grzhegorzhevskiy, 1874.

[5] Hajji Ali, 1873, pp. 10-11 (1992, pp. 15-16); Bodenshtadt, 1855, p. 247. Russian authors give the year of his birth as 1798 – Drozdov, 1899, vol. XX, p. 251; Baratov, 1910, no. 1, p. 10; Isaevich, in *TsGA GSSR*, fond 1087, opis' I, delo 268, list 2-7.

[6] Commentary on the Qur'an.

[7] According to Isaevich, Shamil came to Jamal al-Din when he was twelve years old. Isaevich, *TsGA GSSR*, opis' I, delo 268, list 2. This is unlikely, for Ghazi Muhammad started preaching only in the early 1820s. The version of Baratov, according to which Shamil accepted the tariqa when he was twenty-seven. i.e. some time around 1824, seems much more plausible. Baratov, 1910, no. 1, p. 10.

[8] Hajji Ali, 1992, p. 15.

[9] Bodenshtadt, 1855, p. 250.

Although deeply sympathetic to Ghazi Muhammad's decision to declare *ghazavat*, Shamil abstained from joining him until Jamal al-Din lifted his prohibition on military action following Muhammad al-Yaraghi's orders. Once the prohibition was lifted, Shamil eagerly took the side of the first imam as one of his close and most loyal assistants.[10] He accompanied Ghazi Muhammad in all his military campaigns and was with the imam during his last battle at Gimrah in 1832.[11]

Appointed by Ghazi Muhammad as his deputy in the Koysubu (Hindal) *jama'ats*, Shamil soon became the head of the Naqshbandi branch in that province and one of the most prominent Naqshbandi leaders in Daghestan.[12] However, due to the severe wounds he had received at Gimrah, Shamil did not raise serious claims to the imamate after the death of the first imam, and accepted the appointment of Hamza Bek after his confirmation by Muhammad al-Yaraghi. He joined the new imam as his deputy in the Koysubu province and participated in most of his military campaigns.[13]

At the battle of Khunzakh, Shamil stood at Hamza Bek's side, but after the assassination of the Avar khans he left the Avar capital and returned to his native Gimrah. 'It would be better for us' – said Shamil to his companions on their way back [to Gimrah] – 'if we leave Hamza for a year until people forget all that we have done, for we have been cruel to them and enraged them.'[14]

It was in Gimrah that Shamil learned about Hamza Bek's assassination. On hearing the news he acted quickly. He immediately assembled a small party of his *murids* and summoned a gathering of the Naqshbandi mullahs, *qadis* and military leaders at Ashilta.[15]

The meeting took place on 20 September 1834. Shamil opened it with a speech in which he announced the death of Hamza Bek and urged that a new imam should be elected immediately. The gathering unanimously chose Shamil as their imam but Shamil thrice refused the offer and accepted the nomination only when the people gave him an oath of their full and complete obedience.[16]

Shamil's initial refusal did not really stem from any reluctance on

10 On Shamil's activities as a deputy of the first imam see al-Qarakhi, 1946, pp. 42-3, 49-60. Also Chapter 18, above.

11 On Shamil's escape from the battle at Gimrah see above, Chapter 18.

12 *AKAK*, vol. VIII, pp. 589-90.

13 Al-Qarakhi, 1946, pp. 61-8.

14 *Ibid.*, p. 66. He tried to convince Hamza Bek to do the same and strongly opposed his decision to stay in Khunzakh. See above, Chapter 19.

15 On the meeting see Drozdov, 1899, vol. XX, pp. 254-5; Hajji, Ali, 1992 pp. 15-16; Runovskiy, in *AKAK*, vol. p. 1472; al-Qarakhi, 1946, p. 68. In his account al-Qarakhi claims simply that Shamil 'inherited the imamate from Hamza'.

16 On his election, see Drozdov, 1899, pp. 254-5; Baratov, 1910, no. 1, p. 11.

his part to accept the title. The place of the gathering – the birthplace of his mother where he enjoyed popular following – and the urgency with which he held the meeting – thereby preventing Naqshbandi leaders from other areas of Daghestan and Chechnya attending – clearly indicate that it was intended to guarantee Shamil's election as new imam. Furthermore, the presence and support of Sheikh Jamal al-Din al-Ghazi-Ghumuqi, who after the death of Muhammad al-Yaraghi had become the chief *murshid* of Daghestan and Chechnya, ensured the legitimation of Shamil's election by the supreme Naqshbandi spiritual authority. As for his repeated refusal to accept the title, this was the first manifestation of the tactics that he applied on several later occasions and which were to ensure Shamil's full power and control over his followers.[17]

Two weeks after the gathering, fifty of Shamil's *murids* seized the late imam's treasury and transferred it to Ashilta.[18] It seemed that the new imam had been nominated. However, his power was recognised neither by other Naqshbandi leaders nor by the ordinary people of Daghestan and Chechnya. Only a few villages of the Koysubu *jama'ats* and a few dozen of his *murids* accepted him as imam.

The opposition to the Naqshbandis and their cause increased after the Russian military expeditions in September-October 1834 during which Gimrah was destroyed, Akusha and Hutsal were made to swear an oath of submission and the people of the Avar khanate accepted Russian citizenship.

Back in Gimrah,[19] Shamil tried to demonstrate his power by ordering and promptly carrying out the execution of a traitor who had served as a pathfinder for the Russians[20] and threatened others with similar punishment. However, a few days later, a delegation led by Hasan Muhammad al-Harikuli, the chief *qadi* of Gimrah, went to the Russians to express their full and complete obedience.[21]

Shamil's attempts to reinforce the *shari'a* were hampered by the general opposition of both the religious authorities and ordinary Muslims of Gimrah,[22] and he was soon forced to leave. He moved to Ashilta where he stayed for almost two years, but even there his support was

---

[17] The same tactics were repeated in 1840 when after the defeat at Akhulgoh Shamil arrived in Chechnya to lead the revolt. See below, Chapter 21.

[18] This consisted of the treasury of the Avar khans, which Hamza had taken after the khans were assassinated, and held in Hutsatl. Hajji Ali, 1992 (reprint), pp. 16-17.

[19] On hearing the news that the Russians had entered Gimrah, Shamil immediately left Ansal, where he had gone after the meeting at Ashilta. When he approached Gimrah, he found it destroyed and the last Russian soldiers leaving. He attacked the Russian rearguard and had several clashes with them. *AKAK*, vol. VIII, pp. 589, doc. no. 477; al-Qarakhi, 1946, p. 69.

[20] Drozdov, 1899, pp. 255-6.

[21] Al-Qarakhi, 1946, p. 71.

[22] *Ibid.*, pp. 71-5

less than certain and at least on one occasion he had to leave the village and stay elsewhere.[23]

The strengthening of the Naqshbandi opposition led to the revival of the religious debate concerning the legitimacy of the imam's office in the North Caucasus which had originated at the time of Ghazi Muhammad. Those opposed to Naqshbandi political teaching and activities maintained that only one living spiritual leader (imam) could exist in the Muslim world at a given time and that the Ottoman Sultan was the only possible leader. For their part the Naqshbandis, while recognising the authority of the Ottoman Sultan, claimed that since he could not exercise his authority over the remote areas of *Dar al-Islam* (the Muslim World) there was a need for other leaders so that Muslims would not be left without spiritual guidance. At the core of this argument was the attitude to Russian rule, for the implication was that the war against the Russians was illegal, once the Sultan himself had concluded peace with them.

Shamil's position among other Naqshbandis was also less than certain, his credentials being recognised only by the Naqshbandis in the Koysubu *jama'ats*, while Naqshbandi deputies in other parts of Daghestan and in Chechnya did not accept his authority and refused entry to his deputies. Several Naqshbandi leaders challenged Shamil's claims over the imamate – Qibid Muhammad al-Tilitli and Tashou Hajji al-Enderi, to name but the two most prominant ones.

From the poor family of Hachulaw Muhammad, Qibid Muhammad received a good religious education and became one of the best scholars of Daghestan. He allegedly received initiation into the *tariqa* from Jamal al-Din, although this seems doubtful, since he disregarded Jamal al-Din's confirmation of Shamil as imam and made his own claim to the imam's title.[24] Whatever his spiritual background there is little doubt that Qibid Muhammad was more of a military than a religious leader[25] and, to establish his authority, he relied mostly on force.[26]

A more serious challenge was presented to Shamil by another rival, Tashou Hajji, the leader of the Naqshbandis in Chechnya who, unlike Qibid Muhammad, was both a prominent military leader and an accomplished Naqshbandi sheikh.

---

[23] At some point Shamil was forced to leave Ashilta and move to 'Isha, but was expelled from there as well and returned to Ashilta. *Ibid.*, pp. 68-76.

[24] In Russian captivity Shamil recognised Qibid Muhammad's qualities as a leader and claimed that he was the only man capable of uniting the mountain peoples and leading them in battle after his surrender (Tashou Hajji had died earlier, in 1843). Dnevnik Runovskogo, entry of 6 July, 1860; list 18.

[25] Rumyantsev, 1877, p. 33. In his account Rumyantsev presents Qibid Muhammad as an extremely courageous but simple-minded man. See *idem.*, pp. 40-51.

[26] In 1834 he executed thirty-three elders from Tilitl who refused to accept his authority. Al-Qarakhi, 1941, p. 73; Hajji Ali, 1992, p. 20.

Tashou Hajji al-Enderi[27]

Tashou Hajji was born in the Qumyq village of Enderi.[28] One of the largest centres of the North Caucasus, Enderi had a considerable population of Chechens as well as Qumyqs, and it has not been established whether Tashou Hajji was a Chechen or a Qumyq.[29] He received a sound religious education and while still a young man went on the pilgrimage to Mecca. On his return from the hajj, he acquired the honorary title of Hajji, and established himself as a respected mullah, well known among both the Qumyq and the Chechen people. His fame spread rapidly throughout the Qumyq plain, and from there into the high-mountain Chechen *tuqums*, which used the Qumyq plain as their winter pasture and thus had close links with the Qumyq.

When Muhammad al-Yaraghi started propagating the Naqshbandi *tariqa*, Tashou Hajji accepted it. Little is known about his spiritual education, but his writings reveal him as an accomplished scholar and mystic.[30] He had attained the rank of sheikh in his own right and was appointed by Muhammad al-Yaraghi as 'a *murshid* with full permission (*idhn mutlaq*) to preach in the land stretching from Chechnya to Anapa'.[31]

When Ghazi Muhammad declared *ghazavat* (1829-30), Tashou Hajji was among the first to join him.[32] At that point he left the Qumyq plain and established himself in the high mountain Sayasan village in

---

[27] There is very little written and published on Tashou Hajji-al-Enderi. The only scholar to study his life and activities was A.B. Zaks. She published only a few articles: Zaks, 1941; 1976; 1992. I have largely based my research on Tashou Hajji's own writings. I am extremely grateful to Magomed Galaev for providing me with copies of several manuscripts written by Tashou Hajji. For the purposes of this book I have utilised only that material which helps to elucidate some unclear points in his struggle for power. His writings, however, are of a highly abstract, esoteric character.

[28] Grzhegorzhevskiy, 1876, vol. I, p. 147. According to some other sources, Tashou Hajji was born in Michik, in Chechnya. See Zaks, 1976, p. 140.

[29] He spoke both languages fluently and could gain access to the Chechen *tuqums*, something other Daghestanis could not.

[30] In his treatise *Sharh Tifl al-Ma'ani*, Tashou Hajji discussed a variety of religious, mostly mystical, matters such as the attributes and manifestations of God; ways to achieve vision of God, (*ru'yat Allah*); ways of return to God; relations between spirit (*arwah*) and body; ways to escape from darkness (*dhulmaniyya*) and enter light (*nuraniyya*); as well as practical Sufi matters such as the way to adopt *tauba*, perform *dhikr*, etc.

[31] From the claim of Tashou as mentioned in his treatise *Al-As'ila al-'Adida min al-Makan al-Ba'id* (hereafter, *al-As'ila al-Adida...*), p. 9.

[32] Gammer claims that Tashou was one of the followers of Sheikh Abdalla al-Ashilti, Ghazi Muhammad's deputy in Chechnya. Gammer, 1994, p. 79. Unfortunately, he does not give any reference for this information. The manuscript of Tashou Hajji directly points to Muhammad al-Yaraghi as his *murshid* and although Abdallah and Tashou Hajji must have acted together while in Chechnya, I have no evidence to substantiate Gammer's claim.

Greater Chechnya as Ghazi Muhammad's deputy.[33] Having overcome the initial opposition of Udi Mullah, a local Chechen Naqshbandi sheikh in the Godali village, Tashou Hajji firmly established himself as the head of the Naqshbandis in the high mountains along the imaginary Chechen-Daghestani border. He selected the Almak village next to the Chechen Aukh *tuqum* in Salataw as his place of residence and it soon became the main stronghold of the Naqshbandi brotherhood in the area.[34]

By the time of Ghazi Muhammad's death, Tashou Hajji already felt strong enough to claim the title of imam for himself. He held the banner of the late imam and continued his cause independently of Hamza Bek. However, when Muhammad al-Yaraghi confirmed Hamza as the new imam, Tashou Hajji withdrew his claims, openly recognised the second imam and continued his activities in Chechnya as his deputy.[35]

After Hamza's assassination in 1834, Tashou Hajji came forward again as a major candidate for the title. He issued an appeal in which he denounced the local *'adat*, called upon people to abandon blood feuds and entrust all matters to the *shari'a*, of which he claimed to be the main interpreter.[36] This appeal was remarkably similar to that of the first imam, and put together with the invitation to continue Hamza's struggle against the infidels and his intention to go on a *ziyara* (visit) to the grave of Hamza Bek,[37] stated a clear claim to the imam's title.

When Shamil held the meeting at Ashilta and was elected as the new imam, Tashou Hajji did not recognise him as such and continued to act as leader in his own right. Even the support that Jamal al-Din al-Ghazi Ghumuqi gave to his favourite student did not change the balance in Shamil's favour. Although respected for his deep knowledge and spiritual achievements, Jamal al-Din was seen by other Naqshbandi sheikhs as an equal and did not wield the authority commanded by Muhammad al-Yaraghi before him. Furthermore, once Jamal al-Din took Shamil's side and tried to assist his claims by sending the *khalifas* (deputies) loyal to both himself and Shamil to various parts of Chechnya and Daghestan he encountered serious opposition from Tashou Hajji and other Naqshbandi leaders.

Rising to the challenge, Tashou Hajji dismissed the authority of Jamal al-Din and claimed to have achieved a superior rank (*martaba*) in the *tariqa* than that of Jamal al-Din, by having 'fully seized the

---

33 Tashou Hajji escaped into the Chechen mountains among a number of other Ghazi Muhammad's Qumyq followers after their defeat at Vnezapnaya. See Volkonskiy, 1888, vol. XII, pp. 20, 24; Zaks, 1992, p. 12.

34 Runovskiy, in *AKAK*, vol. XII, p. 712.

35 Volkonskiy, 1888, vol. XII, pp. 20-1.

36 Zaks, 1992, p. 12.

37 In his appeal he wrote: 'The time has come for us to go to the land of Hamza and pray at his grave', as quoted in Zaks, 1992, pp. 12-13.

inward *batin* and outward (zahir) [dimensions of the Divine Knowledge]'
and being only 'one step behind the Prophet Himself'.[38] Moreover,
Tashou Hajji accused Jamal al-Din of violating the main principles of
Naqshbandi ethics by sending new deputies into the Chechen lands in
an attempt to undermine his position there.

> He ought not to appoint anyone in my domain as all the sheikhs have agreed that
> there should not be more than one *murshid* in one quarter for fear of the moral
> decline of the contemporary sheikhs, for...if someone appeals to another sheikh
> and asks his assistance by extending *imdad* and *shafa'* and if he is accepted, the
> heart of the applicant leaves his sheikh and that is the worst abdication.[39]

Tashou Hajji supported his claim over Chechnya with more than purely
religious and mystical arguments:

> God willing, I shall satisfy the Chechen people for I know their state better than
> anyone else and I know how to preach to them according to their circumstances.[40]

Indeed, he knew the people he was preaching to well and his message
varied depending upon which *tuqums* he addressed. Among the better
educated and more religious Qumyq, Tashou Hajji laid the main stress
upon the shari'a and the importance of its strict implementation; addressing the Chechens, and especially those in the high-mountain *tuqums*,
he emphasised the importance of *ghazavat* against the Russians and
boasted of his military victories, which were the main source of legitimation among this less religious and more militant people.[41]

At the beginning, the position of Tashou Hajji appeared to be at
least as strong as that of Shamil and, perhaps, even more so. Whereas
in Daghestan, the scene of Shamil's activities, the people were dissatisfied
with the Naqshbandis and ready to turn to the Russians; in Chechnya
anti-Russian feelings rose high and contributed to strengthening Tashou
Hajji's position as a military-religious leader.

His leadership credentials were extremely strong and, according to
one Russian source, 'Tashou Hajji surpassed Shamil in his enterprising
and steadfast character. He enjoyed exceptional influence over the
Chechens and commanded their full trust and respect.'[42] Despite his
accomplishments, Tashou Hajji had little chance of becoming imam
without the support of the Daghestani Naqshbandis, who did not know
him well and were far away.

---

[38] Tashou Hajji, *al-As'ila al-'Adida*...p. 8-9. These claims are almost identical to those
expressed by Sheikh Shamil. See al-Qarakhi, 1946, p. 68.

[39] Tashou Hajji, *al-As'ila al-'Adida*..., p.8.

[40] *Ibid.*, p. 10.

[41] *Materialy k Istorii Pokoreniya Vostochnogo Kavkaza i Bor'by s Myuridizmom*,
(hereafter *Materialy...*) 1912, vol. XXXII, pp. 240-7; Zaks, 1992, pp. 12-14.

[42] Grzhegorzhevskiy, 1876, vol. XV, p. 147.

Thus, both Tashou Hajji and Shamil were confined to their respective domains and for several years channelled their efforts into consolidating support from their traditional followings.

Fostering of Shamil's spiritual image

Throughout 1835 Shamil was 'absorbed in reading and interpreting the Qur'an, preaching sermons and sending appeals to the Daghestani communities...and praying for the sinners who deviated from the rules of the shari'a'.[43] This period of spiritual retreat helped to create his image as a saintly figure upon whom God had bestowed His grace.

Much in line with Naqshbandi teaching, Shamil concentrated on propagating the necessity to uphold the shari'a as the ultimate duty of all Muslims. He argued that since the Prophet had preached God's message directly, all those who violated God-given legislation were committing the worst sin and deserved to be punished by death. Advocating strict implementation of the *shari'a*, Shamil claimed that God had chosen him as the main guardian of the Muslims in the North Caucasus.

Our Lord has extended His grace and mercy upon me and revealed to me that a humble pauper [*miskin*][44] would reach Divine Heaven easier than a rich man and would be sooner heard by God. And I am the first among these paupers.[45]

Shamil modelled his image after that of the Prophet Muhammad. Imitating the Prophet, he used small pieces of paper for his messages and appeals. Shamil likened his departure from Gimrah to the *hijra* of the Prophet from Mecca, and on leaving his house, he addressed it with the words:

Indeed, I part with you at a time when I cannot establish faith while [living] in you. For did not Muhammad the best of creatures of God Almighty leave the best land of God – Mecca, when he could no longer spread the faith there.[46]

It seems that it was also at that time that the stories of Shamil's childhood started to be modelled after those of the Prophet. It is well established that Shamil was born into the family of an *uzden*. However, stories spread that he was an orphan who, driven by poverty, had to go from one village to another selling dried peaches or taking work as a shepherd.[47] According to this version, he first started to see visions in the solitude of mountain pastures.[48]

---

[43] Drozdov, 1899, p. 264. The quotation is based on Gammer, 1994, p. 77.

[44] Miskin is also a common name for Sufis.

[45] *TsGVIA*, VUA, delo 6457, list 52-3.

[46] Al-Qarakhi, 1946, p. 76.

[47] Chichagova, 1899, pp. 44-5.

[48] The emergence of this legend suggests how similar stories about the childhood and early years of Sheikh Mansour emerged.

Even those who recognised the truth of Shamil's birth and childhood portrayed him as an extraordinary boy. The events of his life were reinterpreted in a different light to suggest his special destiny. Thus the story of his sickness in early childhood and 'miraculous' recovery after his parents changed his name – from Ali – came to be seen as a miracle and as Divine indication that he was predestined for an eventful life and entrusted with a special mission.

As a child Shamil was reputed to have been different from other boys: he spent hours in solitude on a rock nobody else dared to go to for fear of the legendary Samurg – the huge bird of Solomon – which was believed to have nested there.

Another story bears a striking resemblance to that of the Prophet. Once, on his way to the village of Tansu, where Shamil was taking lessons from a knowledgeable scholar, he saw a huge, smooth rock. Nobody could climb it and they would have to make a detour. However, Shamil 'flung himself onto it like a bird, engraving his footprint on its surface'.[49] This was the first miracle attributed to the young Shamil. In a similar way his escape in 1832 from the battlefield at Gimrah was interpreted as a manifestation of Divine protection.[50]

Shamil's strict adherence to the *shari'a* became legendary. Stories spread that even as a child he had never violated the shari'a and did his best to prevent his relatives and friends from committing any sins. Thus, feeling strong disgust towards wine, unusual among his contemporaries, Shamil tried to stop his father from drinking and even threatened to kill himself if he did not give it up.[51]

Consolidation of Shamil's power

Early in 1836 Tashou Hajji issued an appeal to the Daghestani Naqshbandis in which he reproached them for indecisiveness and called on them to join him in *ghazavat*, threatening otherwise to raid their villages and punish them 'with an army so strong nobody could resist it'.[52] Following the appeal, Shamil and Qibid Muhammad al-Tilitli held a meeting at Chirkah, during which they made an oath to act jointly.[53]

---

[49] On popular stories about Shamil's childhood, see Drozdov, 1899, p. 252-3.

[50] Some people even came to believe that Shamil had been killed but that God restored him to life to carry out His mission. Bodenshtadt, 1855, p. 270. Similarly, Shamil's escape from the besieged Akhulgoh in 1839 was later seen as a miracle. On his flight from Akhulgoh, see below.

[51] Drozdov, 1899, p. 252; Chichagova, 1899, p. 15. Extreme and strict obedience to the Shari'a law is a feature common to Sufi sheikhs. Many of them were reputed to possess an inborn virtuousness which prevented them from committing any minor sin, even before they had become aware of them.

[52] Text of the appeal in Grzhegorzhevskiy, 1876, vol. XV, p. 147; Zaks, 1992, p. 13.

[53] al-Qarakhi, 1946, p. 82; Zaks, 1992, p. 14.

This was an agreement between equals, each of whom claimed independent authority over the people in his domain. Despite the agreement Qibid Muhammad entered into negotiations with Mullah Ramazan of Hindal in order to bring the Hindal *jama'at* under his authority.[54] Tashou Hajji also upheld his full autonomy in Chechnya, where he was recognised as imam.[55]

However, the meeting at Chirkah led to the first joint military campaign during which both Tashou Hajji and Qibid Muhammad acted under the general command of Shamil, and which brought under his authority the Koysubu *jama'ats* along the left bank of the Avar Koysu river, Ihali, Orota, Greater and Lesser Hardayrik, Tsatanykh, Andi, Kialal and the outlying villages of the Avar khanate.[56]

By mid-1836 the balance of power changed in Shamil's favour. He had won most of his Naqshbandi peers over to his side. These included Akhberdy Muhammad, Surkhay al-Kulawi and Ali Bek al-Khunzakhi, who now acted under his command and formed the nucleus of his army.[57] In July 1836 he stated that 'this time...no one dares to oppose me any more'.[58]

While consolidating his forces, Shamil avoided any clashes with the Russians. After the assassination of Hamza Bek and with most Inner Daghestani *jama'ats* forced to take the oath of submission, the Russian command concentrated on the Right Flank in the North-western Caucasus.[59] Not able to carry out more than one strategic initiative at a time, they turned a blind eye to the strengthening of Shamil's position in Daghestan. Furthermore, Shamil succeeded in establishing indirect negotiations with Kluki von Klugenau through the *shamkhal* Sulayman Khan. On several occasions he assured the Russian command of his loyalty, formally accepted Russian citizenship, took an oath not to undertake any raids in the lowlands and restrain people 'in his domain' from doing so.[60]

In return Shamil tried to guarantee their non-interference in the domes-

---

54 Grzhegorzhevskiy, 1876, vol. XV, p. 148.

55 See *AKAK*, vol. VIII, p. 712, doc. 609; Tsagareyshvili (ed.), 1953, pp. 91-2.

56 Only few of these were brought under Shamil's control by force, many recognised the imam's authority voluntarily. Al-Qarakhi, 1941, pp. 82-5; Genichutlinkiy (Genichutli), 1992, pp. 73-5; Grzhegorzhevskiy, 1876, vol. XV, pp. 146-62; Gammer, 1994, p. 79.

57 Grzhegorzhevskiy, 1876, vol. XV, p. 153.

58 Shamil's letter to Kluki von Kluginau as quoted in *AKAK*, vol. VIII, pp. 601-2 doc. no. 505.

59 Drozdov, 1899, p. 266; Gammer, 1994, p. 74.

60 Nineteenth-century Russian historians vigorously opposed Shamil's claims that he had 'concluded peace' with the Russian command. Grzhegorzhevskiy, 1876, vol. XV, pp. 378-80. Although there was probably no direct agreement, Shamil must have conducted his negotiations with the *shamkhal* with the knowledge and general agreement of Kluki von Klugenau.

tic affairs of Daghestan. 'Do not prevent us from fighting amongst ourselves. No doubt that the bravest of us will win, order will prevail and, God willing, peace will be established.'[61]

Shamil claimed to have obtained agreement from the *shamkhal* and from the Russians that he would be allowed to establish the shari'a in mountain Daghestan.[62] Rendering the Russians small services,[63] Shamil made full use of the temporary 'truce' with them to consolidate his power. Thus, when Qibid Muhammad tried to bring the *jama'ats* of Hindal, Tilitl and Qarakh under his full control, Shamil informed Klugenau and presented him as the main challenger to peace and Russian authority in Daghestan.[64]

This correspondence with the Russian command also rendered Shamil additional legitimation in the eyes of the Daghestani people. By negotiating with the Russians the terms of a truce, Shamil acquired the standing of a recognised leader who entered into negotiations not as a defeated enemy, but as an equal party and an ally. It also allowed him to claim that he undertook his actions to reinforce the shari'a with the agreement and even support of the Russian command.[65] This was particularly important since most of those who opposed his rule made the threat of Russian punitive measures an excuse for not accepting his authority.

The reason behind the Russian policy of non-interference in the internal affairs of mountain Daghestan was not simply the lack of sufficient forces to carry out an offensive on the Left Flank. Unlike the majority of Russian officers, Kluki von Klugenau gave clear preference to peaceful means in subduing the Caucasus, and was prepared to negotiate and seek compromises with the local people. In return, he enjoyed the rare respect of both the ordinary people and local Daghestani authorities, some of whom claimed that 'he had no deficiency apart from non-recognition of the two *shahadas*', i.e. not being a Muslim.[66]

However, this did not mean that the goals of the Russian government in the North Caucasus had been modified. Rather it meant a temporary change of tactics, whereby means other than violence were deployed to ensure the subjugation of the area. Thus, they arranged for Taj al-Din

---

[61] From Shamil's letter to Klugenau of 6 April 1836, as quoted in Drozdov, 1899, p. 279.

[62] Shamil's letter to Klugenau in *AKAK*, vol. VIII, pp. 601-2, doc. no. 505; Shamil's letters to General Reut of 7 and 16 August 1836, as quoted in Drozdov, 1899, p. 276.

[63] On at least one occasion he prevented a party from mountain Daghestan from raiding the Qumyq lowlands. On another occasion he solicited the release of the Russian tradesmen taken as hostages by the people of the mountain *jama'ats* and encouraged them to return the goods stolen from the Russians. Grzhegorzhevskiy, 1876, vol. XV, p. 162.

[64] Grzhegorzhevskiy, 1876, vol. XV, p. 149.

[65] As Shamil stated in his letter to the elders of Chirkah. Grzhegorzhevskiy, 1876, vol. XV, p. 378.

[66] Al-Qarakhi, 1946, p. 71.

ibn Mustafa (Tazeddin Mustafin in Russian translation), a Muslim scholar from Tatarstan, to preach loyalty and submission to the Russian tsar among the mountain peoples of Chechnya and Daghestan.[67] The latter arrived on 29 June 1836 in Tiflis and set off on a tour around the North Caucasus. During his tour he visited and preached in the lands of the Khanates of Ilisu, Ghazi-Ghumuq, Kurah, Mehtuli, *shamkhalat* of Targhu, the Qumyq district and the Avar khanate. Although Taj al-Din was treated with respect in all the *jama'ats* he visited, his tour was of little help to the Russian authorities, for he was allowed entry only into the provinces under Russian control. The mountain *jama'ats* which recognised Shamil's authority did not allow him to enter their lands and announced that they did not need 'the Russian mullah' to preach to them.[68] Similarly, Taj al-Din's attempts to visit the Chechen *tuqums* failed after Tashou Hajji accused him of being a Russian spy and threatened him with death if he tried to enter Chechen territory.[69]

The beginning of military confrontation[70]

Klugenau's preference for peaceful means in dealing with the North Caucasian peoples was not shared by other Russian military and civil authorities, either in the Caucasus or in St. Petersburg. In 1836 Baron Rozen planned an offensive into Chechnya and Daghestan which was designed to force the unconditional surrender of the imam and stop the spread of *muridizm'* in the area.[71]

However, instead of undermining Shamil's authority and cowing him into full submission, the campaign achieved the opposite. On 9 September 1836 the Russians stormed and took Zandaq, the residence of Tashou Hajji in mountain Chechnya. The capture of Zandaq which was accompanied by extreme Russian brutality brought but a nominal recognition of Russian power, and even the Russian command had to recognise that by this action they only increased the prestige of the Naqshbandi teaching and its leaders in the area.[72]

---

[67] On Taj al-Din's mission, see Ramazanov and Khadzhiev (eds), 1959, p. 167, doc. no. 106; Bushuev (ed.), 1939, pp. 351-6, doc. no. 136, 140; pp. 359-60, doc. no. 140; Drozdov, 1899, pp. 290-2.

[68] A letter of the people of Andal to Taj al-Din, as mentioned in *ibid.*, p. 291.

[69] See the letter from Tashou Hajji to Taj al-Din, as quoted in *ibid.*, p. 292.

[70] Apart from the above-mentioned source, the following publications were of particular importance for research on Shamil's military confrontation with the Russians: published documents in *AKAK*, vol. VIII, IX; Ramazanov and Khadzhiev (eds), 1959; Tsagaresh-vili (ed.), 1953; Bushuev (ed.), 1939; Yurov, 1884-5; Baddeley, 1908; Gammer, 1994.

[71] According to Rozen, Shamil had to stop preaching the shari'a as a token of his unconditional acceptance of Russian citizenship. See Ramazanov (ed.), 1959, pp. 150-1 doc. no. 97. For more on Russian tactics, see Gammer, 1994, pp. 81-2.

[72] For the Russian evaluation of the military campaigns of 1836, see *AKAK*, vol. VIII, p. 501, doc. no, 503; p. 503 doc. no. 510; pp. 515-16, doc. no. 613; Drozdov, 1899,

In April 1837 the Russians brought their troops to Khunzakh,[73] took Ashilta, Shamil's residence for over two years, stormed Akhulgoh[74] and besieged the imam and his supporters in Tiliq.[75] The siege of Tiliq lasted more than a month and was a case unique in military history. While the Russians besieged Shamil in the village, the imam's supporters imposed their own blockade on the Russians, cutting off the road to Tiliq and depriving them of any possible reinforcements.[76] After forty days of this double blockade, General Faezi[77] had to conclude peace on the terms offered to him by Shamil. The tone of Shamil's letter in which he concluded peace with the Russians was that of a victor rather than a defeated subject:

We are hearby concluding peace with the Russian emperor, which none of us shall break unless one side commits an offence against the other. If, however, one side breaks the agreement, they shall be considered traitors and be damned by God and the people.[78]

Some time later Faezi requested an 'elucidation' of the meaning of the first letter, in the hope of receiving a more face-saving document. In his reply Shamil stated bluntly that 'peace had been concluded between the Russian emperor and Shamil'.[79] Shamil clearly benefited most from the treaty, in that he had consolidated his power over almost all of Inner Daghestan and mountain Chechnya and boosted his prestige in other parts of the North Caucasus.

In the course of the Russian campaigns of 1836-7 the process of turning Shamil's adversaries into loyal supporters was finally completed.[80] The destruction of Tashou Hajji's stronghold at Zandaq and

---

pp. 282-4.

[73] On the Russian Avar campaign, see Bodenshtadt, 1855, p. 277; Baddeley, 1908, pp. 294-5; Grzhegorzhevskiy, 1876, vol. XV, pp. 380-1; Gammer, 1994, p. 84; Yurov, 1884, vol. VIII, pp. 13-37.

[74] For more on the Russian military campaigns, see Yurov, 1884, vol. VIII, pp. 63-7; Gammer, 1994, p. 86.

[75] On the Tiliq campaign, see *AKAK*, vol. VIII, p. 617, doc. no. 530; Grzhegorzhevskiy, 1876, vol. XV, issue 3, pp. 645-9; Gammer, 1994, pp. 86-7; Ramazanov and Khadzhiev (ed.) 1959, 168-9, doc. no. 107; Yurov, 1884, vol. VIII, pp. 70-2.

[76] Brought to the brink of starvation, the Russian soldiers exchanged their clothes and bullets for bread. Yurov, 1884, vol. VIII, p. 72.

[77] General Faezi led the Tiliq campaign. On him see *AKAK*, vol. IX, p. xxix; Baddeley, 1908, p. 304; Gammer, 1994, p. 83.

[78] As quoted in *AKAK*, vol. VIII, p. 602; Grzhegorzhevskiy, 1876, vol. XV, issue 3, pp. 648-9. For a translation of the letter, see in Baddeley, 1908, p. 305-6; reprinted in Gammer, 1994, p. 89.

[79] Yurov, 1884, vol. VIII, p. 1 (of Appendix 2).

[80] The process of Tahsou Hajji's recognition of Shamil as imam started some time earlier and the first document in which Tashou Hajji referred to himself as 'Imam Shamil's vazir' is his letter to Taj al-Din. As quoted in Drozdov, 1899, p. 292.

the killing of many of his supporters weakened Tashou Hajji's position *vis-à-vis* the imam.[81] Later, at Tiliq, both he and Qibid Muhammad had to recognise Shamil's strategic vision and accept his military command over their unified forces.[82] Furthermore, the Russian command itself, by virtue of holding negotiations and signing peace with Shamil, reluctantly recognised his authority as ruler of Chechnya and Daghestan.[83]

Shamil was quick to build on his success. Shortly after the campaign he issued an appeal to all *jama'ats* under his control, in which he presented the peace at Tiliq as a victory granted to him and his faithful supporters by God and lured the hesitant to his side:

Ye warriors of Daghestan! When the leader of the Russians sent forth his call to you in the month of Shawwal [January/February] to seduce you from your faith in the truth of my mission, there arose doubt and murmuring among you; and many of you became unfaithful and forsook me.[...] But with the few, they who remained faithful, I went forth against the unbelievers, slew their leader and drove them away in flight.[...] Ye have seen how small was the number of the warriors in comparison with the hosts of the enemy, and yet they gave way to us, for strength is with the believers.[...] Verily God is with those who do His will! Ye have seen that however great the numbers of the unbelievers, they must always fail. When they sent to Hamza Bek and summoned him to surrender, they said 'Lay down your arms, all opposition is in vain, the armies which we send against you are like the sands on the seashore innumerable. But I answered them in his name and said, 'Our hosts are like the waves of the sea which wash the sands and devour them!'[84]

Furthermore, Shamil sent numerous letters to the more remote areas of Kubah and Samur. In his letters he boasted of his achievements at Tiliq and called people to rise in arms under his leadership against the infidels.[85]

Negotiations between Shamil and the Russians

On paper the Russians claimed victory. In their reports to St. Petersburg, the Caucasian military command declared that the Tiliq campaign had attained all its aims and brought Shamil and his supporters to heal.[86]

---

[81] Zaks attributes Tashou Hajji's acceptance of Shamil's authority precisely to this time. See Zaks, 1992, p. 16.

[82] At Tiliq, Qibid Muhammad and, especially, Tashou Hajji wanted to leave the besieged village but had to submit to Shamil's decision to stay. This was the first time the imam demonstrated his power over his former rivals and compelled them to accept his tactics.

[83] In early September 1837, Faezi tried to counterbalance Shamil's growing popularity by issuing a proclamation in which he disputed Shamil's role as a ruler of Daghestan. This, however, had little effect on the people in Daghestan. *AKAK*, vol. VIII, pp. 617-18.

[84] The Russian text of the appeal, see in Bodenshtadt, 1885, pp. 287-91. The translation is based on Gammer, 1994, p. 90.

[85] Tsagareshivili, 1953, pp. 90-1, doc. no. 81.

[86] See the letter of Faezi to Rozen 12 July 1937 as quoted in Yurov, 1884, vol. VIII, p. 75. The version was later repeated in Rozen's report to St. Petersburg, thus creating a completely false impression of the situation in the Caucasus.

Nicholas I and his ministers were led to believe that the whole of Daghestan had been finally subdued and Shamil subjugated.[87] The emperor scheduled a visit to his new province for the autumn of 1837. He requested that during this visit Shamil, Tashou Hajji and Qibid Muhammad should come and swear an oath of loyalty to him and accept Russian citizenship. This was, however, not an easy aim to achieve, as the Russian command in the Caucasus were only too well aware. Baron Rozen ordered that the imam and his companions should be brought to the emperor 'voluntarily or by force' and entrusted Kluki von Klugenau with the task of negotiating with Shamil his oath of submission.

Shamil met Klugenau on 30 September 1837 near Chirkah. It seemed that following Klugenau's long and earnest speech, Shamil was almost convinced to accept the offer.[88] He announced, however, that he was unable to give a final answer until he had consulted Tashou Hajji, Qibid Muhammad and his other allies. In an answer that reached Klugenau a few days later, Shamil wrote that due to the joint position of the respected elders and '*ulama* who had allegedly 'disagreed [with his decision to go to Tiflis to meet the emperor], expressed displeasure and, finally, taken an oath that if I really intended to go, they would kill me',[89] he had to refuse the offer.

It remains unclear whether Shamil referred to Tashou Hajji, Qibid Muhammad and others merely as an excuse not to offend by his refusal the one Russian general whom he respected, or whether he was genuinely not in a position to take such an important decision without consulting other North Caucasian leaders.[90] However, after the Russians tried to pressure him into meeting the emperor, Shamil became suspicious of their true intentions and in his final letter to Klugenau bluntly stated the reason for his refusal as his mistrust of the Russians. 'I have finally decided not to go to Tiflis...for I have often experienced treachery on your part as everyone knows.'[91]

---

[87] Grzhegorzhevskiy, 1876, vol. XV, issue 3, p. 650; Yurov, 1884, vol. VIII, p. 77.

[88] There is a detailed description of the negotiations in al-Qarakhi, 1946, pp. 91-2; Grzhegorzhevskiy, 1876, vol. XV, issue 3, pp. 653-4; Yurov, 1884, vol. VIII, p. 77; Gammer, 1994, pp. 92-4.

[89] Yurov, 1884, vol. VIII, p. 84; Grzhegorzhevskiy, 1976, vol. XV, issue 3, p. 654-5. The letter is partly quoted in Gammer, 1994, p. 93.

[90] On the one hand, by 1837 his position among both the ordinary people of Daghestan and Chechnya and his former Naqshbandi rivals was finally confirmed and he was generally recognised as an imam with full authority. On the other hand, Shamil's power was far from being absolute, and in the North Caucasian social setting, he had to take into consideration the views of other secular and religious authorities.

[91] For the text of this letter, see Ramazanov and Khadzhiev (eds), 1859, p. 371, doc. no. 144; Grzhegorzhevskiy, 1876, vol. XV, issue 3, p. 657; Yurov, 1884, vol. VIII, p. 86. The English translation is based on Gammer, 1994, p. 94.

Nicholas I arrived in the Caucasus in October 1837 and spent a whole month touring the area. During this tour he came to realise that despite enormous material and human resources and military efforts having been committed to the subjugation of the area, it still defied Russian control. Even the rulers of the Daghestani principalities under Russian supremacy regarded the emperor as a superior ally rather than as their sovereign. As to the *jama'ats* in Inner Daghestan and the Chechen *tuqums*, they remained beyond Russian reach and free from any foreign rule. Disappointed and angered at what he had seen in the Caucasus, the emperor made subjugation of the North-eastern Caucasus the immediate priority for 1838-9.[92]

The Russian assault at Akhulgoh

Well aware of the inevitable Russian campaign against him, Shamil was preparing to meet the challenge. He ordered the construction of a formidable fortification in rocky Akhulgoh. The choice of the fortress was excellent, for its topography made Akhulgoh a natural fortress; Shamil perfected it with technical devices which 'would have done credit to any European architect'.[93] Confident that his new fortress was impregnable, Shamil intended to lure the Russian army to Akhulgoh, where it was to be attacked from the rear by the forces of Tashou Hajji.[94]

However, the Russians modified their initial plan and started the campaign from Chechnya, defeated Tashou Hajji and deprived the imam of his vital support.[95] Shamil then made an unsuccessful attempt to raise the spirits of his Chechen followers and bring them to the battlefield. He sent his deputy Qadi Gabats to Chechnya, where he accused Tashou Hajji of indecisiveness and cowardliness and tried to mobilise the Chechens to act under his own command. This was a futile exercise as the reason behind Tashou Hajji's decision not to join Shamil at Akhulgoh was the Chechen's reluctance to fight outside their land, reluctance exacerbated by the recent defeat. Qadi Gabat's accusations were unfair and his attempts to bring the Chechen forces to the imam fruitless. His arrival only aggravated the situation. Tashou Hajji, annoyed at the un-

---

[92] On the Russian plans, see Yurov, 1884, vol. VIII, pp. 13-22.

[93] Bodenshtadt, 1855, p. 299. At the construction of Akhulgoh Shamil used the experience of the Polish engineers who had deserted the Russian army and joined him. Ibid., pp. 299-300.

[94] On Shamil's plans see *TsVIA, VUA*, delo 6306, list 35, 59, 70-5; Bodenshtadt, 1855, pp. 301-2.

[95] The defeat of Tashou Hajji was so decisive that the latter even lost his much treasured banner of Ghazi Muhammad. See Zaks, 1992, p. 18. On the Russian military campaign in Chechnya, see Bushuev, 1939, pp. 414-5, doc. no. 157; Yurov, 1884, vol. VIII, pp. 14-22; Baddeley, 1908, p. 316.

deserved reproach, released his *murids* and went to the Benoy *tuqum* in Ichkeria.[96]

On 5 June 1839 the Russians started their campaign against Shamil. Albeit with some difficulty, they overcame Shamil's positions at Irghin village and on 24 June 1839 besieged Akhulgoh and trapped the imam in the fortress.

As Shamil no longer had the support of Tashou Hajji, and with the Russians determined to crush him resistance was condemned to failure. Still, he withstood the blockade for eighty days and entered into negotiations with the Russians only under pressure from his supporters.[97]

At these negotiations, Shamil expressed his willingness to accept all their conditions in return for permission to remain in the Caucasus where he promised to resign himself to a quiet life far removed from all worldly politics. As a token of his word, Shamil handed over his favourite son, Jamal al-Din, as a hostage. The Russians, however, did not leave any room for compromise. They demanded full and unconditional surrender, after which the imam was to be transferred to Groznaya and left to the mercy of the emperor.[98]

Still, no matter how desperate Shamil's position he was not prepared to give in. He refused to go to the Russian camp and formally surrender. The Russian command realised that Shamil would not surrender voluntarily and on 21 August started a major assault.[99] This was one of the fiercest battles ever fought in Daghestan. The Russian soldiers had orders to take no prisoners. 'Surrounded from all sides...with no hope for retreat or mercy, [the defenders of Akhulgoh] fought with unimaginable ferocity.'[100] Not one of the defenders sought mercy or offered their surrender, 'even women in frenzy for defeated [Akhulgoh] throwing themselves on the [Russian] bayonets'.[101] Many women and children committed suicide, while men were slaughtering their horses so that they would not fall

---

[96] Yurov, 1884, p. 13-27.

[97] It is beyond the scope of this work to give a detailed description of the military campaign. For more information on one of the most important campaigns in the course of the whole Caucasian War, see al-Qarakhi, 1946, pp. 101-9; Baratov, 1909-10, no.3, pp. 1-22; Grzhegorzhevskiy, 1876, vol. XV; Yurov, 1884, vol. IX, pp. 23-83; Milyutin, 1850, pp. 100-27; Gammer, 1994, pp. 99-109.

[98] Milyutin, 1850, pp. 102-27; Shigabuddinov, 1992, pp. 39-108; Gammer, 1994, pp. 99-109.

[99] In fact this was the third major assault. The first one was undertaken at the end of July, the second on 16 August. For more see Gammer, 1994, pp. 103-7. (His dating is given in the new style. I quote the dates as they are given by the Russian sources. i.e. thirteen days earlier). For a description of the attack see Milyutin, 1850, pp. 117-18; Yurov, 1884, pp. 79-80.

[100] *AKAK*, vol. IX, p. 333.

[101] Milyutin, 1850, p. 117.

into the hands of the Russians.[102] When Shamil's fortification[103] finally fell, the Russians did not find a single defender alive.[104] However, some of them, including Shamil, managed to escape and hid in caves nearby. For several days the Russians tried to seize numerous caves around Akhulgoh and capture the imam. Despite these efforts Shamil, several surviving members of his family[105] and a handful of his supporters cut through the line of Russian soldiers and crossed the Andi Koysu river to make a daring escape from Russian captivity.[106]

The Russians, although somewhat disappointed by Shamil's escape, celebrated their 'full victory'.[107] Following the fall of Akhulgoh all Daghestan gave an oath of submission to the Russian Emperor. Even the people of Chirkah village, who were among the most ardent supporters of the imam and took pride in the fact that the Russians had never set foot on their soil, invited the Russian army to come to their village, as a token of their full loyalty and submission. On the arrival of the Russian detachment they handed over all Naqshbandi followers from the village, paid tribute[108] and agreed to cut down their famous vineyards to make space for the new Russian fort to be built nearby.[109]

In Chechnya the people also submitted: they handed over *amanats*, paid tributes, cut down forests at the request of the Russian command[110] and accepted the Russian-appointed *pristavs* into their villages.[111] In January 1840 Grabbe reported to the minister of war that 'full and complete peace had been established on the Left Flank'.[112] With no

---

[102] Al-Qarakhi, 1946, pp. 108-9; Genichutlinskiy, 1992, p. 82; Shigabuddinov, 1992, pp. 97-8.

[103] Shamil's fortification beyond the village became known as New Ahulgoh as opposed to Old Akhulgoh, i.e. the village itself.

[104] On the losses on both sides, see Shigabuddinov, 1992, pp. 101-2; Gammer 1994, pp. 109.

[105] Jawharat, one of Shamil's wives, and her baby son were killed in the retreat from Akhulgoh. al-Qarakhi, 1946, p. 113.

[106] On Shamil's escape, see *ibid.*, pp. 109-13; Shigabuddinov, 1992, pp. 100, 103-5; Yurov, 1884, vol. VII, p. 83.

[107] The Emperor even issued a special medal for the seizure of Akhulgoh, which was distributed among the surviving participants of the campaign. Bodenshtadt, 1855, p. 320.

[108] 40,000 sheep out of the village's 120,000.

[109] The Naqshbandi followers in Chirkah tried to resist the decision and even undertook a small military action against the Russian detachment. They, however, had lost their influence in the village and could not change the prevailing mood of submissiveness. On the events in Chirkah, see Bodenshtat, 1855, pp. 317-18.

[110] Several clearings were made in the forests of Gekhi, and at Valerik in between Lesser Ataghi and Shali.

[111] Yurov, 1886, vol. X, p. 268. Only at the villages of Batash-yurt and Kazbek-yurt did the Russians encounter some resistance, *ibid.*, p. 269.

[112] *Idem.*

major uprising anticipated, the Russian command devised plans to incorporate the area into the empire. Three more fortresses were to be
built to secure Russian communications,[113] while the system of *pristavs*
was to guarantee the establishment of Russian administration.[114] The
Russians all but forgot about Shamil. They rejected his offers of submission, which he made on the condition that he would be allowed to
stay in Daghestan, and set a mere 100 roubles as a price on his head.
In just a few months he proved that he was worth much more than
that.

[113] At the entrance to the Argun gorge on the Chechen Plato, in the Qumyq lands and
in Salataw near Chirkah.

[114] On the Russian plans for 1840-1, see *ibid.*, pp. 268-71.

21

RESURRECTION OF SHAMIL'S POWER[1]

The capture of Akhulgoh shook the whole of Daghestan. The people struggled to come to terms with the idea that even their inaccessible mountains could no longer offer them protection from the enemy. In despair people turned against the Naqshbandi order and blamed the imam and his supporters for all their troubles. All Daghestani *jama'ats* denounced the imam and refused him entrance into their villages. Even in his native Gimrah, Shamil was met by patrols that opened fire on him.[2]

Forced to travel only at night, Shamil was provided for by the members of the Naqshbandi order, who secretly brought him and his companions provisions and warned him of possible dangers. However, they were in no position to offer the imam more substantial help or invite him to their villages.[3]

The Naqshbandi order also experienced a deep crisis, its position being considerably undermined by the devastating losses. About 500 of the most loyal Naqshbandis were killed and another 900 captured at Akhulgoh. Many others were handed over to the Russians as hostages by their *jama'ats*. Those who remained in the area lost virtually all their prestige and influence, while the people openly expressed their hostility towards the *murids*.

Among his Naqshbandi followers Shamil's authority also seemed to have been somewhat shaken. Some Naqshbandi leaders rendered an oath of submission to the Russians,[4] some laid claims to the succession,[5] while others treated Shamil as their companion rather than imam.[6] Defeated and abandoned by most of his followers, Shamil arrived in Chechnya at the end of 1839 at the invitation of Tashou Hajji.[7] He settled in

---

[1] In addition to the above-mentioned sources on Shamil, this chapter is based on Dubrovin, 1871; Potto, 1870; Potto, 1887-97; Potto, 1901-4; Yurov, 1882; Yurov, 1883; Yurov, 1884-5.

[2] Al-Qarakhi, 1946, p. 118.

[3] On Shamil's flight, see al-Qarakhi, 1946, pp. 111-22.

[4] E.g. Qibid Muhammad.

[5] Milyutin, 1850, p. 132.

[6] As is clearly seen in the description of Shamil's flight from Akhulgoh provided by al-Qarakhi, 1946.

[7] Zaks, 1992, p. 19

Gharashkiti village in the Shatoy *tuqum* (Shubut in the Russian translation) in mountain Chechnya.[8]

Unlike Daghestan, the Chechens of Greater Chechnya disregarded
all Russian appeals to denounce Tashou Hajji and other Naqshbandi
leaders and refused to expel them from their lands. They remained
loyal to their Voqqh Hajji[9] and gave Shamil a warm welcome. Tashou
Hajji, Shuayib Mullah and Jawad Khan, who were among those who had
laid claim to succeed Shamil, renewed their allegience and expressed
their full loyalty. Welcoming Shamil to Chechnya, Shuayib Mullah
promised that: 'Soon other supporters will gather around you here, more
worthy than the old ones. As far as I am concerned, I am your devoted
slave...and shall fulfil all your orders.'[10]

Shamil's rise to power in Chechnya

The encouraging words of Shamil's Chechen deputy proved to be
prophetic. Assisted by his supporters, Shamil made a phoenix-like rise
to power in an incredibly short space of time. In Gharashkiti he established
himself first and foremost as a religious authority. His vast knowledge
of the *shari'a* and his pious way of life earned him the respect of the
people in the Shatoy and neighbouring *tuqums*.

Shortly after Shamil's arrival in Gharashkiti a remarkable incident
occurred. A Chechen decided to sell a Muslim woman as a slave, and
Shamil intervened on her behalf. He accused the Chechens of violating
the *shari'a*[11] and threatened to kill his host if this woman was not
released immediately. His threats against his Chechen host were a clear
violation of the local *'adat* according to which host-guest relations were
inviolable. In other circumstances such behaviour would have caused
outrage among the Chechens but in Shamil's case it only emphasised
his uniqueness and reinforced his reputation as a holy man. The Chechens
released the woman and acknowledged Shamil's right to institute the
shari'a among them.[12]

His very defeat at Akhulgoh was turned in his favour. People saw
his escape from the besieged fortress as a manifestation of Divine Providence and a sign of the special destiny assigned to him by God.

One day Shamil sat in the open exposed to the gaze of the Russians.[...] He longed

[8] The idea to take Chechnya as imam's residence was first advocated by Shamil's
supporters in 1837 after his defeat at Ashilta. Then, however, Shamil declined to move
his capital to Chechnya, driven primarily by his doubts about Chechen loyality.

[9] Great Hajji – the nickname given by the Chechens to Tashou Hajji.

[10] Al-Qarakhi, 1946, p. 121.

[11] According to the *shari'a* no Muslim could be a slave, and especially not be sold as
such by another Muslim.

[12] Al-Qarakhi, 1946, p. 122-3.

for death but it comes only from God Almighty. And how could God have desired Shamil's...death, for he charged him with what he designed to be done to the infidels, to conquer the *munafiq*, glorify Islam and to arrange the affairs of the Muslims in This World and Hereafter. And it is said in the Book [Qur'an 13:18]; 'As to what is useful to people, it remains on earth'.[13]

Word of his piety quickly spread throughout the area and people started to come and visit him. Some sought his *baraka* and initiation into the *tariqa*, others asked his advice on various religious matters and invited him to be their judge. Gradually he acquired a number of devoted followers who settled around his residence and put themselves under his spiritual patronage. Delegations started to arrive inviting him to settle in their villages and assume religious authority over them.

The establishment of Shamil's position in the Shatoy and the neighbouring Chechen *tuqums* was assisted by the efforts of Tashou Hajji, Shuayib Mullah and his other deputies,[14] who mobilised support on his behalf in other parts of Chechnya.[15] In these efforts Shamil and his companions were unwittingly assisted by the Russians, just a few months of whose rule had stretched the limits of the Chechen's endurance. Later Russian historians laid the blame for Shamil's raise to power on the Russian-appointed *pristavs*. These virtual outcasts were recruited by the Russian command from among the local militia men and received no fixed salary. They felt free to compensate for their service to the Russian government by taking bribes, appropriating taxes and abusing their power in every other possible way.

Under the pretext of collecting taxes and fines the people's best arms and other harmless yet valuable belongings were expropriated. It happened that completely innocent people were arrested at the instigation of false and untrustworthy interpreters. Prisoners and even *amanats* were treated inhumanely.[16]

True as these accusations were, the actions of the local *pristavs* were but a manifestation of the vices existing throughout the Russian empire, now merely transplanted onto Caucasian soil. The fault lay with the Russian system of government, based on authoritarian misrule and the use of force.

General Pullo, appointed as the head of the Russian administration on the Left Flank, was an embodiment of this system. A talented officer,

---

[13] *Ibid.*, p. 107.

[14] One of Shamil's deputies active in Chechnya at the time was Muhammad al-Quduqli. He had performed the piligrimage to Mecca and assumed the title of Hajji and Effendi. Thus in the historiography of that period he became known as Hajji Muhammad Effendi. Yurov, 1886, vol. X, p. 277.

[15] While Shamil mobilised the support in northern Chechnya, Tashou Hajji was active in the Aukh *tuqum* in the north-west and Ahberdy Muhammad in Lesser Chechnya and among the Ingush. Al-Qarakhi, 1946, pp. 123-5.

[16] Yurov, 1886, vol. X, p. 271.

he was 'extremely cruel, unscrupulous and often unjust'.[17] Hated by the Chechens, he had already inspired the outbreak of hostilities in Chechnya in 1838, but at that time the people's anger was checked by the defeat of Tashou Hajji at Zandaq and Shamil at Akhulgoh and they submitted to his rule.

However, unlike the people in Daghestan, the Chechens soon recovered from this shock, which in any case had never been as strong as in Daghestan. By the spring of 1840 'more than enough explosive material had been amassed in Chechnya and only a spark was needed to create a comprehensive explosion'.[18]

This spark came when General Pullo ordered the confiscation of the best firearms. This meaningless order, issued to demonstrate complete Russian authority over the Chechens, was interpreted by the local people as the worst kind of humiliation.[19] Their dismay was exacerbated by rumours that the Russians intended to supplement this order by forcing all men and women into slavery[20] and to introduce conscription into the Russian army.[21]

In January 1840 a delegation of Chechens from lowland Chechnya came to Shamil. The delegates offered their total obedience to the imam and asked him to assume authority over them. Just as he had done at the time of his first election as imam, Shamil first refused the offer and yielded to their pleas only after they gave him an oath of their absolute obedience and handed over hostages from respected families. These were transferred to Akhberdy Muhammad, his Daghestani lieutenant who had arrived in Chechnya shortly before hand.[22]

In March 1840 the whole of Chechnya was in uproar: now Shamil joined his deputies in their campaigns. He criss-crossed Chechnya trying to bring the whole area under his control and stir up insurrection against the Russians.[23]

The accounts of Shamil's campaigns in various Chechen *tuqums* bear strong resemblance to Ghazi Muhammad's early campaigns in Daghestan. In every *tuqum* people held a communal gathering (*jama'at*)

[17] *Ibid.*, p. 271.

[18] *Ibid.*, p. 272.

[19] Handed down from father to son, weaponry in the Caucasus is still seen as the most precious posession and the symbol of manhood and family honour.

[20] I.e. to introduce the system of serfdom as it existed in the mainland of Russia and of which the Caucasians knew well from the Russian soldiers they had captured or who had deserted to them.

[21] Yurov, 1886, vol. X, pp. 272-3; al-Qarakhi, 1946, pp. 123-4.

[22] On the description of the meeting, see Ocherk, 1876 p. 354; Dubrovin, 1871, p. 465; Yurov, 1886, vol. X, pp. 274-5. They also destroyed before Shamil's eyes the medals which they had received for their loyalty to the Russians. Al-Qarakhi, 1946, p. 122.

[23] Report of General Grabbe to the Minister of War, Chernyshev, 31 March 1840, in *AKAK*, vol. IX, p. 248.

to discuss whether they should seek accommodation with the Russians or accept Shamil as imam. The outcome often had a direct link with the position of the Naqshbandi order in a particular *tuqum*, for during his campaign Shamil relied heavily on his Naqshbandi followers who usually belonged to the younger generation.

In some *tuqums* Shamil had to use force to overcome opposition. He took *amanats* from the most respected families and publicly denounced his opponents. Such 'dispensations of justice' provoked the resistance of the independent-minded Chechens, and on one occasion Shamil was nearly killed. In the Ingush village of Gu, Shamil had executed several elders and blinded another. The latter broke into Shamil's room and stabbed him several times.[24]

Notwithstanding such temporary setbacks, Shamil's power grew rapidly and by May 1840 he had won over the majority of Chechens in both Greater and Lesser Chechnya, including those living in Nazran district and the Qarabulaq *tuqums* along the Assa, Sunja and Fortanga rivers. They expelled all Russian appointed *pristavs* and gave Shamil an oath not to enter into any negotiations with the Russians.

To secure his position in Chechnya, Shamil resettled whole villages from the easily-accessible lowland areas into the mountain forests.[25] By doing so he ensured that the Chechens under his authority had no links with the Russians and drew a clear border between the territories under Russian control and his domain. Thus, by early summer 1840 almost all Chechens had left the upper Terek and upper Sunja areas and resettled beyond the left bank of the Sunja.[26]

In parallel with gaining control over Chechnya, Shamil and his deputies organised regular raids against the Russian military line. After the disaster at Akhulgoh, Shamil changed his military tactics and avoided direct clashes with the Russian army, resorting to guerrilla warfare. Here, mobile parties of the mountain peoples who, unlike the Russian army, were familiar with the terrain, gained a clear advantage over the clumsy Russian army. Furthermore, it allowed the parties of North Caucasian warriors to fight simultaneously in several places.[27] This, coupled with the tactics of misinformation applied successfully by Shamil

---

24 Al-Qarakhi, 1946, pp. 127-9; Yurov, 1886, vol. X, pp. 291-2. This incident checked the spread of Shamil's authority in the Ingush lands.

25 This tactic Shamil "borrowed" from the Russians who had resettled the local people to suit their own aims. See above.

26 Dubrovin, 1871, p. 465; al-Qarakhi, 1946, p. 125.

27 Thus, for example, on 26 April 1840 Shamil fought at Aukh, Akhberdy Muhammad threatened Groznaya and Tashou Hajji – Vnezapnaya. Ramazanov and Khadzhiev (eds) 1859, pp. 243-9, doc. no. 130-4.

and his companions,[28] frustrated the Russians, who by May 1840 had once again lost the initiative.[29]

This loss of initiative was at least partly due to the fact that the Russian command found it impossible to believe that only a few months after their decisive victory at Akhulgoh, the Chechens could stage a comprehensive revolt.[30] They mobilised all available force to the Chechen theatre, but their actions were ambiguous and indecisive. While chasing, usually unsuccessfully, the parties of Shamil's warriors, they continued to implement their original plans for the construction of new fortifications, which consumed much of their efforts and prevented them from taking the offensive.[31]

Although Shamil was the ultimate leader of the Chechen uprising of 1840, it was his Chechen deputies, Tashou Hajji and Shuayib Mullah, who prepared and conducted it. Furthermore, taking advantage of the deployment of the Russian forces in Chechnya, from July 1840 Shamil concentrated his efforts in Daghestan.

Consolidation of Shamil's authority in Daghestan

Shamil first established secret contacts with the people of Koysubu and Untsukul in March 1840. In April he sent numerous written appeals to the Inner Daghestani *jama'ats*. These appeals coincided with the first Chechen military victories, and coupled with the news of Russian defeats on the West Flank, gradually started to change the general mood of the Daghestanis. In early June 1840 the people of Salataw, Andi and Gumbet (including Chirkah village) allowed Shamil's *murids* to enter their *jama'ats* and accepted Shamil's authority. This gave Shamil the necessary base and provided him access to the *shamkhalat* and Avaria.

Throughout the summer and early autumn of 1840 Shamil was busy in Daghestan where he preached in the Avar *jama'ats*, threatened the Avar khanate and raided the Qumyq plain.[32] In August several villages in the *shamkhalat*, eight Avar villages and the *jama'ats* in low Sulaq and Gimrah recognised his authority. More importantly still, Qibid Muhammad, Shamil's former associate, who had, after Akhulgoh, sworn

---

[28] On conflicting reports that the Russian command received at that time, see Yorov, 1886, vol. X, pp. 284-5.

[29] *AKAK*, vol. IX, pp. 248-51, doc. no. 255.

[30] Failure to assess the situation in the North Caucasus was aggravated by the deep enmity in the Caucasian Command between Golovin and Grabbe, one of whom was *dejure* and another *defacto* commander of the Caucasian troops. On this enmity, see Yurov, 1886, vol. X, p. 330.

[31] On the assessment of the Russian tactics in 1840, see *ibid.*, p. 286; Gammer, 1994, pp. 119-20.

[32] *AKAK*, vol. IX, pp. 338-42, doc. No. 300-4; Yurov, 1886, vol. X, pp. 308, 332-4, 345-60; Grzhegorzhevskiy, 1976, vol. 6, pp. 355-7.

an oath of submission to the Russians, once again joined Shamil and swore loyalty to him. This brought under Shamil's authority the *jama'ats* to the north of the Andi Koysu river, which had kept their alliance with Qibid Muhammad.[33]

In October 1840 Shamil returned to Chechnya, leaving Daghestan transformed by his activities. The morale of the people was largely restored, while the Russians had lost the initiative; their prestige, so fiercely won during the Akhulgoh campaign was shattered, to restore it 'many years and numerous heroic deeds were required'.[34]

Furthermore, shortly after Shamil left Daghestan a very important event occurred which unexpectedly brought to him one of the most influential men in Daghestan and his former sworn enemy: Hajji Murad, the assassin of Hamza Bek and *de facto* ruler of the khanate. In 1834 Hajji Murad's defection cost the Naqshbandis the Avar khanate, which under him recognised Russian rule and on numerous occasions successfully resisted Shamil's campaigns. However, the general mistrust of the Russian command for any local leader made Hajji Murad prone to the elaborate intrigues of his traditional enemy, Ahmad Khan of Mehtuli.[35] The latter persuaded the Russian command that Hajji Murad had maintained secret links with the Naqshbandis. As proof Ahmad Khan used the fact that Hajji Murad continued to wear a white turban on his *papakh*. Although this was officially allowed by the Russians, it was worn mainly by the Naqshbandis, and thus seen as a sign of anti-Russian hostility.

On 22 November 1840 Hajji Murad was arrested; he was to be transported to Temir-Khan-Shura with an escort of forty soldiers and four officers. Enroute, with Hajji Murad tied to a rope held by two Russian soldiers the party passed along a narrow mountain path. At a sharp bend in the path Hajji Murad suddenly pulled the rope towards him thus freeing himself from the Russian officers and jumped into a deep abyss. The deep snow softened the fall and saved him from certain death.[36]

Immediately after Hajji Murad's escape, Kluki von Klugenau tried to improve the situation and lure him back through negotiations.[37] However,

[33] According to N.V, Qibid Muhammad joined Shamil not in 1840, but in 1841; N.V., 1888, vol. XII, p. 219.

[34] Yurov, 1886, vol. X, p. 329.

[35] Ahmad Khan was an official ruler of Avaria since the death of Aslan Khan of Ghazi-Ghumuq until his own death in 1843. From 1843 the khanate was put under direct Russian rule with prince Orbeliani appointed as the head of the administration.

[36] On Hajji Murad and his endeavours, see Potto, 1870, pp. 159-82; Shulgin, 1909, vol XL, pp. 54-70; Kvinitadze, 1934, pp. 8-12; Baddeley, 1908, p. 352; Gammer, 1994, pp. 122-4.

[37] Klugenau in fact was the only Russian officer who tried to oppose the arrest of Hajji Murad from the very beginning. The order to arrest Hajji Murad was issued during his short period of absence from the area.

the usual lack of co-ordination between the Russian officers made any negotiations impossible. When Hajji Murad arrived in Tselmes, his native village, he found his house destroyed, his property ransacked and his three close relatives taken hostage by Ahmad Khan and executed. The Russians blamed Ahmad Khan for these actions, but as far as Hajji Murad was concerned they clearly demonstrated that the Russian command was only after his head.[38] In reply to Klugenau's letter, Hajji Murad bitterly wrote: 'I do not trust you at all, because I know positively that you, Russians, dislike a brave man.'[39]

On hearing the news of Hajji Murad's escape, Shamil reacted immediately. He let Hajji Murad know that he was ready to forget the past and accept him into the ranks of his distinguished lieutenants. Determined to revenge the humiliation inflicted on him by the Russians, Hajji Murad accepted the offer and gave an oath of loyalty to the imam. In return Shamil appointed him as his deputy in Avaria with full authority over it.

The defection of Hajji Murad profoundly changed the balance of power in Daghestan. Situated in a strategic location between Chechnya, Andi and Gumbet on the one hand and the rest of Daghestan on the right bank of the Avar Koysu river on the other, the Avar khanate was key to the domination of both southern and northern Daghestan.[40] Now the most prominent Avar leader, who had fought Shamil on numerous occasions, brought the imam the support of his many followers in the Avar lands.[41]

Furthermore, the defection of Hajji Murad triggered that of Hajji Yahya, a member of the Ghazi-Ghumuq ruling family,[42] and brother of Harun Bek and Mahmud Bek, the two regents of Kurah and Ghazi-Ghumuq respectively. This significantly reinforced Shamil's positions in central Daghestan and opened the Ghazi-Ghumuq khanate to his influence. Thus, in 1842, both his brothers appealed through Hajji Yahya to Shamil to give them support against the Russians.[43] As a result, in the spring of 1842 Shamil entered Ghazi-Ghumuq, seized the rich treasury

---

[38] See N.V., 1888, vol. XII, pp. 219, 236-9.

[39] Yurov, 1886, vol. X, p. 368; also quoted in Gammer, 1994, p. 123.

[40] The loss of Khunzakh by the Russians in 1843 also deprived them of their only base in the heart of Daghestan. Grzhegorzhevskiy, 1876 vol. VI, pp. 368-9.

[41] Al-Qarakhi, 1946, p. 164.

[42] He was the nephew of Aslan Khan of Ghazi-Ghumuq and the son of Tahir Bek. On him, see Gammer, 1994, p. 125.

[43] This appeal came after they learned about the Russian plans to build a fortress in Ghazi-Ghumuq accompanied by rumours about Russian intentions to dispose of Mahmud Bek, the regent of Ghazi-Ghumuq, in favour of his cousin.

of the khans and put the villages of the khanate and the neighbouring *jama'ats* under his rule.[44]

The following year Shamil's main attention was drawn to the Avar khanate where the Russians had massed their forces and laid down more than a dozen fortified points. Following the death of Ahmad Khan of Mekhtuli in 1843, the khanate was put under direct Russian control with Prince Orbeliani as the head of its administration. However, the loss of Hajji Murad's support significantly undermined the Russian position in the area, and this could only partially be compensated for by their military might. Thus, in the autumn of 1843 Shamil fought two most successful campaigns in the Avar lands which brought him control over the whole of Avaria.[45] This was followed by Shamil being able to recruit the people of Akusha and Tsudaqar, who had previously been loyal to the Russians.[46]

By 1845 Shamil's domain was at its largest and his power at its peak. It included all the *jama'ats* along the Avar Koysu river, parts of Ghazi-Ghumuq khanate in the east, Vladikavkaz in the west, Qaytaq, Tabarsaran, Terekem and the *jama'ats* along the Lezgin line in the south, and well into the Qumyq lands in the north.[47] In 1846-7, exploiting his successes in Daghestan and Chechnya, Shamil attempted to extend his domain and bring first the Kabardians in the central North Caucasus and then people in southern Daghestan under his control, an ambition which he had long held.

Shamil's aspirations in the Central and West Caucasus

The resistance of the Circassian tribes in the central and western Caucasus produced as many fearless fighters and intelligent leaders as in the east. However, Islam failed to unite the various Circassian tribes, and they did not co-operate as readily as in Chechnya and Daghestan where 'people were less hostile to each other and united more easily'.[48] It had been Shamil's long-felt ambition to extend his power over the central West Caucasus and bring the resistance of both lines under his unified leadership.

It was primarily the Kabardians who would have to provide a bridge

---

[44] See the Russian reaction to Shamil's campaign in Ghazi-Ghumuq in *AKAK*, vol. IX, pp. 391-2, doc. no. 348. For Shamil's account of the events, see his letter as quoted and translated by Gammer, 1994, p. 131. On the military history of Ghazi Ghumuq campaign and Shamil's confrontation with the Russians, see Gammer, 1994, pp. 131-6.

[45] On the Avar campaign, see Gammer, 1994, pp. 139-48.

[46] Grzhegorzhevskiy, 1876, vol. VI, p. 370.

[47] In 1841-2 Shamil carried out raids beyond this border into the Tusheti and Khevsurety lands. See Yurov, 1886, vol. XII, pp. 22-33, 258-60; Ramazanov and Khadzhiev (eds), 1959, pp. 305-6, doc. no. 163; Tsagareshvili, 1959, pp. 199-202, doc. no. 159-60, 162.

[48] Yurov, 1885, vol. IX, p. 7.

between the East and West Caucasus. In the first half of the nineteenth century they were settled in the central North Caucasus, bordering on Pyatigorsk and Mozdok *uezd* (province) in the north, Ossetia and Svanetia in the south, the lands of Abadzekhs (one of the Circassian tribes, present day Abkhaz) in the west and the Vaynakh (Ingush) lands in the east.[49]

Due to their central location, the Muslim Kabardians had always maintained close links with both their western and eastern neighbours. When the Russians advanced into their territory, the Kabardians joined with the Vaynakh in raiding their settlements. After the construction of the Russian fortification line between the upper Tahtamysh and the Urukh rivers, the links between the two further intensified. Those Kabardians who did not recognise Russian authority escaped into the lands of free Abadzekh or more often Chechen communes, where they formed 'fugitive' communities.[50]

Through these Kabardians the ideas of the Naqshbandi brotherhood started to penetrate into areas to the west of Chechnya. In their turn the people of the West Caucasus despatched their emissaries to seek aid and advice from Shamil, who readily sent his agents to their lands.

In 1842 Shamil dispatched Hajji Muhammad al-Daghestani, who settled in the Shapsugh lands[51] and started preaching beyond the Kuban' river. His preaching brought him a certain number of followers who became famous for their fearless raids against the Russians. However, the efforts of Hajji Muhammad in spreading the Naqshbandi *tariqa* were curtailed by his early death in 1844.[52]

His successor, the Daghestani *'alim* Sulayman Effendi' was a deeply religious but uncharismatic person who failed to inspire enthusiasm or lead the resistance. Besides, in 1846 – less than a year after his arrival – he turned to the Russians and denounced Shamil.[53]

---

[49] After the change of borders by the Russian administration, the Kabardians were pushed away from their eastern lands, which were resettled by Ossetians, predominantly Christian and loyal to the Russians. Thus the present Kabardino-Balkar republic has no administrative border with the Checheno-Ingush republic.

[50] This migration further intensified after the Russians unleashed their campaign of terror, during which they carried out 'exemplary' executions of individuals and whole villages. However, instead of bringing the Kabardians into submission this had an opposite effect. As recognised even by official Russian historians, these measures 'finally embittered the people of Kabarda, who now began to run away not in ones or twos or separate families but in whole *auls* with their elders'. Volkionskiy, 1879, vol. IV, p. 148.

[51] The term Circassian was applied to various tribes. The Shapsugh, Abadzekh, Natukhay, Ubykh, Djiget tribes lived in classless tribal groups similar to that of the Chechens. Beslenji, Mahoshi, Temirghoy, Egirukay, Biedukh had developed a local aristocracy and a limited class of landlords similar to that in the khanates in Daghestan. On the Western Caucasus, see Olshevskiy, 1895, vol. VI, pp. 179-80.

[52] *Ibid.*, p. 180; *AKAK*, vol. IX, pp. 890, 897-901.

[53] Prozritelev, 1927, vol. III, pp. 125-9.

The third and the most successful of Shamil's emissaries in the west was Muhammad Emin. Born in the Koysubu *jama'at*, Muhammad Emin had accepted the Naqshbandi *tariqa* directly from Shamil and in 1846 went to propagate it in the Kabardian lands. He successfully overcame the initial mistrust of the Kabardian people, learned the local language and finally became integrated into the local society after his marriage into a well-established Adygh Temirghoy princely family. It was this marriage rather than his Naqshbandi association that allowed him to rise to an important social position in the Temirghoy tribal association. This is hardly surprising, since among the Circassians, where the missionaries had traditionally arrived from the west, the Daghestanis lacked the religious prestige that they enjoyed among the Chechens. Thus, the authority of Muhammad Emin was interpreted in traditional and largely secular terms and he never managed to implant the Naqshbandi order firmly among the Circassians. He was first and foremost a military leader and never reached a prominence similar to that of Shamil in the east.

However, he successfully overcame the opposition of Effer Bey, a famous leader from a local family, well known both among the Caucasians and the Ottomans, and carried out a set of reforms similar to those administered by Shamil in the east.[54] In the late 1840s, the links between Muhammad Emin and Imam Shamil were gradually reduced to a subordination which was purely that of a religious hierarchy. Muhammad Emin turned into a leader in his own right with no real co-ordination in military activities between him and Imam Shamil. However, throughout his life he kept the spiritual link with Shamil based on the *murshid-murid* relationship.[55]

In his effort to bring the central and western Caucasus under his authority Shamil did not rely exclusively on his Naqshbandi deputies. In the early 1840s he and his deputies ventured on several military campaigns into the Kabardian lands. The first was undertaken in 1840 by Akhberdy Muhammad, Shamil's closest ally, who raided the Russian Mozdok fortress. Akhberdy Muhammad planned and executed his campaign independently of Shamil and its only result was rich booty but no strategic gains.[56] Similarly, the campaign into Lesser Kabarda, undertaken under Shamil's direct leadership in the spring of 1841, did

---

54 He organised the *mahkama* (shari'a court), recruited the *murtaziqa* (police) from among his most loyal followers and thus concentrated both judicial and executive powers under his control.

55 After he finally surrendered to the Russians, Muhammad Emin went to visit Shamil in Kaluga to receive his final blessing before leaving for Ottoman Turkey.

56 Perhaps the most significant gain during this raid was a beautiful Armenian hostage, Anna Uvarova, whom Akhberdy gave as a gift to Shamil. She converted to Islam and became the imam's favourite wife, known as Shuanet.

not achieve its aims.[57]

In 1846, at the pinnacle of his military and political career, Shamil organised a large-scale campaign into the Kabardian lands.[58]

The invasion of Ghabarta [Kabarda] was Shamil's peak, and with it his power reached its furthermost limits. For Shamil this campaign had a very special – one is tempted to use the word sacred – meaning and witnesses described that he was in a very festive, merry and affable disposition. The force marched in somewhat solemn order. The imam explicitly forbade plundering or using force against local people, saying: 'I shall coerce no one, they themselves will follow whatever is agreeable to God.'[59]

Although carefully prepared and skilfully executed, this campaign failed to achieve Shamil's ultimate goal to incorporate Kabarda into his state.[60] Furthermore, it clearly demonstrated Shamil's shortcomings and 'revealed his huge disadvantage in the overall balance of power with Russia...So large was the disparity that he had no chance of winning a strategic victory.'[61]

Shamil tried to compensate for his failure in the west by bringing southern Daghestan under his authority.[62] In 1847 the Didoy, Antsukh, Kapuch and other *jama'ats* of southern Daghestan broke out in open revolt. They expelled the Russian-appointed *pristavs* and invited Shamil to assume authority over them. Despite his military successes, Shamil's political gains in southern Daghestan turned out to be short lived. Only a year later the imam's deputy, Hajji Muhammad, was expelled by the people; all southern Daghestani *jama'ats* denounced Shamil's authority and continued their anti-Russian efforts independently of the imam.[63]

The loss of southern Daghestan, along with the imam's failure to bring under his authority the lands west of Chechnya, marked the limitation of Shamil's efforts to extend his domain. From 1846-7 his state stopped growing in size.

Both Shamil's campaign in Kabarda and southern Daghestan indicate the crucial importance of the Naqshbandi brotherhood in cementing Shamil's power. It seems that it was not accidental that Shamil had succeeded in firmly establishing his authority only in those areas where

---

[57] The aim of this campaign was to cut off Russian communications along the Georgian military way which linked the North Caucasus with the Transcaucasus.

[58] On the campaign, see al-Qarakhi, 1946, pp. 198-200.

[59] Gammer, 1994, p. 170.

[60] On Shamil's military campaigns in Kabarda, see Gammer, 1994, pp. 162-71.

[61] *Ibid.*, pp. 169-70.

[62] On Shamil's military campaigns in southern Daghestan, see *Ibid.*, pp. 195-207.

[63] On the Lezgin people and their Russian/Shamil relations, see Volkonskiy, 1885, vol. IX, pp. 160-216.

the Naqshbandi brotherhood had put down deep roots,[64] while in the communes with no Naqshbandi following, Shamil could achieve only a temporary victory.

The assassination of the second Naqshbandi imam which coincided with the death of the chief *murshid* of the North Caucasus presented the first serious challenge to the integrity of the Naqshbandi order in the area. With no generally recognised supreme spiritual authority, the Naqshbandis lacked a vehicle to ensure the smooth transfer of the imam's office. This resulted in the outbreak of rivalry between several antagonist parties.

In the absence of an authority capable of bolstering the new imam, the contenders had to rely on their own achievements. Those claiming the imam's office not only had to demonstrate administrative and military skills, but had to have reached an advanced rank in the Naqshbandi spiritual hierarchy to win credibility as the foremost religious authority with both the Naqshbandi order and ordinary Muslims.

In the ensuing power struggle two principal claimants combining the necessary qualities emerged. Characteristically, they represented the two main constituent parts of the Naqshbandi domain in the North Caucasus – Daghestan and Chechnya, which themselves corresponded to the two centres of the Naqshbandi order that had crystallised in the North Caucasus.

Furthermore, each of the two leaders representing their domain personified differing concepts of power and modes of interaction between the ruler and the ruled in their 'constituencies'. Thus, for several years two poles of the Naqshbandi order existed in the North Caucasus, each with its independent local leader: Tashou Hajji in Chechnya and Shamil in Daghestan.

Although each of the two leaders commanded the loyal support of the Naqshbandis in his respective domain, the split among the Naqshbandis of the Northern Caucasus clearly demonstrated the military and logistical limitations of each of the two parts. Of the two Naqshbandi peers, Tashou Hajji had fewer chances of becoming the new imam of the North Caucasus, for tradition and history were strongly against him. There was no precedent of a Chechen religious authority extending his power to Daghestan. On the other hand, the whole history of the spread of Islam in Chechnya was closely linked to the activities of the Daghestani preachers, mullahs and scholars, who were held in extremely high esteem by the Chechens. It took Tashou Hajji a number of military defeats

---

64 Characteristically the positions of the Naqshbandi brotherhood are still strongest in the same areas where Shamil's influence had been most stable, i.e. mountain Chechnya and western Daghestan: Ichkeriya (Vedeno district in the Soviet administrative system), the former territory of the Avar khanate (present-day Khunzakh district in Daghestan) and Andalal society (present-day Ghunib district in Daghestan).

finally to recognise the limitations to his ambitions and to concede to Shamil the stewardship of the overall Naqshbandi brotherhood and the movement.

Immediately after Tashou Hajji recognised Shamil as imam, the Chechens readily accepted his leadership. Furthermore, it was in Chechnya that Shamil found his spiritual and political rescue after his devastating defeat at Akhulgoh. From then onwards Chechnya replaced Daghestan as Shamil's main base from which he mounted a spectacular return to eminence both in Chechnya and Daghestan. Shamil never failed to appreciate the strategic importance of Chechnya for the survival of his cause. As long as Chechnya remained with him and under his control, he could, and indeed did, weather many failures and tactical defeats. Indeed, it was only when Chechnya was irrevocably lost to the Russians that Shamil's defeat became inevitable.

Shamil's remarkable recovery from near oblivion and his rise to prominence among the Chechens revealed a new trend in the political set-up of the region. Defeated, abandoned by his followers and ousted from his native Daghestan, the imam represented everything that a new leader of Chechnya should not be. Yet, he was accepted by the Chechens as such. This change in attitude to power and leadership was one of the main achievements of the Naqshbandi *tariqa*. Previously all the Chechen leaders had to 'earn' their credibility mainly on the battlefield and through following the *'adat*. In contrast, Shamil's main credentials lay in the spiritual sphere by being a link between God and the Muslims and a supreme judge who ruled on the basis of the *shari'a* which was above tribal and clan concepts of justice.

The existence of the network of *murids* in the main *tuqums* and *jama'ats* of Chechnya and Daghestan was yet another reason behind the success of Shamil's mission despite the number of military defeats. In a sense, the Naqshbandi order acted as 'Shamil's clan' which permeated all the existing clan and tribal formations of Daghestan and Chechnya and served as a vehicle for Shamil's influence and power. The fact that Shamil only ruled temporarily small parts of the areas beyond the Naqshbandi grasp, such as southern Daghestan and Kabarda, serves as best evidence to that effect.

Part VIII. THE STATE OF GOD: ITS CREATION, PEAK AND DECLINE

22

SHAMIL'S IMAMATE[1]

The viability and longevity of Shamil's undertaking was attributed by many historians and by the imam himself[2] to his administrative reforms, which led to the creation of the first unified state on the territory of Inner Daghestan and Chechnya. The formation of the North Caucasian imamate was a gradual and lengthy process. It had already been started by the first two imams, who had laid the foundations of the reform by introducing a common *shari'a*-based legislation throughout the area. By doing so they assumed the role of spiritual guides and supervisors of the local rulers and claimed a higher religious authority over them.

This idea originated in the Naqshbandi-Mujaddidi tradition, which advocated the responsibility of a Sufi sheikh to safeguard the rulers of the Muslim *umma* in order to ensure the strict implementation of the *shari'a* at all levels of social life. However, while in the Middle East or Muslim India the Sufi sheikhs had to provide religious guidance to a commonly accepted and well-established ruler, in the North Caucasus the Naqshbandi imams had to carry out their *shari'a*-reinforcing activities in a number of independent state-like formations governed by independent rulers or councils of elders. To ensure their acceptance by the local rulers and ordinary people they had to overcome the opposition of traditional non-Naqshbandi religious authorities and the pressures of Russian military administration. They could achieve their aims only

---

[1] The main sources for the present chapter are Bushuev, 1937; Linevich, 1877; Nakhcho, 1886; Makarov, 1859; Nizam Shamilya, 1970; Pokrovskiy, 1923 (1991); Przhetslavskiy, 1863; Rumyantsev, 1877; Runovskiy, 1860; Runovskiy, 1862; Runovskiy, 1862(a); Runovskiy, 1862(b); Dnevnik Runovskogo, *AKAK*, vol. XII, p. 13; Sharafutdinova, 1970; Sharafutdinova, 1974; Sharafutdinova, 1975; Shamil i Chechnya, 1859; Saget, 1900.

[2] 2 *AKAK*, vol. IX, p. 346; Runovskiy, 1862, p. 329.

through a combination of both political and military means. Thus, when elected as the first Naqshbandi imam, Ghazi Muhammad assumed both religious and military leadership.

In order to reach the remote areas of Chechnya and Daghestan Ghazi Muhammad applied the traditional Sufi practice of dispatching his deputies into various communes. These deputies were to watch over and report to the imam on the progress made in introducing the *shari'a* and, in the event of a joint military campaign, the deputies were to mobilise people's support and recruit warriors into the imam's army.

This was the first step towards bringing the isolated North Caucasian communes under a unified shari'a-based legal system and to ensure their co-ordination in resisting the Russians. However, the lack of law-reinforcing means available to either the imam or his deputies hindered the further consolidation of power.

Neither the first nor the second imam attempted to modify the existing social and political order of the North Caucasus. In their activities they did not try to change the traditional power structure and at most sought to substitute those rulers who opposed their authority with more compliant ones.[3] Even when Hamza Bek removed the dynasty of the Avar khans, he did not attempt to replace it by an alternative Sufi institution.[4]

Shortly after Shamil was elected an imam in 1834, he applied tactics similar to those of his predecessors. He dispatched deputies, tried to win the support of local rulers and make them recognise his religious and military supremacy. Gradually, however, Shamil came to realise the limitations imposed by the existing order, and embarked on a far-reaching course of reform. Through a comprehensive set of administrative, fiscal and military measures Shamil eliminated the power base of the traditional elite and created a state which became known as the Imamate of Shamil.

Religious and administrative officials in Shamil's imamate

One can identify three sources for Shamil's administrative reform: firstly the Sufi framework which he adapted into a lay form of social organisation; secondly the structure of the Ottoman empire, of which he learned mainly through his association with a certain Hajji Yusuf;[5] and thirdly what he had seen of a centralised Russian autocracy.

---

[3] In 1831 Ghazi Muhammad nominated Ummalat Bek as the new *shamkhal* and Umar Bek as new *utsmiy*. See *AKAK*, vol. VIII, pp. 543-4, doc. no. 422; vol IX, pp. 375-7, doc. no. 334; Volknoskiy, vol XIII, p. 307; *ibid.*, vol. XIV, p. 103.

[4] Hamza Bek was assassinated shortly after the annihilation of the family of the Avar khans and he may not have had time to implement his plans. For, unlike his predecessor, he showed no inclination to pass the title of the Avar khan to anybody, but rather assumed the prerogatives of the ruler himself.

[5] Hajji Yusuf was a Chechen, who had spent many years in Egypt, where he studied

The whole organisation of the imamate was based on the religious, or, to be more precise, Naqshbandi structure which Shamil had transformed to suit the needs of his state. At the top of the pyramid was the imam – the supreme temporal and religious authority who exercised his power through an elaborate system of deputies and representatives.

Shamil had divided the territory under his control into large military-administrative districts – *vilayat*[6] or *naibstvo*[7] (in Russian Sources) – headed by deputies.[8] Outwardly similar to the traditional Sufi *khalifas*, the institution of *naibs* in Shamil's imamate turned into an administrative structure with well-defined functions.

Initially, the *naibs* had full authority over all military, administrative and judicial matters in their *vilayat*, and recognised Shamil merely as commander-in-chief and as a point of reference in religious matters. In 1847 Shamil issued a special decree which significantly narrowed the scope for the *naibs'* ambitions as Shamil's competitors and ensured their greater subordination to the imam.[9] This decree confined the *naibs'* powers to military issues, and transferred all judicial matters to the jurisdiction of specially appointed *muftis* and *qadis*.[10] The *naibs* were to see to the mobilisation of soldiers, collection of taxes and oversee the general implementation of the shari'a leaving 'all judicial matters to *muftis* and *qadis*...even if they [*naibs*] were well educated '*ulama*'.[11]

To avoid the *naibs* opposing his decree, Shamil issued a supplement, according to which those who did not approve of his orders or did not feel in any way capable of carrying them out were to step down and leave their office.[12]

In addition to issuing the decree on the *naibs'* powers, Shamil divided

---

mathematics and engineering. In the early 1840s he joined Shamil and took an active part in organising both the army and administration in his state. On him, see Genko, 1941(a); Tsagareshvili (ed.), 1953, pp. 215-6. doc. no. 160; Ramazanov and Khadzhiev (eds), 1959, p. 483, doc. no. 257; Gammer, 1994, p. 261.

6 As used by Shamil and other North Caucasians. From Arabic *wilaya* – an administrative district (in the Ottoman Empire).

7 From *naib*, the title of the head of a province. This term is usually used in Russian sources.

8 The number and the composition of the *vilayats* in Shamil's state changed throughout the history of the imamate. From the four *vilayats* introduced by Shamil in 1842, their number increased up to thirty-three in 1856. On the *vilayat* system in the imamate, see al-Qarakhi, 1946, p. 126; Dubrovin, 1871, vol. I, book I, p. 468; Linevich, 1877, p. 4.

9 This decree was issued under the pretext that *naibs* abused their authority. Shamil i Chechnya, 1859, p. 145. It seems, however, that it was one of the important steps taken by Shamil to prevent the concentration of too much power in the hands of his deputies and to ensure their subordination.

10 Nizam Shamilya, 1870, vol. III, pp. 8-11.

11 *AKAK*, vol. X, p. 527, also Nizam Shamilya, 1870, vol. III, p. 10.

12 Nizam Shamilya, 1870, vol. III, pp. 13-14.

the *vilayats* into smaller districts.[13] They were headed by a *ma'zun*[14] or *dibir*[15] in Daghestan and a *turqkh* in Chechnya. The *ma'zuns* and *turqkhs* were elected by the people in their area or appointed by *naibs* to whom they were directly answerable. The smallest administrative unit in the imamate was a single village governed by its elders[16] who were elected by the people of the village and responsible for its military, administrative and fiscal duties.[17]

The supreme religious and judicial authority in a *vilayat* rested with a *mufti* accountable directly to the imam.[18] On a district and village level this authority was invested in the local *qadis*, who were responsible to the *mufti*. To ensure the respect and trust of the local people, both *muftis* and *qadis* were to be elected by the people in the *vilayat* or district they lived and served in.

In practice, the division between the *naibs'* and *muftis'* authority was not clear-cut. The *naibs* often refused to give up their jurisdiction over the settlement of legal disputes, which formed an important part of their income. Under the pretext of overseeing the implementation of the *shari'a*, they continued to interfere in judicial matters and largely maintained their function as religious judges. Furthermore, although officially *muftis* and *qadis* were elected by the people, the *naibs* had the final say in the nomination of the candidates and their elections to the post.

At the district level the division of administrative and judicial power between *ma'zun* and *qadi* remained in principle only. This was, however, of lesser importance. All significant matters were raised directly to *naibs* and the office of a *ma'zun* was, in effect, reduced to the position of the local head of police.[19]

In their activities, *naibs* had to account for their actions to the imam through the institution of *mudirs* – superintendents, specially appointed by Shamil to keep a watchful eye on his deputies. A *mudir* supervised *naibs* and *muftis* in several *vilayats* and at the same time acted as a *naib* in his own right in the area of his residence. Apart from *mudirs*,

---

[13] In Russian – *uchastok*.

[14] A traditional administrative authority with some religious functions. From Arabic *ma'zun* – an official authorised by a *qadi* to perform marriages.

[15] Local mullah.

[16] It is noteworthy that the head of the Sufi lodge in the village or village quarter was also called a *turqkh*.

[17] In the late 1840s, when the administrative system had crystallised, the general size of a *vilayat* was roughly 1,000 households and that of the district (*uchastok*) 30. Pokrovskiy, 1991, p. 17. His accounts Pokrovskiy based on the documents from *Chechenskiy Oblsatnoy Arkhiv* (Chechen District Archive), delo 104, copy in Severokavkazskiy Gorskiy nauchno-Issledovatelskiy Institut. Pokrovskiy, 1991, p. 26, fn. 67. See also Okolnichiy, 1859, vol. II, p. 400; Runovskiy, 1862, p. 361.

[18] *AKAK*, vol. X, p. 527.

[19] *Dnevnik Runovskogo*, entry 28 June 1860.

Shamil also appointed *muhtasibs* – members of the imam's secret police. The *muhtasibs* were recruited from the most loyal and knowledgeable people of the imamate, and as a rule were respected Naqshbandi sheikhs. They travelled from one commune to another, usually incognito, and reported on their observations directly to the imam.[20] Furthermore, at least in principle, anybody had the right to appeal against the decision of a *naib* or a *mufti* directly to the imam. Shamil designated two days of public audience to receive such complaints during which he could exercise his authority as chief judge, passing sentences and executing them on the spot.[21]

By establishing this strictly defined system of government in the imamate, Shamil profoundly changed the existing order under which the North Caucasus had lived for centuries. He not only dismantled the traditional power structure and deprived the old elite of their power base, but, far more importantly, he introduced what amounted to a concept of citizenship, whereby for the first time the ruler and the ruled were accountable to one system of law and in theory were at least equal in their obligations and rights as far as the system of law was concerned.[22]

Although many of Shamil's *naibs* belonged to the traditional ruling houses[23] they had reached their posts through their service to the imam and their personal merits rather than their noble origin. Furthermore, their power was now interpreted not in traditional but religious terms, but rather derived from their association with the imam.

Fiscal reform in the imamate[24]

To maintain a centralised system of government, Shamil needed to put in order the financial affairs of his imamate. The imam's treasury had

---

[20] Runovskiy, 1862, p. 361

[21] The days appointed were Saturday, Sunday and Monday.

[22] This fact has inspired elaborate discussion within Russian/Soviet historiography on the class nature of his state. Some authors saw the transformation of the power from the traditional Daghestani aristocracy as the manifestation of an egalitarian or even 'revolutionary, character of his state. Pokrovskiy, 1991, pp. 13-4. In pre-revolutionary Russia, when the local traditional nobility were seen as natural allies for the Russians, Shamil was portrayed as 'a plebeian who supports commoners to anihilate aristocracy'. In Soviet historiography the treatment of the nature of Shamil's state differed greatly depending on the ideological climate of the moment and varied from the 'revolutionary' to the 'oppressive clerical-feudal'. Perhaps the best Marxist analysis of the class structure in Shamil's imamate is in Pokrovskiy, 1991, pp. 14-25.

[23] E.g. Daneil-Bek of Ilisu, Hajji Murad of Avaria, Hajji Yahya of Ghazi Ghumuq, etc. Their noble origin was in certain ways an advantage to Shamil, for having joined the imam they brought with them a significant following of people in their domain.

[24] On Shamil's tax system, see Dubrovin, 1871, pp. 491-2; Shamil and Chechnya, 1859, pp. 136-44.

already been set up by Ghazi Muhammad,[25] but it was Shamil who systematised the sources of revenue and their distribution.

One of the main sources of revenue in Shamil's state, especially at the beginning of his rule, was military booty. In the traditional Muslim manner, Shamil divided it into five equal parts. One fifth (*khums*) went to the imam's treasury, and four-fifths were divided among the participants of a raid. However, Shamil reserved the right to expropriate anything at his own discretion before the division, which in effect considerably increased the share which went into the treasury.[26]

According to the shari'a, the *khums* was to be distributed between the descendants of the Prophet Muhammad (*sayyids*); the needy (*masakin*); the poor (*fuqara*); the wayfarer (*ibn al-sabil*) and those worthy of a special reward (*masalih*). Following the *shari'a*, Shamil established special 'pensions' for the Daghestani *sayyids* – there were about 100 people, mainly in Ghazi-Ghumuq, who claimed descent from the Prophet.[27] The orphans, the disabled, and those who had lost all their possessions in the cause of war received support from the funds set up for *masalih* and *fuqara*. A special fund was set up to give rewards for outstanding bravery.[28] As for the funds designated for *ibn al-sabil*, they were used to provide for the special emissaries dispatched by Shamil into the neighbouring Muslim countries, particularly the Ottoman lands. However, due to the small number of such emissaries, the spare resources were utilised for the reconstruction of roads, bridges, construction of fortifications, etc.[29]

Military booty was, however, not sufficient to maintain the centralised state apparatus. Thus, Shamil introduced regular taxation. The first attempts to introduce the idea of levying taxes had already been made by Shamil's predecessors, who imposed a small tax of one rouble on every tenth household.[30] Following their example, Shamil at first introduced a similar tax,[31] but as he made progress in building up a centralised state, the need for a regular source of revenue and, subsequently, regular taxation became all too apparent. In the early 1840s, Shamil introduced

[25] It was Ghazi Muhammad, the first imam of the North Caucasus, who had set up the imam's treasury, known as *bayt al-mal*.

[26] Zaks, 1941, p. 21.

[27] This money was kept by a special treasurer who announced the time of the distribution of pensions in advance so that those eligible could arrive to collect the money or send their trustees. The abuse of the right to collect this pension led to a gradual tightening of the category of those who could collect the money instead of the pensioner himself. Runovskiy, 1862, pp. 376-7.

[28] Bodenshtadt, 1855, pp. 346-7.

[29] On the distribution of military spoils see Zaks, 1992, pp. 22-3.

[30] E.g. Ghazi Muhammad.

[31] The first to be obliged to pay this tax in 1836 were the people of Ighali. *AKAK*, vol. VIII, p. 607.

a traditional Muslim system of taxation, which consisted of two types of levies: *kharaj* (land tax) and *zakat* (income tax).[32]

At first *kharaj* was collected only from the villages that had previously paid land tax to the hereditary rulers.[33] However, in 1853, when contributions from military raids became scarce, Shamil had to cancel tax exemptions enjoyed by the free *jama'ats* and force all the communes in the imamate to pay it.[34]

Apart from taxes and military spoils, Shamil set up a system of fines for various offences such as stealing[35] and avoiding conscription.[36] According to another decree, the estates of deserters and of people who did not leave any direct heirs were expropriated into the treasury and became government property.[37] The amount of 'state' land was never significant but its importance increased in the last years of the imamate when Shamil lost low land Chechnya,[38] the main 'bread-basket' of his state, and had to rely on other resources. The land was cultivated by peasants as a special duty, which resulted in the emergence of a class of peasants dependent directly on the state.

Military reform

One of the key reforms undertaken by Shamil was in the military sphere. These reforms were aimed at the reorganisation of his forces in order to make them capable of sustaining large-scale campaigns.

Shamil's military system was based on the principle that all able-bodied males in the imamate were armed, trained and available for combat or could contribute to military operations in one way or another.[39]

[32] It is not clear whether *zakat* was allocated exclusively for religious purposes, or was channelled into the treasury and used for financing the war effort. Bodenshtadt, 1855, pp. 147-8.

[33] I.e in the villages of the Avar khanate, Ghazi-Ghumuq, Mehtuli, etc.

[34] Zaks, 1941, p. 41.

[35] Shamil introduced a law by which a thief had not only to return the stolen goods (or the equivalent of their value) to the owner, but also to pay a penalty equal to half of the value to the treasury.

[36] The fine for draft evasion was introduced in the early 1850s. According to this a deserter was put in prison – usually a pit in the ground – and had to pay a fixed amount of money for each night spent there, until he agreed to enter military service. This penalty became a particularly important source of revenue from the mid 1850s, when the imamate stopped growing in size, Shamil's power started to decline and discipline in his 'army' deteriorated. Dubrovin, 1871, pp. 475-8; Bodenshtadt, 1855, p. 352.

[37] Runovskiy, 1862, pp. 376-8; Bodenshtadt, 1855, pp. 345-6.

[38] On the period when Shamil lost the lowlands of Lesser and Greater Chechnya, see below, Chapter 23.

[39] Nizam Shamilya, 1870, vol. III, pp. 11-12. There were several categories exempted from the obligatory military service: citizens of the salt-producing villages of Andalal and Hindal, those involved in manufacturing gunpowder and casting cannon, merchants

Thus, in military terms the *vilayat* corresponded to the largest military unit – the regiment or 1,000 (*alf*), divided into two battalions or 500 (*khamsa mi'a*), companies of 100 (*mi'a*) platoons of fifty (*khamsin*), and squads of ten (*'ashara*). The corps were divided into cavalry (*fawaris*) and infantry (*mushat*).[40] Russian deserters who found refuge in the imamate and accepted Islam formed the imam's artillery brigades.

Furthermore, Shamil introduced a corresponding system of command structure and military ranks. Each of the sub-units had a commander (*rais*) whose rank corresponded to the number of people under his command (*rais al-alf, rais khamsa mi'a*, etc.). Each rank was assigned an appropriate military insignia comprising various signs, tokens and orders. A head of every unit had a special silver badge with an inscription corresponding to his rank. Three of the imam's favourite *naibs*, Akhberdy Muhammad, Shu'ayib Mullah and Ullughbey Mullah received a rank equivalent to that of general in the Russian army marked by a special silver star. To ensure more uniformity, Shamil also introduced the semblance of a uniform with distinct colours corresponding to each of the 'services' (cavalry, infantry, *murtaziqa*, etc.) in his armed forces.[41]

Apart from the distinction of rank Shamil introduced medals and personal presents – usually a weapon with special engravings. Thus, Akhberdy Muhammad and Ostemir each had the following phrase engraved on their swords: 'There is no braver man than Akhberdy (or Ostemir) and no sharper blade than his *kinzhal*.' As a mark of favour Shamil gave Idris Effendi a dagger with an inscription which read: 'This is the sign of courage of the one who is like a lion.'[42]

There were also special signs to mark cowardice, indecisiveness or other similar vices. For instance someone who behaved in cowardly fashion during a battle had a piece of felt sown on the back of his sleeve. This seemingly harmless punishment in fact amounted to the worst kind of public humiliation which made the person in question a virtual social outcast.[43]

The 'army' received no maintenance from the imam. Each fighter was to be armed, fed and maintained by his own family.[44] During

particularly from the most important trade centres of the imamate such as Adni, Chokh and Salataw, and the *tariqa murids* (see below).

[40] Dubrovin, 1871, p. 486.

[41] Nizam Shamilya, 1870, vol. III, pp. 8-10, 12-13. Chichagova claimed that each category of citizens in Shamil's imamate had a distinctive colour turban: mullahs – green, *naibs* – yellow, public criers – red, hajjis – brown, executioners – black, and the rest – white. Chichagova, 1889. p. 50

[42] For a detailed description of signs and medals, see Zaks, 1941, pp. 155-7; Dubrovin, 1871, vol. I, part 1, p. 491, Zheleznov, 1902, pp. 96-9; Prushanovskiy, 1902, vol. XXIII, pp. 63-5.

[43] He could restore his honour only through exceptional bravery or some heroic deed, after which the felt was removed from his clothes.

[44] The family of the fighter had to provide him with provisions, a horse if they had

lengthy military campaigns the obligation to maintain and feed the fighters was put on the people of the commune in which they fought. On rare occasions the imam designated special sums from the treasury to be paid to the *naibs* from which they had to make provision for a lengthy campaign.[45] This was implemented only during general mobilisation which happened very rarely.[46]

This 'self-maintained' character presented one of the main challenges to the creation of a regular army. The warrior's readiness as well as ability to fight depended upon the good-will of the people and their ability to provide him with food and ammunition. Thus, although Shamil had significantly improved the moral and fighting standards of the North Caucasian warriors, his 'army' constituted, in essence, a people's volunteer corps.

Murtaziqas

The *murtaziqa* formed the nucleus of Shamil's army – armed horsemen – who constituted the only regular military unit in the imamate. The *murtaziqa* were recruited by Shamil and his *naibs* from among the best horsemen and masters of sword and dagger. Shamil's *murtaziqa* formed his 'personal brigade' and, about 180 of them – the *crème de la crème* – his bodyguards. For their service, the imam's *murtaziqa* received a fixed income from the imam's treasury. The *murtaziqas* who were recruited by *naibs*, received a limited income – no more than one rouble a month or ten measures of grain, which from the early 1850s was constantly reduced – and were largely maintained at the expense of the people in a *vilayat*.[47]

The *murtaziqa* regiments were set up and run along Sufi lines. The *murtaziqa* were the imam's or *naibs' murids*.[48] On entering the service they had to adopt *tauba* and swear on the Qur'an an oath of allegiance to the imam (or a *naib*) whom they accepted as their sheikh and *murshid*. By adopting the *tauba* they denounced all previous ties and loyalties and put themselves body and soul at the disposal of imam (or *naib*).[49]

Unlike the proper Sufi *murids* their religious knowledge consisted of the basic minimum. They had to memorise several *suras* from the

---

one and weaponry.

[45] Usually a *naib* bought sheep and cattle which were transported with the fighters and slaughtered at need. See Leontovich, 1869, vol. II, p. 108; Dubrovin, 1871, pp. 490-1.

[46] In Daghestan in 1843, 1845 and Kabarda in 1846.

[47] Dubrovin 1871, vol. I, book 1, p. 472.

[48] In Russian they were called *naibskie* or *imamskie myuridy* (the *naib's* or imam's *murids*), see Runovskiy, 1862, pp. 362-3.

[49] The *murtaziqas'* oath included a vow to kill anybody at the commander's orders, even be it their close relative.

Qur'an, know the obligatory prayers and strictly follow the *shari'a* laws in all their deeds. Their service to God was principally interpreted in terms of devoting their whole lives to *ghazavat*, which was seen as the most pious of all deeds and the supreme manifestation of one's love of God.[50] In the pursuit of this goal, the *murtaziqa* forsook all obligations imposed by the traditional code of *'adat* and put themselves entirely at the disposal of their sheikh-commander.

This translation of the Sufi ethics of *murshid-murid* relationship into the military language created a unique category of warriors whose full devotion to the cause of *ghazavat* and loyalty to their commanders became legendary. The ties between a commander and his *murids* were so strong that the loyalty of the *naib murids* to their patrons was equal if not greater than to the imam himself.[51]

Spiritual warfare and the tariqa murids

Not all *murids*, however, saw the military struggle as the only or indeed the best way of service to God. Some continued their *jihad fi-sabil allah* (endeavour for the sake of God) in purely religious terms and sought enlightenment through following the traditional Sufi path of mystical purification. These followers formed a group of *tariqa murids* distinct from the imam's or *naib's murids*.

Generally looked down on by the *naib's* or imam's *murids* as cowards, the *tariqa murids* nonetheless were held by the imam in an extremely high esteem. Not only did Shamil appreciate their importance in strengthening and deepening the Islamic faith in the imamate, but he also relied upon them in his campaigns. Even though the *tariqa murids* were spared from armed struggle they contributed fully to Shamil's military efforts by providing the ideological support and propaganda back-up to all his undertakings, for the imam obliged those who were not fighting 'with arms' to 'fight with their tongues'.[52]

Ideological warfare was one of the key elements in Shamil's undertakings. His success wholly depended upon the willingness of people to follow him and fight under his command. In order to guarantee this following, he had to win people's trust and respect. Furthermore, the human and military resources of his 'army' were no match for one of the strongest European armies at the time, and in carrying out his military

---

[50] In a similar way, in the present-day war in Chechnya, those who take the title *ghazi* imply that they have resigned themselves to inevitable death and devoted themselves heart and soul to war in the name of God, breaking all traditional ties and obligations.

[51] Thus, when Hajji Murad clashed with the imam in 1851, his *murids* remained loyal to him and were ready to fight Shamil. Only the mediation of the spiritual Naqshbandi authorities prevented a civil war. Al-Qarakhi, 1946, pp. 226-7; Zisserman, 1851, pp. 655-80.

[52] Dubrovin, 1871, p. 485; Nizam Shamilya, 1870, vol. III, p. 12; Zaks, 1941, p. 153.

campaigns he had to rely largely on people's morale. For their part, the Russians mostly relied on the use of brute force, but they too could not disregard the importance of ideological warfare. In their propaganda campaign they relied heavily on local mullahs and *'ulama* loyal to them as well as Muslim clerics brought in from Tatarstan and Crimea[53] to propagate the 'true meaning of Islam and teach people loyalty to the Russian Emperor as a main guardian of his Christian and Muslim subjects'.[54]

However, Muslim scholars seconded from the Russian Empire to the North Caucasus encountered a great deal of hostility and suspicion from the local people who regarded them as Russian spies and agents, and repeatedly denied them access to their communes. Moreover, from the late 1840s the Russian officials in St. Petersburg came to the conclusion that the main source of the Caucasian War was not so much religious fanaticism but 'Shamil's dictatorial powers'. They tended to link the pacification of the area exclusively with the imam's full and complete defeat. Furthermore, they came to see any links between the North Caucasian Muslims and those of inner Russia as potentially dangerous on the grounds that they could facilitate the spread of rebellious ideas among the empire's Muslims.[55]

Thus, in the mid 1840s Russian officials decided that their main effort should be focused on educating the indigenous clerics as loyal subjects of the Russian tsar. In order to achieve this objective, eight schools were opened throughout the Caucasus – three for the Sunnis and five for the Shi'i Muslims – in which students were taught to be loyal to the Russian government.[56] The education of a new religious elite, however, required time and effort while the Russians felt an immediate need for loyal and qualified supporters. As an alternative solution they tried to win over respected mullahs and *'ulama* both from among Shamil's Naqshbandi supporters and, especially, from those who were in opposition to Shamil and the *tariqa*.

Among scholars who came forward with arguments denouncing Shamil's claims to the imamate were Mama Kash, the *qadi* of Enderi; Ayyub, the *qadi* of Pangutay, Yusup, the *qadi* of Aqsay, Hajji Abdulla from the Lak village of Kay, and most importantly the *qadi* of Akusha.

---

[53] Apart from Taj al-Din, the Russians summoned to the Caucasus Qadi Asker Sayyid Halil Effendi from Crimea. The latter arrived in Groznaya in 1845 and spent less than a year there. Although he was denied access to any mountain communes and achieved no results at all, the Russian command solicited for him a reward and a medal for promoting better understanding between the Russian and the mountain peoples. Smirnov, 1963, p. 97.

[54] *TsGVIA, VUA*, delo 6448, chast' 1841, list 18-19.

[55] Smirnov, 1963, pp. 97-8.

[56] *Ibid.*, p. 78; *AKAK*, vol. X, pp. 127-8.

One of the main Criticisms voiced against Shamil by these *'ulama* was that he had inspired enmity among the North Caucasian Muslims and led them into war against a far superior enemy.[57] In 1846 Sulayman Effendi, a Naqshbandi follower and Shamil's deputy in the Adygh lands, defected to the Russians and wrote a treatise in which he accused Shamil of violating Sufi ethics by becoming directly involved in worldly and, especially, military affairs.[58]

However, the North Caucasian Muslims distrusted the arguments of the local opposition who used language almost identical with the proclamations distributed by Russian officials. Furthermore, Shamil tried to prevent the distribution of any such appeals and Russian-sponsored proclamations by introducing the death sentence for holding any public or private gatherings to read or discuss them.[59] At the same time, he employed the Naqshbandi scholars from among his supporters to compose treatises with counter-arguments.[60]

Shamil also successfully used the Naqshbandi network to win over the people's support and guarantee the success of his military campaigns. The Naqshbandi *tariqa murids* penetrated the areas which the imam or *naib murids* could not reach and paved the road for the imam's advances. In fact, virtually all the imam's military operations were preceded and accompanied by a propaganda campaign undertaken by the Naqshbandi *tariqa murids*.

The first of these 'spiritual warriors' was Jamal al-Din al-Ghazi-Ghumuqi who used his prestige and exceptional influence to win Shamil the support of the local people. In the words of a Russian author:

Jamaluddin [Jamal al-Din] was not at all a militant person, but without taking up arms, through his exceptional fame and popularity, he inspired irreconcilable hatred of us through his preaching and correspondence with the elders and scholars.[61]

Shamil's legislative and judicial powers: shari'a and nizams

Further concentration of power in the imam's hands found its reflection in Shamil's change of his title. If at the beginning of his rule he used the title of *al-imam al-a'zam* (Great Imam) from the mid 1840s it was replaced by that of *amir al-mu'minin*, (Commander of the Faithful). Identical to the title used by Ottoman Sultan, it highlighted Shamil's claims to have full authority as the sovereign ruler of the North Caucasian Imamate.

---

[57] The letter of the *qadi* of Akusha published in Ramazanov and Khadzhiev (eds), 1959, pp. 56-63.

[58] Sulayman-Effendi, 1847, pp. 30-5.

[59] 1844 god na Kavkaze, 1883, p. 160.

[60] One of these was the treatise of al-Qarakhi, much quoted in the present work.

[61] Runovskiy, 1862, p. 220.

However, even at the peak of his power Shamil was hardly a despotic and autocratic ruler, contrary to persistent claims made by Russian and Soviet historians.[62]

At the beginning of his rule, Shamil's power was legitimised by his election at the gathering of religious leaders. First held at the time of Ghazi Muhammad[63] and later summoned for the elections of all subsequent imams, these gatherings had supreme legislative power and in Shamil's imamate were institutionalised as the *shura al-'ulama*.[64] Held at times of crucial importance in the life of the imamate,[65] the *shura al-'ulama* gathered to discuss the imam's domestic and military policy and played a significant role in giving or withholding approval for the imam's plans.

Gradually the importance of the *shura al-'ulama* started to decline. In the early 1840s it was replaced by the congress of *naibs* known as *majlis al-nuwwab*, which by 1847 had turned into a consultative rather than legislative body dealing almost exclusively with military rather than administrative or judicial matters.[66]

This process corresponded to the general tendency in Shamil's state towards greater consolidation of authority in the imam's office, which started in the early 1840s and culminated at the Andi gathering in 1846 when Shamil finally formalised his administrative system, codified the laws and defined the authority of each official in his imamate.[67]

To guarantee the success of his reforms Shamil summoned an extended gathering of the *shura al-'ulama* at which many non-religious officials

[62] Some Russian historians even used it as a justification for the Russian military expansion under the pretext that they came to assist the local peoples to liberate themselves from the despotic power of the imam.

[63] Volkonskiy, 1887, vol. XI, p. 123; Shamil i Chechnya, 1859, p. 136.

[64] It is not clear whether *shura al-'ulama* in Shamil's imamate included the non-Naqshbandi representatives from various Daghestani and Chechen communes, although it seems very likely that it did. Hajji Ali, 1873, p. 11. For more on *shura al-'ulama* see Runovskiy, 1861; al-Qarakhi, 1946; Shamil i Chechnya, 1859; Pokrovskiy, 1991, pp. 15-6, Abdurahman, 1862, pp. 9-12.

[65] The *shura-al-'ulama* met in 1837, 1838, 1843.

[66] Pokrovskiy, 1991, p. 16.

[67] Some authors claim that Shamil started his reforms as early as 1837. However, although the creation of the imamate was a gradual and continuous process, it seems that till the 1840s Shamil's activities were not much different from those of his predecessors. He appointed his first deputy in 1836 during the campaign against Untsukul. Al-Qarakhi, 1946, p. 87. However, the role of his deputy was almost identical to that of the earlier deputies. In 1841-2, Shamil started his full-scale changes which eventually resulted in the creation of a state with an essentially different character. This change of policies can at least be partly explained by the defeat suffered by Shamil at Akhulgoh, which deprived him of his power base in Daghestan, revealed the limitations of his power and compelled him to introduce a comprehensive set of reforms to avoid such devastating effects from a single military defeat.

and even ordinary Muslims were present. The imam opened it with a speech in which he deplored the fact that, despite all his efforts, the war was to continue for a long time and asked to be spared the burden of the imamate, promising his full support to whomever would be elected as new leader. As at the Akusha gathering and later in Chechnya this threat of resignation was used as a tactical ploy to guarantee the full loyalty and obedience of his followers. After the gathering had repeatedly asked him to remain in power, Shamil agreed on the condition that they should obey him and follow all his orders.[68]

Immediately after winning this impromptu vote of confidence, Shamil made a forceful attempt to make his rule hereditary and laid the foundation of a ruling dynasty. Having secured the support of the Naqshbandi religious dignitaries, particularly that of Jamal al-Din al-Ghazi-Ghumuqi, Shamil suggested to the gathering that his eighteen-year-old son Jamal al-Din[69] should be elected as his legitimate successor.[70] Despite the opposition of many of his *naibs*,[71] Jamal al-Din was 'elected' as such.[72]

However, even after the Andi gathering, Shamil's power was hardly that of an absolute monarch. He never had absolute legislative power. This was controlled by the 'imam's council' – the *shura al-imam* or the *divan-khaneh*, the official supreme legislative and judicial power established by Shamil in 1841. As the importance of the *shura al-'ulama* and later *majlis al-nuwwab* as legislative bodies declined, that of the *divan-khaneh* increased. It was comprised of Naqshbandi religious leaders,[73] trustworthy *naibs* and respected elders, who met regularly to discuss matters of domestic and military policy and settle disputes raised by *naibs* or other people in the imamate.[74] All laws and initiatives of the imam had to be approved at the *divan-khaneh*,[75] in order to gain legitimacy and achieve compliance with the *shari'a*.

---

[68] Dubrovin, 1871, p. 470.

[69] Named so after Jamal al-Din al-Ghazi-Ghumuqi.

[70] Following the precedent, many of the *naibs* tried to ensure that their post was to be made hereditary as well. *AKAK*, vol. X, p. 527; Pokrovskiy, 1991, p. 16; Shamil i Chechnya, 1859, pp. 141, 145.

[71] Especially Hajji Murad.

[72] Shamil's decision to appoint his son as his successor was legitimised by Naqshbandi religious authorities, who claimed that they had received inspiration according to which Jamal al-Din was named as Shamil's lawful successor. See al-Qarakhi, 1946, pp. 223-4.

[73] Some of its permanent members included Jamal al-Din al-Ghazi-Ghumuqi, Muhammad Effendi Ghazi-Ghumuqi, Rajabil Muhammad Chirkavi, Hajji Yahya, Dibir Hajji Karanawi, Mitlik Murtazali (the head of Shamil's bodyguard).

[74] There were special days assigned for each *vilayat* – Mondays and Tuesdays for those situated in proximity to the imam's capital; Wednesdays and Thursdays – for more remote ones. *AKAK*, vol. XII, p. 1459; Shamil i Chechnya, 1859, p. 137; Pokrovskiy, 1991, p. 16.

[75] *AKAK*, vol. XII, p. 1459.

All members of the *divan-khanesh* had an equal voice, but Shamil had the right to veto its decision. However, there are no accounts of open clashes between the imam and the members of the *divan-khanesh*. It seems that generally members of the *divan-khaneh* tended to support Shamil's decisions, while the imam showed respect towards the opinion of its members. The latter is particularly true respect to Jamal al-Din al-Ghazi-Ghumuqi, who as Shamil's *murshid* enjoyed his full obedience and respect, for not even the imam could break the ethics of a traditional Sufi *murshid-murid* bond.[76]

Most importantly, Shamil's authority was bound by the *shari'a*, which was the supreme 'constitution' in the imamate.[77] In principle every Muslim ruler was obliged to follow and to strictly implement the shari'a. In Shamil's state the importance of the *shari'a* was further enhanced as the main source of legitimation of the imam's power, as his position as a ruler was largely based on his role as a guarantor of the *shari'a* and safeguard of the Muslim *umma*.[78]

In conclusion, it is fair to say that Shamil largely carried out his legislative efforts on the basis of and in accordance with Muslim law. However, in as wide-ranging reforms as his, Shamil discovered that in narrowly legalistic terms the *shari'a* could not provide all the answers to his needs. Therefore Shamil, being not only a ruler but a learned Muslim scholar and a Sufi sheikh, passed his own judgement or qualified opinions, which under the circumstances amounted to a separate set of laws known as *nizams*.[79] Each of these *nizams* in accordance with the concept of *ijma'* was to be passed through the *divan-khaneh* which gave its approval. These *nizams* embraced a vast range of domestic, religious, political and military matters.

Nizams and the shari'a

There were two broad categories of Shamil's *nizams*: those which promoted and reinforced the shari'a laws in opposition to the local *'adat* and laws induced by the Russian administration, and those which supplemented the shari'a or interpreted it in a different way.

---

76 It even seems that the very institution of the *divan khaneh* was introduced at Jamal al-Din's initiative. Neitgart, p. 403. Gammer also suggests that Shamil's campaign into Ghazi-Ghmumuq was undertaken by Shamil on Jamal al-Din's initiative. See Gammer, 1994, p. 238. On many occasions Jamal al-Din acted as a mediator between Shamil and his enemies and the imam always followed his sheikh's advice. Even the Russian command showed great respect towards the *murshid* and sought his mediation.

77 In this sense Shamil's imamate can perhaps best be described as a constitutional monarchy.

78 Runovskiy, 1862, p. 329.

79 They were similar to *qanuns* passed by the Ottoman Sultan, and like these had to be approved by the religious authorities, who ensured that they did not contradict the shari'a.

The shari'a-reinforcing *nizams* had crucial importance for the whole of Shamil's law-making activities. It was through the introduction and implementation of these rules that he exercised his role as a guardian of the Muslim *umma* and derived his legitimation as imam. There were several types of *nizams* in this category, some of which regulated matters of criminal and civil justice while others dealt with the religious life of the imamate.

One of the first and most important of Shamil's *nizams* which enforced the *shari'a* law as opposed to the local *'adat* was that concerning killing and blood revenge. In an attempt to limit the harmful effects of this common crime, Shamil ordered the strict implementation of the *shari'a*. This allowed blood revenge to be directed only against the party immediately responsible for a crime, but strongly advocated settlement of any blood disputes through peaceful means. Reinforcing the shari'a concerning blood revenge, Shamil introduced the concept of differentiation between intentional and non-intentional killing[80] and elucidated which types of killing excluded any revenge at all.[81] Similarly, Shamil's *nizam* on settling disputes on inheritance reinforced the *shari'a* law as opposed to the local *'adat* and obliged mullahs to exclusively apply the *shari'a* in their resolutions.[82]

Another group of Shamil's *shari'a*-reinforcing regulations aimed at strengthening the Muslim way of life in its entirety. Thus, Shamil introduced the concept of crime against state and religion, which had hitherto been known only in the Avar khanate.[83]

Following the tradition of the Naqshbandiyya-Mujaddidiyya-Khalidiyya and in the spirit of the time, Shamil's interpretation of the shari'a was that of a fundamental character. He obliged all people physically fit to observe the fast of Ramadan;[84] ordered women to cover their heads and faces, dress modestly and avoid mixing with men;[85] and prohibited music and dancing on any occasion, with the exception of chanting Naqshbandi religious hymns.[86]

In his drive to root out all non-Islamic practices such as drinking

---

[80] The distinction between intentional and non-intentional killing is one of the concepts characteristic to Islamic as opposed to pre-Islamic legislation. For more details, see Chapter 6 above.

[81] One such case was a killing of a trespasser. Runovskiy, 1862, p. 344. For more on the law concerning blood revenge see Runovskiy, 1860, pp. 199-216.

[82] Inheritance law was one of the most complicated in the North Caucasus and often led to lengthy disputes which disrupted the life not only of one family, but the whole commune. See Runovskiy, 1862, p. 345.

[83] See Chapter 6 above.

[84] Nizam Shamilya, 1870, vol. III, p. 14.

[85] al-Qarakhi, 1946, pp. 57-60.

[86] Runovskiy, 1860, pp. 384-5; Bodenshtadt, 1855, p. 352.

alcohol and smoking, Shamil went much further than even the *shari'a* required. He devised a system of retribution which was as much a means of humiliating an offender[87] as punishing him.[88] He supplemented a shari'a law banning wine with an additional *nizam* by which even the selling of grapes to those who were likely to be making wine was forbidden.[89]

Although these regulations had a clearly religious character, they served as much practical as religious purposes. As Shamil himself later admitted, he was a great admirer and lover of music and dancing. However, he found it inappropriate that anyone would engage in such pleasant and joyful activities during the war and feared that they could deter people from fighting and undermine their morale. Similarly, smoking and, especially, drinking could undermine the fighting spirit of the North Caucasian Muslims as well as lead to the erosion of Muslim ethics. The practical purposes of Shamil's reforms should not, however, be exaggerated, for in the end he saw his main aim as much – and, perhaps, even more – in establishing the 'truly Muslim state' as sustaining a war against the Russians.

Apart from the prohibitive regulations, Shamil set up 'positive measures' aimed at strengthening Islam in the North Caucasus. He established traditional Muslim schools at each mosque and introduced obligatory primary religious education for boys.[90] At the same time he entrusted *naibs* with the task of educating people during the Friday congregational prayers and obliged all men to attend them.[91]

In his policy towards non-Muslims Shamil was also guided by the shari'a, which in respect of his non-Muslim subjects was a more liberal interpretation.[92] The latter enjoyed full religious freedom and had never been forced to Islamise. They were settled in separate villages – usually close to the imam's residence – where they were allowed to practise their religion and customs, drink, smoke, dance and play music.[93] Those who chose to convert to Islam voluntarily were fully integrated into

---

[87] A smoker was put on a donkey, his face to its tail, with a thread put through his nose to which a pipe or a snuff box was attached, and paraded through the village.

[88] Drinking was punishable from forty lashes to the death penalty for persistent and heavy drinking. Runvoskiy, 1862, p. 284.

[89] *Ibid.*, p. 384; Sharafutdinova, 1975, p. 169.

[90] Sharafutdinova, 1975, p. 169.

[91] Nizam Shamilya, 1870, vol. III, p. 14; Sharafutdinova, 1975, p. 169.

[92] In fact Shamil's attitude towards people of the various faiths proved to be far more tolerant than that of the Russians. Hence many members of the Christian sects widespread throughout the Caucasus found refuge in Shamil's imamate. Russian run-away soldiers and officers constituted another considerable group of Shamil's Christian subjects.

[93] On the community of the Russian deserters near Vedeno, see Atarov, 1853; Volkonskiy, 1879, pp. 173-4; Zaks, 1941, pp. 158-60.

local society and had to observe all religious obligations and prohibitions imposed by the *shari'a*.

Supplementary nizams

The largest category of the supplementary *nizams* were of a general non-religious administrative and military character. They defined the authority and responsibilities of various officials in the imamate, regulated domestic[94] and foreign affairs[95] and military conduct.[96] They also established the degree and methods of punishment for various offences.[97]

In addition to this category, there were *nizams* which provided further commentary on *shari'a* laws without entering into obvious contradiction with them.[98] Family law was one such matter generally governed by the *shari'a* and supplemented by Shamil with several additional *nizams*.

Thus, in the 1840s Shamil issued a *nizam* concerning marriage, which was inspired by an alarming tendency in Chechen society. On his arrival in. Chechnya, Shamil found 'a great number of unmarried girls with grey hair and ancient elders who had all their lives lived as bachelors'.[99] The decline of the number of marriages was largely due to the prohibitively high *kalym* (bride money), which varied from eighty to 100 silver roubles. This, in the circumstances of continuous devastating war, made marriage extremely difficult. To improve the situation, Shamil issued a law according to which no one was allowed to take more than 20 silver roubles as bride money for a virgin and 10 silver roubles for a divorcee. At the same time he forbade the mullahs to officiate at a marriage through elopement without the consent of the bride's parents.[100]

Shamil legitimised this law in religious terms, claiming that enforced celibacy could lead to extra-marital liaisons and a deterioration of

---

[94] Such as *nizams* on financial affairs in the imamate, one of which obliged the acceptance of Russian coins minted in Tiflis. Another established a fine for falsifying Russian coins. Sharafutdinova, 1975, p. 169; Ramazanov and Khadzhiev (eds) 1959, p. 575, doc. no. 329; *ibid.*, p. 619. doc. no. 370; Runovskiy, 1862, pp. 342-4.

[95] Such as the prohibition against maintaining any contacts with Russians, see Sharafutdinova, 1975, p. 169.

[96] On administrative *nizams* concerning army, treasury, *naibs*' and other officials' prerogatives, see above.

[97] Shamil established two types of death sentence – humiliating and honourable, depending on the merits of the one facing execution. Honourable execution implied cutting off the head while one was sitting in a praying pose with opened eyes. Humiliating execution was carried out by cutting the head off on a special block with the convict's eyes blindfolded. See Bodenshtadt, 1855, p. 153.

[98] After all, Shamil was an *'alim* and a Sufi sheikh in his own right and had full authority to interpret the *shari'a* and pass his verdicts on it.

[99] Runovskiy, 1862, p. 345.

[100] *Ibid.*

morals.[101] In fact, this law served as much practical as religious aims. The decrease in the number of marriages led to a fall in the population growth, which in turn could potentially lead to a dangerous fall in the male population and jeopardise people's ability to wage war. Equally, the elopement of brides often triggered blood feuds between the clans of a bride and groom which could result in disruptive social tension and violence.

There was a potential danger that once the conditions of marriage were eased, there would be a corresponding increase in the divorce rate. To prevent this undesirable consequence of his marriage law, Shamil issued several supplementary *nizams*. He forbade girls being forced into marriage or marrying without their consent.[102] At the same time, he put in order the financial elements of the divorce settlement. Thus, he obliged a man to pay *kalym* back in full, even if he had spent only several minutes alone with his bride.[103] In cases when a man and wife had lived together before the divorce, the man had to settle all his financial obligations towards his wife regardless of his own circumstances.[104]

Shamil's laws had at times limited geographic jurisdiction and were meant to come into effect in a particular province. Thus, when he issued a *nizam* on bride money, he issued a commentary to the effect that this law applied only to Chechnya. In Daghestan where the bride money was lower than the amount established by Shamil and where his *nizam* could lead to its artificial increase, he forbade the taking of a larger *kalym* than that which already existed.

Despite Shamil's deep commitment to the *shari'a*, he often had to test the limits of its flexibility. Some of the requirements of Islamic legal practice were simply not feasible in the reality of the North Caucasus and needed reinterpretation. This category involved mainly the *nizams* concerning punishment for various crimes.

One of the most obvious examples was the law on theft. The traditional North Caucasian *'adat* was soft on theft especially if committed outside one's *tuqum* or *jama'at*.[105] Therefore, the introduction of *shari'a* law on theft – which called for the amputation of limbs for repeated stealing – the right hand for the first offence, the left for the second, right leg

---

101 Runovskiy, Diary, entry 10 November 1859, in *AKAK*, p. 1398.

102 In issuing this *nizam*, Shamil made one provision: it applied to all girls apart from those 'renowned for their joyful disposition'. Runovskiy, 1862, p. 347.

103 In contrast to the *shari'a* law, according to which if at the divorce a wife had remained a virgin, her husband had to return only half of the bridal money. In practice this law had been abused. The most notorious case being when a man claimed that his wife remained a virgin after they had lived eight years together but did not have children. *Ibid.*, p. 353.

104 This law hindered another common abuse of marital law, when a husband provided false witnesses to claim that his property was mortgaged or sold in order to avoid payments to his divorced wife.

105 On *'adat* concerning theft, see above.

for the third, the left for the fourth, and finally beheading – was socially and culturally unacceptable. Besides, as Shamil himself later admitted, it could have damaged the fighting efficiency of his army and could leave many of his fighters disabled. Thus, according to a special *nizam*, he substituted the amputation of limbs by fine and imprisonment.[106] Only in rare cases did Shamil reserve the right to apply the *shari'a* to the most persistent offenders.[107]

Challenges to Shamil's state

In his state building efforts Shamil had to overcome both the general fragmentation of North Caucasian society and numerous local peculiarities in social practice and historic tradition. The people of Daghestan were generally less militant than their Chechen neighbours[108] and hence more difficult to summon to arms against the Russians.[109] However, when they accepted Shamil as imam, they were more law-abiding and disciplined. In contrast, the more militant Chechens were exceptionally good warriors,[110] but resisted Shamil's new laws and vigorously guarded their full independence and autonomy. Even when Shamil enjoyed the Chechens' full support as a religious and military leader, this did not automatically ensure their subordination to his deputies. They resisted any interference in self-administration and on more than one occasion rebelled when Shamil appointed a *naib* without their consent.[111]

One of the earliest in the series of such rebellions broke out in 1841, shortly after the Chechens gave Shamil an oath of their full allegiance. It was provoked by Shamil's decision to replace Tashou Hajji, the *naib* of Aukh, by Bulat Mirza. In the course of the revolt, the people killed Bulat Mirza and made Shamil reinstate Tashou Hajji as their legitimate *naib*.[112]

Similarly, Shamil's attempts to introduce central taxation and to reorganise the distribution of military booty met the most violent opposition from his Chechen followers. Not only was the idea of taxation completely

---

[106] Nizam Shamilya, 1870, vol. III, pp. 3-8.

[107] In principle the third offence was to be punished by death. In practic this was often substituted by a fine and imprisonment and even if the verdict had been passed, *naibs* did their best to help with escape from captivity.

[108] Among all the Daghestanis, Shamil singled out the people of Sugratl and Andalal, whom he described as the most diligent and militant of all Daghestanis.

[109] This can be at least partly explained by their greater involvement in manufacturing and trade, which was considerably undermined during the war.

[110] Among all the Chechens, Shamil noted the particular bravery of the Gekhi *tuqum*. Dnevnik Runovskogo, entries of 6, 31 July and 25 August 1860.

[111] On the Chechen rebellions, see *AKAK*, vol. XII, pp. 1467-8.

[112] Yurov, 1887, p. 206; Tarkhanov, 1868, p. 59; Zaks, 1992, p. 24.

alien to the Chechens, they in fact had to bear the main burden of it. According to Shamil's tax regulations, *zakat* was taken to be equivalent to twelve per cent of the grain harvest; one per cent of cattle and two per cent of cash-money (and only from those who had over 40 roubles in cash),[113] which implied that grain-producing Chechens in low-land Chechnya had to pay twelve times as much as their cattle breeding, high-mountain neighbours.

The introduction of regular taxation immediately led to unrest. People refused to pay the tax and expelled *naibs* who tried to force them to do so. For example, when in 1841 Jawad Khan tried to collect taxes and force people in his *vilayat* to maintain a cordon on the Argun river, the people accused him of violating the *shari'a* law according to which no tax was to be taken from the poor, and expelled him from their *tuqum*.

Likewise the Chechens tried to resist the newly-introduced system for the centralised appropriation of military spoils and demanded that it should instead be distributed equally among all participants in the raid.[114] When Akhberdy Muhammad, Shamil's *naib* in Lesser Chechnya, following the raid against Mozdok in 1840, tried to appropriate all military booty for the central treasury, the people rebelled and made him hand it over to the elders for equal distribution. Unable to crush the resistance, Akhberdy Muhammad not only gave into people's demands but also dismissed all his Daghestani *murids* whom the Chechens held responsible for overtaxing and robbing them.[115]

Such manifestations of insubordination and free will were incompatible with Shamil's centralising policies. To overcome the Chechens' centrifugal tendencies, he resolved to make minor concessions combined with persistent measures aimed at greater centralisation. Thus following the expulsion of Jawad Khan, Shamil assured the Chechens that he had ordered all his *naibs*, Jawad Khan including, not to abuse their power and granted them temporary tax exemption. At the same time he forced the Chechens to accept Jawad Khan back and ordered the latter to use all means available, including force, to crush any act of further insubordination.

To bring the Chechens to order, Shamil appointed *naibs* from among the Daghestani *muhajirun*,[116] for he believed that those deputies who

---

113 Hajji Ali, 1873, vol. VII, p. 74.

114 This was the traditional manner upheld both by Beybulat and Tashou Hajji.

115 Yurov, 1886, vol. X, pp. 207-8.

116 *Muhajir* – lit. emigrant. In Islamic tradition, the Companions of the Prophet Muhammad who had emigrated with him from Mecca to Madina. In the North Caucasus this term was applied to those who left the communes which had recognised Russian supremacy and joined the imam. Sometimes it referred specifically to those Daghestani followers of Shamil who joined him in Chechnya.

had no personal links with the people in their *vilayat* were less prone
to regional and tribal loyalties and, not having any conflict of interests,
would serve the interests of the state best.[117]

At the same time Shamil introduced an elaborate system of both
individual and collective punishments. The forms of individual punishments ranged from imprisonment and monetary fines to the death sentence. A particular form of non-violent collective punishment, called
ekzekutsii in Russian sources, was invented by Shamil. Such *ekzekutsii*
were carried out by the imam's or *naibs' murids*, usually Daghestanis,
who would arrive in any village that showed some form of insubordination, quarter themselves in the houses of those who had instigated
it and stay there until the people agreed to follow the imam's or *naib*'s
orders.[118] If *ekzekutsii* did not work, Shamil applied the Russian-inspired
policy of resettling people from insubordinate villages in another territory
or dispatching them to other communes.[119]

Although some scholars have drawn parallels between the policies
of Shamil and the Russians,[120] there were important differences between
the two. In a hostile territory with intelligence sources failing to provide
accurate information on the situation in each village, the Russians applied
their punitive policies indiscriminately and on a much larger scale than
Shamil. Furthermore, their actions lacked any legitimation in the eyes
of the local people. Shamil on the other hand knew the country and
people well and had an excellent intelligence service – *mudirs* and *muhtasibs*
– who provided him with the most accurate information on the mood
in each commune. Thus his punishment was swift and aimed at those
directly responsible for insubordination. Most importantly, in his dis-
pensation of justice, Shamil drew legitimation directly from God:

Usually, before important decisions, the imam would go into a *khalwa*. After
several days of fasting, prayer and (silent) *dhikr* he would pass out. Afterwards,
he would emerge and announce that the Prophet had appeared to him when he was
unconscious and had given him certain instructions.[121]

---

[117] This differed dramatically from the tactics earlier applied by both Beybulat and
Tashou Hajji, who chose their deputies from among people's representatives. By doing
so they preserved the traditional order and maintained the principle of self-administration,
but failed to unify the Chechens into one state.

[118] On *ekzekutsii*, see Shamil i Chechnya, 1859 p. 143; Dubrovin, 1871, pp. 476-7;
Runovskiy, 1862, p. 341.

[119] Thus, for example, Shamil resettled the people of Karachay village, situated on the
most convenient trade road between Chechnya and Daghestan (Andi – Black mountains
– Vedeno) for robbing the trade caravans. However, Shamil later dismissed the usefulness
of these measures. Dnevnik Runovskogo, entry of 6 July 1860.

[120] e.g. Baddeley, 1908, pp. 479-81.

[121] Gammer, 1994, p. 239. On the illustration of such practicies see *ibid.*, pp. 239-40;
'Shamil i Chechnya', 1859, p. 130; Volkonskiy, 1882; vol. VI, pp. 502-3.

For as long as Shamil was victorious, and his followers were determined to continue *ghazavat*, he could successfully justify his resort to violence as being necessary to maintain unity and solidarity for the sake of God and victory. Even Russian historians admitted that through his reforms Shamil succeeded in greatly improving the behaviour and morals of the mountain peoples and promoting a union among them which had never existed before.[122] However, once military fortunes started to betray Shamil, it seemed that no persuasion – peaceful or violent – could prevent the growing dissent of his subjects. The internal contradictions and tensions within his imamate resurfaced and contributed to the decline of his power.

---

[122] Ramazanov and Khadzhiev (eds), 1959, pp. 401-8, doc. no. 219 (a letter by Neidhart to Chernyshev, 20 November 1843); also pp. 412-23, doc. no. 221 (a report by Orbeliani who was in Shamil's captivity in 1842).

23

THE DECLINE OF SHAMIL'S POWER AND THE FALL OF THE IMAMATE[1]

In the late 1840s-early 1850s a critical change in the military-political climate of the North Caucasus occurred, brought about by the modification of Russian tactics. The first signs of the change in the Russian approach towards the war in the North Caucasus date back to 1845, when Vorontsov first realised the need to make more persistent and permanent advances based on 'siege strategy'.[2] The new strategy recalled that of Ermolov's policies and involved the consolidation of Russian gains and a gradual systematic advance into hostile territory.[3] In 1846 the Russians transferred a considerable military force to stop all gaps in the Russian defence line, started to reinforce the existing forts and to construct new ones, to repair and build military roads and communications. This was accompanied by the persistent campaign in Lesser Chechnya to cut down the Chechen forests and clear the most fertile low-land areas of all the Chechen population.[4]

The result was the gradual formation of a broad belt of uninhabited land between the Russian and Murid lines, and the advantage lay undoubtedly with the invaders from the north; for the desert thus created was of itself fertile, and had served as a granary not only to the wilder and more barren parts of Tchetchnia, to which Shamil's hold of this country was not reduced, but in great measure to Daghestan as well. Nor did the matter end there; for the ties of blood were strong amongst the Tchetchens, and the transference of whole villages to the security of the northern plains led to the defection of many of Shamil's nearest adherents, including even some of his trusted naibs. At the same time the Cossack colonies were

---

[1] On the last period of Shamil's activities in addition to the above-mentioned sources the following ones are used: Rusogly, 1859; Shabanov, 1866; Soltan, 1884, 1885, 1887 and 1888; Volkonskiy 1879, 1879(a) and 1880.

[2] This plan was suggested by Vorontsov in 1845. However, it was not until 1853 that the Russians finally realised the futility of punitive expeditions and embraced the siege strategy. More on Vorontsov's plan, see Gammer, 1994, p. 175; Baddeley, 1908, p. 446.

[3] On siege policy as worked out by Vorontsov, see Gammer, 1994, pp. 175-82.

[4] In 1850 the Russians rounded up and deported all Chechens living between Sunja and the newly constructed Great Russian Highway beyond Terek. *AKAK*, vol. X, pp. 509-10, doc. no. 460.

strengthened and advanced, while the felling of the forest trees was supplemented by the construction of strategic roads.[5]

In 1853 the Russians cleared their way through the forests of Greater Chechnya and forced its population beyond the Black Mountains. As a result Shamil lost most of lowland Chechnya.[6] Although the imam continued to fight the Russians, at times rather successfully,[7] he did not fail to appreciate the long-term effect of the Russian campaign in Lesser and Greater Chechnya. In his own words, watching over the increasingly systematic nature of Russian advances into his domain, he had already in 1846 recognised their fatal danger to his state.[8]

The decline of his power was finally made irreversible in the early 1850s, when both sides resorted to a defensive strategy. This allowed the Russians to build on their strategic advantage and await a favourable moment to resume their systematic advance. Shamil, on the other hand, was faced with the most difficult challenge of holding his state together and defending it from both internal and external enemies.

Internal decline

Once the imamate stopped growing in size and with no significant campaign into hostile territory in sight, the war stopped 'feeding itself'. Furthermore, the loss of lowland Chechnya, the main grain supplier in the imamate, forced Shamil to increase taxes and other payments in the remaining parts of his state and to impose strict control of foreign and domestic trade. He issued a set of regulations which forbade the 'export' of grain from the imamate and introduced fixed prices, much lower than in the Russian-ruled territories.

The newly-introduced regulations and the tightening of Shamil's fiscal policy – however inevitable – proved to be counterproductive. It served to raise tensions in the imamate and widened the gap between Shamil and his people. Furthermore, the morale of both ordinary people and officials in the imamate deteriorated. As a result Shamil's lieutenants frequently began to abuse their powers. From the very beginning the institution of the *naib* created much tension in the imamate, especially in Chechnya. For their service Shamil's *naibs* and *mudirs* received land which was usually confiscated from the people for various offences or

---

[5] Baddeley, 1908, p. 445.

[6] He later gained back his positions in greater Chechnya, which finally fell out of his imamate in winter 1856-7 in the aftermath of the Russian campaign. On the Russian winter campaign in Greater Chechnya see *AKAK*, vol. XII, pp. 1028-38, doc. no. 907-11; Soltan, 1884, pp. 335-97.

[7] On Shamil's campaigns in central Daghestan see Gammer, 1994, chapter XVIII, pp. 183-94; in southern Daghestan, *ibid.*, chapter XIX, pp. 195-209.

[8] *Dnevnik Runovskogo*, entry 16 March 1860, in *AKAK*, vol. XII, p. 1419.

allotted from the communal lands. This acquisition of land by people from outside one's *tuqum* or *jama'at* violated the foundation of the land-ownership system in the North Caucasus, which did not permit foreigners and outsiders to come into possession of land and forbade communal land to be transferred to private property.[9] Furthermore, in Chechnya it created a class of private land-owners which had never existed there before and challenged the very foundation of the social order.

The process of land acquisition[10] as well as the expression of people's discontent were somewhat checked by Shamil's power. However, starting from the early 1850s the situation swiftly began to deteriorate.[11] With the war nearing its end *naibs* were concerned with enriching themselves by all means available, and, when any clash between them and the imam occurred, they defected to the Russians. The first in the line of defections was Hajji Murad. After a number of conflicts between him and Shamil,[12] he defected to the Russians in 1851. Following him, Bata, another of Shamil's *naibs*, defected to the Russians.

At the same time Shamil started to lose the support of the ordinary people in the imamate. A local chronicler noted that 1853 was the year when 'people's war weariness and hunger increased [beyond endurance]'.[13] The hitherto muted opposition to Shamil's policy spilled out in open revolt. People reproached the imam for impoverishing them, refused to pay taxes or to join his military campaigns, especially if fought in territory other than that of their own *tuqum* or *jama'at*. This shifted the base of Shamil's military force from the voluntary people's

[9] On land acquisition by Shamil's *naibs* see Ivanenkov, 1910, pp. 53-4; Zaks, 1941, p. 154, n. 37.

[10] Shamil made his *naibs* swear an oath before taking up the office whereby they promised to obey all his orders and never violate the law. Since this oath was taken on the Qur'an, any violation of *naibs* authority was treated not merely as administrative crime but also blasphemy. 'Shamil i Chechnya', 1859, p. 143.

[11] Later Shamil and his official chronicler ascribed the fall in Shamil's power to the abuse and treachery of his *naibs*: al-Qarakhi, 1946, pp. 240-3.

[12] First the tension between Shamil and Hajji Murad spilled out immediately after the gathering of Andi, when Hajji Murad openly expressed his discontent with the 'election' of Jamal al-Din, Shamil's son, as the next imam. However, Shamil did not take any measures against him. In 1851 the people of Tabarsaran and Qaytaq raised charges against Hajji Murad. Shamil tried to depose him from his office and ordered the confiscation of his property. Defended by his *murids*, Hajji Murad kept his position for several more months and, only after hearing the rumours that Shamil had passed a death sentence on him, escaped into the Russian-held territories. However, he left behind his family who became virtual hostages of Shamil. Not being able to face life in the Russian camp and with Shamil's refusal to allow his family to join him, Hajji Murad once again tried to escape into the mountains but was killed by Russian soldiers. On Hajji Murad, see Zisserman, 1851-2. For a literary account of Hajji Murad's life and adventures, see Tolstoy, 1912, pp. 3-125.

[13] Al-Qarakhi, 1946, p. 231; Runovskiy, 1862, p. 341.

corps to *murtaziqa* units. Devoid of its most significant strategic advantage, i.e. the popular nature of the war, Shamil was left with scarce military and human resources, insufficient to sustain a war of this scale for long.

Through his strong will and military genius, Shamil managed to arrest the process of his military and political decline for a short period of time. When the Crimean War broke out in 1853 Shamil used it to boost the morale of his warriors. Seizing the opportunity provided by the re-deployment of some Russian units from the North Caucasus to the Crimean front, he staged a number of successful campaigns,[14] entered into negotiations with the Russian command and established commercial links between the imamate and the Russian-held territories.[15] This temporary recovery in the imam's fortunes was dealt a fatal blow when the Crimean War ended in the signing of the Paris Peace Treaty on 30 March 1856. In the Caucasus the end of the war was seen as the victory of the Russians and it finally crushed the people's resolve to fight.[16]

This change in the mood of the North Caucasians found its reflection in the emergence of an alternative non-Naqshbandi Sufi teaching and structure. Expressed within the framework of the Qadiri Sufi order, it was preached by a Chechen from Eliskhan-yurt, Sheikh Kunta Hajji.[17]

Kunta Hajji was born some time in the 1830s in Isti-su-*aul* to a poor family of a Chechen *uzden* called Kishi. When he was still a little boy, his family moved to Eliskhan-yurt, where Kunta Hajji studied Arabic and the Qur'an.[18] In 1848-9, at the age of eighteen together with his father, Kunta Hajji went on his first *hajj* to Mecca. It was

---

[14] As result of one of his campaigns carried out across the border with Georgia, he captured a Georgian Princess Chavchavadze with her entourage, whom he was later able to exchange for his eldest son Ghazi Muhammad. On the raid, see Baratov, 1876, pp. 237-67.

[15] These negotiations were held through Jamal al-Din al-Ghazi-Ghumuqi. On negotiations between Shamil and the Russians, see Gammer, 1994, pp. 275-6.

[16] Delegations from all over the imamate came to Shamil demanding peace. Fadeev, 1856, no. 10, pp. 63-4.

[17] The early history of the Qadiri order in the North Caucasus is one of the most under-researched subjects. In the course of my fieldwork I have collected copies of several Qadiri manuscripts from Chechnya. However, they require separate study which remains outside my present scope. Here I base the account of Kunta Hajji and his order on Akaev, 1994; Borusevich, 1893; Gatuev, mauscript, 282, fond 1, opis' 1, 1539, list. 1-51; Ippolitov, 1869; Salamov, 'Pravda o Sheikhakh i Svyatykh Mestakh v Checheno-Ingushetii', unpubl. paper; Salamov, 'Myuridizm v Checheno-Ingushetii', unpubl. paper; Umarov, 1985; Umarov and Shamilova, 1984; Vertepov, 1914.

[18] Russian sources present Kunta Hajji as illiterate, but this is challenged by the fact that he wrote letters and appeals in Arabic. Furthermore, his childhood falls within the years of Shamil's rule, when the imam introduced obligatory primary education for boys and established a school at each quarter's mosque.

during this journey that he apparently was initiated into the Qadiri order and, on his return to Chechnya, started to preach the new *tariqa*.[19]

His message differed dramatically from that of the Naqshbandis. Preaching self-purification and religious devotion, Kunta Hajji denounced violence and called for full withdrawal from worldly and especially military affairs. At the same time he introduced a characteristically different practice of vocal *dhikr*, which involved music and dancing.[20]

On learning of the new preacher, Shamil immediately summoned him to his residence at New Dargho (Vedeno) and forbade his religious preaching and *dhikr* ceremonies, under the pretext that the latter contradicted the *shari'a*, which forbids dancing and music during *dhikr*. However, the reasons for tension between the two religious leaders appear to be somewhat different. The non-violent character of Kunta Hajji's teaching appealed to a people exhausted and impoverished by war. Moreover, it provided them with a doctrine by which one could remain a true Muslim without following *ghazavat* but through asceticism and withdrawal from worldly activities. Not surprisingly Shamil saw it as a challenge to his authority as a religious and political leader, which might undermine his efforts to sustain the resistance. Thus, in 1859 Kunta Hajji was forced to leave Chechnya and to go on *hajj* for a second time. However, by that time many of traditional Naqshbandi 'lay' followers and the *tariqa murids* had accepted the teaching of Kunta Hajji and joined the Qadiri order.

The fall of the imamate

In this general atmosphere of physical and moral exhaustion, Shamil could not fail to recognise that the end of war was inevitable. Shortly after the Paris Peace Treaty between the Russians and the Ottoman-British-French coalition, he openly stated that if the Ottoman Sultan Abdul Majid had made peace with the Russians, he should do the same.[21] However, when presented with a choice between peaceful negotiations or military victory, the Russians always opted for the latter.[22] Convinced

[19] Akaev, 1994, p. 30.

[20] The most common musical instrument which accompanied the Qadiri *dhikr* in the North Caucasus was the drums. The *dhikr* 'dance' involved quick movement around a circle accompanied by special head movements and the exclamation '*Ulillah*'. There is no single explanation of what *Ulillah* stands for – Wali Allah [*waliullah*] or a considerably shortened phrase '*la ilaha illa allahu*'.

[21] Gammer, 1994, p. 276.

[22] The Russian military successfully blocked any negotiations and advocated purely military means to ending the conflict. Thus, when Shamil's representative in Istanbul approached the Russian embassy to offer Shamil's surrender, the Emperor seemed to have been inclined to accept the offer. However, he was strongly advised against any negotiations by Prince Baratinskiy, who was anxious to test Shamil's defeat and surrender.

that the days of the imam were numbered, they saw the negotiations merely as an obstacle to complete military triumph. In 1857 they broke off all negotiations with the imam and launched a two-pronged attack from the north-west and north-east.

In June 1857, despite strong resistance led by the imam himself,[23] the Russians cleared avenues through the forests, paved roads and established a new fort at Burtinay...stormed and destroyed Shamil's fort opposite Burtinay (17 October) and received submission of part of the population of Salatawh...between 12 and 28 November destroyed Zandaq, Dilim and the country in between them...destroyed all the villages along Jalka, Shavdon and Khulkhulaw rivers and transferred their population beyond the Sunja. After a months rest...Evdokimov dealt his master-blow: on January 1828 he conquered the Argun defile.[...] Strategically the Upper Argun defile was of great importance, being the very centre of Shamil's dominions.[...] Ending the winter campaign...Evdokimov immediately moved to Lesser Chechnya, where between 13 and 28 April he received the submission of ninety-six villages inhabited by 15,000 people. Ten weeks later he started the summer campaign.[...] Although encountering bitter resistance, the Russians advanced step by step, continually clearing the forest and cutting through roads. On 12 August Shubut was captured.[...] On 26 August the community of Shubut submitted. It was followed by that of Chanti on 27 August.[...] By 12 September...fifteen Chechen communities had submitted to the Russians.[24]

The first stage of the general offensive was completed with the seizure and destruction of Shamil's capital in New Dargho (Vedeno) on 13 April 1859. The fall of New Dargho delivered the final blow to the people's resolve to fight. One by one the remaining Chechen *tuqums*, including the most militant people of Chaberloy, Ichkeria, and the upper Aukh, submitted.[25] In Daghestan, Daniel Bek, the *naib* of Ihali and Qibid Muhammad al-Tilitli defected to the Russians and submitted along with the people they ruled.[26] Furthermore, Qibid Muhammad seized the imam's treasury and handed over to the Russians one of the most ardent Naqshbandi preachers, Aslan al-Tsudaqari, as a proof of his loyalty to them.[27] By 19 August 1959, following a Russian assault on Shamil's last stronghold in Ichiqale, all villages remaining under Shamil's control

---

See Ramazanov and Khadzhiev (eds), 1959, p. 676, doc. no. 432; Volkonskiy, 1879, p. 401; Gammer, 1994, p. 285.

[23] On Shamil's attempts to check the process and his military and political efforts, see Gammer, 1994, pp. 284-5.

[24] *Ibid.*, pp. 279-83.

[25] *AKAK*, vol. XII, pp. 1139-40, doc. no. 1010-1; p. 1143, doc. no. 1013-4; pp. 1132-4, 1139, doc. no. 997-8; 1008; Anoev, 1877, no. 5, pp. 188-204; Volkonskiy, 1879, pp. 151-69, 199-203, 228-30.

[26] They were followed by other of Shamil's *naibs*, see al-Qarakhi, 1941, pp. 242-3; 246-50.

[27] Pokrovskiy, 1991, p. 24.

had submitted to the Russians. The imam, with his family and no more than 400 followers reached his last refuge in the high mountain village Ghunib.[28]

On 21 August 1859 the Russian forces approached Ghunib and laid siege to it. Eager to capture the imam alive, they tried to negotiate with him through his former *naib*, Daniel Bek al-Ilisu, but Shamil refused to surrender. He established his defence line around the flat summit of Ghunib mountain and for several more weeks held his positions. On 6 September 1859, despite the desperate defence put up by Shamil and his *murids*, the Russians finally seized the village and the imam's camp.[29] Shamil along with the members of his family and several dozen remaining followers retreated to the village mosque. According to Shamil's biographer, the imam was determined to follow the fate of his predecessor, Ghazi Muhammad, and die in battle rather than allow the Russians to imprison him. He made a passionate speech to those few who remained with him in the mosque, urging them to seek death as martyrs and to fight to the last. However, his emotional appeal failed to inspire his close circle. Both his own sons and lieutenants pleaded with him to surrender, hinting at the presence of women and children with them. The imam finally succumbed to their pleas, especially those of his son Ghazi Muhammad and the women and gave himself up.[30]

Thirty years had passed since, fired by religious enthusiasm and love of liberty (or, as the Russians have it, of fanaticism and licence) he had raised with Kazi Moulla the standard of the Holy War. During all that time, through good and evil fortune, he had remained faithful to the Cause and to himself. While the First Imam lived he had served with a rare devotion and it was only by little less than a miracle that he had failed to share his fate. During Hamza's brief rule he had shown equal fidelity, though he might justly have claimed the succession himself. Chief of the Faithful since 1834, he had achieved an astonishing measure of success and the merit was mostly his own. Now, when three decades of ceaseless strife against the colossal might of Russia had brought him face to face with complete and final failure, his conscience acquitted him of blame, and with that verdict the impartial historian must agree.[31]

Shamil's surrender finally marked the end of the Caucasian war. There still remained small pockets of resistance, but these were no more than the last sparks of a dying fire. For the imam and his supporters this symbolised not merely military defeat, but defeat for the cause of Islam in the North Caucasus.

---

[28] For a description of Ghunib, see Baddeley, 1908, pp. 476-7; Soltan, 1859, pp. 390-410.

[29] On the defence staged by both men and women, see al-Qarakhi, 1941, pp. 247-8.

[30] This decision somewhat tarnished his image in the collective memory of the North Caucasians, especially the Chechens, for several generations to come.

[31] Baddeley, 1908, pp. 477-8.

Captivity and the last days of Imam Shamil[32]

Shamil and his two sons were first sent to the Russian camp on the Kahal mountain, then to Temir-Khan-Shura, from where they were escorted to St. Petersburg to the Emperor's court. Throughout his journey, Shamil, although a prisoner of the Russian empire, was treated with full military honours. In St Petersburg the Emperor met Shamil in a personal audience, presented him with a golden sword and allocated to him a generous government retainer of 20,000 roubles a year and a house in Kaluga.[33]

Jamal al-Din al-Ghazi-Ghumuqi, Shamil's *murshid* and the most prominent Naqshbandi sheikh, was spared captivity, which Shamil and many other Naqshbandi leaders faced. After Shamil's surrender he was allowed to remain in the North Caucasus and stayed first in Tiliq and later in Kazanischa, where he was cared for by the family of the *shamkhal* of Targhu, Abu Muslim Khan, and Russian officials, including Baron Rozen and the Georgian Prince Orbeliani. In 1864 Jamal al-Din decided to leave his native Daghestan for the Ottoman lands. He settled first at Kars and some time later in Istanbul were 'he lived venerated till his death in 1283 (1866/7)'.[34]

At Ghunib, Shamil had surrendered on the condition that he and his family would be allowed to go to Mecca. However, years passed by and his wish was not granted. Despite all the respect and honours rendered, Shamil was tormented by his captivity and pressed his captors for permission to leave for Mecca.

Meanwhile, even in Russia he maintained to the best of his ability the 'truly Muslim way' of life. He tried to abstain from contacts with Christians, spent all his time reading the Qur'an and other religious books and supervised the regular prayers of his family.[35] Although he had lost his political power, he retained his position as a Naqshbandi Sufi sheikh and as such continued to enjoy the respect of the Muslims both in the North Caucasus and in other Muslim areas of the Russian empire.[36] His house was frequented by visitors from the Caucasus, the

---

[32] On Shamil in captivity, see Puteshestvie Shamilya of Guniba do St. Peterburga, 1859; Przhetslavskiy, 1877-8; Runovskiy, 1859 and 1861; Ryndin, 1895; Shamil Polveka Nazad v Moskve, 1909; Zakharin, 1898.

[33] Al-Qarakhi, 1946, 254-5.

[34] *Ibid.*, p. 258. At his grave a *mazar* ('mausoleum') was built, which came to be frequented by Naqshbandis from all over the world.

[35] Przhetslavskiy, 1877, no. 10, p. 256.

[36] Even in captivity Shamil safeguarded his image. Thus, he once enquired about the possibility of transferring himself and his family to Moscow, for nobody in the Caucasus had heard of Kaluga and there they could have thought that he was an 'ordinary captive', see Przhetslavskiy, 1877, no. 10, p. 262.

Volga basin and Central Asia who asked for religious instruction and sought his *baraka*.[37]

In 1869, following his repeated requests, Shamil was finally granted permission to go on the *hajj*, provided that he left one of his sons behind. On 4 April 1869 Shamil and his family set off for Mecca, leaving Ghazi Muhammad and his wife as 'hostages'.[38] Shamil travelled through the Ottoman lands and everywhere he went he was met with honour and respect. Crowds of people awaited the arrival of his ship from Anapa eager to see the great imam and greet him on Ottoman territory.[39]

In Istanbul he was granted an audience with the Sultan, who bought a special residence for him and allocated him a pension. Shamil stayed in Istanbul for several months,[40] after which he went to Cairo. In Cairo, Shamil was met by Isma'il Pasha who showed him the honours reserved for the most important dignitaries and statesmen.

In August 1870 Shamil finally arrived in Mecca. It was his wish to end his life in the holy land[41] and, perhaps, one would be forgiven for believing that God had answered the prayers of his most loyal servant and blessed him by putting his soul to rest in the land where Shamil desired most to remain. The great imam, who had glorified the name of his country and its people in the name of Islam, died in Madina on 4 April 1871. Shamil's burial was attended by all the prominent sheikhs of the holy cities who led his funeral procession and offered their prayers for him at the site of the Prophet's grave. He was buried in the al-Baqiyya cemetery amongst the greatest men of Islam for the glory of which he lived and died.[42]

[37] Though, both imam and his visitors were under the constant surveillance of the Russian authorities.

[38] Al-Qarakhi, 1946, p. 304.

[39] *Ibid.*, pp. 310-1.

[40] One of the first things he did his arrival in Istanbul was to visit the grave of his *murshid.*

[41] On Shamil's wishes and prayers see al-Qarakhi, 1946, pp. 310-13.

[42] *Ibid.*, pp. 312-13.

Imam Shamil in Russian captivity.

EPILOGUE
THE SUFI LEGACY IN THE NORTH CAUCASUS

In a little less than fifty years of activity, the Naqshbandi order introduced new ideas and concepts which transformed the whole fabric of North Caucasian society and changed the political and religious landscape of the area. Initially preached as a set of ethics and mystical exercises aimed at gaining insight into the Divine wisdom and unity with God, Naqshbandi ideas became intertwined with the complex political situation arising from growing Russian interference into the affairs of the North Caucasus. As a result, the activity of the Naqshbandi sheikhs almost immediately acquired a political dimension.

Although the Naqshbandi order, especially the Mujaddidi-Khalidi branch, was known to have a high degree of political involvement with Muslim rulers through an established Muslim hierarchy, in the North Caucasus the situation was different. As the imams discovered, the majority of the local rulers and the Muslim elite, fearful of antagonising Russia, came to view the Naqshbandi order as troublemakers and were hostile to them. The leaders of the new movement, on the other hand, realised that preaching the virtues of the *shari'a* without the means to enforce it, i.e. political power, was futile. Having challenged the existing political and social order, the Naqshbandi leaders initiated a series of reforms that overhauled it and introduced an entirely new order based principally on the *shari'a* and Naqshbandi political principles. Shamil's imamate came as a culmination of this process.

The most spectacular result of the thirty-year rule of the Naqshbandi imams, and that of Shamil in particular, became apparent in the transformation which North Caucasian mountain society underwent. Divided by tribal codes, clan and territorial affiliations and by the geographic terrain itself, this fragmented society was for the first time united under the Naqshbandi imams.

Having identified *'adat* as the main obstacle in the way of the unification of the numerous tribal groups in the Caucasus, the imams pressed on with the introduction of the shari'a into the legal system and wider societal context (relationships within and between families, villages, communes, state and individuals, etc.) To this day North Caucasians refer to the period of the imams, particularly Shamil's rule as 'the time of the *shari'a*'.

On a cultural level, Naqshbandi rule contributed to the profound Islamisation of the mountain societies of Chechnya and Daghestan. The established network of the Sufi lodges, Muslim schools, the use of

235

Arabic as an official language of the imamate, as well as the cultivation
of the class of the Muslim officials – *qadis, 'ulama'* and *tariqa* sheikhs
– significantly raised the standards of Muslim learning and created the
Muslim elite whose position became far more important and influential
than ever before.

The replacement of the *'adat* laws by those of the shari'a above all
Islamised the legal culture of the North Caucasus, which retained but
slight elements of customary law. Furthermore, it transformed Islam
from a vague concept into a way of life and dramatically changed the
identity of the whole society. The Naqshbandi reforms significantly
undermined the sense of clan and communal affiliation by introducing
a broader sense of universal Daghestani (understood as the mountain
country, including Chechnya) political affiliation and an association
with the Muslim world at large.

Shamil's imamate was the first and only experience of a state for
many of the North Caucasian peoples. The introduction of a regular
army, taxation, treasury, administration and government, and foreign
and domestic policy for the first time generated a concept of citizenship
and a loyalty far greater and stronger than that of clan, tribe and commune.
Short-lived as it was, this experience had a 'civilising' effect in the
sense that all the subjects of the imamate could identify with the idea
of a North Caucasian body politic in an Islamic form, even long after
it had ceased to exist.

The 'civilising' effect of Shamil's rule was recognised even by the
Russians, who kept his system of administration, including the administrative division and the titles of the governors – *naibs* and *naibstvo*
– almost intact for many years after the fall of the imamate.[1] However,
having outwardly recognised the practical usefulness of Shamil's system
of administration, the Russian authorities sought to deprive it of its
Islamic, and especially, Naqshbandi essence. They saw the shari'a and
the institutions associated with it as the main source of hostilities and
tried to remove all matters of law and administration from the jurisdiction
of the Muslim religious officials and replace the *shari'a* by the *'adat*
and, whenever possible, Russian imperial law.

The policy of eradicating the shari'a had a limited effect. Although
excluded from official Russian administrative and legal institutions, the
Sufi brotherhoods never ceased to wield influence and formed an alternative system of administration. This system permeated all levels of
social, religious and political life in Chechnya and Daghestan and, based
as it was on a clandestine network of *murid* organisations, remained
totally outside Russian reach.

Furthermore, the Qadiri order which initially preached non-interference in political affairs, experienced a dramatic transformation only

---

[1] On the Russian administrative system see Esadze, 1907.

a few years after the Russian conquest and adopted many features of Naqshbandi doctrine and organisation.[2] Despite the 'peaceful' character of Kunta Hajji's preaching, the Qadiri followers grew increasingly hostile to Russian rule due to both the inflow of former Naqshbandi adepts into the order and the corrupt and arbitrary nature of the Russian administration.

The time of the imamate became seen increasingly as the 'golden era', the return to which was a goal and an obligation of every true Muslim. All those who were dissatisfied with the existing state of affairs, which amounted virtually to the whole of Chechnya and northern Daghestan, became associated with one of the two Sufi orders.

The growing number of adepts lent the brotherhoods the political and spiritual credibility that Shamil strove to achieve. By joining one of the orders, people not only sought the spiritual guidance and protection of a sheikh, but also recognised him as the only credible authority that stood for the values and principles lost with the fall of the imamate. Many people simply refused to refer to the Russian administration for justice, settlement of disputes and the running of the Russian of their communes, but appealed to the Sufi sheikhs instead.

Having assumed the role of political and spiritual leadership, the Sufi orders became the focal point of the anti-Russian opposition in the area and the main vehicle of its expression. Thus there emerged a characteristic pattern of protest which took the form of popular uprisings led and inspired by the Sufi orders. All these uprisings shared a common goal – i.e. the restoration of the imamate – and were led by an imam[3] and always originated in the territory that had constituted Shamil's imamate.

The whole discourse surrounding the history of the Naqshbandi order in the North Caucasus becomes inevitably dominated by the political and military confrontation between the local peoples and Russia which followed the introduction of the order into the area. The significance of the Naqshbandiyya was, however, by no means confined to its political role. Perhaps more important was the way in which it transformed the fundamental principles and relationships along which North Caucasian

---

[2] Its organisation came to resemble Shamil's hierarchy with Kunta Hajji accepted as the imam or *ustadh* who had two deputies (*vakils*), eight *naibs*, whose number corresponded to the eight provinces in which the Qadiri order operated (mainly in Lesser Chechnya and among the Qumyqs of Daghestan), and numerous *turqkhs*, who organised the Qadiri activities on the scale of a village or village quarter. Ippolitov, 1869, pp. 2-3; Salamov, 'Pravda o Svyatykh Mestakh v Checheno Ingushetii', pp. 9-10.

[3] e.g. the revolts of 1877-8 by Imam Alibek Hajji Aldanov; 1917-20 by imam Najmuddin Hotso (Gotsinskiy); and the North Caucasian Emirate of Uzun Hajji. The tendency was disrupted only in the late 1930s, when the modern secular elite took over the leadership in the national liberation struggle, e.g. Hasan Israilov in 1939-44, Djohar Dudaev in 1991-6.

society operated. In hindsight, the continuity of traditional Muslim values, institutions and way of life over more than a century of foreign domination must be largely attributed to the Sufi legacy.

The Naqshbandi movement in the Northern Caucasus staged the first serious effort to modernise North Caucasian society. It introduced hitherto unknown or weak concepts of state, citizenship, and a coherent social order. The defeat of the movement by the Russians and the establishment of Russian control disrupted the natural course of the state-building experiment. Russian and consequently Soviet rule was in itself an unprecedented attempt at social and political restructuring. However, the Russian efforts being entirely alien in both ideology and political terms failed to promote a sense of citizenship and create modern nations in the Northern Caucasus. The Naqshbandi movement on the other hand was a genuinely indigenous phenomenon and as such it preserved and even increased its appeal. On the eve of the twenty-first century all politicians in the Northern Caucasus, from secular nationalists to Islamists refer to the Naqshbandi era as a role model of an ideology and social order that enjoys popular support and legitimacy. In this sense the Naqshbandi legacy continues to dominate political and cultural discourse in the area.

BIBLIOGRAPHY

ARCHIVAL SOURCES

TsGVIA Tsentral'ny Gosudarstvenny Voenno-Istoricheskiy Arkhiv (Central State Military-History Archive), Russian Federation, Moscow.

Fond VUA (Voenno-Uchetny Arkhiv) 52; 428; 718.

TsGADA Tsentral'ny Gosudarstvenny Arkhiv Drevnikh Aktov (Central State Archive of Ancient Documents), Russian Federation, Moscow.

Razdel VII; XIII; XXIII.

TsGA Dag. Tsentral'ny Gosudarstvenny Arkhiv Dagestanskoy SSSR (Central State Archive of Daghestan), Daghestan, Mahachqala.

Fond Kizlyarskogo Kommendanta; 150; 133.

RF IIYaL DAG Rukopisny Fond Instituta Istorii, Yazyka i Literatury Dagestanskoy Akademii Nau (Manuscript Collection of the Institute of History, Languages and Literature, Daghestan Academy of Sciences).

TsGA GSSR Tsentral'ny Gosudarstvenny Arkhiv Gruzinskoy SSR (The Central State Archive of Georgian SSR), Georgian Republic, Tbilisi. (I acquired a copy from this archive before the change of status of the Republic, when it was still GSSR.)

Fond 1087.

Private Archive of Prof. Salamov, Grozny.

UNPUBLISHED SOURCES

Arabic

Hajji, T., manuscript, *Sharh Tifl al-Ma'ani*, RF IIYah, Mahachqala.

———, manuscript, *Al-As'ila al-'Adida min al-Makan al-Ba'id*, RF IIYAL, Mahachqala.

Al-'Uradi, M.A., manuscript *Al-Murham*.

Muhammad, Ghazi, manuscript, Bahir al-Burhan Li-'Irtidat 'Urala Daghestan, RF IIYAL, Mahachqala.

Russian

Gatuev, D., 'Sheykhizm v Chechne. Sostavleno v 1925-6 g', In *RF IIYAL DAN, fond 1, opis' 1; delo 1539, list 1-51.*

'Isaevich Iz Neizdannoy Rukopisi Polkovnika Isaevicha. Kharakteristika Deyatelnosti Imama Chechni i Dagestana Shamilya', in *TsGa GSSR, fond 1087, opis' I, delo 268, list 2-7.*

Kotsebu, L.-C, 'Svedeniya o Gorskikh Vladeniyakh Sostvlennaya v 1826 gody'. In *TsGVIA,* VUA, delo 18498, list 1-11.

Kusheva, E. N, 'Chechnya i Ingushetiya v XVI-XVII vekakh', in Salamov's private archive.

240 *Bibliography*

Makatov, M., 1965, 'Preodolenie Kul'ta svyatykh v protsesse ateisticehskogo vospitaniya', Ph.D. thesis, Moscow State University.
Potemkin, P, '1785 Pis'ma Imperatritse', in *TsGVIA*, fond 52, opis' 2/203, delo 32, god 1783-89, list 2-5 ob.
Runovskiy, A., 'Dnevnik Runovskogo', Salamov's Private Archive.
Salamov, A., 'Pravda o Svyatykh Mestakh v Checheno-Ingushetii', Salamov's Private Archive.
——— 'Myuridizm v Checheno-Ingushetii', Salamov's Private Archive.
'Yyur'ev Obschiy Vzglyad na Prichiny i Posledstviya Besporyadknov, Voznikshikh v Dagestane ot Rasprostraneniya Fanatizma Sekty Myuridov Mezhdu Gortsami'. In *TsGVIA*, fond VUA, delo 6550, list 2-21.

Western

Abu-Manneh, B., 1971, 'Some Aspects of Ottoman Rule in Syria in the Second Half of the 19th Century. Reforms, Islam and Khaliphate', D.Phil, Oxford University.
Damrell, D., 1992, 'Islam and Mysticism in the Mughal Empire: the Naqshbandi Reaction's Reconsidered', paper presented at South Asian History Seminar June 9, 1992, St. Antony's College, Oxford. I am grateful to the author for allowing me to have a copy of his paper and to quote from it.
———, 1992, 'The Naqshbandi Order in Transition. A Central Asian Shaykh in Mughal India', unpublished paper. I am grateful to the author for allowing me to use and quote from it.
Fusfeld, W. E., 1981, 'The Shaping of Sufi Leadership in Delhi: The Naqshbandiyya-Mujaddidiyya, 1750 to 1920', Ph.D., University of Pennsylvania.

PUBLISHED SOURCES

Arabic

1326 (1908), *Silsila al-Khawajakan Adab 'Ubudiyat al-A'yan*, Temir-Khan-Shura.
al-Ghazi-Ghumuqi, Jamal al-Din, 1905, *al-Adab al-Mardiyya fi al-Tariqa al-Naqshbandiyya*, Petrovsk.
al-Khani, A., 1308, *al-Hada'iq al-Wardiyya fi Hada'iq Ajilla' al-Naqshbandiyya*, Cairo.
al-Qadari, H., 1894-5, *Kitab Asar-i Daghestan*, St. Petersburg.
al-Qarakhi, M.T., 1946, *Baraqat al-Suyyuf al-Dagistaniyya fi Ba'ad al-Ghazawat al-Shamiliyya*.
al-Shawqani, I.A. 1348 AH (1929/30 AD), *al-Badr al-Tali' bi Mahasin man Ba'ad al-Qarn al-Sabil*, Cairo.
al-Thughuri, A., 1907, *al-Mashrab al-Naqshbandiyya*, Temir-Khan-Shura.
al-Tsudaqari, I., 1904, *Sullam al-Murid*, Kazan.
al-Yaraghi, M., 1910, *Athar al-Sheikh al-Yaraghi*, Temir-Khan-Shura.
Sahib, A., 1334 (1915), *Bughyat al-Wajid fi Maktubat Hadrat Mawlana Khalid*, Damascus.
Sulayman, I., 1313, *Al-Hadiqa al-Nadiyya fi Adab al-Tariqa al-Naqshbandiyya wa al-Bahja al-Khalidiyya*. Printed on the margin of Usman ibn Snana al-Wali Asfa al-Mawarid min Silsal Ahwal al-Imam Khalid, Cairo.

Russian

1836, *Obozrenie Rossiyskikh Vladeniy za Kavkazom v Statisticheskom, Etnografi-cheskom, Topograficheskom i Finansovom Otnosheniyakh* IV, St. Petersburg.

1859, 'Puteshestvie Shamilya ot Guniba do St. Peterburga', in *Russkiy Mir*, pp. 941-5.

1859, 'Shamil v Publichnoy Biblioteke', in *Russkiy Mir*, pp. 9-75. vol. 56.

1859, 'Shamil' i Chechnya', *Voenny Sbornik* IX: 121-164.

1859, 'Shamil' v Sankt Peterburge', in *Russkiy Khudozhstvenny Listok*, pp. 101-4.

1859, 'Vzyatie Shamilya', in *Odesskiy Vestnik*, pp. 454-5.

1862, 'Chechenskiy Aul', *Kalleydoskop* 42: 2-3.

1866-1906, *AKAK-Akty Sobrannye Kavkazskoy Arkheologicheskoy Komissiyey* XII vols, Tiflis.

1870, 'Nizam Shamilya. Materialy dlya Istorii Dagestana', *Sbornik Svedeniy o Kavkazskikh Gortsakh* III: 1-8.

1871, 'Chechnya. Topograficheskoe i Geograficheskoe Opisanie Postepennoe Zaselenie, Grazhdanskoe Ustroystvo, Soslovnoe Delenie', *Kavkaz* XI:336-71.

1872, 'Ermolov, Dibich i Paskevich, 1826-27', *Russkaya Starina* V, VII, IX: 706-26 (V), 39-69 (VII), 234-80 (IX).

1883, '1844 God na Kavkaze', *Kavkazskiy Sbornik* VII:1-155.

1884, 'Avantyurist XVII Veka. Sheikh Mansur', *Russkaya Mysl'* VII: 294-314.

1889, *Snosheniya Rossii s Kavkazom. Materialy Izvlechennye iz Moscovskogo Glavnogo Arkhiva Ministerstva Inostrannykh Del.* I, Moscow.

1898, *Derbend-nameh*, Tiflis.

1909, 'Shamil' Polveka Nazad v Moskve', *Russkaya Starina* X:576.

1911, 'Gamzat-Bek – Vtoroy Imam Chechni i Dagestana', *Kavkazskiy Sbornik* XXXI:1-30.

1911, 'O Volneniyakh Obnaruzhivshikhsya v Avarii i o Deystviyakh dlya Sokhraneniya Spokoystviya v Dagestane Voobsche protiv Khadzhi Murata', *Kavkazskiy Sbornik* XXXI:1-30.

1911, 'Smert' Khanshi Pakhi-Bike', *Kavkazskiy Sbornik* XXXI:31-7.

1912, 'Materialy k Istorii Pokoreniya Vostochnogo Kavkaza i Bor'by s Myuridizmom', *Kavkazskiy Sbornik* XXXII:1-479.

1912, *Obzor Dagestankoy Oblsti za 1911 God*, St. Petersburg.

1915, 'Dva Imama ili Istreblenie Doma Avarskogo. Istoricheskoe Povestvovanie o Kavkaze', *Russkiy Arkhiv* I, II, III:116-146 (I), 231-258 (II), 358-385 (III).

1940, *Materialy po Istorii Chechni i Dagestana. Dagestan i Chechnya v Period Zavoevaniya Russkim Tsarizmom* III, part I, Mahachqala.

1959, *Dvizhenie Gortsev Severo-Vostochnogo Kavkaza v 20-50kh godakh XIX vv. Sbornik Dokumentov*, Mahachqala.

1967-9, *Istoriya Dagestana*, Moscow.

1977, *Katalog Arabskikh Rukopisey IIYaL im. G. Tsadasy, Dagestanskiy Filial Akademii Nauk SSSR*, Mahachkala.

1859, 'Shamil' i Chechnya', *Voenny Sbornik* IX:121-64.

A.D.G., 1859, 'Pokhod 1845 goda v Dargo', *Voenny Sbornik* V.

Abdullaev, M.A., 1968, *Iz Istorii Filosofskoy i Obshestvenno-Politicheskoy Mysli Narodov Dagestana v XIX v.*, Moscow.

Abdurahman, S. (Sayyid Abd al-Rahman), 1862, *Vyderzhka iz Zapisok Ab-durahmana*, Tiflis.

————, 1869, 'Predislovie k Rukopisnomu Sochineniyu Dzhemaleddina o Tarikate', *Sbornik Svedeniy o Kavkazskikh Gortsakh* II:2-5.

Aglarov, M.A., 1988, *Sel'skaya Obshchina v Nagornom Dagestane v XVII-Nachale XIX vv. Issledovanie Vzaimootnosheniya Form Khozyaystva, Sotsialnykh Struktur i Etnosa*, Moscow.

Akhmadov, S.B., 1991, *Imam Mansur*, Grozny.

Akhmadov, Y.Z., 1975, Iz Istorii Chechensko-Russkikh Otnosheniy. *Voprosy Istorii Dagestana* III.

Akhriev, Ch., 1871, 'Prisyaga u Ingush', *Sbornik Svedeniy o Terskoy Oblasti* I:280-3.

————, 1875, 'Ingushi', *Sbornik Svedeniy o Kavkazskikh Gortsakh* V:1-40.

Al-Qarakhi M., 1929, Asari-Daghestan (Russian translations), Mahachkala.

————, 1946 *Khronika Muhammeda Tahira al-Qarakhi* (The Russian translation of *Bariqat al-Suyuf al-Daghistaniyya fi Ba'd al-Ghazawat al-Shamiliyya*). Translated by A.M. Barabanov, Moscow-Leningrad.

Alferyev, P., 1909, *Kazi Mulla i Myuridizm v Istorii Pokoreniya Dagestana*, Kazan'.

Ali, Hajji, 1873 (reprinted in 1990), 'Skazanie Ochevidtsa O Shamile', in Sbornik Svedeniy o Kavkazskikh Gortsakh (SSKG), vol. VII, pp. 1-75.

Ali, Zamir, 1990 (reprint), 'Istoricheske Ocherki', in Sovetskiy Dagestan, issues 3; 4, pp. 23-31; 32-5.

Aliev, M.H., Sh.M., Akhmedov, and M.-S.K. Umakhanov, 1970, *Iz Istorii Srednevekovogo Dagestana*, Mahachqala.

Alimova, B. M., 1992, *Tabasarantsy*, Mahachqala.

Alqadari, M.H.E., 1929, *Asari-Daghestan* (Russian translation), Mahachqala.

Anoev, A., 1887, 'Vospominaniya o Boevoy Sluzhbe na Kavkaze', *Voenny Sbornik* IV, V, VI:398-412(IV), 188-204(V), 393-414 (VI).

————, 1906, 'Iz Kavkazskikh Vospominaniy', *Istoricheskiy Vestnik* IX:820-51.

Arsakhanov, I., 1959, *Akkinskiy Dialekt v Sisteme Checheno-Ingushskogo Yazyka*, Grozny.

Atarov, M., 1853, 'Rasskaz Mozdokskogo Grazhanina Kuptsa Minaya Shaeva syna Atarova', *kavkaz* 85:62-98.

Avksentev, A.V., 1973, *Islam na Severnom Kavkaze*, Stavropol'.

Avtorkhanov, A., 1931, 'K Voprosam Izucheniya Teypa, Tukumov i Klassovoy Bor'by v Chechenskoy Derevne', *Revolyutsiya i Gorets* I-II:24-30.

Aytberov, T.M., 1977, 'Dagestanskie Dokumenty XV-XVII Vekov', *Pis'mennye Pamyatniki Vostoka* 4-11.

————, 1978-9, 'Pis'mo Seyyida Muhammeda Kazi-Kumukhskogo Dzhamaatam Kazi-Kumukha, Kala-Kureysha i Zerikhgerana, i Osobenno Seyyidu Akhmadu (XV v.)', *Pis'mennye Pamyatniki Vostoka*:4-8.

Bakikhanov, A.K., 1926, *Gulistam-Iram* (Russian translation), Baku.

Barabanov, A.M., 1945, 'Poyasnitel'nye Znachki v Arabskikh Rukopisyakh i Dokumentakakh Severnogo Kavkaza', *Sovetskoe Vostokovedenie* III:183-214.

Baratov, N., 1876, 'Opisanie Nashestviya Skopisch Shamilya na Kakhetiyu v 1854 G', *Kavkazskiy Soborник* I:237-67.

————, 1909-10, 'Okonchatel'noe Pokorenie Vostochnogo Kavkaza – Chechni i Dagestana', *Voenny Sbornik* XI (1909); I, III, IV, IX (1910): 223-40 (XI); 1-16 (I); 1-22(III); 17-32(IV); 51-66 (IX).

Bartold, V.V., 1928, *Istoriya Tyurko-Mongolskikh Narodov*, Tashkent.

————, 1964, 'Ulugbek i Ego Vremya.', in *Sochineniya*, edited by Barthold, pp. 25-177. vol. II, part 2, Moscow (also published as a separate book in Moscow, 1918).

Bazorkin, A., 1875, 'Gorskoe palomnichestvo', *Sbornik Svedeniy o Kavkazskikh Gortsakh* VIII:1-12.

Belyaeva, V.A., and A.M. Leskov, 1990, *Kul'turnye Svyazi Narodov Sredney Azii i Kavkaza v Drevnosti i Srednie Veka*, Moscow.

Berzhe, A.P. 1858, *Kratkiy Obzor Gorskikh Plemen na Kavkaze*, Tiflis.

————, 1859, *Chechnya i Chechentsy*, Tiflis.

Bokarev, E.A., 1961, *Vvedenie v Sravnitel'no-Istoricheskoye Izuchenie Dagestanskikh Yazykov*, Mahachqala.

Borusevich, K.I. 1893, 'Sektantstvo Sredi Ingushey', *Etnograficheskoe Obozrenie* III: 139-44.

Bronevskiy, S., 1823, *Noveyshie Geograficheskie i Istoricheskie Izvestiya o Kavkaze* I, Moscow.

Bushuev, S.K., 1937, 'Gosudarstvennaya Sistema Imamata Shamilya', *Istorik Marksist* VI:77-104.

————, 1939, *Bor'ba Gortsev pa nezavisimost' pod rukovodstvom Shamilya*, Moscow.

————, 1956, 'O Kavkazskom Myuridizme', *Voprosy Istorii Religii i Ateizma* XII:72-9.

Butkov, P.G., 1869, *Materialy Dlya Novoy Istorii kavkaza s 1722 po 1803 God* I-III, St. Petersburg.

————, 1958, 'Svedeniya of Kubinskom i Derbentskom Vladeniyakh', in *Istoriya, Geografiya i Etnografiya Dagestana XVIII-XIX vv. Archivnye materialy*, edited by Kh.O. Khashaev, and M.O. Kosven, pp. 209-13, Moscow.

Butkovskiy, A.M., 1958, 'Vyderzhki iz Opisaniya Kavkazskoy Gubernii i Sosednikh Gorskikh Oblastey, 1812', in *Istoriya, Geografiya i Etnografiya Dagestana XVIII-XIX. Archivnye materialy*, edited by Kh.O. Khashaev, and M.O. Kosven, pp. 239-47, Mahachqala.

Celebi, Evliya, 1979, Kniga Puteshestviy, Moscow.

Chekovich, A.D., 1974, *Samarkandskie Dokumenty XV-XVI vv.,* Moscow.

Chichagova, N.M., 1889, *Shamil' na Kavkaze i v Rossii*, St. Petersburg.

Chikovani, G.A., 1986, 'Iz Istorii Byta Vaynakhov', *Kavkazskiy Etnograficheskiy Sbornik* VI:115-40.

Dakhkil'gov, I.A., 1991, *Mify i Legendy Vaynakhov*, Grozny.

Dalgat, B., 1893, 'Pervobytnaya Religiya Chechentsev', *Terskiy Sbornik* III(2):41-132.

————, 1905, 'Rodovoy Byt u Chechentsev i Inugeshey v Proshlom', *Izvestiya Insgushskogo Nauchno-Issledovatel'skogo Instituta Kraevedeniya* IV(2):135-78.

————, 1929, 'Materialy po Obychnomu Pravu Ingushey', *Izvestiya Ingushskogo Nauchno-Issledovatel'skogo Instituta Kraevedeniya* II(2-3):301-64.

————, 1968, *Iz Istorii Prava Narodov Dagestana*, Mahachqala.

Danel-Bek, 1861, 'Pis'mo Daniel'-Beka o Ego Otnosheniyakh k Shamilyu', *Kavkaz* VIII.

Drozdov, I., 1899, 'Nachalo Deyatel'nosti Shamilya (1834-1836)', *Kavkazskiy Sbornik* XX:250-96.

Dubrovin, N., 1890-1, 'Iz Istorii Voyny i Vladychestva Russkikh na Kavkaze'.

Voenny Sbornik X (1890); III-VI (1891):197-240 (X); 5-39 (III); 77-206 (IV); 5-38 (V); 197-217 (VI).

Dubrovin, N.T., 1871-1888, *Istoriya Voyny i Vladychestva Russkikh na Kavkaze*, St. Petersburg.

Dzhevdet-Pasha, 1888, 'Opisanie Sobytiy v Gruzii i Cherkesii po Otnosheniyu k Ottomanskoy Imperii s 1192 po 1202 God Khidzhry (1775-1784)', *Russkiy Arkhiv*.

Ermolov, A.P., 1865-8, *Zapiski A.P. Ermolova*, Moscow.

Esadze, S., 1907, *Istoricheskaya Zapiska ob Upravlenii Kavkazom* II, Tiflis.

————, 1909, *Shturm Guniba i Plenenie Shamilya*, Tiflis.

Fadeev, A. F., 1955, 'O Vnutrenney Sotsial'noy Baze Myuridicheskogo Dvizheniya na Kavkaze', *Voprosy Istorii* VI:67-77.

————, 1958, 'Protiv Fal'sifikatsii Istorii Narodov Kavkaza', *Vestnik Moskovskogo Universiteta*(3):232-6.

————, 1958(a), *Rossiya i Vostochnyi Krizis 20kh Godov XIX veka*, Moscow.

————, 1958(b), 'Vopros o Sotsial'nom Stroe Kavkazskikh Gortsev XVII-XIX VV v Novykh Rabotakh Sovetskikh Istorikov', *Voprosy Istorii* (5):130-7.

————, 1960, 'Vozniknovenie Myuridistskogo Dvizheniya na Kavkaze i Ego Sotsial'nye Korni. Postanovka Voprosa', *Istoriya SSSR* V:37-58.

————, 1960(a), *Rossiya i Kavkaz Pervoy Treti XIX veka*, Moscow.

Fadeev, R.A. 1890, *Shest'desyat Let Kavkazskoy Voyny*, St. Petersburg.

Farfarovskiy, S., 1913, 'Shamil' i Chechentsy (Neizvestny Eshche Epizod iz Zavoevaniya Kavkaza)', *Russkiy Arkhiv* VI:770-4.

Farfarovskiy, S.V., 1914, 'Bor'ba Chechentsev s Russkimi. Velikiy Sheikh Mansour', *Russkiy Arkhiv* OI(4):455-7.

Fedorov, Y.A., and G.S. Fedorov, 1978, *Ranniye Tyurki na Severnom Kavkaze. Istoriko-Etnograficheskiye Ocherki*, Moscow.

Freytag, 1843, *Kratkoe Opisanie Proiskhozhdeniya Chechentsev i Sostoyaniya Obschestv do Poyavleniya Shamilya*, St. Petersburg.

————, 1883, 'Adaty Chechentsev', in *Adaty Kavkazskikh Gortsev*, edited by F. I. Leontovich, pp. 1-261, Odessa.

Gadzhiev, V.G., 1981, *Obshchestvenny Story Soyuzov Selskikh Obshchestv Dagestana v XVIII-Nachale XIX Vekov*, Mahachqala.

Gadzhieva, S.S., 1960, *Materiyal'naya Kul'tura Kumykov v XIX-XX Vekakh*, Mahachqala.

————, 1985, *Sem'ya i Brak u Narodov v XIX-Nachale XX Vekov*. Nauka, Moscow.

Gamzatov, G.G., 1990, 'Dagestan: Istoriko-Literaturny Protsess', *Voprosy Istorii Teorii i Metodologii* III:211-46.

Gapurov, S., 1906, 'Laki i Ikh Proshloe', *Sbornik dlya Opisaniya Mestnostey i Plemen Kavkaza* XXXVI:1-30.

Gapurov, S.A., 1988, 'Nekotorye Voprosy Istorii Dvizheniya Gortsev pod Predvoditel'stvom Mansura vo Vtoroy Polovine 80kh Godov XVIII Veka',. in *Voprosy Istoriografii Dorevolyutsionnoy Checheno-Ingushetti*, Grozny.

Gavrilov, P.A., 1869, 'Ustroystvo Pozemelnogo Byta Gorskikh Plemen Severnogo Kavkaza', *Sbornik Svedeniy o Kavkazskikh Gortsakh* II:1-78.

Genichutlinskiy, H.G., 1992, *Istoriko-Geograficheskie i Istoricheskie Ocherki*. Translated from Arabic into Russian by T.M. Aytberov, Mahachqala.

Genko, A.N. 1930, 'Iz Kul'turnogo Proshlogo Ingushey', *Zapiski Kollegii Vostokovedov pri Aziatskom Muzee Akademii Nauk SSSR* V:681-761.

————, 1933, 'Arabskaya Karta Chechni Epokhi Shamilya', *Zapiki Instituta Vostokovedeniya Akademii Nauk SSSR* II:31-6.

————, 1941, 'Arabskiy Yazyk i Kavkazovedenie', *Trudy Vtoraoy Sessii Assotsiatsii Arabistov*, Moscow-Leningrad.

Gerber, I., 1958, 'Izvestiya o Nakhodyashchikhsya s Zapadnoy Storony Kaspiyskogo Morya Narodakh i Zemlyakh. Sochineniya i Perevody k Pol'ze i Uveseleniyu Sluzhashchikh. Sostavleno v 1760 Godu', in *Istoriya, Geografiya i Etnografiya Dagestana XVII-XIX Vekakh. Archivnye Materialy*, edited by K.O. Khashaev, and M.O.Kosven, pp. 60-121, Moscow.

Glinoetskiy, N., 1862, 'Poezdka v Dagestan', *Voenny Sbornik* XXIII; XXIV(1, 2); XXIV (3): 119-64 (1); 387-422 (2); 61-90 (3).

Golenishchev-Kutuzov, V. I., 1843, *Opisanie Grazhdanskogo Byta Chechentsev s Ob"yasneniem Adatnogo Ikh Prava i Novogo Upravleniya Vvedennogo Shamilem*, St. Petersburg.

Golovinskiy, N., 1878, 'Zametki o Chechne i Chechentsakh', *Sbornik Svedeniy o Terskoy Oblasti* I:8-24.

Gordelevskiy, 1962, 'Bahauddin Nakshband Bukharskiy', in *Izbrannye Sochineniya*, pp. 369-386. vol. III.

————, 1962(a), 'Sheikh Suleyman. Iz Zhizni Naqshbendi v Turtsii', in *Izbrannye Sochineniya*, pp. 387-90. vol. III.

Grabbe, K.K., 1958, 'Zamechaniya ob Akhtakh i Rutule, 1835 G', in *Istoriya, Geografiya i Etnografia Degestana XVIII-XIX. Archivnye materialy*, edited by K.O. Khashaev, and M.O.Kosven, pp. 335-52, Moscow.

Grabovskiy, N.F., 1870, 'Ekonomicheskiy i Domashniy Byt Zhiteley Gorskogo Uchastka Ingushevskogo Okruga', *Sbornik Svedeniy o Kavkazskikh Gortsakh* III(1): 1-27.

————, 1876, 'Ingushi. Ikh Zhizn' i Obychai', *Sbornik Svedeniy o Kavkazskikh Gortsakh* IX:21-111.

Gren, A., 1892, 'Kratkoe Izlozhenie Osnov Shariata', *Terskiy Sbornik* II(2):3-25.

Grzhegorzhevskiy, I. 1874-6 General-Leytenant Klyuki fon Klyugenau. Ocherk Voennykh deystviy i Sobytiy na Kavkaze v 1818-1850 Godakh', *Russkaya Starina* IX, X (1874); III (1875); I, II, III, VI (1876): 131-52 (IX); 497-515 (X); 545-54 (III); 144-62 (I); 377-87 (II), 645-58 (III); 352-82 (VI).

Gul, K., S. Vlasova, I. Kisin, and A. Terterov, 1959, *Fizicheskaya Geografiya Dagestankoy ASSR*, Mahachqala.

Guldenshtadt, 1834, *Geograficheskoe i Statisticheskoe Opisanie Gruzii Kavkaza*, St. Petersburg.

Gvozdevskiy, N.A., 1958, *Fizicheskaya Geografiya Kavkaza* II, Moscow.

I-skiy, V., 1859, 'Shamil' v Rossii', in *Kavkaz*, VIII, pp. 483-5.

Ippolitov, A., 1869, 'Uchenie Zikr i Ego Posledovateli v Chechne i Argunskom Okruge', *Sbornik Svedeniy o Kavkazskikh Gortsakh* II:1-17.

Ippolitov, A.P., 1868, 'Etnograficheskie Ocherki Argunskogo Okruga', *Sbornik Svedeniy o Kavkazskikh Gortsakh* I:1-52.

Isaev, S.A., 1975, 'Agrarnaya Politika Rossii v Chechne i Dagestane v 50-60 GG. XIX Veka', *Voprosy Istorii Dagestana* II.

Ivanenkov, I., 1910, 'Gornye Chechentsy', *Terskiy Sbornik* VII.

Ivanov, A.I., 1940, 'Sotsial'no-Ekonomicheskoe i Politicheskoe Polozhenie

Dagestana do Zavoevaniya Tsarskoy Rossiey', *Istoricheskiy Zhurnal* (II): 62-72.

K-n, V., 1900, 'Pod Kazbekom', *Kavkazskiy Vestnik* X:88-108.

Kantaria, M.V., 1986, 'Agrikul'turnye Sposoby Polevodstva v Checheno-Ingushetii', *Kavkazskiy Etnograficheskiy Sbornik* IV:41-70.

Kazem-Bek, M.A.K., 1859, 'Myuridizm i Shamil', *Russkoe Slovo* XII(1):182-242.

Khalilov, A., 1988, 'Shamil'v Istorii i Pamyati Narodnoy', *Sovetskiy Dagestan* V:30-35.

Khanykoff, N.V. 1843, *Opisanie Bukharskogo Khanstva*, St. Petersburg.

————, 1847, 'O Myuridakh i Myuridizme', *Sbornik Gazety Kavkaz* I:136-56.

Kharuzin, N.N., 1888, 'Zametki o Yuridicheskom Byte Chechentsev i Ingushey', *Sbornik Etnografii Kavkaza* III:115-42.

Khashaev, K-M.O., 1956, 'K Voprosu o Tukhumakh, Sel'skikh Obschinakh i Vol'nykh Obshestvakh Dagestana v XIX Veke', *Uchenye Zapiski Instituta Istorii Yazyka i Literatury Dagestanskogo Filiala Akademii Nauk SSSR*; 1:42-79.

————, 1957, *Feodal'nye Otnosheniya v Dagestane, XIX – Nachalo XX Veka.* *Arkhivnye Materialy*, Mahachqala.

————, 1961, *Obshchestvenny Story Dagestana v XIX Veke*, Moscow.

Khashaev, K.O., and M.O. Kosven, 1958, *Istoriya, Geografiya i Etnografiya Dagestana XVIII-XIX. Archivnye materialy*, Moscow.

Khashaev, K.O., 1965, *Pamyatniki Obychnogo Prava Dagestna. XVII-XIX VV.*, Moscow.

Khozhaev, D.A.A., and A.A. Musaev, 1992, *Beybulat Taymiev*, Grozny.

Khrisanf, 1958, 'Svedeniya ob Avarskom Khanstve', in *Istoriya, geografiya i etnografiya Dagestana XVIII-XIX. Archivnye materialy*, edited by K.O. Khashaev, and M.O. Kosven, pp. 265-75, Moscow.

Klimov, G.A., 1965, *Kavkazskie Yazyki*, Moscow.

Klinger, 1859, 'Nechto o Chechne', *Kavkaz* (97).

Kobychev, V. P., 1982, *Poselenie I zhilische naradov Severnogo Kavkaza, v XIX-XX vekakh*, Moscow.

Kokurkhaev, K., 1989, *Obschestvenno-Politicheskiy Story i Pravo Chechentsev i Ingushey*, Grozny.

Kolokolov, P.F., 1958, 'Opisanie Tabasarani, 1831', in *Istoriya, Geografiya i Etnografiya Dagestana XVIII-XIX. Arkhivnye Materialy*, edited by K.M. Khashaev, and M.O. Kosven, pp. 313-8, Moscow.

Kolosenko, L., 1887, *V Gostyakh u Emira Bukharskogo*, St. Petersburg.

Kolosov, L.N., 1991, *Slavny Beybulat*, Grozny.

Komarov, A.V., 1868, 'Adaty i Sudoproizvodstvo po Nim', *Sbornik Svedeniy o Kavkazskikh Gortsakh* I:1-88.

————, 1873, 'Narodonaselenie Dagestanskoy Oblasti (s Etnograficheskoy Kartoy)', *Zapiski Kavkazskogo Otdela Rossiyskogo Geograficheskogo Obschestva* VIII.

Korol'kov, M.Y., 1914, 'Sheikh Mansur Anapskiy', *Russkaya Starina*:410-7.

Kosven, M.O., 1955, 1958, 1962 'Materialy po Istorii Etnograficheskogo Izucheniya Kavkaza v Russkoy Nauke', *Kavkazskiy Etnograficheskiy Sbornik* I (1955); II (1958); III (1962).

————, 1963, *Sel'skaya Obshchina i Patronimiya*, Moscow.

Kotsebu, M.A., 1958, 'Svedeniya o Dagestanskikh Vladeniyakh, Sostavlennoe v 1826 Godu', in *Istoriya, Geografiya i Etnografiya Dagestana XVII-XIX VV. Arkhivnye Materialy*, edited by K.O. Khashaev and M.O. Kosven, pp. 252-64, Moscow.

Kovalevskiy, M.K., 1888, 'Rodovoye ustroystvo Dagestana', *Yuridicheskiy Vestnik* XXIX(3).

————, 1890, *Zakon i Obychay na kavkaze* I, II, Moscow.

————, 1958, 'Opisanie Dagestana, Sostavlennoe v 1831 Godu', in *istoriya, Geografiya i Etnografiya Dagestana XVII-XIX VV. Archivnye Materialy*, edited by K.O. Khashaev, and M.O.Kosven, pp. 306-12, Moscow.

Krachkovkiy, I.Y., 1960(c), 'Novye Rukopisi po Istorii Shamilya Muhammeda Takhira al-Karakhi',*Izbrannye Sochineniya* VI:585-608.

Krachkovskiy, I.Y., 1945, 'Arabskie Pis'ma Shamilya v Severnoy Osetii', *Sovetskoe Vostokovedenie* III:36-58.

————, 1960, 'Arabskaya Literatura na Severnom Kavkaze', in *Izbrannye Sochinenie*, pp. 609-22. vol. IV, Moscow.

————, 1960(a), 'Dagestan i Yemen', in *Izbrannye Sochineniya*, pp. 574-84. vol. VI, Moscow-Leningrad.

————, 1960(b), 'Neizdannoe Pis'mo Shamilya', in *Izbrannye Sochineniya*, pp. 551-8. vol. VI, Moscow-Leningrad.

————, 1960(c), 'Arabskie Materialy o Shamile v Sobraniyakh Akademii Nauk SSSR', *Izbrannye Sochineniya* VI:559-70.

————, 1960(d), 'Arabskaya Literatura na Severnom Kavkaze', *Izbrannye Sochineniya* VI:609-24.

Krestovskiy, V.S., 1887, *V Gostyakh u Emira Bukharskogo*, St. Petersburg.

Krovyakov, N., 1990, *Shamil'. Ocherk iz Istorii Bor'by Narodov Kavkaza za Nezavisimost'*, Cherkessk.

Krupnov, E. I., 1938, *Arkheologicheskie Raskopki v Checheno-Ingushetii*, Grozny.

————, 1947, 'Gruzinskiy Khram Thaba-Erdy na Severnom Kavkaze', *Kratkie Soobscheniya Instituta Istorii Material'noy Kul'tury Akademii Nauk SSSR* XV:116-25.

————, 1971, *Srednevekovaya Ingushetiya*, Moscow.

Kundukhov, M.P., 1936-7, 'Memuary', *Kavkaz* (Paris) (1, 2, 3, 4, 5, 8, 10, 11, 12 (1936); 3, 5, 7, 8, 10 (1937)): 12-7 (1); 13-9 (2); 14-8 (3); 19-23 (4); 20-5 (5); 31-4 (8); 24-30 (10); 26-9 (11); 31-6 (12); 26-30 (3); 24-8 (5); 24-7 (7); 24-9 (8); 22-5 (10).

Kusheva, E.N., 1963, *Narody Kavkaza i lkh Svyazi s Rossiey v 16-17 VV.*, Moscow.

Kuzanov, 1861, 'Myuridizm v Dagestane', *Raduga* I; II; III; IV:1-8 (I); 28-37 (II); 50-7 (III); 65-71 (IV).

Kvinitadze, G., 1934, 'Khadzhi Murat', in *Kavkaz*, VII: 8-12, Paris.

L'vov, N., 1870, 'Domashnyaya i Semeynaya Zhizn' Dagestanskikh Gortsev Avarskogo Plemeni', *Sbornik Svedeniy o Kavkazskikh Gortsakh* III: 1-25.

Laudaev, U., 1872, 'Chechenskoe Plemya', *Sbornik Svedeniy o Kavkazskikh Gortsakh* VI: 1-62.

Lavrov, L.I. 1951, 'O Prichinakh Mnogoyazychiya Dagestana', *Sovetskaya Entsiklopediya* II: 202-3.

————, 1966, *Epigraficheskie Pamyatniki Severnogo Kavkaza na Arabskom,*

Persidskom i Turetskikom Yazykakh Teksty, Perevody, Kommentarii I, II, Moscow.

———, 1968, *Epigraficheskie Pamyatniki Severnogo Kavkaza* I, II, Moscow.

———, 1978, *Istoriko-Etnograficheskie Ocherki Kavkaza*, Moscow.

Leontovich, F.I., 1882-3, *Adaty Kavkazskikh Gortsev*, 2 vols, Odessa.

Linevich, I.P., 1877, 'Karta Gorskikh Narodov Podvlastnykh Shamilyu', *Sbornik Svedeniy o Kavkazskikh Gortsakh* VI:1-4.

Litvinov, M., 1884, 'Kavkaz. Voyenno-Geograficheskiy Ocherk', *Voenny Sbornik* (II, III, IV):304-20 (II); 149-64 (III); 328-46 (IV).

Lobanov-Rostovskiy, M.B., 1865, 'Nachalo Myuridizma na Kavkaze', *Russkiy Arkhiv* XI:13-79.

M., 1884, 'Avantyurist XVIII Veka', *Russkaya Mysl'* VII:297-314.

Magomedov, R.M., 1991, *Bor'ba Gortsev za Nezavisimost' pod Rukovodstvom Shamilya*, Mahachqala.

———, 1957, *Obshchestvenno-Ekonomicheskiy i Politicheskiy Stroy Dagestana v XVIII – nachale XIX VV.*, Mahachqala.

Mahmudbekov, 1898, 'Myuridicheskaya Sekta na Kavkaze', *Sbornik Materialov dlya Opisaniya Mestnostey i Plemen Kavkaza* XXIV:14-40.

Makarov, 1859, 'Shamil – Voenny i Grazhdanskiy Pravitel', *Kavkaz* (94):352-81.

Maksimov, E., 1893, Chechentsy. Istoriko-Geograficheskiy i Statstiko-Ekonomicheskiy Ocherk', *Terskiy Sbornik* III(2):3-100.

Malyavkin, G., 1893, 'Karanogaytsy', *Terskiy Sbornik* X:133-73.

Mamakaev, M.A., 1936, *Pravovoy Institut Taypizma*, Grozny.

———, 1973 *Chechenskiy Taip (rod) v Period ego Razhlozheniya*, Grozny.

Marr, N.Y., 1916, 'K Istorii Perdvizheniya Yafeticheskikh Narodov s Yuga na Sever i na Kavkaz', *Izvestiya Akademii Nauk* V:1379-1408.

———, 1920, *Plemennoy Sostav Naseleniya Kavkaza. Klassifikatsiya Narodov Kavkaza (Rabochiy Prospekt)*, Petrograd.

Marshaev, R.G., 1958, *Russko-Dagestanskie Otnosheniya XVII-pervoy chetverti XVIII Vekov. (Dokumenty i Materialy)*, Mahachqala.

Martirosyan, G.K., 1928, 'Nagornaya Checheno-Ingushetiya', *Izvestiya Ingusevskogo Nauchno-Issledovatel'skogo Instituta Kraevedeniya*, I:7-155.

———, 1933, *Istoriya Ingushii*, Ordzhonikidze.

———, 1940, *Materialy po Istorrii Dagestana i Chechni*, Moscow.

Maslov, E.P., A.I. Gozulov and S.N. Ryazantsev (eds), 1957, *Severny Kavkaz*, Moscow.

Miller, F.M., 1888-93, *Materialy po Arkheologii Kavkaza* I, III, Moscow.

Milyutin, D.A., 1850, *Opisanie Voennykh Deystviy v Sevenrom Dagestane v 1839 g.*, St. Petersburg.

N. V., 1888, '1840, 1841 i 1842 Gody na Kavkaze', *Kavkazskiy Sbornik* XII:217-344.

N. Z., 1864, 'Voenno-Akhtynskaya Doroga i Samurskiy Okrug', *Kavkaz* (1).

Nadezhdin, P.P., 1895, *Kavkazskiy Kray. Priroda i Lyudi*, Tula.

Nakhcho, 1886, 'Epizod iz Vremeni Rasprostraneniya Imamstva Shamilya nad Gornoy Chechnyey', in *Severny Kavkaz*, pp. 1-2.

Neverovskiy A.A., 1847, 'Kratkiy Vzglyad na Severny i Sredniy Dagestan v Statisticheskom i Topograficheskom Otnosheniyakh', *Voenny Zhurnal* V:1-64.

———, 1847(a), *O Nachale Bespokoystv v Severnom i Srednem Dagestane*, St. Petersburg (also printed in *Voenny Zhurnal*, 1947, no. 1, pp. 1-36).

————, 1848, *Istreblenie Avarskikh Khanov v 1834 Godu*, St. Petersburg.

Nordeenstam, I.I., 1958, 'Opisanie Atl' Ratlya', in *Istoriya, Geografiya i Et-nografiya Dagestana XVIII-XIX VV. Archivnye Materialy*, edited by K. O. Khashaev and M.O. Kosven, pp. 319-28, Moscow.

Ogranovich, 1866, 'Poezdka v Ichkeriyu', *kavkaz* XXIII:579-643.

Okol'nichiy, N., 1859, 'Perechen' Poslednikh Voennykh Sobytiy v Dagestane (1843 god)', *Voenny Sbornik* I, II, III, IV, VI: 107-72 (I); 337-406 (II); 1-54 (III); 305-48 (IV); 311-80 (VI).

Olshevskiy, M.Y., 1850, *Venno-Strategicheskoe i Topograficheskoe Opisanie Bol'shoy i Maloy Chechni*, Moscow.

Olshevsiky, M.I., 1893-5, 'Zapiski Olshevskogo. Kavkaz s 1841 po 1866 god', *Russkaya Starina* VI-IX (1893), I, II, VI, VII, IX, XI, XII (1894); III, IV, VI, IX, X (1895):573-610 (VI); 89-124 (VII); 287-319 (VIII); 563-89 (IX); 133-81 (I); 131-71 (II); 63-94 (VI); 44-108 (VII); 22-43 (IX); 179-89 (XI); 155-97 (XII); 165-75 (III); 179-89 (IV); 171-84 (VI); 115-7 (IX); 129-66 (X).

Omarov, A., 1868-9, 'Vospominaniya Muttaalima', *Sbornik Svedeniy o Kav-kazskikh Gortsakh* I, II: 13-64 (I); 1-70 (II).

Omarov, A.S., 1964, *Pamyatniki Obychnogo Prava Dagestantsev. XVI-XVII VV.*, Moscow.

————, 1968, *Iz Istorii Prava Narodov Dagestana. Materialy i Dokumenty*, Mahachqala.

Oshaev, K., 1929-30, 'Myuridizm v Chechne', *Revolyutsiya i Gorets* (3-5; 9-10): 39-45; 48-55.

Petrushevskiy, I.P., 1934, *Dzharo-Belokanskie Vol'nye Obshchestva v Pervoy Polovine XIX Stoletiya*, Tiflis.

Pigulevskaya, N.V., 1941, *Siriyskie Istochniki po Istorii SSSR*, Moscow-Leningrad.

Pikman, A.M., 1956, 'O Bor'be Gortsev s Tsarskimi Kolonizatorami', *Voprosy Istorii Religii i Atezma* III: 75-84.

Pogodin, M., 1863, *Aleksey Petrovich Ermolov. Materialy Dlya Ego Biografii*, Moscow.

Pokhvistnev, M.N., 1872, 'Aleksey Petrovich Ermolov. Po Povodu pomesh-chennykh v Russkoy Starine Materialov pod Zaglaviem "Ermolov, Dibich i Paskevich"', *Russkaya Starina* XI: 475-92.

Pokrovskiy, M.N., 1924, *Diplomatiya i Voyny Tsarskoy Rossii na Kavkaze v XIX Stoletii*, Moscow.

Pokrovskiy, N.I., 1923, 'Myuridizm u Vlasti', *Istorik Marksist* II (36):30-75.

————, 1936, 'Obzor Istochnikov po Istorii Imamata',. *Problemy Istoch-nikovedeniya Akademii Nauk* SSSR XVII(2): 187-234.

————, 1991 (reprint), 'Myiridizm u Vlasti', *Niyso* (4): 10-28.

————, 1936, 'Obzor Istochnikov po Istorii Imamata', *Problemy Istoch-nikovedeniya* 2 (XVII): 187-234.

Popke, I, 1880, Terske Kazaki so starodavnikh urenien do nashikh dney, St. Petersburg.

Potto, A., 1887-97, *Kavkazskaya Voyna*, St. Petersburg.

Potto, N.N.B. and V.A., 1901-4, *Utverzhdenie Russkogo Vladychestva na Kav-kaze* I-IV, Tiflis.

Potto, V.A., 1870, 'Khadzhi Murat', *Voenny Sbornik* (XI) (1): 159-82.

250   Bibliography

———, 1912, *Dvsa veka terskogo kazachestva*, vols I, II, Vladikavkaz.
Pozhidaev, V.P., 1926, *Gortsy Severnogo Kavkaza Ingushi, Chechentsy, Khevsury, Kabardintsy*. *Kratkiy Istroiko-Etnograficheskiy Ocherk*, Moscow-Leningrad.
Prezhetslavskiy, P.G., 1877-78, 'Shamil'i Ego Sem'ya v Kaluge. Zapiski Polkovnika P. G. Przhetslavskogo', *Russkaya Starina* X, XI (1877); I, II (1878): 253-76 (X); 471-506 (XI); 41-46 (I), 265-80 (II).
Prozritelev, G.N., 1912, *Sheikh Mansur*, Stavropol'.
———, 1927, 'Posol'stvo Shamilya k Abadzekham', *Dagestanskiy Sbornik* III: 125-9.
Prushanovskiy, 1847, 'Kazi Mulla. Iz Zapisok Kapitana Prushanovskogo', *Sbornik Gazety Kavkaz* II: 22-39.
———, 1902, 'Vypiska iz Putevogo Zhurnala Kapitana Prushanovskogo s 1823 po 1843 Godakh', *Kavkazskiy Sbornik* XXIII: 1-73.
Przhetslavskiy, P.G., 1863, 'Neskol'ko Slov o Voennom i Grazhdanskom Ustroystve Sushchestvovavshem v Chechne i Dagestane vo Vremya Pravleniya Imama Shamilya', *Kavkaz* (62): 155-72.
———, 1867 Dagestan, Ego Nravy i Obychai. *Vestnik Evropy* III: 141-92.
———, 1864, 'Vospominaniya o Blokade Goroda Derbent v 1831 Godu', *Voenny Sbornik* II: 155-78.
Ramazanov, Kh. Kh. and V.G. Khadzhiev (eds), 1959, Divizhenie Gortsev Severo-Vostochnogo Kavkaza v 20-5-kh godakh XIX stoletiya. Sbornik Dokumentov, IIYAL Dag., Mahachqala.
R-v, N., 1859-60, 'Nachalo i Postepennoe Razvitie Myuridizma na Kavkaze', in *Russkiy Khudozhestvenny Listok*, 33, 34, 35, 36: 113-16 (33); 117-20 (34); 123-28 (35); 129-30 (36).
Robakidze, A.I., 1986, 'K Voprosu o Formakh Poseleniya na Severnom Kavkaze', *Kavkazskiy Etnograficheskiy Sbornik* VI: 3-10.
Rozen, R., 1830, 'Opisaniye Chechni i Dagestana', in *Istoriya, Geografiya i Etnografiya Dagestana XVII-XIX vv. Arhivnye Materialy*, edited by Kh.O. Khashaev and M.O. Kosven, , pp. 181-92, Moscow.
Rtishchev, N.R., 1958, 'Svedeniya o Dagestane, 1813', in *Istoriya, Geografiya i Etnografiya Dagestana XVII-XIX vv. Arhivnye Materialy*, edited by K.O. Khashaev and M.O. Kosven, pp. 247-51, Moscow.
Rumyantsev, I.N., 1877, *V Plenu u Shamilya. Zapiski Russkogo*, St. Petersburg.
Runovskiy, A., 1859, 'Moe Znakomstvo s Shamilem', *Voenny Sbornik* XI: 172-224.
———, 1860, 'Kanly v Nemirnom Krae', *Voenny Sbornik* XII(4):269-318.
———, 1860(a), 'Semeystvo Shamilya', *Voenny Sbornik* V:189-218.
———, 1860(b), 'Shamil', *Voenny Sbornik* II:531-82.
———, 1861, 'Shamil' v Kaluge', *Voenny Sbornik* I:133-200.
———, 1862, 'Kodeks Shamilya', *Voenny Sbornik* II:327-86.
———, 1862(a), 'Vzglyad na Soslovnye Prava i Vzaimnye Otnosheniya Sosloviy v Dagestane', *Voenny Sbornik* XXVI(8):373-404.
———, 1862(b), 'Myuridizm i Gazavat v Dagestane po Ob''yasneniyu Shamilya', *Venny Sbornik* XII:646-85.
Runovskiy, A.I., 1904, 'Vypiski iz Dnevnika', *AKAK* XII: 1395-1529.
———, 1904, 'Dnevik Runovskogo', *AKAK* XII: 1395-1529.
Runovskiy, A.N., 1862(b), 'Legendy, Narodnaya Meditsina, Predrassudki i

Verovaniya Dagestanskikh Gortsev, Sostavlennye so Slov Shamilya i Chlenov Ego Semeystva', *Biblioteka Dlya Chteniya* (172, 173).

Rusogly, 1859, 'Nekotorye Zamechaniy po Povodu Sdache Shamilya', in *Moskovskie Vedomosti*, pp. 134-44.

Ryndin, A., 1895, 'Imam Shamil'v Rossii', *Istoricheskiy Vestink* XI:529-42.

Saget, D., 1900, 'O Grazhdanskikh, Dukhovnykh i Voennykh Postanovleniyakh Shamilya', *Voenny Sbornik* III:210-4.

Saidov, M., 1963, 'Dagestanskaya Literatura XVIII-XIX VV. Na Arabskom Yazyke', in *Trudy XXV Mezhdunarodnogo Kongressa Vostokovedov*, Moscow Leningrad.

Savinov, G., 1852, 'Sheikh Mansur', *Panteon* 1:23-9.

Scherbakov, 1888-1904, *General-Fel'dmarshal Knyaz' Paskevich. Ego Zhizn' i Deyatelnost'*, 7 vols, St. Petersburg.

Serebrov, A.G., 1958, 'Istoricheskoe i Etnograficheskoe Opisanie Dagestana. 1796', in *Istoriya, Geografiya, Etnografiya Dagestana XVII-XVIII VV. Arkhivnye Materialy*, edited by K.O. Khashaev and M.O. Kosven, pp. 173-97, Moscow.

Serov, F., 1927, 'Naezdnik Beybulat Taymazov', in *O Tekh Kogo Nazyvali Abrekami*, pp. 125-40, Grozny.

Shabanov, I., 1866, 'Vospominanie o Zimney Ekspeditsii 1859 Goda v Chechne', *Voenny Sbornik* X:297-333.

Shamilyev, A.I., 1963, 'K Voprosu o Khristianstve u Chechentsev i Ingushey', *Checheno-Ingushskiy Nauchno Issledovatel'skiy Institut* III(1):83-96; and 'Puti Proniknoveniya Islama k Chechentsam i Ingusham', *Checheno-Ingushskiy Nauchno Issledovatel'skiy Institut.* III(1):97-107.

Shamilova, M.S. and S-T.S Shamilov, 1984, *Myuridizm Pered Sudom Vremeni*, Grozny.

Sharafutdinova, P.S., 1975, 'Eshche Odin Nizam Shamilya', *Pis'mennye Panyatniki Vostoka*:168-9.

Sharafutdinova, R.S., 1970, 'Arabskie Pis'ma Shamilya iz Arkhiva Dorna', *Pismennye Pamyatniki Vostika*: 485-502.

———, 1974, 'Arabskiy Dokument iz Arkhiva Akademika Dorna', *Pismennye Pamyatniki Vostoka*: 162-9.

———, 1977, 'Pis'mo Naiba Tashev-Hadzhi k Shamilyu', *Pis'mennye Panyatniki Vostoka*: 86-9.

Shcherbachev, A.P., 1958, 'Opisanie Mekhtulinkogo, Kaysumskogo Khanstva, i Khanstva Avarskogo, Okolo 1830', in *Istoriya, Geografiya, Etnografiya Dagestana XVII-XVIII VV. Arkhivnye Materialy*, edited by K.O. Khashaev and M.O. Kosven, pp. 293-9, Moscow.

Sheripov, Z., 1927, 'Sheikh Mansur', in *O Tekh Kogo Nazyvayut Abrekami*, pp. 151-9, Grozny.

Shigabuddinov, D.M., 1992, *Akhulgo*, Mahachqala.

Shikhsaidov, A.R., 1957, 'O Pronikonvenii Khristianstva i Islama v Dagestan', *Uchenye Zapiski IIYaL* III:54-76.

———, 1958, 'Rasprostranenie Islama v Yuzhnom Dagestane. Uchenye Zapiski', *IIYaL* VI: 127-1961.

——— 1969 *Islam v Srednevekovom Dagestane*, Mahachqala.

———, 1978, 'Dagestanskaya Istoricheskaya Khronika "Tarikh Daghestan"

Muhammada Rafi (K voprosu ob Izuchenii)', *Pis'mennye Pamyatniki Vostoka*:90-113.

———, 1978, 'Nadpisi iz Khnov', *Pis'mennye Pamyatniki Vostoka*:262-76.

———, 1979, 'Mul'k v Daghestane X-XV vv', Moscow.

———, 1984, *Epigraficheskiye Pamyatniki Dagestana X-XVII vv. kak istoricheskiy Istochnik*, Nauka, Moscow.

Shilling, E., 1931, *Ingushi i Chechentsy*, Moscow-Leningard.

———, 1935, 'Kul't Tushouli u Ingushey', *Izvestiya Ingushevskogo Nauchno-Issledovatel'skogo Instituta Kraevedeniya* IV(2):98-117.

———, 1949, *Kubachintsy i lkh Kul'tura*, Moscow-Leningrad.

Shnitkov, F.A., 1958, 'Opisaniye Kubinskoy Provintsii', in *Istoriya, Geografiya Etnografiya Dagestana XVII-XIX VV. Arkhivnye Materialy*, edited by K.O. Khashaev and M.O. Kosven, pp. 329-34, Moscow.

Shubin, P., 1892, 'Ocherki Bukhary', *Istoricheskiy Vestnik* (10): 110-8.

Shulgin, S.N., 1903, 'Rasskaz Ochevidtsa o Shamile i Ego Sovremennikakh', *Sbornik Materialov dlya Opisaniya Mestnostey i Plemen Kavkaza* XXXII(1):10-24.

———, 1909, 'Predanie o Shamilevskom Naibe Khadzhi Murate', *Sbornik Materialov dlya Opisaniya Mestnostey i Plemen Kavkaza* XL(I):57-70.

Simonovich, F.F., 1958, 'Opisanie Yuzhnogo Dagestana, 1896', in *Istoriya, Geografiya, Etnografiya Dagestana XVII-XVIII. Arkhivnye Materialy*, edited by K.O. Khashaev and M.O. Kosven, pp. 138-57, Moscow.

———, 1958, 'Opisaniye Tabasarana, in *Istoriya, Etnografiya, Geografiya Dagestana XVII-XIX VV. Arkhivnye Materialy*, edited by K. Khashaev, pp. 197-200, Moscow.

Sitnyakovskiy, N., 1900, 'Bukharskie Svyatyni. Mazar Emira Bukharskogo s Planom', *Protokoly Zasedaniy i Soobshcheniy Chlenov Turkestanskogo Kruzhka Lyubiteley Arkheologii* V:49-56.

Skitskiy, B.V., 1932, 'Sotsialny Kharakter Dvizheniya Imam Mansura', *Izvestiya 2-go Severokavkazskogo Pedinstituta im. T. Gadieva* IX:97-119.

Smirnov, N.A., 1950, 'Turetskaya Agentura pod Flagom Islama (Vosstanie Sheikha Mansura na Severnom Kavkaze)', *Voprosy Istorii Religii i Ateizma* 1:11-63.

———, 1954, 'O Reaktsionnoy Ideologii Myuridizma', *Voprosy Istorii Religii i Ateizma* IV:45-8.

———, 1958, *Politika Rossi na Kavkaze, v XVI-XIX vekakh*, Moscow.

———, 1959, 'Kharakternye Cherty Ideologii Kavkazskogo Myuridizma', *Voprosi Istorii Religii i Ateizma* VII:175-86.

———, 1963, *Myuridizm na Kavkaze*, Moscow.

Soltan, V., 1856, 'Obzor Sobytiy v Dagestane v 1855 i 1856 GG', *Kavkazskiy Sbornik* XII:479-530.

———, 1884, 'Zanyatie Salatavii v 1857 Godu', *Kavkazskiy Sbornik* VIII:335-97.

———, 1885, 'Ocherk Voennykh Deystviy v Dagestane v 1852 i 1853 Godakh', *Kavkazskiy Sbornik* IX:475-521.

———, 1887, 'Ocherk Voennykh Deystviy v Dagestane v 1854 Godu', *Kavkazskiy Sbornik* XI:525-71.

———, 1888, 'Obzor Sobytiy v Dagestane v 1855 i 1856 Godakh', *Kavkazskiy Sbornik* XII:479-532.

———, 1892, 'Na Gunibe v 1859 i 1871 Godakh', *Russkaya Starina* V: 390-410.

Suleyman-Effendi, 1847, 'Opisanie Postupkov Shamilya Protivnykh Musul'manskomu Shariatu Kotorye Byli Zamecheny Suleiman Efendiem vo Vremya Ego Nakhozhdeniya Pri Nem', *Sbornik Gazety Kavkaz* I:30-5.

T., 1869, 'Vospominaniya o Kavkaze i Gruzii', *Russkiy Vestnik* (I, II, III, IV): 1-36 (I); 401-43 (II); 102-55 (III); 658-707 (IV).

Tagirova, N.A., 1988, 'Iz Istorii Araboyazychnoy Rukopisnoy Traditsii v Dagestane', *Izuchenie Istorii i Kultury Dagestana* II:124-46.

Takaev, I., 1936, 'Missionerstvo v Sisteme Kolonial'noy Politiki Tsarizma na Severnom Kavkaze', *Revolyutsionny Vostok* II-III:48-76.

Tarkhanov, 1868, 'O Mukhadzhirakh v Zandakovskom Naibstve (Nagornogo Okruga)', *Terskie Vedomosti* (15):78-86.

Tereshchenko, A., 1856, 'Lzheprorok Mansur', in *Syn Otechestva*, pp. 54-57, 73-75, St. Petersburg.

Tikhonov, L.I., 1958, 'Opisaniye Severnogo Dagestana 1796', in *Istoriya, Geografiya, Etnografiya Dagestana, Arkhivnye Materialy*, edited by K.O. Khashaev and M.O. Kosven, pp. 135-8, Moscow.

Tolstoy, L.N., 1912, 'Khadzhi Murat', in *Posmertnye Khudozhestvennye Proizvedeniya*, pp. 3-125. vol. III, Moscow.

Tomay, A., 1935, 'Materialy k Voprosu o Feodalizme i Istorii Dagestana', *Revolyutsionny Vostok* V:116-37.

Tormasov, A.P., 1958, 'Vyderzhki iz Vedomostey Soderzhashchikh Svedeniya o Chislennosti Naseleniya Dagestana, 1811', in *Istoriya, Geografiya, Etnografiya Dagestana XVII-XIX VV. Arkhivnye Materialy*, edited by K.O. Khashaev and M.O. Kosven, pp. 237-8, Moscow.

Tsadasa, G., 1958, 'Adaty o Brake i Sem'e Avartsev v XIX-Nachale XX Vekov', in *Pamyatniki Obychnogo Prava Narodov Dagestana. XVII-XIX VV.*, edited by K.O. Khashaev and M. O., Kosven, Mahachqala.

Tsagareshvili, Sh.-V (ed.), 1953, *Shamil Stavlennik Sultanskoy Turtsii i Angliys kikh Kolonizatorov. Sbornik Dokumental'nykh Materialov*, Tbilisi.

Umarov, S.T., 1985, *Evolyutsiya Osnovnykh Techeniy Islama v Checheno-Ingushetii*, Grozny.

Uslar, P.K., 1888, *Chechenskiy Yazyk*, St. Petersburg.

Vartapetov, A.S., 1932, 'Problemy Rodovogo Stroya Ingushey i Chechentsev', *Sovetskaya Etnografiya*(4).

Verderevskiy, E.A., 1856, *Plen u Shamilya*, St. Peterburg.

Vertepov, G.A. 1892, 'sud'ba Religiozno-Politicheskikh Ucheniy v Chechne', *Terskie Vedomosti* (52-54).

———, 1914 Sektanstvo v Chechne. *Zapiski Terskogo Obschestva Lyubiteley Kazach'ey Stariny* II:75-80.

———, 1892, 'Ingushi', *Terskiy Sbornik* III:71-139.

———, and E.D. Maksimov, 1892-4, *Tuzemtsy Severnogo Kavkaza*, Vladikavkaz.

———, 1903, 'V Gorakh Kavkaza', *Terskiy Sbornik* V-VI:94-148.

Veydenbaum, E.G., 1888, *Puteshestvie po Severnomu Kavkazu*, Tiflis.

Vinogradov, A., 1934, *Sheikh Mansur*, Moscow.

Volkonskiy N.A. 1879, 'Okonchatel'noe Pokorenie Kavkaza', *Kavkazskiy Sbornik* IV:69-436.

———, 1879(a), '1858 God v Chechne', *Kavkazskiy Sbornik* III: 377-591.

———, 1880, 'Pogrom Chechni v 1852 Godu', *Kavkazskiy Sbornik* V:1-234.

———, 1882, 'Sem' Let v Plenu na Kavkaze (1849-56). Ocherk Politicheskogo i Domashnego Byta Kavkazskiykh Gortsev', *Voenny Vestnik* V:217-83.

————, F.A. Klieman., and P. Klubitskiy, 1886-1899, 'Voyna na Vostochnom Kavkaze s 1824 po 1834 God v Svyazi s Myuridizmom', *Kavkazskiy Sbornik* X (1886), XI (1887), XII (1888), XIII (1889), XIV (1890), XV (1894), XVI (1895), XVII (1896), XVIII (1897), XX (1899): 1-224 (X); 1-185 (XI); 1-216 (XII); 152-335 (XIII); 1-211 (XIV); 506-76 (XV); 405-80 (XVI); 323-409 (XVII); 288-351 (XVIII); 97-141 (XX).

————, 1885, 'Trekhletie na Lezginskoy Kordonnoy Linii (1847-9)', *Kavkazskiy Sbornik* IX:157-366 and 22 pages of Appendix with separate pagination.

Voronov, N.I., 1868, 1870, 'Iz Puteshestviya po Dagestanu', *Sbornik Svedeny o Kavkazskikh Gortsakh* I, III:1-36; 1-40.

Yakovlev, N.F., 1927, *Voprosy Izucheniya Ingushey i Chechentsev*. Grozny. (Reprint in 1992 in Grozny),

Yandarov, A.D., 1975, *Sufizm i Ideologiya Natsional'no-Osvoboditel'nogo Dvizheniya*, Alma-Ata.

Yaqubi, 1927, 'Istoriya. Tekst i Perevod', in *Materialy po Istorii Azerbaydzhana*. Translated by P. K. Juze. vol. III, IV, Baku.

Yaroshenko, S.P. (ed.), 1898, *Materialy po Obychnomu Pravu Kavkazskikh Gortsev*. XXXV, Novorosiysk.

Yashnikov, T.N., 1958, 'Granitsy Vladeniya Elisuyskogo Sultanatsva, 1831', in *Istoriya, Geografiya, Etnografiya Dagestana XVII-XIX VV. Arkhivnye Materialy*, edited by K. O. Khashaev and M.O. Kosven, pp. 304-5, Moscow.

Yudin, P., 1914, 'Lzheprorok Ushurma, Shikh Mansur Anapskiy', *Russkaya Starina* III (10):217-28.

Yurov, A., 1882, '1843 God na Kavkaze', *Kavkazskiy Sbornik* VI:1-219 (and 40 pages of Appendix with separate pagination).

————, 1883, '1844 God na Kavkaze', *Kavkazskiy Sbornik* VII:157-382.

————, 1884-5, 'Tri Goda na Kavkaze. 1837-9', *Kavkazskiy Sbornik* VIII; IX:1-120; 1-155.

Yurov, A., and N.V. Yurov, 1886-90, '1840, 1841 i 1842 Gody na Kavkaze', *Kavkazskiy Sbornik* X-XIV:225-404 (X); 187-301 (XI); 217-344 (XII); 335-424 (XIII); 303-444 (IV).

Yushkov, S.V., 1939, 'K Voprosu of Osobennostyakh Feodalizma v Dagestane', *Uchenye Zapiski Sverdlovskogo Gosudarstvennogo Pedagogicheskogo Instituta* I:66-70.

Yuzefovich, 1869, *Dogovory Tossii s Vostokom. Politicheske i Torgovye*, St. Petersburg.

Zakharin, I., 1898, 'Poezdka k Shamilyu v Kalugu v 1860 g', *Vestnik Evropy* VIII:601-40.

Zakharov, A.A., 1935, 'Ingushskaya Boginya Tusholi i Dea Syrio Lukman', *Izvestiya Ingushskogo Nauchno-Issledovatel'skogo Instituta Kraevedeniya* IV(2):118-28.

Zaks, A.B., 1941, 'Severo-Kavkazskaya Istorichesko-Bytovaya Ekspeditsiya Gosudarstvennogo Istoricheskogo Muzeya 1936-7', *Trudy Gosudarstvennogo Istoricheskogo Muzeya*: 151-95.

————, 1976, *Tashev Khadzhi. Lyudi, Sobytiya, Fakty*, Moscow.

————, 1992, *Tashev-Khadzhi – Spodvizhnik Shamilya*, Grozny.

Zasedateleva, L.B., 1974, *Terskie Kazaki (Seredina XVI-Nachalo XX vv.) Istoriko-Etnograficheskie Ocherki*, Moscow.

Zeydlits, N.K., 1894, 'Poezdka v Galgaevskoe i Dzherakhovskoe Uschelya',

Izvestiya Kavkazskogo Otdela Russkogo Geograficheskogo Obschestva
II:161-3.

Zisserman, A. I., 1851, 'Khadzhi Murad. Pisma o Nem Knyazya M. S. Vorontsova
i Rasskazy Kavkaztsev. 1851-2 gg', *Russkaya Starina* III:655-80.

Zubov, P., 1834-5, *Kartina Kavkazskogo Kraya, Prinadlezhaschego Rossii i
Sopredel'nykh Onomu Zemel' v Istoricheskom, Strategicheskom, Etnograficheskom i Topograficheskom Otnosheniyakh*. IV St. Petersburg.

Western

A.M., 1832, 'Guerre des Russes dans le Daghestan', *Nouveau Journal Asiatique*
(9): 466-72.

Abu Manneh, B., 1982/84, 'The Naqshbandiyya-Mujaddidiyya in the Ottoman
Lands in the Early 19th Century', *Die Welt Des Islam* 22:1-36.

———, 1985, 'Khalwa and Rabita in the Khalidi Suborder', in *Naqshbandis.
Historical Developments and Present Situation of a Muslim Mystical Order*,
Istanbul, 1985, pp. 289-302.

Adams, Charles J. 1985, 'The Naqshbandis of India and the Pakistan Movement',
in *Naqshbandis Historical Developments and Present Situation of a Muslim
Mystical Order*, Istanbul 1985, pp. 221-30.

Adighe, R., 1947, 'Literature on Daghestan and Its People', *Caucasian Review*
(4): 101-8.

Ahmad, Aziz, 1964, *Studies in Islamic Culture in the Indian Environment*,
Oxford.

———, 1967, *Islamic Modernism in India and Pakistan*, London.

———, 1969, *An Intellectual History of Islam in India*, Edinburgh.

Algar, Hamid, 1975, Bibliographic Notes on the Naqshbandi Tariqat', in A.
Hourani (ed.) *Essays on Islamic Philosophy and Science*, pp. 254-9. New
York.

———, 1976, 'The Naqshbandi Order: A Preliminary Survey of Its History
and Significance', *Studia Islamica* 44:123-52.

———, 1985, 'A Brief History of the Naqshbandi Order', in *Naqshbandis.
Historical Developments and Present Situation of a Muslim Mystical Order*,
Istanbul, 1985, pp. 3-44.

———, 1985(a) *Political Aspects of Naqshbandi History*, Istanbul, pp. 123-52.

Allen, W.E.D., 1953, *Caucasian Battlefields: A History of Wars on the Turco-
Caucasian Border* 1828-1923, Cambridge.

Ansari, Muhammad A., 1986, *Sufism and Shari'a: A Study of Sheikh Ahmad
Sirhindi's Efforts to Reform Sufism*, London.

Arberry, Arthur J., 1943, *An Introduction to the History of Sufism*, London.

———, 1950 (2nd edn 1979), *Sufism: An Account of the Mystics of Islam*.
London.

Baddeley, John F., 1908 *The Russian Conquest of the Caucasus*, London.

———, 1940, *The Rugged Flanks of the Caucasus*, Oxford.

Baldick, Julian, 1989, *Mystical Islam: An Introduction to Sufism*, London.

Bartold, V.V., 1962, *Four Studies on the History of Central Asia*.

Bennett, J.G., 1982, *Sufi Spiritual Techniques*, Masham.

Bennigsen, A., 1964, 'Un Movement populaire au Caucase XVIII Siecle', *Cahiers
du Monde Russe et Sovietique* II(5):159-204.

————, 1988 'The Qadiriyya Tariqa in the North-Eastern Caucasus', *Islamic Culture* (2-3):63-78.

Berg, L.S., 1950, *Natural Regions of the USSR*, New York.

Blanch, L., 1960, *The Sabres of Paradise*, London.

Bodenshtadt, Friedrich von, 1855, *Volker des Kaukasus und ihre Freiheits Ramphe gegen die Russen*, (Narody Kavkaza i ikh borba za Svobody protiv Russkikh. Russian translation in manuscript), Berlin.

Boldyrev, A.N., 1985, 'Eshche Raz k Voprosu o Khodzhe Akhrare', in *Dukhovenstvo i Politicheskaya Zhizn'na Blizhnem i Srednem Vostoke v Period Feodalizma*. Moscow.

Bregel, Yuri, 1991, 'Turko-Mongol Influence in Central Asia', in *Turko-Persia in Historical Perspective*. R. L. Canfield (ed.) pp. 53-78. Cambridge.

Brown, J.P., 1968, *The Darvishes or Oriental Spiritualism*, London.

Broxup, Marie Bennigsen, 'Caucasian Miuridizm in Soviet Historiography' in *Jemaleddin of kazi-kumukh. Adab ul Marzia. Naqshbandi Treaty*. Society for Central Studies, Series N10, Caucasus Series N1, pp. 5-14.

———— (ed.) *The North Caucasus Barrier: The Russian Advance Towards the Muslim World*. London, 1992.

Bruinessen, Martin van, 1985, 'The Naqshbandi Order in 17th-Century Kurdistan', In *Naqshbandis. Historical Developments and Present Situation of a Muslim Mystical Order*, Istanbul.

————, 1992, *Agha Shaikh and State. The Social and Political Structures of Kurdistan*, London and New Jersey.

Burkhart, T., 1990, *An Introduction to Sufism*. Matheson, transl, London.

Canfield, Robert L., 1991, 'Introduction: The Turko-Persian Tradition', in R. L. Canfield (ed.), *Turko-Persia in Historical Perspective*, pp. 1-34. Cambridge.

————, 1991(a), 'Theological 'Extremism' and Social Movements in Turko-Persia', in R. L. Canfield (ed.) *Turko-Persia in Historical Perspective*, pp. 132-60. Cambridge.

Cannynghame, A.T., 1872, *Travels in the Eastern Caucasus on the Caspian and Black Seas and on the Frontiers of Persia and Turkey During the Summer 1871*, London.

Cehajic, D., 1986, *Derviski Redovi u Jugoslovenskim Zemljama sa Posebnim Osvrtom na Bosnu i Hercegovinu*, Sarajevo.

Chittick, W.C., 1989, *The Sufi Path of Knowledge. Ibn al-Arabi's Metaphysics of Imagination*, Albany, NY.

Chodkevicz, M., 1995, *Spiritual Writings of Amir Abd al-Kader*, New York.

Damrel, David, 1985, 'The Spread of Naqshbandi Political Thought in the Islamic World', in *Naqshbandis. Historical Developments and Present Situation of a Muslim Mystical Order*, Istanbul 1985, pp. 269-88.

Danzier, R., 1977, *Abd al-Qadir and the Algerians. Resistance to the French and Internal Consolidation*, New York.

Dewasse, D.A., 1993, *An Uwaysi Sufi in Timurid Mawarannahr. Notes on Hagiography and the Taxonomy of Sanctity in Religious History of Central Asia*, Bloomington.

Digby, Simon, 1985, 'The Naqshbandis in the Deccan in the late Seventeenth Century and Early Eighteenth Century', in *Naqshbandis. Historical Developments and Present Situation of a Muslim Mystical Order*, Istanbul, 1985, pp. 167-207.

———, 1986, 'The Sufi Sheikh as a Source of Authority in Medieval India', *Purusartha* 9:60-2.

Donia, R., 1981, *Islam under the Double Eagle*, New York.

Faruqi, Burhan Ahmad, 1977, *The Mujaddid's Conception on Tawhid*, Delhi.

Fishel, A., 1970, *The Russian Annexation of Crimea*, Cambridge.

Friedman, Yohanan, 1971, *Shaykh Ahmad Sirhindi: An Outline of His Thought and a Study of His Image in the Eyes of Posterity*, Montreal.

——— 1975, 'Medieval Muslim Views of Indian Religions', *JAOS* 95(2):214-21.

——— 1985, 'The Naqshbandis and Aurangzeb: A Reconsideration' in *Naqshbandis. Historical Developments and Present Situation of a Muslim Mystical Order*, Istanbul, 1985, pp. 209-20.

Gammer, M., 1992, 'Russian Strategies in the Conquest of Chechnia and Daghestan 1825-1859', in M. Broxup-Bennigsen, (ed.) *The North Caucasus Barrier. The Russian Advances towards the Muslim World.* pp. 45-62, London.

———, 1994,*Muslim Resistance to the Tsar. Shamil and the Conquest of Chechnia and Daghestan.* London.

Geiger, B., A.H., Kuipers, T., Halasi-Kun, and K.H. Menges, 1959, *Peoples and Languages of the Caucasus: A Synopsis*, Columbia.

Gellner, Ernest, 1969, *Saints of the Atlas*, Chicago.

———, 1985, *Islamic Dilemmas: Reformers, Nationalists and Industrialization.* Berlin.

Gilsenan, Michael, 1973, *Saint and Sufi in Modern Egypt: An Essay in the Sociology of Religion*, Oxford.

Gordelevskiy, 1910, *Bahauddin Naqshband Bukharskiy*, Bukhara.

Gross, Jo-Ann, 1985, 'A Multiple Role and Preconceptions of a Sufi Shaikh: Symbolic Statements of Political and Religious Authority', Istanbul, 1985, pp. 109-121.

Haar, Jonathan G.J. ter, 'The Importance of the Spiritual Guide in the Naqshbandi Order', in L. Lewisohn (ed.), *The Legacy of Mediaeval Persian Sufism.* pp. 311-21, London-New York.

Habib, M., 1962, 'Some Notes on the Naqshbandi Order', *Muslim World*: 49-59.

———, 1969, 'Some Notes on the Naqshbandi Order', *Muslim World*(59):40-9.

Hakim, Halkawt, 1985, 'Mawlana Khalid et les Pouvoirs' in *Naqshbandis. Historical Developments and Present Situation of a Muslim Mystical Order*, Gaborieau, M., Popovic A., Zarcone Th. (eds), Istanbul, 1985, pp. 361-71.

Hamid, Algar, 1971, 'Some Notes on the Naqshbandi Tariqat in Bosnia', *Die Welt des Islam* 13:168-203.

Hauner, Milan 1991, 'Russia's Geopolitical and Ideological Dilemmas in Central Aisa', in R.L. Canfield (ed.), *Turko-Persia in Historical Perspective.* pp. 189-216, Cambridge.

Henze, P., 1983, 'Fire and Sword in the Caucasus', *Central Asian Review* II(1):243-73.

———, 1992, 'Circassian Resistance to Russia', in M. Broxup Bennigsen (ed.), *The North Caucasus Barrier. The Russian Advance towards the Muslim World.* pp. 62-112. London.

Heper, M., 1984, *Islam and Politics in the Modern Middle East*, London.

Hourani, Albert, 1981, 'Sufism and Modern Islam: Maulana Khalid and the Naqshbandi Order', in H. Albert (ed.), *The Emergence of the Modern Middle East.* pp. 75-90, Oxford.

Huart, C.I., 1922, 'Les Mosafirides de L'Adherbaidjan', in R.A Nicholson (ed.), *A Volume of Oriental Studies*, pp. 228-54, Cambridge.

Jong, S.F. de, 1978, *Turuq and Turuq Linked Institutions in 19th Century Egypt*, London and Amsterdam.

Keddie, N., 1972, *Scholars, Saints and Sufis: Muslim Religious Institutions in the Middle East since 1500*, Berkeley, CA.

Kedourie, Elie, 1980, *Islam in the Modern World*, London.

Klans, Ferdinand, 1988, *Islam: State and Society*, London.

Lapidus, I., 1991, *A History of Islamic Societies*, Cambridge.

Lemercier-Quelquejay, Ch., 1992, 'Cooptation of the Elites of Kabarda and Daghestan in the Sixteenth Century', in M. Broxup-Bennigsen (ed.), *The North Caucasus Barrier. The Russian Advance towards the Muslim World*, pp. 18-45, London.

Luzbetak, L. J., 1951, *Marriage and the Family in Caucasia. A Contribution to the Study of North Caucasian Ethnology and Customary Law*, Vienna-Modling.

Mardin, S., 1989, *Religion and Social Change in Modern Turkey*, New York.

Massignon, Louis, 1989, *Testimonies and Reflections*, Notre Dame, IN.

Minorskiy, V., 1953, *History of Shirvan and Derbend*.

Mole, M. 1963, 'Traites Mineures de Najm al-Din Kubra' *Annals Islamologiques* IV:15-22.

Monteith, W., 1856, *Karz and Erzerum. With the Campaigns of Prince Paskiewitch in 1828-1829 and an Account of the Conquests of Russia beyond the Caucasus from the Time of Peter the Great to the Treaty of Turcuman Chie and Adrianopole*, London.

Nasr, S. H., 1991, *Islamic Spirituality*, London.

Nickolson, R.A., 1921, *Studies in Islamic Mysticism*, Cambridge.

Nickolson, Reynold A., 1963, *The Mystics of Islam*. London.

Nizami, Khalid A., 1965 'Naqshbandi Influence on the Mughal Rulers and Politics', *Islamic Culture* 39(1):41-52.

———, 1980, 'Shah Waliullah of Delhi: His Thought and Contribution', *Islamic Culture* 54: 141-52.

O'Fahey, R.S., 1990, *Enigmatic Saint*, Evanston.

Piscatori, J.P., 1983, *Islam in the Political Process*, New York.

Popovic, Alexandre, 1986, *Les Orders Mystique dans l'Islam*, Paris.

Qureishi, I.H., 1962, *The Muslim Community of the Indo-Pakistan Subcontinent (610-1947)*, The Hague.

Rizvi, Athar Abbas S., 1975, *A History of Sufism in India*, New Delhi.

———, 1965, *Muslim Revivalist Movements in Northern India in the 16th and 17th Centuries*, Agra.

———, 1985, 'Sixteenth Century Naqshbandiyya leadership in India', in *Naqshbandis. Historical Developments and Present Situation of a Muslim Mystical Order*, Istanbul, pp. 153-66.

Robinson, Francis, 1991, 'Perso-Islamic Culture in India from the Seventeenth to the Early Twentieth Century', in R. L. Canfield (ed.), *Turko-Persia in Historical Perspective*. pp. 104-31, Cambridge.

Sayed, Sabzavari S.M. Ibn, 1989, *Islamic Political and Judicial Thought in the 18th Century*, Tehran.

Schimmel, A., 1973, 'The Sufi Ideas of Shaykh Ahmad Sirhindi', *Die Welt Des Islams* 14:199-203.

————, 1976, *Pain and Grace*, Leiden.

————, 1975, *Mystical Dimensions of Islam*, North Carolina.

Scholem, G.G., 1955, *Major Trends in Jewish Mysticism*, London.

Shushud, H., 1983, *The Masters of Wisdom*, Oxford.

Smith, Clancy, 1994, *Rebel and Saint: Muslim Notables, Populist Protest, Conlonial Encounters (Algeria and Tunisia 1800-1904)*, Berkeley, CA.

Tor, Andrea, 1960, *Islamische Mystiker*, Stuttgart.

Trimmingham, J. Spencer, 1971, *The Sufi Orders of Islam*, Oxford.

Troll, D., 1928, *Sayyid Ahmad Khan*, New Delhi.

Vambery, Armenius, 1971 (2nd edn, Ist edn 1868), *Sketches of Central Asia: My Travels, Adventures and Ethnography of Central Asia*, Taipen.

Vikør, Knut S., 1995, *Sufi and Scholar on the Desert Edge: Muhammad b. 'Ali al-Sanusi and his Brotherhood*, London.

Watt, W. M., 1988, *Islamic Fundamentalism and Modernity*, Edinburgh.

Zelkina, A., 1993, 'Islam and Politics in the Nothern Caucasus', *Religion, State and Society in ex-Communist Countries*, vol. 21, no.1.

————, 1996, 'Islam and Society in Chechnya. Late Eighteenth-First Half of Nineteenth Century', Journal of Islamic Studies, vol. 7, no.2.

INDEX

Abbas Mirza, 132
Abbasid caliphate, 27
Abd al-Khaliq al-Ghujduwani, 78-80, 83, 94
Abd al-Qadir al-Germenchuki, 121-2
Abdallah al-Ashilty, 155
Abu Bakr al-Derbendi, 47
Abu Bakr al-Siddiq, 77
Abu al-Hasan al-Kharaqani, 78
Abu Jahl, 49-50
Abu Maslama, 26-7
Abu Muslim, 25
Abu Muslim Khan, 233
Abu Yazid al-Bistami, 77-8
'adat: 5, 17-18, 32, 40, 43, 45-6, 212; and
    the shari'a, 40-6, 217-18, 221, 235-6;
    and oaths, 43; and blood-revenge, 44,
    218; and matters of inheritance, 45; and
    intermarriage, 45-6; and theft, 221
Ahkberdy Muhammad, 169, 179, 192, 199,
    210
Ahmad Khan (of the Avar khanate) 146,
    194, 197
Akhulgoh: construction of, 185-6, 189; Rus-
    sian assault on, 186-7, 189, 193, 202
Akusha, 15, 30, 41-2, 54, 70-1, 140, 164,
    172, 213, 216
Aldy, 58-9, 63, 65
Alexander I, Tsar, 69, 133
Ali ibn Abu Talib, 77
Andi, 143, 216
Aqsay, 64, 131
Arab-Muslim learning in the North Cau-
    casus, 30-2, 35
Arabic language, 24, 31-2
Arabistan, 30
Arabs in the North Caucasus, 13, 26-7, 31,
    50, 236
Archi, 30
Ashilta, 172, 175
Aslan Khan, 108, 116-19, 145, 156, 165, 167
Aslan al-Tsudaqari, 231
Astrakhan, 52
Ataghi, 130
Avar (Avaria), 10-12, 18-19, 27, 29, 43,
    64, 70, 118, 146-7, 152, 160, 164-6,
    168, 171-2, 181, 194
Ayyub, 213
Azeri, Azerbaijan: 13, 48, 69; as base of
    Sheikh al-Shirwani, 100-5
Azeri Turkish language, 24

Baghdad, 13
Baha al-Din al-Naqshband, 80-1, 113
Bashkir, 48
Bata, 228
Berke Khan, 28
Bersa, Sheikh, 49
Beybulat Taymi, 8, 122-34
blood-revenge, 44, 218
Bolshevik revolution, 2
Britain, 2, 93
Bukhara, 52, 67, 75
Bulach Khan, 147, 165
Bulat Mirza, 222

Catherine the Great, 54
Chechnya: political geography, 3-4, 9-11,
    16-17; society, 4-5, 14-15, 19; Tugum
    as social and political unit, 15-18, 21;
    Tuqum as economic unit, 21-5; legal
    system in Tuqum, 40-6; Islamization of,
    33-6; teips, 16, 25, 33-6
Chernyshev, Russian Minister of War, 147
Chirkah, 141
Christianity, Christian: 28, 29, 39; influence
    from Georgia, 34, 35-6; Russian colonial
    policy towards, 56, 62-3
Circassia, Circassian, 4, 64, 66, 197, 199
Cossacks, 4, 53-5, 63, 123, 125, 226
Crimea, 52, 54-5
Crimean War, 229

Daghestan: political geography, 3-4; physi-
    cal geography, 9-10; population (ethnic
    make-up), 11-13; society, 4-5, 14-19;
    Jama'at, 16-10, 21-24; legal system of
    17, 25, 40-6; administration of, 17-20
Daniel Bek, 231-2
Dar-waq, 31
Dargho (Darghins), 12-13, 15, 43
Derbend: 5, 10, 13, 69, 71, 153; as stron-
    ghold of Arab-Muslim caliphate, 26-7;
    Hashimids of, 27; as a trading centre,
    28; culture and learning in, 30-2
dhikr, 80
Didoy, 12, 27, 30, 43
Dihlawi, Sheikh Waliullah, 91-2
divan-khaneh, 216-17

Egypt, 234
Enderi, 32, 48, 64, 71

261